Meaning in Texts

MEANING IN TEXTS

The Historical Shaping of a Narrative Hermeneutics

by
EDGAR V. McKNIGHT

FORTRESS PRESS   Philadelphia

Library of Congress Cataloging in Publication Data

McKnight, Edgar V.
  Meaning in texts.

  Includes index.
   1. Bible. N.T.—Hermeneutics. 2. Hermeneutics. 3. Structuralism (Literary analysis)
  I. Title.
BS2331.M3   225.6′3   77-15238
ISBN 0-8006-0518-7

6522B78   Printed in the United States of America   1-518

Dedicated to my father
William Gotehre McKnight
and to the memory of my mother
Carrie Belle DeMars McKnight

Table of Contents

Part Three
STRUCTURES AND MEANINGS
IN NEW TESTAMENT NARRATIVE

Preface

Meaning in Texts relates the structural study of narrative to New Testament hermeneutics. It is concerned with the philosophical hermeneutics of Schleiermacher, Dilthey, Heidegger, and Gadamer and the New Testament hermeneutics of Bultmann, Fuchs, and Ebeling. The goal of narrative hermeneutics, then, must be differentiated from the goal of historical interpretation on the one hand and the goal of theological, religious, or homiletical application on the other hand. Its focus is the relationship or the application of the New Testament to the present day, even to the point where the text facilitates present-day "language-event." But it is also concerned that the event in the present be related to the original text and author and not merely to the reader or hearer in the present situation. To answer the question as to how a historical text can be unfolded beyond the historical flux, hermeneutics has transformed the question of interpretation into the question of knowledge ("How do we know?") and the question of being ("What is the mode of being of that being who only exists through understanding?"). Can hermeneutics now engage the New Testament text more fruitfully by adopting insights and methods of structuralism?

The structuralism involved in narrative hermeneutics is not that doctrinaire structuralism of early structuralists who saw themselves as ideologically opposed to the hermeneutical tradition. It is the structuralism of a later generation concerned with narrative, and students of the structural study of narrative in large measure see their work as based on the theory of perception developed by M. Merleau-Ponty, a French philosopher in the hermeneutical tradition. A. J. Greimas, for example, considers "perception as the non-linguistic place where the apprehension of signification is located," but his concern is perception *of the work* not merely perception as genius or imagination. (See below, p. 167.) The

structuralism of narrative hermeneutics is clearly not that of those structuralists who perceive meaning in any or all grammatical patterns in such
an idiosyncratic way as to preclude any necessary relationship of the
meaning of the author and the meaning for the reader. The structuralism
which can be related to hermeneutics is concerned explicitly with the
nature of the creator of meaning (author and reader) and implicitly about
questions of meaning and knowledge; it is the structuralism of "narratologists" who are discovering the logical and human constraints of narrative
or the way that the human as human creates narrative in order to understand and be understood.

The narrative hermeneutics which results from the wedding of hermeneutics and the structural study of narrative is not merely hermeneutics
or narratology. It retains major ideas of both of these fields but becomes
something new as these ideas are combined. Although utilization of
developments in both hermeneutics and structuralism in this century
makes narrative hermeneutics something new, in a very real sense the
method is the application of the comprehensive approach to language
and meaning advocated by Wilhelm Dilthey at the turn of the century.
Wilhelm Dilthey held language and meaning (ranging from denotation
of individual terms to life itself) in creative tension in a comprehensive
systematic approach which centered in man's mental structure. This
mental structure was a continuously developing system integrating and
equilibrating various stages of inner and outer development. The key as
well as the barrier for Dilthey's overcoming of the hermeneutical problem
(a problem which has continued although it has been viewed from
different perspectives in this century) was language. The concepts in
Dilthey's tradition were too limited for the use he wished to make of
language. At the very time Dilthey was dealing with the hermeneutical
question in terms of a limited view of language, however, C. S. Peirce and
F. de Saussure were working independently on studies in semiology and
linguistics. These studies have resulted in a very much broader concept
of language which can be applied to Dilthey's comprehensive view and
result in a structural or at least a narrative hermeneutics.

The opposition of the "art" of hermeneutics and the "science" of structuralism is mediated by the work of Dilthey. The hermeneutics of Dilthey
is often characterized as an epistemology of the human sciences in contrast with the epistemology of the natural sciences. Dilthey wished to
move beyond romantic caprice and skeptical subjectivism, but he could
not accept any a priori in his hermeneutics. Life, experience, and history

constituted the focus of Dilthey, and his epistemology was empirical.
The goal of Dilthey was not some absolute knowledge, therefore; but
his program was not a capitulation to historical finitude. Dilthey's attempt
to find a theoretical universality of interpretation in face of the finite
historical nature of man and understanding is important in the attempt
to find help for hermeneutics in structuralism.

Some may deny that structuralism assists hermeneutics in any more
than an accidental way because the application of structural insights
in literature does not result in absolute, scientifically objective results.
Philip Pettit claims that structural analysis is not scientific because a
reader cannot "definitely say that a text lacks structure and is unallow-
able" and because "there is no single structure in virtue of which the text
is allowable." (See below, pp. 253, 265.) In the light of the conceptualization of Dilthey, the lack of absolute knowledge is precisely what we
should expect in analysis which involves human capacity. Yet this need
not lead either to skepticism toward analysis or caprice in use of the
method. No knowledge, at least in the literary area, is absolute. No
approach to literature is, in Pettit's strict sense, a science. Narrative
hermeneutics, then, is not positivistic; but neither does it lack a clear
method which is based on actual data and which can be carried out with
rigor.

Meaning in Texts, then, accomplishes two tasks at the same time. First,
it applies studies in narrative from a structural perspective to hermeneutical studies. It also traces hermeneutical and structural developments
in the twentieth century to their source in Dilthey, and in his mediation
of the two traditions finds a new and fruitful approach to hermeneutics
and structuralism—narrative hermeneutics.

This book began to take shape in 1973–74, during a sabbatical year
at Oxford University, and numerous individuals at Oxford played a
part in the process of research and writing. Of particular value were
lectures, seminars, and conferences with Dr. Peter Seuren in linguistics,
Dr. Jonathan Culler in literary studies, and Professor John Macquarrie in
philosophical theology. I am especially indebted to Professor Macquarrie
for his encouragement throughout the project and for his careful reading
and suggestions concerning the entire manuscript. The administration of
Furman University and the faculty committee on Research and Profes-
sional Growth have supported the project by means of a sabbatical and
several research grants.

MEANING AND
LANGUAGE IN HERMENEUTICS

Introduction

Part One examines hermeneutical developments in the areas of meaning and language to discover common ground between the structural and hermeneutical traditions. The initial chapter centers on Dilthey, because he not only was not opposed to structural perspectives but actually attempted to develop what can be called structural hermeneutics. In order for the vision of Dilthey to become useful in today's hermeneutical situation, however, the traditional interpretations of his work must be modified. The tradition which posits a break between the anthropological and psychological emphases of Dilthey and his later textual interpretation (poetics versus hermeneutics) was possible because of the nature and method of Dilthey's scholarship and the relative lateness of the collection and publication of his works. The traditional reading was also the result of the literary situation of those critics who interpreted Dilthey. René Wellek, for example, cites Dilthey as important only because of Dilthey's alleged recognition of failure to reconcile his poetics with his theory of interpretation and alleged disavowal of his poetics.

To read Dilthey from today's perspective is to see clearly a poetics of creation which emphasizes the structure of the mind as a dynamic structure incorporating and equilibrating inner and outer developments, and it is also to see clearly a hermeneutics which rests upon this subjective but real structure. Poetics and hermeneutics for Dilthey, however, have to do with life and the meaning of life, which are more central for him than either poetics or hermeneutics. The meaning of life, spoken most fully in the poetic work, could not be obtained from the literary work by means of the linguistic tools then available. Hence, Dilthey could not unite the two poles of his concern—poetic creativity and textual interpretation. Yet his conceptualization continued to contain both elements.

The second chapter traces the post-Diltheyan developments in general hermeneutics through Heidegger and Gadamer in order to show the growing importance of "language" in hermeneutics but also to show that the approach to language has not really resulted in a satisfying hermeneutics. Heidegger in *Being and Time* postulated that language is related to a superior and prior "discourse" which is an *existentiale* equiprimordial with state-of-mind and understanding. This allows man or *Dasein* to be questioned for existence or Being. After *Being and Time* "language" assumed a more central position, displacing or incorporating state-of-mind, understanding, and discourse.

Dilthey's attempt to understand the experience of life in their structural and developmental inner connections is seen by Heidegger as evidence that Dilthey was on the way toward the question of life. Heidegger's goal, however, is not life but Being. Hence, *Dasein*, for Heidegger, is a means for questioning Being. Heidegger's failure to be concerned with the psychological nature of the text or even with the ideas of "expression," "symbolic form," "communication as assertion," "the making known of experience," and "the patterning of life" distinguishes Heidegger from Dilthey. Heidegger is concerned with the ontological locus of the phenomenon of language in "*Dasein's* state of Being."

Dilthey envisioned a relationship between poetics and hermeneutics. Heidegger broadened both of these poles, postulating a relationship between *Dasein* and language on the one hand and between language and Being on the other. But Heidegger, like Dilthey, could not find in contemporary linguistics and grammar a way of connecting the poles.

Gadamer affirms the ontological view of Heidegger but attempts to move back to less ultimate levels of knowledge by using Humboldt's view of language as an unbordered creative power of thought and speech that makes unlimited use of limited materials. The attempt of Gadamer does not appear to have effectively wed the ontological participation of belonging of the interpreter with the critical methodological attitude of the interpreter. Gadamer comes basically to the same dialectic as Dilthey when he speaks of the means of understanding. The means of understanding is the content of tradition, but every meaning of tradition finds its reality in relationship to the one who is doing the understanding. Language mediates the two poles. Tradition brings itself to language; and human consciousness is linguistic. In this mediation, human consciousness is not dissolved. Gadamer admits that there is no possible consciousness in which the "matter" which is passed down in tradition appears in light of eternity. Gadamer, then, drives us back forcefully to the problem of man's linguistic ability.

Chapter Three shows that the problems of general hermeneutics are recapitulated in New Testament hermeneutics. Rudolf Bultmann's theological context brought him to approach the New Testament as source for proclamation, and the work of Heidegger gave Bultmann direction in his search for the subject matter of the New Testament, human existence, and in the categories used to speak of human existence. Bultmann's approach is valid in that human existence is obviously one level of meaning in the New Testament—for the author and reader. His approach is limited in that some levels of meaning and language are ignored in existential interpretation.

The New Hermeneutic, in contrast to Bultmann who emphasized the early work of Heidegger on *Dasein,* utilizes Heidegger's later work on language as the speaking of Being. In Fuchs especially the difficulty of locating "language" in relation to ordinary human language, in relation to linguistics and grammar, makes the New Hermeneutic difficult to understand much less to use for theology and New Testament interpretation. Fuchs does not seem to be concerned to relate "language" to ordinary human language in anything more than a figurative way, but students who find the goal of the New Hermeneutic compelling, particularly the vision of "language-event" in the present, would like to situate Fuchs's view of "language" in relation to recognizable linguistic landmarks.

The hermeneutical tradition in general and New Testament hermeneutics in particular view language and meaning not only in ways that parallel the structuralist conceptualization but also in ways that are capable of being related to recent approaches in the structuralist tradition. Three particular conclusions which follow from the discussion of Part One will prepare for a discussion of the structuralist program.

1. "Language" for hermeneutics is not identical with language as it is ordinarily known. Yet, the language of hermeneutics is not unrelated to ordinary language. The language of the New Testament, then, is not unrelated to the broader hermeneutical concepts of language. While the New Testament is language in the more limited sense, it is also language in the broader sense.

2. Language in hermeneutics involves levels of meaning beyond the meaning of words and sentences. It involves existential, theological, and

ontological levels. Clearly it is not merely the material, physical side of language (the sound, the letters on a page, etc.) which accomplishes these levels of meaning. But the material aspect of language is involved. The material of language is a means to the meaning which the author intends to communicate in the text and to the various levels of meaning which impinge upon the author and reader.

3. Language for New Testament hermeneutics involves the reader or hearer in such a way that the result of reading or hearing is to be thought of as an event in the present. Although reading is not merely the deciphering of an ancient text, the ancient text is necessary for the "language-event" in the present day.

CHAPTER ONE

Dilthey's ·
Poetics and Hermeneutics

The anarchy which Wilhelm Dilthey claimed was characteristic of literary criticism at the end of the nineteenth century continues although he wished to overcome it with a new poetics. The poetics based upon Aristotle had given a dependable basis for the work of the writer and critic until the middle of the eighteenth century, Dilthey asserted. However, with the rationalism of the seventeenth century, the romanticism of the eighteenth century, and the historicism of the nineteenth century, no one approach has been developed to accomplish what the poetics of Aristotle had accomplished. Dilthey envisioned a poetics which would develop universal laws to serve as both rules of creation and norms of criticism.[1]

The history of literary criticism since Dilthey, however, has been marked by increasing variety. The various elements of literature and the relationship of the elements are viewed in radically different ways. The author of a work is ignored completely or, either through emphasis on the external situation of the author or the creative powers of the author or the author-in-general, made the dominant factor in interpretation. The text is seen as communicating information which can be verified, the thought of an author, the "world" of an author, or other matters of which the text is a derivative; the work is also seen as participating or even dominating in perception and meaning. The reader is viewed as a passive instrument or as a creator of meaning who is just as important as the original creator of the work. It will be observed that the history of literary criticism is a continuation of the conversation that began with the philosophical consideration of Plato, the interest in creative techniques on the part of the Sophists, and the balance proposed by Aristotle. Yet the history of literary criticism is not circular, for each development

7

concerning one element of the literary process (creator—this term in-cludes reader as well as author—text, meaning) alters the concep-tualization of the other elements. Moreover, the levels of language and literature studied and the vectors from which study is approached constantly change, and literature and its criticism are then always con-tinually new.

A change *has* occurred in biblical criticism, however. It is not a change from anarchy to the reign of a particular method. On the contrary, biblical criticism has moved from a situation of relative calm where there was general agreement on the methods and perimeters of criticism to the vortex of the conflict in general literary criticism. For the major part of the life of biblical criticism (higher criticism) there has been general agreement regarding the method of biblical interpretation, although there has not been total agreement in the application and the results of biblical criticism. Now, the anarchy characteristic of general literary criticism and practice has come to characterize biblical interpre-tation.

Not only do we see a growing variety in literary theory in general and in biblical interpretation in particular; we also see opposing method-ologies claiming exclusive allegiance. This allegiance is often demanded and acceded, perhaps because of ignorance of other possibilities. The major opposing methodologies of today may be seen as either having their source in Dilthey or flowing through Dilthey from earlier scholars such as Schleiermacher. It is the purpose of this work to attempt to present the various approaches in a productive relationship. This chapter will show how Dilthey attempted to hold together seemingly opposing perspectives which today are represented in hermeneutics and structural-ism. Two results should follow from such an attempt: (1) Dilthey's opposing perspectives may stimulate reconsideration of the exclusivism of competing methodologies. (2) The successes and failures of Dilthey's attempt to hold differing views together in creative tension may point the way to patterns of relationships for today.

CURRENT MISUNDERSTANDING OF DILTHEY

Students of literature and New Testament interpretation may have to be convinced that Dilthey is worthy of consideration, for they often have the impression that Dilthey gave up his attempt at a theory of interpretation involving poetics and hermeneutics and that his particular suggestions in hermeneutics have long since been forgotten by scholars.

In his important *History of Modern Criticism: 1750–1950* René Wellek cites Dilthey's recognition of his failure to reconcile a poetics of creativity with his theory of interpretation and the repudiation of the "very basis of Dilthey's own early poetics."[2] In the opinion of Kurt Müller-Vollmer, literary historians see Dilthey as a completely out-of-date figure, as the "originator and principal exponent of . . . a view which defined literary studies as a species of intellectual history," and as responsible for a "procedure which emphasizes the intellectual and emotional content of literature at the expense of its aesthetic and literary qualities, interpreting a given work in terms of the metaphysical world view held by its author and of that mysterious and ubiquitous force called 'spirit of the times.'"[3] Rudolf Bultmann has made Dilthey's name known in New Testament studies through his use of the insight that genuine comprehension of poetry and art as well as works of philosophy and religion is "oriented . . . to the *inquiry into the understanding of one particular existence in history.*" But Bultmann limits his use of Dilthey because of a view that Dilthey's basic concepts are no longer tenable. He sees that Dilthey is caught up in the "ultimately aesthetic approach of romanticism" while Bultmann wishes to reemphasize real understanding as arising from "the possibilities of human being which are revealed" in a work.[4] The major point to be made in this section is that the later hermeneutical efforts of Dilthey did not involve a repudiation of his poetics. Other misunderstandings of Dilthey will be clarified in the presentation of his poetical and hermeneutical ideas and in the discussion of Bultmann's hermeneutics.

Different interpretations of the writings of Dilthey are inevitable, at least in part, because of the very nature and method of his scholarship. Even in his own time, his ideas were not confidently understood by his disciples or even by his own children. After Dilthey's death, no clear picture of his contribution could be drawn because his works were so diverse and scattered. The first volume of the collected works was not published until 1928, with publication of other volumes continuing until 1958. Even with the collection and publication of the works, the problem of determining the central point around which to interpret all of the writings of Dilthey continues to be a matter of debate. Richard E. Palmer, who traces hermeneutics from Schleiermacher to Gadamer, criticizes Dilthey's "psychologism" which he inherited from Schleiermacher and says that Dilthey eventually moved away from an emphasis on the process of creation to the *expression* of lived experience itself. Earlier, however,

Palmer rightly cautions that the "bogey" of psychologism "should not frighten us away from considering the relation of the theory of artistic creation to the theory of literary understanding and, therefore, to literary interpretation."[5]

Hans-Georg Gadamer is heir of the hermeneutical tradition through Heidegger; he rereads the history of hermeneutics from a post-Heideggerian perspective and wishes to follow Hegel's "integration" rather than Schleiermacher's "reconstruction" and therefore uses hermeneutics for a goal that he sees as differing from Dilthey's. Gadamer speaks of the transition of Dilthey's foundation of the human science from psychology to hermeneutics, that is, from a concern to define the *Zusammenhang des Lebens* with the help of a psychology to the understanding of the expression. A broader and truer foundation than either psychology or hermeneutics, however, and one which may serve as a mediation between the two, is "life" (*Leben*). In "Hermeneutik and Historismus," which was printed in the second edition of *Wahrheit und Methode*, Gadamer acknowledges the continuity of Dilthey's attempt to find his epistemological foundation in psychology.[6]

Two complementary views which relate poetics and hermeneutics in Dilthey are those of Kurt Müller-Vollmer and Frithjof Rodi. Müller-Vollmer assumes a unity of purpose in the writings of Dilthey and interprets the poetics against the background of the philosophical writings.[7] Rodi feels that a correct understanding of Dilthey is gained only from a genetic study and stresses that Dilthey's concept of understanding must be studied in light of his aesthetics in which the concept of meaning is the ultimate unifying factor. The question of Dilthey's aesthetics, therefore, is "the question of the possibility of a hermeneutical system which is in the genuine sense open and makes experiences of life understandable according to their meaning."[8]

Dilthey himself gives broad hints if not plain evidence that he continued to see a relationship between poetics and hermeneutics. His *Poetik* was published in 1887. A sequel to this work, *Die drei Epochen der modernen Ästhetik und ihre heutige Aufgabe*,[9] published in 1892, maintained continuity with the basic ideas in the work of 1887. Even after publications in hermeneutics, Dilthey continued to be concerned with poetics in itself. Until his death in 1911, he maintained notebooks in which he gave his plans for the reworking and expansion of the text of *Poetik* into a full-sized book. Volume VI of *Gesammelte Schriften*, the same volume containing *Poetik* and *Drei Epochen*, contains notes concerning the projected revision from two different periods of Dilthey's life.

In the early 1890s notes for a revision call for uniting the *Poetik* with the *Drei Epochen* with some reorganization of the content. The major thrust of the *Poetik* was to remain intact.[10] The second plan from 1907–8 called for a more radical reworking, and it is from these notes that Wellek concludes that Dilthey repudiated his psychological poetics. The editor of the collected works does indicate that, according to the notes, "the writing would be radically recast by means of a changed ordering of the text, deletions of large sections, and additions of whole parts."[11] The recasting, however, is not a repudiation of the earlier poetics. Wellek correctly cites a changed concept of *Erlebnis* in the notes and an emphasis of *Bedeutsamkeit* over against feeling. But Dilthey emphasized in his notes of 1907–8 that he maintained continuity in terms of the very matters cited by Wellek: "The coherence of the concept of life, experience . . . , meaningfulness as a characteristic of life, psychology of inwardness, mission, poetry as a happening of meaningfulness, etc., were already contained in my early publications."[12]

Wellek also quotes from "Die Abgrenzung der Geisteswissenschaften," which was read at the Berlin Academy of Sciences in 1909, to the effect that Dilthey at that time realized that the work of literature is not based on " 'inner processes within the poet,' but rather a 'nexus created by him and detachable from them. . . . Thus the subject with which literary history and poetics have to deal primarily is totally distinct from psychic events in the poet or his readers.' No sharper rejection of the very basis of Dilthey's own early poetics could be imagined."[13] Wellek clearly misunderstands and mistranslates Dilthey at this point. Dilthey says that the subject of poetics is not psychic processes in the poets or readers. The impossibility of isolating these processes for study was emphasized by Dilthey in his earliest publications. In the paper cited by Wellek, Dilthey actually says that the subject is the nexus (*Zusammenhang*) "created by them" (i.e., "the inner processes in the poet") and that this nexus is "separable from them" (from the inner processes). There is no question but that Dilthey indicates in the notes that he would use a terminology in his new work which moves away from the orientation toward feeling and hedonistic satisfaction toward one favoring experience and meaningfulness. But this represents no absolute turn from an explanation of poetic creativity on the basis of psychology and the use of this in hermeneutics. Indeed, the notes indicate that he planned to utilize his work on structural psychology in the projected work, and in the notes there is a fragment on structural psychology which was to form a part of the work.[14] The editor of *Gesammelte Schriften*, in a preface to Volume V, declared that poetics along with the theory of history were the general bases for Dilthey's ideas of life and the understanding of life and that he continued an active interest in poetics throughout his life.[15]

In the realist literary interpretation of English and American critics, the question of the process of creation is irrelevant, and it is attractive to read Dilthey in that light. But I propose to read Dilthey in another light, in light of the history of hermeneutics through Heidegger to Gadamer and through Bultmann to the new hermeneutic and in light of the history of poetics of the twentieth century which takes its impetus from Dilthey and which includes the various structural approaches to the text. José Ortega y Gasset declares that Dilthey was among the first discoverers of the "Idea of life," but that his writings served little or not at all to "promote the subsequent advances in the conception of the Idea of life." He declares, however, that the advances independent of Dilthey lend meaning and importance to the thought of Dilthey which "without them and by itself it would be lacking." Here, he says, we "have the case of an idea carrying water to its 'source.' "[16]

I propose to attempt to carry back to Dilthey some advances in the study of interpretation which have been made independently of Dilthey in hopes that these ideas may lend meaning and importance to Dilthey's thought which can in turn be reapplied to literary criticism in general and biblical hermeneutics in particular.

THE POETICS OF DILTHEY

In *Drei Epochen*, Dilthey gives evidence of his reaction to the historical developments in critical theory during the previous two centuries and indicates the elements of the various "epochs" which can contribute to a new poetics comparable in value to that of Aristotle and which will serve artists, critics, and the public in general. The three movements treated by Dilthey are: (1) the rationalism of the last half of the seventeenth century; (2) the eighteenth century's analysis of aesthetic impressions, and (3) the historical method of the nineteenth century.

The abiding contributions of rationalism (the full effects of which were not felt in creative writing, especially poetry, until the mid-eighteenth century), in Dilthey's view, are those of Leibniz, and his school. Rational aesthetics on the basis of the insights of Leibniz "grasps beauty as the appearance of the rational in the sensual and art as a sensual realization of the harmonious world order."[17] Expressions of the creative imagination follow certain rules which are "ultimately grounded in the rational order of the universe."[18] Not only was this rational aesthetics valuable for its own time, it also has a valuable core of truth which remains valid. "There are rules of the arts which flow universally out of the nature of the things themselves,"[19] but it is necessary to isolate the rules from the historical variability of aesthetic taste.

In the course of the first half of the eighteenth century, the constraints upon art and aesthetics altered, and aesthetic theory, influenced by the success of the analytic method in the human sciences following Locke and Hume, came to emphasize the analysis of the aesthetic impression. Dilthey sees Henry Home's work as "the most mature and most complete analysis of beauty in the eighteenth century."[20] ". . . Home found the mental stimulus of aesthetic impression simply joined by nature to a definite characteristic of the aesthetic object or of the process."[21] The real site of aesthetic perception was sentiment and feeling, and aesthetic analysis was a methodological dissection of these feelings. "We grasp the nature of the aesthetic impression, however, only when we separate the emotion which is roused through the real presence of the object from the emotion which the ideal presence calls forth."[22] The ideal presence is related to reality as the image called up by memory is related to the object it represents.

Dilthey states a problem for Home which did not exist for the rationalists: how is a universal aesthetic science possible? Home's answer is that an analysis of the sensitive part of our nature provides the fundamental basis for a universal aesthetic. "Definite aesthetic impressions are regularly bound with definite characteristics of the aesthetic objects in accord with the nature of our minds."[23] The common aspects of human nature, then, establish the universality of aesthetic taste.

Dilthey acknowledges his indebtedness to Home, particularly as the work of Home anticipates the work of G. T. Fechner a century later. Yet Dilthey points out weaknesses in the method of psychological analysis of aesthetic impressions which influence his own poetics: (1) the method falls into a circle in that analysis is dependent upon a previous notion of the beautiful which is not gained from the method itself; (2) the necessary procedures for obtaining objective and universally valid results are not possible because the people tested are always from a particular place and time. Historically constrained aesthetic tastes cannot be distinguished from universally valid canons of taste; (3) regular simple relationships between items capable of producing effects and the effects produced cannot be observed; (4) even when individual relationships are observed, there is no way to insure that there is not a deeper hidden unity explaining the observed relationships; (5) the most important concern of aesthetics cannot be satisfied by the isolated analyses of impressions. Aesthetics must be directed to the function of art in the life of man.[24]

Dilthey sees four motifs in the development of German aesthetics in the historical method of the nineteenth century following the work of Winckelmann and Lessing. (1) German transcendental philosophy had brought the idea of the creative potential of the nature of man to apply in all areas; (2) this creative potential was applied to the copying of natural objects of beauty; (3) the artistic effect was related to the constraints and the medium of the artistic product; and (4) the development of the arts was seen as interwoven with the course of culture and the life of the mind by means of an inner coherence.[25]

Dilthey, in his introduction of *Poetik*, simply mentions the three epochs in passing, for his purpose was to emphasize the anarchy which, in Dilthey's opinion, was a sign of a new way of experiencing reality, a new way which could not be contained in the existing forms and rules and which, therefore, was attempting to construct new forms. It was the nature of new developments which made the task of poetics so difficult: "How are we to overcome the difficulties besetting the human sciences and develop general statements out of the inner experiences which are so personal, so undefined, so confused, and yet so indivisible?"[26] Is it possible for poetics "to develop universal laws which are useful as rules of creation and norms of criticism?"[27]

Literary history, by Dilthey's definition of his task, is not the answer. More than a literary history is needed. A *science* which deals with the elements and laws which form the foundation of literary writings is necessary. But the material for literary history is precisely the material for poetics as a science. "The point of departure," however, "must be in the analysis of the creative capacity, the processes of which govern poetry."[28] For as long as ten years Dilthey had felt that "the imagination of the poet in its relation to the world of experiences"[29] is the necessary point of departure for poetics.

Part One of *Poetik* sets forth the relationship between traditional viewpoints and the new task of poetics. The views of Aristotle which reigned until the eighteenth century emphasized form and a technique dependent upon the doctrine of forms. Aristotle used the procedure of abstraction and analysis: he abstracted forms from specific works, coordinated them, and analyzed the composition of these forms into smaller units. The poetics of Aristotle was a doctrine of forms, then, analogous to the way that language or music is analyzed into its component parts or the way that an argument is decomposed into its units from beginning to end. The parts may be arranged into columns, and rules may be discovered which account for the organization, which tell why the units are organized as they are in order to carry out the purpose.

The poetics of Aristotle, then, is not derived from general aesthetic principles, such as beauty or artistic creativity; it is the result of descriptive analysis. The effect of the work upon the spectator is the result of imitation induced by the elements of the work itself. Like logic and epistemology, the principle of imitation is to be viewed objectively: there is a basic agreement between perception and thought on the one hand and reality (*Sein*) on the other hand. "Being is portrayed in thought."[30]

The downfall of Aristotle's poetics resulted from a radically changed view of the nature of man in Dilthey's time. "The Aristotelian principle of imitation was objective in a way analogous to Aristotelian epistemology. Since the research into the subjective capacity of man's nature was deepened generally and its independent powers established, . . . the principle of imitation in aesthetics became impossible."[31] The altered view of human consciousness based on Descartes and Locke could only result in a new aesthetics.

It was in the work of Schiller that Dilthey found the real impetus for a new aesthetics. For Schiller, beauty is a living, breathing Gestalt, which comes into existence when perception (*Anschauung*) captures life in an image or when a Gestalt is filled (*beseelen*) with life (*zum Leben*). "The form must become life and life must become form."[32] Dilthey quotes the formulation of Schiller:

> . . . a human being, although he lives and has form, is far from being on that account a living form; that would require his form to be life and his life form. As long as we only think about his form, it is lifeless, a mere abstraction. As long as we only feel his life, it is shapeless, mere impression. Only as the form of something lives in our sensations, and its life takes form in our understanding, is it a living form, and this will everywhere be the case where we judge it as beautiful.[33]

Dilthey entitles "Schiller's law" the principle of the aesthetic process which captures life in form or transforms life into form, therefore, the translation of experience (*Erlebnis*) into form and of form into experience. The fundamental basis of the German aesthetics formulated by Schiller was Kant's thesis that the aesthetic impression lies in the same process as the aesthetic creation. The meaning of feeling for the processes of creation, the metamorphoses of images and compositions, can, therefore, be examined, and this aspect of aesthetic thought will allow the necessary generalization and psychological grounding for a proper poetics. Since "the creativity of the artist mounts characteristics which already lie in reality,"[34] the possibility exists of recognizing the characteristics and the relationships.

The traditional belief in the universality of aesthetic principles continued to influence German aesthetics, and Dilthey sees this as one of the difficulties which he must overcome. Aristotle's technique claimed universality. Kant intended to transfer the idea of timeless universality from the realm of logic to the area of aesthetics—as well as to the areas of law, religion, and ethics. In agreement with this tradition, Schiller undertook to develop a universal technique of all poetry upon the foundation of aesthetic ideas. Herder is taken as Dilthey's model in this respect, for Herder stressed the historical variety of national tastes. Unfortunately, from Dilthey's point of view, Herder was unable to prevail against Aristotle, Kant, and Schiller because his ideas lacked clarity and his formulations firmness.

In spite of failure to resolve the problem of universality and historicality, German aesthetics did attempt to establish the relationship between the creativity of the artist and the product of his activity. Yet, Dilthey asserts, idealistic speculation hindered full development of the potential in German aesthetics. Dilthey is not to be hindered by such speculation, for he brings to recognition the historical essence (*Wesen*) of man which could have prevented romantic theories in German aesthetics from falling prey to idealistic speculations.

The conclusion of Part One logically focuses on the means which are available for the project of contemporary poetics. The task as Dilthey sees it is to examine the problems of the various periods of aesthetic speculation in light of modern research and experience and to make use of scientific observation and general principles in the spirit of empirical study. Rhetoric and hermeneutics ought to offer help because of their close relationship to poetics. Rhetoric, however, has not approached the modern empirical method, and hermeneutics was in the same condition as literary theory in general and was not yet in a position to assist literary theory. Linguistics was more promising because of advances of scientific approaches, yet linguistics approaches language as a physical system which can be studied with the method of natural science. The living process out of which poetry comes cannot be so studied. Laws which are valid for past, present, and future will come only from insight into human nature. Poetics once had a firm point in ideal pattern, then in a metaphysical idea of beauty, but now the only firm point is to be sought in the life of the mind.

The second part of Dilthey's *Poetik* is an attempt to apply psychological insights to the artistic life and activity so as to answer the questions which natural science cannot answer. First must come some understanding of the elements and functions of art. The elements of poetry are also present in philosophy, natural science, and politics. They are images of the outer world, realities which are experienced by all. No inner element of man can become a component of poetry unless it (or a combination of such elements) stands in a relationship with concrete life experiences. The basis for all true poetry is consequently experience (*Erlebnis*). With this vital experience, however, inner elements of all kinds are also related. This operation of understanding, which generalizes, orders, and strengthens the usefulness of experience, is no more unique to the poet than are the images of the outer world. But this relationship of an elementary, powerful intellect to life experience and generalization, which is a potential to all, *must* be a reality with every great poet. As Goethe said, "Man must be something in order to make something."[35]

The elements of poetry, then, such as motif, plot, character, and action, are all transformations of representations from life. "The material ground of all true poetry is a historical reality. . . . The poetic technique is historically conditioned."[36] How does poetic creativity grow out of the material ground of historical reality? The essence and function of art are related to this question. Art is something which satisfies the viewer or hearer. It is something in a sensory media which is not designed to make facts known nor is it to be borne factually, but it is to satisfy the viewers or hearers by what it is. It is this value of satisfaction for the viewer which is characteristic of every work of art. The poet as an artist creates by means of a series of words, but it is not the series of words that distinguishes poetry from other arts. The nature and function of poetry in society are due to its own "nuclear content."[37]

As our body breathes, so our soul longs for completion and extension of
its existence in the pulsations of its inner life. The feeling of life wants to
express itself in sound and word and picture. The vision satisfies us completely only to the extent that it is completed with such a force of life
and the pulsation of feeling; this reciprocal relationship of our primitive,
total life, a view of a deepened and satiated feeling, a feeling of life radi-
ating in the brightness of the image: that is the internal essential mark of
all poetry.[38]

In Dilthey's presentation, the poetic experience is not a matter of
thought or idea. The function of poetry, in light of this essential nature,
is to maintain, strengthen, and awaken a vitality in man. It is in light of
this essence and function that we speak of a "poetic nature" and of works
of art in other than poetic forms as "poetic." The essence and function
of poetry, in Dilthey's conception, must be a potential for every man
and every class of mankind. Yet the creative imagination of some men
is intensified in a way to mark them off.

The chief problem of the undertaking of a contemporary poetics is
noted by Dilthey as precisely those processes in the poet by which he
achieves his creative work. Psychology should solve the problem, but
contemporary psychology is unable to clarify the life of images in man,
for "the reigning psychology moves from the presupposition that mental
acts are fixed and stable elements. It accounts for the changes of these
mental acts from the outside. . . ."[39] The experience of artistic creation
cannot be explained by such a stimulus-response view. The perceptions
and images which come from outside are inspired, colored, and invigo-
rated by feelings.

In his attempt to transcend the limited views of contemporary psychology, Dilthey sees mental processes in man which move beyond the
elementary ones in which there is a unity of perception of outer reality
and inner representation. Some processes exist in which perception and
representations (or their component parts) are called into consciousness
by one another. The inner processes, then, are processes of creation which
are characterized by the total structure of the inner life (*der ganze Zusammenhang des Seelenlebens*). This structure of the inner life alters and
gives form to perceptions, representations, and circumstances. In addition,
it embraces the evaluations resulting from our feelings and the purposes
of our will. The structure consists not only in contents but also in relationships which arise out of all these contents. Relationships are as real as
contents. Although elements of this inner structure can be isolated, it is
so greatly united that it operates as a total unity.

That which is in consciousness is oriented to the inner structure: it is bordered, defined, and grounded by it. Statements have their certainty in it; ideas have their sharp boundaries through it; our position in space and time has its orientation in it. Just so, feelings receive from it the means for the coherence of our life. Our will, which is mainly employed with means, remains constantly certain of the feeling of its purpose through the same inner structure in which the means are grounded.[40]

Although inner experience is a unity, Dilthey distinguishes three classes of creative processes which take place in the structure of the inner life: cognitive, volitional, and affective. The simplest class of operations is the cognitive. All of the logical processes which are borne by language are a part of this type of creative process which can be called "scientific imagination."[41] The will is as primary a fact as thinking and feeling. This creative volitional imagination is directed toward the outer realities of economics, law, society, and technology, and toward the inner moral and ethical life. Dilthey speaks of this type of imagination as "practical imagination."[42] The process of imagination of feeling, not grounded in the will or directed toward the will, is a process which ranges from the creation of an image by a hypochondriac to the *Venus de Milo*, Raphael's *Madonna*, and Goethe's *Faust*. The fundamental principle of this process is that "representations which are formed from a basis of feeling can be called up again in an orderly fashion."[43] It is in the formation of the higher feeling that these processes of creation make possible continuity in individual experience and in the development of mankind.

The importance of the life of feeling for artistic creation is expressed by Dilthey:

Out of the experience of the relations of forms to our feelings comes the meaning which the relations of lines, the distribution of force and weight and symmetry have in architecture and construction. From perception of relations of our feelings to the change of voice in height and depth, rhythm and intensity, comes the synthesis of stressed address and melody. Out of the acquired insights into the effect of characters, events, and actions on our feelings is created the ideal formation of character and the feeling of action. Out of the secret relations between differences of the inner life which are felt and the variety of the observable bodily forms arises the ideal in the art of painting.[44]

The logical conclusion to these facts, says Dilthey, is that "the analysis of feeling will hold the key for the explanation of the artistic creativity."[45]

Feeling varies in a quantitative manner from displeasure to indifference to great pleasure and can obviously be analyzed in specific instances according to quantitative standards. Likewise, however, and more importantly for Dilthey, feeling varies in qualitative ways. Dilthey undertakes to analyze the qualitative varieties of feelings into elementary components. He is aware that just as feeling may be seen as forming a continuum quantitatively from displeasure to great pleasure, so feeling may be seen as forming a continuum qualitatively from those feelings which have truly physical causes with no mental representations to those feelings by which we experience consciously the general characteristics and worth of the impulses of the will.

It is vital to remember that Dilthey is not attempting to introduce new distinctions into poetics; he is attempting to translate traditional distinctions in works of art into psychological terms. The first four circles of feeling refer to what is traditionally called "form," and the last two circles refer to "content." In ascending order, Dilthey distinguishes: (1) feelings which have physical causes with no mental representation; (2) feelings which arise out of the content of sensory perception; for example, the effect resulting from the response to color; (3) feelings resulting from the relation of different sensual perceptions; for example, in tone and color there are feelings of harmony or contrast; (4) feelings which spring from a contemplative uniting of the mental representations noted above rather than from the content of the mental representations; Dilthey indicates that it is with this circle of feeling that we enter into the area of the total form of the poem from which stem aesthetic effects; (5) feelings which result from physical drives which are the "strong springs" of our lives and the "muscles" which effect society; (6) feelings by which we consciously experience the general characteristics and worth of the impulses of the will. The feelings which originate here are of special importance, for the images of these great characteristics of the will and the feelings which stem from them become an ideal of life and the soul of the work of the poet.[46]

On the basis of the model which Dilthey has set up to help explain poetic creation and on the basis of the analysis of the circles of feeling, he deduces laws of aesthetic effect and creation and discusses ways that representations transform themselves beyond the limits of the real. Just as experiences can be reproduced as mental representations, feelings may also be called back and changed into drives. There are causal relationships which allow Dilthey to deduce laws of aesthetic effect and creation. These laws are principles or an application of principles which G. T. Fechner set forth in *Princip der Wahrheit*: the principle of total effect—a variety of elementary feelings combine to make a total effect which is greater than the sum of its component elements; the principle of the aesthetic threshold—there is a certain threshold which must be exceeded before a stimulus can call forth a feeling; the principle of the relativity of feelings—the impulse of desire is more effective in a situation where this desire is at a minimum at the time of the entry of the impulse; the principle of association—one mental representation may call forth another which will be the stimulus for yet another feeling; the principle of conciliation—there is a tendency to establish harmony, and the work of art not only expresses experiences but attempts to bring about a lasting satisfaction and inner calm.[47]

In Dilthey's opinion, the real problem of the psychological foundation of poetics is to be found in the changes which transform the elements of representation beyond the limits of reality. Dilthey sees that all creations of the inner life are composed from the elements of perception. The images and the combinations of the images of the real world are altered freely by the creativity of the poet (unconstrained by reality), and the unified and unifying structure of the mind which is responsible for this free creativity is as recognizable as the structure of physical bodies. Dilthey lists three ways that images are altered. These laws of transformation are obviously related to what are traditionally called principles of style. The important point is that Dilthey is attempting to view traditional elements not from a descriptive point of view but from the point of view of a creative poetics. Images change when some of the parts are excluded or expanded or contracted, by the strengthening or weakening of the intensity of the sensation which calls the images forth, and by the entry of new components into the inner core of the images. Dilthey's contribution is his vision that the alteration of the images is an automatic process in the artistic or poetic mind. This process is designed to bring about a satisfying impression upon readers or hearers. The creativity of the poet and the impression upon the reader or hearer are based on the same principle of satisfaction. The artist (and the reader or hearer) in his own creative imagination produces a feeling of equilibrium in which all tensions and conflicts are reconciled. It is this goal of satisfaction toward which the processes of exclusion, heightening, and unfolding are directed.[48]

Part Three[49] is a short but significant discussion of the "type" in poetry. The concept of the type is introduced to solve the problem of literary communication. How is it that a work grasps a person? How is it that the reality of a work is grasped? What is it that allows a writer to communicate to a reader? The essential nature of a work is called by Dilthey its "type or the 'typical.' " It is the type of a work, or a work seen as a type, which makes it effective. Those aspects of a work which form its essence or type are generality and necessity (*Allgemeingultigkeit* and *Notwendigkeit*).

The generality of a work may be described in contrast with its singularity, with the actual work containing a mixture of essential and purely accidental elements. Dilthey agrees with Otto Ludwig that what grips the reader is not the singular, not the undifferentiated mixture of features. The reader must be grasped through "generalizing," through sorting out the accidental, lifting out that which is essential and meaningful for the feeling of life, fixing his mind and heart on those essential images, and having the deepest content of his own being grasped by those images. It is because the work contains "generality" that every heart can experience the work. "Necessity" is a feature of the type or essence of a work in that every work has a structure (*Zusammenhang*) which is as compelling for the reader as it was for the artist who created it. The secret of the power of art, then, is in the typical. "The characters and situations presented to us in a poem, and the feeling-responses evoked by them in us, are *typical* of a segment of possible human experience, and of its value or significance for us. By contemplation of the type, our acquaintance with what it represents is widened, and our power to see its true significance is heightened."[50]

The last part of the *Poetik* is the treatment of the specific poetic technique which can be built on the psychological foundation. If norms of technique can be given, they will not be derived from metaphysical presuppositions but from human nature itself in the structure of historical life. In such an analysis, perhaps, the question of the relationship of the historical variety of poetic works to universally valid principles, the problem of historicality and universality, can be solved.

In the initial chapter of Part Four, Dilthey discusses the implications of poetic creativity and aesthetic impression for technique. The two sides of aesthetics, the creative process of the author and the impression made upon the hearer or reader, find their unity and source in the vitality of the mind (*das Gemut*). It is true, Dilthey says, that the process in creation is more powerful than that in appreciation, but the impression is possible because of processes in the hearer or reader which are similar to those in the author.

In the work of the writer, rational understanding is united with involuntary creativity. From this, Dilthey formulated the "law of poetic technique": "The intention which calculates means for impression must dissolve behind the appearance of completely automatic forms and free realities."[51] Poetics makes an error when it concentrates on only one of these aspects. The poetics which begins with the impression upon the reader or hearer sees poetry as a work of understanding and calculates poetics effects. This was true with the poetics of Aristotle. To concentrate solely on the unconscious creativity of source, however, is to despise rules, educated insights, and intelligent analysis. This occurred in the Romantics. The poetics which Dilthey supports must "open both doors of its experiences as wide as possible so that no sort of fact or experience is excluded!"[52]

When poetics "studies impression, it enjoys the advantages of being able at will to call upon the changes of the impressions themselves from the change of objects and to analyze the complex of processes into its component parts. An experimental aesthetics becomes possible."[53] When poetic begins with creativity, "the store of literary-historical material becomes valuable."[54] The new poetics which wishes to clarify poetry will include all the expressions of poetry beginning with the simplest unit in the expressions of primitive peoples. As a result, the nature of literary creativity will be clarified, its changeless norms traced out, and the historical nature of its technique pointed out in such a way as to understand the past and to point the way of the future.

Dilthey concludes the *Poetik* with applications of the psychological foundation of poetics for artists and critics. Relationships are established between historically oriented conceptions of development and poetic creativity. Of relevance for structural study of narrative is Dilthey's treatment of the creation of epic poetry, drama, and the novel. Before the actual composition, there is a structuring which stands before the eyes of the poet. The structuring is necessary before he can begin the detailed composition. Tradition has called this structure "myth" or "fable." In this fable characters and actions are united, for these are really two sides of the same fact. Since the fable is structured from characters and actions or occurrences, two fundamental forms of the fable arise: the form in which the process in the mind of the hero is central or the form in which the actions with their play and counterplay are central. When the fable is one centering in action or occurrence, the structure must contain as far as possible only those components which are capable of effecting feeling. The number of the units of the action is as limited as possible, with the indispensable elements being generously unfolded in composition. The fable or plot is not an attempt to represent reality: the elements which are contained in the nexus are those which are effective; the elements which are dead insofar as feeling is concerned are eliminated. The fables concerned primarily with characters are formed in something of the same fashion: the essential points are those which are of the strongest interest for the emotions. The comparative study of literature will, in the opinion of Dilthey, help to clarify typical characters and to show the different methods of power of imagination in images.[55]

THE STRUCTURE OF THE MIND

Dilthey clearly sees the operation of poetics as involving a mental structure which man has or which man is. It is this idea which was overlooked, ignored, and, in the case of some critics at any rate, claimed to have been disowned by Dilthey himself in a more acceptable move toward a study of "meaning, structure, and value" which replaced "expression, emotion, and experience."[56]

Dilthey did not first introduce the concept of a mental structure in the *Poetik*. It was a part of his program of a "new criticism of reason" from the very beginning. As early as 1859, Dilthey had concluded that a new criticism of reason must take its point of departure from psychological principles and impulses.[57] Peter Krausser has traced chronologically the development of Dilthey's criticism of historical reason, and he finds the theory of structure as the core of Dilthey's work. "It is a question of a formal-anthropological theory of a unique dynamic structure which constrains the historicality and intelligence of man, a coherence of bodily-physical-mental functions operating with one another and with the changes, especially social and cultural changes, of the outside world."[58] Krausser declares that this theory was and still is a new type of theory which has general theoretical and practical application—not limited to the human sciences.

By the time Dilthey wrote the *Poetik* he had developed a clear theory of the structure of the mind. Numerous terms are used to express his ideas: "*Grundplan der Lebewesens*," "*Struktur des Seelenlebens*," "*Seelische Struktur*," "*Lebenszusammenhang*," "*Zusammenhang des Seelenlebens*," "*Erworbener Zusammenhang*," "*Zweckzusammenhang*," "*Wirkungszusammenhang*," "*Strukturzusammenhang*," among others. At times, Dilthey is speaking of an abstract hypothetical fundamental structure (*Grundstruktur*). But along with this abstract model, he speaks of concrete, real, dynamic systems. There is a physical-biological structure of lower organisms, a psycho-physical system of higher animals, a physical-biological-psychical-mental structure of men, and even structures of society. The structural system is seen at times as a reality independent of content with an emphasis on the systematic processes. The *erworbene Zusammenhang* emphasizes the contents of the structure and the relationships of those contents.[59]

In the *Poetik*, Dilthey sees the structure as regulating all of the details in a fundamental structural system. The basic function is regulatory. Related to this is the function of the structure in the active and passive adaptation between man and his environment. Wellek's observation of the development of the concepts of meaning and value in Dilthey's thought after *Poetik* is valid, but this development means not that the theory of structure is abolished but that the relationship of the dynamic fundamental structural system is seen more and more as purposeful by Dilthey. This development was no doubt influenced by the work of Husserl. Indeed, Paul Ricoeur declares that the "concept of intentionality and of the identical character of the intentional object allowed Dilthey to reinforce his concept of psychic structures through the Husserlian notion of meaning."[60]

The *erworbene Zusammenhang* of Dilthey is of contemporary interest in debate between an ahistorical structuralism and methods of interpretation which are historically oriented. The process whereby the structure of the mind develops is not a purely intellectual process in Dilthey. It does involve the internalizing of social and cultural content and relationships but it is also always a process of physiological and psychic development. The *erworbene Zusammenhang* is not identical with the fundamental structure basic to man but it can never be separated from this fundamental human structure.[61] It is important to note the fine distinctions and dialectical relationships in the thought of Dilthey. Through such a dialectic, Dilthey was able to unite a number of apparently contradictory views. This dialectical containment did not end when Dilthey moved into hermeneutics. Indeed, his hermeneutics must be understood as a deepening and widening of insights in his *Poetik*.

THE HERMENEUTICS OF DILTHEY

The hermeneutics of Dilthey grew out of insights which were expressed in the *Poetik* at its most original points. Dilthey saw no basic contradiction between his poetics and his hermeneutical ideas. Indeed, the projected new edition of his *Poetik* was to include his hermeneutical

efforts. The beginning point for Dilthey was the hermeneutics of
Schleiermacher. In the *Poetik*, Dilthey points out the kinship of poetics
to hermeneutics and indicates that Schleiermacher raised hermeneutics
to the level of an aesthetic form of observation. But, because no real
progress had been made in hermeneutics since the time of Schleiermacher,
hermeneutics could not be used to help in the construction of a contemporary poetics.[62] In *Die Entstehung der Hermeneutik* (1900) Dilthey
takes up the development of hermeneutics to the high point of Schleiermacher. Heinz Kimmerle cautions against the traditional practice of
reading Schleiermacher's hermeneutics from Dilthey's presentation in
Die Entstehung der Hermeneutik. Dilthey, in the judgment of Kimmerle,
read the later works of Schleiermacher in isolation from earlier works
which would have perhaps led to a somewhat different conclusion.
Kimmerle has reconstructed the developments in the hermeneutics of
Schleiermacher in light of the complete manuscript collection,[63] but for
the purposes of understanding Dilthey we are interested in observing
Dilthey's understanding of and use of Schleiermacher. For Dilthey,
hermeneutics involves such questions as: What are the means by which
we know other individuals? Can we raise the understanding of the
individual being to universal validity? Dilthey terms "understanding"
(*Verstehen*) the process by which "we know an inner reality by means
of signs which are given perceptively from without." Understanding
applied to lasting fixed expressions of life is termed "exposition" or
"interpretation" and "the interpretation of the remains of human existence
contained in literature" is a central point in the art of understanding.[64]

The process of the development of hermeneutics is traced through
the development of rhetoric in Greece, the rebirth of classical scholarship
in the Renaissance, and the development of the two streams of classical
and biblical interpretation. Although attempts were made to reunite the
classical and biblical streams in the mid-eighteenth century, it was
Schleiermacher who was able to do this because in him was united "the
masterly skill of philological interpretation" and "the true philosophical
capacity."[65] Schleiermacher worked under certain influences: (1) the
combination of (a) Winckelmann's interpretation of art, (b) Herder's
understanding of the soul of ages and peoples and Heyne's philology,
which was constructed from this new aesthetic viewpoint, and (c) the
philology of F. A. Wolf and his student Heindorf; and (2) the German
transcendental philosophy according to which objects go back to a
creative capacity in the consciousness which unconscious of itself works
in a united way to bring to us the whole form of the world.[66]

Schleiermacher saw all interpretation of literature as dependent upon understanding, but understanding is not to be separated from production. It is in the relationship between understanding and production that rules of interpretation can be defined on the basis of universal human nature shared by the interpreter and the author. The interpreter, then, follows a process with two sides: grammatical and psychological. The grammatical interpretation moves from individual words and their combinations to the total work. The psychological interpretation moves from the arrangement in the creative inner process to the outer and inner forms of the work and from here to the grasp of the unity of the work in the psychology and development of its creator. The final goal of the process is "to understand the author better than he has understood himself."[67] This statement, claims Dilthey, is the necessary consequence of the concept of unconscious creativity.

Dilthey's hermeneutics is not simply a wholesale adoption of his insights into Schleiermacher. Of particular importance is the different epistemological grounding of Dilthey's hermeneutics. In fact, in the last outline for a revision of the *Poetik*, he gave his plan to deal with hermeneutics as a part of epistemology. Dilthey does not, as Schleiermacher, ground human life and the world in God as the whole. He begins with no a priori, not even a philosophy of history, but from the "standpoint of life," and epistemology becomes an empirical study. Life, experience, and history are the focus of Dilthey, not some universal which is presupposed and which cannot be developed out of lived experience. Schleiermacher's philosophical presupposition was such that historical development is only formal change, that what happens in the history of an individual shows what he was in the beginning. Dilthey is not interested in any timeless principle embodied in man but in man's social and historical situation.

The hermeneutics of Dilthey began with his reading of Schleiermacher and emphasizes understanding which allows us to move from the effect of the expression to the cause of lived experience and even to share or relive the experience of another person. What Dilthey has in mind is not an exact reproduction of another's inner processes but an apprehension of the structure or plot and intelligible (not necessarily temporal) order of the sequence. The deeper the understanding, in fact, the more emancipated from the temporal order and the less a near replica of another's thought processes. Selection, abstraction, and symbolization are necessary in the process of understanding that Dilthey envisions, and so "understanding becomes an intellectual process involving the highest concentration, and yet never fully realizable."[68]

Writing in 1900 Dilthey saw the main task of hermeneutics as the establishment "in opposition to the constant inroads of romantic caprice and skeptical subjectivity into the area of history," of "the theoretical universality of interpretation on which all the security of history rests. Taken up into the system of epistemology, logic, and the methodology of the human sciences, this doctrine of interpretation becomes an important element linking philosophy and the historical sciences, a major component of the foundation of the human sciences."[69] Some expressions of man are so fleeting that no method of understanding can be focused on them; some experiences are so simple as to be understood directly or so complex as to preclude understanding in any deep sense; but some expressions are permanently fixed expressions of life, and it is the interpretation of these that Dilthey finds significant.

In manuscripts published after his death, Dilthey lists some principles and postulates of hermeneutics. Among the postulates are the following: (1) The possibility of understanding rests upon the fact that the elementary factors and components of mental life are common to all men. Human nature is everywhere the same. (2) The totality of a work is understood from its parts and its parts from the whole. The understanding of the whole of a work allows access to the individuality of the creator and to literature. That experience, in turn, allows a deeper understanding of the individual parts of the work. (3) "Every mental state is understood by us only from outer stimulation which calls it forth . . . so the context for understanding is indispensable." (4) The key to the question of knowledge and to the human studies is the structure of the mental vitality, the structural coherence (*Zusammenhang*) of the mind. (5) The study of this structure is possible and the procedures will be the same as in natural sciences: induction, analysis, construction, comparison. "Induction . . . takes place here as elsewhere on the foundation of knowledge of a set of relationships. In the physical sciences this is the mathematical knowledge of quantitative relationships . . . ; in the human sciences it is the structure of the mental vitality. So this foundation is not a logical abstraction but a real structure expressed in living; this is, however, an individual and, therefore, a subjective reality."[70]

Unknown to Dilthey, apparently, and to the later hermeneutical tradition until the work of Kimmerle, is the fact that early in his career Schleiermacher had considered a language-oriented approach to hermeneutics. Kimmerle has traced the development of Schleiermacher's hermeneutics from the earliest period by means of Schleiermacher's unpublished papers and he finds that between 1805 and 1819 Schleiermacher was considering language as the basis on which the understanding took place. Language is the basis for both thought and expression. Kimmerle judges that Schleiermacher gave up the conception of the identity of thought and language for philosophical reasons. From transcendental speculative philosophy, he had the concept of an ideal, inner essence; but from the empirical sciences, he had the concept of material outer reality which did not totally match the ideal essence. The text, then, could not be a direct manifestation of thought. Interpretation must indeed go through language but language is not equivalent to thought and must be transcended. This overcoming of language, moreover, is in order to reconstruct the mental process of the author. Schleiermacher in his earlier hermeneutical thinking had held a position "that our thinking, as our own being, are originally and essentially determined through language," in which an understanding of our world is given for us.[71]

In Dilthey's later writings as well as in manuscripts published after his death, the external physical expression is stressed more than in his earlier work. He declares that the linguistic expression must be the basis for the logical operations of induction, and, therefore, the theory of language or grammar is the proper area of study. Dilthey would like to affirm that the philological study of a linguistic expression which results in explanation is a mechanism for delving into the understanding of the reality behind the literary expression. The assertion of Dilthey that grammar and philology are necessary in the total work of hermeneutics and not simply as preliminary activities is interesting in light of Schleiermacher's early work and subsequent developments in the study of language; but even the aesthetic philology of F. A. Wolf, which moves beyond the study of language and literature to the study of the whole cultural life of the nation, was not sufficient to deal with the hermeneutical question as Dilthey had raised it.[72]

The task of Schleiermacher's hermeneutics, "to understand better than the author understood himself," continued to be accepted by Dilthey. Such a task is an art. The process, Dilthey says, is one of "divination." Only through inner affinity and sympathy can it come close to perfection. In fact, the process of hermeneutics goes beyond the limits of logical reflection, beyond the explicit consciousness even of the original author of a work. The interpreter operates with the same creative possibilities of the author and can, by means of the expression of that author, move beyond the author. In the notes published after his death, Dilthey affirms that "in the sense of an unconscious structure which is effective in the organization of the work and is understood from this inner form, an idea is really present (not an abstract thought) of which the poet need not be, and indeed will never be, completely conscious. The interpreter lifts it out and that perhaps is the greatest victory of hermeneutics."[73]

MEANING

In light of developments in structuralism and our attempt to relate the structural study of narrative to hermeneutics, Dilthey's concept of meaning (*Bedeutung*) is very important. In notes for the revision of the *Poetik*, he indicates that the importance of the concept of meaningfulness was clear to him in his early publications, but this concept became more important to him through the years. In the notes from the 1890s, Dilthey lists "The Meaning of Life" as one of the chapters in the third major part of the volume, and he indicates that meaning and meaningfulness are to be emphasized to a larger extent than formerly in the discussion of the satisfaction or harmony which a work of art calls up. The notes of 1907–8 also emphasize meaning. In the outline for Book One (The Poet) Dilthey lists for discussion: "Category of Life: Meaning," and in the second book he lists "Meaningfulness" for discussion as one of the elements of the relationship from which the historicality of the work arises. In places he also substitutes "meaning" for the terms "feeling" and "satisfaction."[74]

"Meaning" is used by Dilthey at times to indicate the relation between a word and its reference, whereby the word "means" the thing to which it refers. In a few places, "meaning" is used with a sense of "importance," but the most profound sense of "meaning" goes beyond the idea of "significance" or "importance." "Meaning is a category of life along with value (*Wert*), purpose (*Zweck*), development (*Entwicklung*), ideal (*Ideal*), and others. Dilthey derives categories from actual experiences instead of on the basis of logic, and he does not define a precise number of categories. Meaning, however, is the "comprehensive category by which life is understandable," for it "shows the relation of the parts of life to the whole that is grounded in the essence of life."[75]

In memory, with which we can see the past flow of life, we grasp the meaning of a moment of the past. It is meaningful because in that moment a commitment for the future took place, or the plan for future life was secured, or the realization of such a plan was hindered, or the engagement of the individual's own being in humanity occurred. The

moment has meaning in the relation of past and future, individual existence and humanity. Since meaning depends upon the relation of the
parts to the whole, our grasp of meaning constantly changes, and meaning must await the end of history.

Dilthey uses analogies to try to express his concept of meaning, and
in the analogies he gives some insight into the use of the concept of meaning for hermeneutics. "As words have a meaning (*Bedeutung*), by which
they point to something, or sentences have a meaning (*Sinn*), which we
construe, so the coherence of the parts of life can be construed to the
defined-undefined meaning of the parts."

> Meaning (*Bedeutung*) is the special kind of relationship which in life the
> parts of life have to the whole. This meaning we recognize as the meaning
> of words in a sentence, in recollections and possibilities of the future. The
> essence of the meaning references is in the relationships which the form
> of a course of life contains in the course of time on the ground of the
> structure of life under the constraints of the environment.[76]

Dilthey sees a real relationship between meaning in the case of
sentences and the meaning of life because of the relationship of meaning
to understanding. He defines this relationship in six assertions: (1) In
the understanding of the sentence, the simplest understanding of meaning
is evident. It is from the meaning or reference of individual words that
understanding of the sentence takes place. But there is a reciprocal
relationship between the sentence and the word. The various possibilities
of word meanings make the meaning of the sentence indeterminant. (2)
In the process of life, the meaning or signification of life (*Sinn*) is the
result of the relationship between the meaning or reference (*Bedeutung*)
of the parts and the whole. (3) The individual events which build the
course of life have a relation to something to which they refer. The coherence of these experiences gives the meaning (*Bedeutung*) of the
course of life. (4) The idea of meaning exists only when we relate it to
the experience of understanding. In this case, what is considered is the
relationship of an external, or an observable reality, to the inner reality
of which it is an expression. The relationship is not a grammatical relationship, for the expression is not simply the reference of the words. (5)
Meaning in this highest sense, understanding, the meaning of life and
history, does not speak of references, does not point to events which are
to be understood through the inner structure. (6) What we seek is the
meaning of life itself. The various manifestations refer to something that
belongs to life but what we seek is life itself which does not mean something else.[77]

For Dilthey, meaning is not ultimately an intellectual relationship; it is not simply a rational process. "Meaning is obtained from life itself."[78] But if one would point to a structure as the meaning (*Sinn*) of a total life as it is given out of the meaning (*Bedeutung*) of the parts, "the poetic work speaks forth the meaning of life by means of the free creation of the structure of meaning."[79] Dilthey, in his *Poetik*, relates this "meaning" to religion. He indicates that since "religion has lost the support of metaphysical arguments for the existence of God and the soul,"[80] for many people an ideal comprehension of "the meaning of life" is available only in art and poetry. Poetry has the difficult task of finding form to express "an immense content."[81] The core of meaning which is to be expressed by the poet is the same for all times. In this sense, the great poets possess something eternal. Man, on the other hand, is a historical being. "When the social order and the meaning of life change, the poets of past ages no longer move us as they once did. This is true today. We await the poet who will speak to us as we suffer, eat and drink, and wrestle with life."[82]

CONCLUSION

In the works of Dilthey in poetics and hermeneutics are discussions of elements which continue to be important in literary theory. But these elements are presented in a conceptual framework which is even more important than the individual elements themselves. It appears that the almost immediate acceptance of some of the peripheral elements of Dilthey's literary theory, and the subsequent disavowal of such ideas, caused Dilthey's comprehensive view to be lost in terms of continuing influence in the development of literary studies. The influence of Dilthey upon the hermeneutics of Martin Heidegger and the influence of Dilthey and Heidegger upon New Testament hermeneutics must be examined to discover to what extent the comprehensive concept of Dilthey was modified and whether a return to some of the basic ideas of Dilthey might help New Testament hermeneutics move beyond its present aporia.

The structural movement, which was beginning in Russia at the same time that Dilthey was working on his phase of poetics, must also be examined, particularly the developments in the structural study of narrative, to ascertain the basic contributions of structuralism. Finally, the possible relationships between hermeneutics and structuralism must be examined and the contribution of structural study of narrative to New Testament hermeneutics proposed.

NOTES

1. Wilhelm Dilthey, *Die Einbildungskraft des Dichters: Bausteine für eine Poetik, Gesammelte Schriften*, VI (5th ed.; Göttingen: Vandenhoeck and Ruprecht, 1968), 103–9. Hereafter *Poetik*.

2. René Wellek, *The Later Nineteenth Century*, vol. IV of *A History of Modern Criticism: 1750–1950* (New Haven: Yale University Press, 1965), p. 323.

3. Kurt Müller-Vollmer, *Towards a Phenomenological Theory of Literature: A Study of Wilhelm Dilthey's "Poetik"* (The Hague: Mouton, 1963), p. 9.

4. Rudolf Bultmann, "The Problem of Hermeneutics," *Essays Philosophical and Theological* (London: SCM, 1955), pp. 248, 250–51.

5. Richard E. Palmer, *Hermeneutics: Interpretation Theory in Schleiermacher, Dilthey, Heidegger, and Gadamer* (Evanston: Northwestern University Press, 1969), pp. 106, 121, 80.

6. Hans-Georg Gadamer, *Wahrheit und Methode* (3d ed.; Tübingen: J. C. B. Mohr, 1972), pp. 211, 477. English translation: *Truth and Method* (New York: Seabury Press, 1975).

7. Müller-Vollmer, *Towards a Phenomenological Theory of Literature*, pp. 41–46.

8. Frithjof Rodi, *Morphologie und Hermeneutik: Zur Methode von Diltheys Ästhetik* (Stuttgart: W. Kohlhammer Verlag, 1969), p. 7. ". . . die Frage nach der Möglichkeit eines im echten Sinn offenen hermeneutischen Systems, das die Erfahrungen des Lebens nach ihrer *Bedeutung* verständlich macht. . . ."

9. Wilhelm Dilthey, *Die drei Epochen der modernen Ästhetik und ihre heutige Aufgabe* (Göttingen, 1892). Hereafter referred to as *Drei Epochen*.

10. *Gesammelte Schriften*, II, 307–10.

11. *Ibid.*, p. 310: ". . . sollte die Schrift radikal umgestaltet werden, durch veränderte Verteilung des Textes, Streichung weiterer Partien, Zusätze von ganzen Abschnitten."

12. *Ibid.*, p. 311: "Der Zusammenhang der Konzeptionen von Leben, Erlebnis. . . , Bedeutsamkeit als einer Eigenschaft des Lebens, inhaltlicher Psychologie, Aufgabe, Dichtung als Erhebung zu Bedeutsamkeit usw. Ist schon in meinen ersten Veröffentlichungen enthalten."

13. Wellek, *The Later Nineteenth Century*, p. 322. The quotation from Dilthey comes from *Gesammelte Schriften*, VII, 85: "Dieses sind night die inneren Vorgänge in dem Dichter, sondern ein von diesen geschaffener, aber von ihnen ablösbarer Zusammenhang. . . . So ist der Gegenstand mit dem die Literaturgeschichte oder die Poetik zunächst zu tun hat, ganz unterschieden von psychischen Vorgängen im Dichter order seinen Lesern."

14. *Gesammelte Schriften*, VI, 317–19.

15. *Ibid.*, V, ix.

16. José Ortega y Gasset, *Concord and Liberty* (New York: W. W. Norton, 1946), p. 134.

17. *Drei Epochen*, p. 253: ". . . begreift das Schöne als die Erscheinung des Logischen im Sinnlichen und die Kunst als eine sinnliche Vergegenwärtigung des harmonischen Weltzusammenhanges."

18. *Ibid.*: ". . . schliesslich in der rationalen Ordnung des Universums begründet."

19. *Ibid.*: "Es gibt Regeln der Künste, die allgemeingültig aus der Natur der Sache fliessen."

20. *Ibid.*, p. 258: ". . . die reifste und vollständigste analytische Untersuchung des 18. Jahrhunderts über das Schöne."

21. *Ibid.*: ". . . fand Home die seelische Bewegung des ästhetischen Eindruckes einfach an eine bestimmte Beschaffenheit des ästhetischen objektes oder Vorganges von der Natur geknüpft."

22. *Ibid.*, p. 259: "Wir erfassen aber die Natur des ästhetischen Eindrucks erst ganz, wenn wir die Emotion, welchedurch die wirkliche Anwesenheit des Gegenstandes erregt wird, von der sondern, welche die blosse ideale Gegenwart des Objektes hervorruft."

23. *Ibid.*: ". . . bestimmte ästhetische Eindrücke regelmässig gemäss der Natur unserer Seele mit bestimmten Eigenschaften der ästhetischen Objekte verbunden sind."

24. *Ibid.*, pp. 263–66.

25. *Ibid.*, pp. 266–70.

26. *Poetik*, p. 107: "Wie überwinden wir doch die überall auf den Geisteswissenschaften lastende Schwierigkeit, allgemeingültige Sätze abzuleiten aus den inneren Erfahrungen, die so persönlich beschränkt, so unbestimmt, so zusammengesetzt und doch unzerlegbar sind?"

27. *Ibid.*: ". . . allgemeingültige Gesetze gewinnen, welche als Regeln des Schaffens und als Normen der Kritik brauchbar sind?"

28. *Ibid.*, p. 108: "Der Ausgangspunkt einer solchen Theorie muss in der Analysis des schaffenden Vermögens liegen, dessen Vorgänge die Dichtung bedingen."

29. *Ibid.*: "Die Phantasie des Dichters in ihrer Stellung zur Welt der Erfahrungen."

30. *Ibid.*, p. 110: ". . . das Sein im Denken dargestellt wird."

31. *Ibid.*, p. 115: "Das Aristotelische Prinzip der Nachahmung war objektivistisch, analog der Aristotelischen Erkenntnistheorie; seitdem die Untersuchung sich überall in das subjektive Vermögen der Menschennatur vertiefte und die selbständige Kraft desselben erfasste . . . wurde auch in der Ästhetik das Prinzip der Nachahmung unhaltbar."

32. *Ibid.*, p. 117: "Die Gestalt muss Leben werden und das Leben Gestalt."

33. *Ibid.*: "Ein Mensch, wiewohl er lebt und Gestalt hat, ist darum noch lange keine lebende Gestalt. Dazu gehört, dass seine Gestalt Leben und sein Leben Gestalt sei. So lange wir über seine Gestalt bloss denken ist sie leblos, blosse Abstraktion; so lange wir sein Leben bloss fühlen, ist es gestaltlos, blosse Impression. Nur indem seine Form in unserer Empfindung lebt und sein Leben in unserem Verstande sich formt, ist er lebende Gestalt, und dies wird überall der Fall sein, wo wir ihn als schön beurteilen."

34. *Ibid.*, p. 119: "Das Schaffen des Künstlers steigert Eigenschaften, die im Wirklichen schon liegen."

35. *Ibid.*, p. 128: ". . . man muss etwas sein, um etwas zu machen."

36. *Ibid.*, p. 129: "So ist schon der mütterliche Boden aller echten Posie ein geschichtlich Tatsächliches. . . . Die dichterische Technik ist historisch bedingt."

37. *Ibid.*, p. 130: ". . . kernhafter Inhalt . . ."

38. *Ibid.*, pp. 130–31: "Wie unser Leib atmet, so verlangt unsere Seele nach Erfüllung und Erweiterung ihrer Existenz in den Schwingungen des Gemütslebens. Das Lebensgefühl will austönen in Klang und Wort und Bild; die Anschauung befriedigt uns nur ganz, sofern sie mit solchem Gehalt des Lebens und den Schwingungen des Gefühls erfüllt ist; dies Ineinander, unser ursprüngliches, volles, ganzes Leben, Anschauung vom Gefühl verinnerlicht und gesättigt, Lebensgefühl ausstrahlend in der Helle des Bildes: das ist das inhaltliche, wesenhafte Merkmal aller Poesie."

39. *Ibid.*, p. 139: "Die herrschende Psychologie ist von Vorstellungen als festen Grössen ausgegangen. Sie lässt deren Veränderungen von aussen. . . ."

40. *Ibid.*, pp. 143–44: ". . . das im Bewusstsein Befindliche ist zu ihm orientiert; es ist von ihm begrenzt, bestimmt und begründet. Sätze haben in ihm ihre Gewissheit; Begriffe haben durch ihn ibre scharfe Begrenzung; unsere Lage im Raum und in der Zeit hat an ihm ihre Orientierung. Ebenso empfangen aus ihm die Gefühle ihr Mass für den Zusammenhang unseres Lebens. Unser Wille, welcher zumeist mit Mitteln beschäftigt ist, bleibt vermittels desselben Zusammenhangs beständig des Gefüges der Zwecke gewiss, in welchem die Mittel begründet sind."

41. *Ibid.*, p. 145: ". . . wissenschaftliche Einbildungskraft . . ."

42. *Ibid.*, p. 147: ". . . praktische Phantasie . . ."

43. *Ibid.*: "Vorstellungen, die von einer Gefühlslage aus geformt sind, wiederum diese regelmässig hervorrufen können."

44. *Ibid.*, p. 148: "Aus der Erfahrung von den Verhältnissen der Formen zu unseren Gefühlen entspringt die Bedeutung, welche die Verhältnisse der Linien, die Verteilung von Kraft und Last und die Symmetrie im architektonischen und bildlichen Aufbau haben. Aus der Wahrnehmung von den Beziehungen unserer Gefühle zu dem Stimme nach Höhe und Tiefe, Rhythmus und Stärke entsteht der Aufbau der betonten Rede und der Melodie. Aus den erworbenen Einsichten über die Wirkung von Charakteren, Schicksalen und Handlungen auf unsere Gefühle bildet sich die ideale Gestaltung der Charaktere und die Führung der Handlung. Aus den geheimnisvollen Beziehungen zwischen den gefühlten Unterschieden des Seelenlebens und dem Mannigfachen der Körperformen erwächst das Ideal in der bildenden Kunst."

45. *Ibid.*: "So wird die Analysis des Gefühls den Schlüssel fur die Erklärung des künstlerischen Schaffens enthalten."

46. *Ibid.*, pp. 150–54.

47. *Ibid.*, pp. 154–63.

48. *Ibid.*, pp. 163–77. At this point Dilthey cites evidence from a number of poets concerning these processes. *Ibid.*, pp. 178–84.

49. *Ibid.*, pp. 185–88.

50. H. A. Hodges, *The Philosophy of Wilhelm Dilthey* (London: Routledge and Kegan Paul, 1952), p. 113.

51. *Poetik*, p. 195: ". . . die Absicht, welche für den Eindruck die Mittel

berechnet, muss hinter dem Schein ganz unwillkürlichen Gestaltens und freier Wirklichkeit verschwinden."

52. *Ibid.*: "Die Poetik öffne beide Tore ihrer Erfahrungen soweit als möglich, damit keine Art von Tatsache oder Verfahren ausgeschlossen werde!"

53. *Ibid.*: "Indem sie die Eindrücke untersucht, geniesst sie des Vorteils, den Wechsel derselben willkürlich vom Wechsel der objekte aus hervorrufen und das Komplexe des Vorgangs in seine Bestandteile zerlegen zu können; hier wird experimentelle Ästhetik möglich. . . ."

54. *Ibid.*: ". . . die Fülle des literarhistorischen Stoffes verwertbar gemacht werden."

55. *Ibid.*, pp. 219–26.

56. Wellek, *The Later Nineteenth Century*, p. 335.

57. Clara Misch-Dilthey (ed.), *Der Junge Dilthey* (Göttingen: Vandenhoeck & Ruprecht, 1960), p. 80. Cited in Peter Krausser, *Kritik der endlichen Vernunft: Wilhelm Diltheys Revolution der allgemeinen Wissenschafts—und Handlungstheorie* (Frankfurt: Suhrkamp Verlag, 1968), p. 28.

58. Krausser, *Kritik der endlichen Vernunft*, p. 210: ". . . es handelt sich um eine formalanthropologische Theorie des eigentümlichen dynamischen, die Geschichtlichkeit und Lernfähigkeit des Menschen bedingenden Zusammenhangs der leibich-seelisch-geistigen Funktionen untereinander und mit den Änderungen der Aussenwelt, insbesondere der sozialen und kulturellen."

59. *Ibid.*, pp. 101–3. The most important references to the mental structure prior to *Poetik* are: *Gesammelte Schriften* I, 14–18, 34–35, 37–78, 81; V, 15–16, 37–39, 60, 63–64, 68–73; VI, 94–96; XIV, 658–59, 661, 708, 722; "Breslauer Ausarbeitung" of the second volume of *Einleitüng in die Geisteswissenschaften* (duplicated but unpublished; contained in an appendix to Peter Krausser, *Kritik der endlichen Vernunft*), 60–61, 96–101; *Das Erlebnis und die Dichtung* (13th ed.; Stuttgart: B. G. Teubner, 1957), pp. 33–34, 171–72.

60. Paul Ricoeur, "The Task of Hermeneutics," *Philosophy Today* 17 (1973), 118.

61. Krausser, *Kritik der endlichen Vernunft*, pp. 145–61, discusses Dilthey's view of the development of the inner structure.

62. *Poetik*, p. 124.

63. Schleiermacher, *Hermeneutik*, newly edited on the basis of manuscripts and introduced by Heinz Kimmerle (2d ed.; Heidelberg: Carl Winter, 1974). See also Heinz Kimmerle, "Hermeneutical Theory or Ontological Hermeneutics," *History and Hermeneutic*, vol. 4 of *Journal for Theology and the Church* (New York: Harper, 1967), pp. 105–21.

64. Wilhelm Dilthey, *Die Entstehung der Hermeneutik* in *Gesammelte Schriften*, V, 318: ". . . in welchem wir aus Zeichen, die von aussen sinnlich gegeben sind, ein Inneres erkennen." P. 319: ". . . der Auslegung oder Interpretation der in der Schrift enthaltenen Reste menschlichen Daseins." Hereafter referred to as *Entstehung*.

65. *Ibid.*, p. 329: ". . . philologischen Virtuosität . . . philosophisches Vermögen . . ."

66. *Ibid.*, pp. 326–27.

67. *Ibid.*, p. 331: ". . . den Autor besser zu verstehen, als er sich selber verstanden hat."

68. *Gesammelte Schriften*, VII, 227: "Das Verstehen wird also ein intellektueller Prozess von höchster Anstrengung, der doch nie ganz realisiert werden kann."

69. *Ibid.*, V, 331: ". . . gegenüber dem beständigen Einbruch romantischer Wilkür und skeptischer Subjektivität in das Gebiet der Geschichte." ". . . die Allgemeingültigkeit der Interpretation . . . auf welcher alle Sicherheit der Geschichte beruht. Aufgenommen in den Zusammenhang von Erkenntnistheorie, Logik, und Methodenlehre der Geisteswissenschaften, wird diese Lehre von der Interpretation ein wichtiges Verbindungsglied zwischen der Philosophie und den geschichtlichen Wissenschaften, ein Hauptbestandteil der Grundlegung der Geisteswissenschaften."

70. See *ibid.*, 334–35: (3) "Sochon jeder einzelne seelische Zustand wird von uns nur verstanden von den äusseren Reizen aus, die ihn hervorriefen. . . . So ist das Milieu für das Verständnis unentbehrlich." (5) "Die Induktion . . . vollzieht sich hier wie überall auf der Grundlage eines Wissens von einem Zusammenhang. Dieser ist in den physikalisch-chemischen Wissenschaften die mathematische Kenntnis quantitativer Verhältnesse, in den biologischen Wissenschaften die Lebenszweckmassigkeit, in den Geisteswissenschaften die Struktur der seelischen Lebendigkeit. So ist diese Grundlage nicht eine logische Abstraktion, sondern ein realer, im Leben gegebener Zusammenhang; dieser ist aber individuell, sonach subjektiv."

71. Kimmerle, "Einleitung," in Schleiermacher, *Hermeneutik*, p. 21: "dass unser Denken wie unser ganzes Sein ursprünglich und wesentlich von der Sprache bestimmt sind."

72. *Gesammelte Schriften*, V, 333.

73. *Ibid.*, p. 335: ". . . im Sinne eines unbewussten Zusammenhangs, der in der Organisation des Werkes wirksam ist und aus dessen innerer Form verstanden wird, vorhanden; ein Dichter braucht sie nicht, ja wird nie ganz bewusst sein; der Ausleger hebt sie heraus und das ist vielleicht der höchste Triumph der Hermeneutik."

74. *Ibid.*, VI, 308, 310–12.

75. *Ibid.*, VII, 233. See Hodges, *The Philosophy of Wilhelm Dilthey*, pp. 277–81.

76. *Gesammelte Schriften*, VII, 233–34: "Wie Worte eine Bedeutung haben, durch die sie etwas bezeichnen, oder Sätze einen Sinn, den wir konstruieren, so kann aus der bestimmt-unbestimmten Bedeutung der Teile des Lebens dessen Zusammenhang konstruiert werden." "Bedeutung ist die besondere Art von Beziehung welche innerhalb des Lebens dessen Teile zum Ganzen haben. Diese Bedeutung erkennen wir, wie die von Worten in einem Satz, druch Erinnerungen und Möglichkeiten der Zukunft. Das Wesen der Bedeutungsbeziehungen liegt in den Verhältnissen, welche im Zeitverlauf die Gestaltung eines Lebenslaufes auf Grund der Struktur des Lebens unter Bedingungen des Milieu enthält."

77. *Ibid.*

78. *Ibid.*, p. 240: "Die Bedeutsamkeit ist aus dem Leben selbst herausge-holt."

79. *Ibid.*: ". . . spricht das dichterische Werk vermittles des freien Schaffens des Bedeutungszusammenhanges den Sinn des Lebens aus."

80. *Poetik*, p. 237: ". . . die Religion den Halt metaphysischer Schlüsse auf das Dasein Gottes und der Seel verloren hat . . ."

81. *Ibid.*, p. 240. ". . . ungeheurer Gehalt . . ."

82. *Ibid.*, p. 241. "Wenn die Ordnung der Gesellschaft und die Bedeutung des Lebens eine andere geworden ist, bewegen uns die Dichter des dann ver-gangenen Zeitalters nicht mehr, wie sie einstmals ihre Zeitgenossen bewegt haben. So ist es heute. Wir harren des Dichters, der uns sage, wie wir leiden, geniessen und mit dem Leben ringen!"

CHAPTER TWO

Post-Diltheyan
Hermeneutics and Language

Schleiermacher and Dilthey endeavored to find a key to hermeneutics in language, Schleiermacher at the beginning of his career and Dilthey toward the end of his work. The logical impossibility of the identity of ideal thought and actual expression caused Schleiermacher to abandon the key of language. The historical and finite character of reason for Dilthey meant that he did not have Schleiermacher's philosophical problem; but still Dilthey did not have the linguistic tools in his time to accomplish the task.

Hermeneutics since Dilthey has continued, nevertheless, to see language as central. Instead of beginning with accepted ideas of language, however, hermeneutics has conceived of language as a reality far beyond the reach of the tools of traditional grammar and philology. The concern with language has become a concern for New Testament theology, and Heidegger is the philosopher from whom New Testament hermeneutics has drawn most directly, beginning with the work of Rudolf Bultmann and continuing on with the "New Hermeneutic." The task of Heidegger has to do with the philosophical question of Being. He approaches language from the perspective of Being and contrariwise Being from the reality of language. The work of Heidegger has been found useful for other less ultimate enterprises, and no limitations can be placed upon such use of Heidegger; but it appears most sensible to keep his major concern in mind while describing his various contributions and evaluating his relationship to the broad hermeneutical program of Dilthey. Gadamer has continued the Heideggerian hermeneutical tradition but he does not confine his interest to Being. Gadamer returns to some of the wider concerns of Dilthey, but from a different perspective.

HEIDEGGER: "BEING AND TIME"

If the question of Being unites the work of Heidegger, different approaches to Being divide his work into at least two periods, the early approach of *Being and Time* and a somewhat different approach in more recent works. *Being and Time* has been very influential in terms of the philosophy of existence, and so it is important to remember that what Heidegger wishes to accomplish in *Being and Time* is nothing other than the clarification of the question of "what belongs to the concept of a science *of Being as such*, and to its possibilities and its variations." The postulate which allows Heidegger to make the investigation is that "Being (not entities) is something which 'there is' only insofar as truth is. And truth *is* only insofar and as long as *Dasein* is. Being and truth 'are' equiprimordially."[1]

The importance of language in the study of Being will be observed by the sensitive reader from the very beginning of *Being and Time*, long before the explicit discussion of language in section thirty-four (page 160). The language which Heidegger uses in *Being and Time* is a clue to his estimation of the worth of language: (1) At the very beginning, *man* is replaced by *Dasein*, and throughout Heidegger avoids current expressions which would have been expected, such as consciousness and mind. This practice of Heidegger must be stressed; otherwise a comparison with Dilthey is problematic. (2) Words which are synonyms of everyday language are often distinguished carefully, with the common usage being disregarded. *Fear* and *anxiety*, for example, are so distinguished. (3) New words are created with the use of prefixes and suffixes; such a word is *Zuhandenheit*. In the case of *Befindlichkeit*, a word which was current several centuries earlier was reintroduced. (4) New meanings of words are created by stressing the original meanings of some of the elements. *Entfernung*, for example, means the opposite of what one would have expected. Jan Aler declares that "the result of these and similar manipulations is a style of writing that is especially accurate, plastic, lively, emphatic, and original."[2] The language used by Heidegger seems to be in harmony with his understanding of language and its significance in the understanding of Being.

The vehicle for Heidegger's research into Being as well as his recording of his insights is language. This is made plain in his discussion of the phenomenological method: "Our investigation itself will show that the meaning of phenomenological description as a method lies in *interpretation*. The *logos* of the phenomenology of Dasein has the character of a *hermeneuein,* through which the authentic meaning of Being, and also those basic structures of Being which Dasein itself possesses, are *made known* to Dasein's understanding of Being. The phenomenology of Dasein is a *hermeneutic* in the primordial signification of this word, where it designates this business of interpreting." In Heidegger's view, "*Legein* is the clue for arriving at those structures of Being which belong to the entities we encounter in addressing ourselves to anything or speaking about it." Heidegger is not satisfied with the traditional philosophical treatment of language as an adequate base on which to establish ontology because in traditional treatment the *logos* gets experienced and interpreted as something "present-at-hand" and the "entities which it points out have the meaning of presence-at-hand." This traditional treatment is the reason why and evidence for the fact that the basis on which ancient ontology arose was not a primordial one.[3]

The bases given by Heidegger for his view of language are the definition of man as "that living thing whose Being is essentially determined by the potentiality for discourse" and the phenomenological method of letting "that which shows itself be seen from itself in the very way in which it shows itself from itself." *Logos* is central in the definitions of man and phenomenology, and Heidegger points out that *logos* is akin to *legein;* hence, he is able to interpret *logos* in such a way as to show language as both the ability to speak and the result of the action, that which is spoken. The concept of the *logos* is treated in the introduction to *Being and Time,* but following a cyclic approach to analysis, Heidegger postpones until the fifth chapter of the first division the explicit treatment of discourse and language. (Heidegger uses "discourse" to designate the *existentiale* equiprimordial with state-of-mind and understanding and "language" as the expression of discourse.) Early in the treatment of discourse and language, state-of-mind and understanding are developed as "the fundamental *existentialia* which constitute the Being of the 'there.' " These are not separate elements of *Dasein,* for "a state-of-mind always has its understanding" and "understanding always has its mood." Primordial understanding (as distinguished from the understanding which is one possible kind of cognition among others) has competence not over a what but over Being as existing. Interpretation is the appropriation of that which is understood. Again, it is not the acquiring of information but the working out of possibilities projected in understanding. State-of-mind, maintaining itself in a certain understanding, also has a certain capacity for getting interpreted.[4]

Heidegger deals with the question of how information is perceived and structured and how disclosure is possible. Perceiving, understanding, interpreting, as Heidegger sees them, are "grounded in something we have in advance—in a fore-having . . . in a foresight . . . in a fore-conception." This grounding is operative on the ordinary level of interpretation of things.

> An interpretation is never a presuppositionless apprehending of something presented to us. If, when one is engaged in a particular concrete kind of interpretation, in the sense of exact textual Interpretation, one likes to appeal to what "stands there," then one finds that what "stands there" in the first instance is nothing other than the obvious undiscussed assumption of the person who does the interpreting. In an interpretative approach there lies such an assumption, as that which has been "taken for granted" with the interpretation as such—that is to say, as that which has been presented in our fore-having, our fore-sight, and our fore-conception.[5]

The basis for perception, understanding, interpretation on whatever level is the fact that discourse and language as the derivative of discourse are existentially equiprimordial with state-of-mind and understanding, and that since Being-in-the-world is the basic state of *Dasein,* "discourse too must have essentially a kind of Being which is specifically *worldly.*" Moreover, discourse, through language, "becomes something which we may come across as ready-to-hand."[6]

In his discussion of hearing, Heidegger again deals with the matter of how perception occurs. Hearing is "an existential possibility which belongs to talking itself." By "hearing" Heidegger is thinking of a reality "more primordial than what is defined 'in the first instance' as 'hearing' in psychology—the sensing of tones and the perceptions of sounds." But "just as linguistic utterance is based on discourse, so is acoustic perception on hearing." The fact that what is heard is not a "pure noise" but the creaking wagon or the motorcycle is evidence that "Dasein, as Being-in-the-world, already dwells *alongside* what is ready-to-hand within-the-world." What is heard, the structuring of what is heard, is the result of the nature of *Dasein.* In the same way "when we are explicitly hearing the discourse of another, we proximally understand what is said, or—to put it more exactly—we are already with him, in advance, alongside the entity which the discourse is about."[7]

Heidegger asserts that in discourse, in talking, *Dasein* expresses itself. We cannot think of this as taking place in an object-subject relationship, as something internal as over something outside, for *Dasein,* "as Being-in-the-world . . . is already 'outside' when it understands." What is expressed in fact can be thought of as this "Being-outside," or "the way in which one currently has a state-of-mind." Heidegger sees disclosure of existence not only in discourse which has this objective but also in other talking. "The items constitutive for discourse are: what the discourse is about (what is talked about); what is said-in-the-talk, as such; the communication; and the making-known." In discourse Being-in and state-of-mind are made known and indicated in language "by intonation, modulation, the tempo of talk, 'the way of speaking.' " "In 'poetical' discourse," moreover, "the communication of the existential possibilities of one's state-of-mind can become an aim in itself, and this amounts to a disclosing of existence."[8] In his treatment of "idle talk" Heidegger gives a summary of his view:

> For the most part, discourse is expressed by being spoken out, and has always been so expressed; it is language. [*Die Rede spricht sich zumeist aus und hat sich schon immer ausgesprochen. Sie ist Sprache.*] But in that case, understanding and interpretation already lie in what has thus been expressed. In language, as a way things have been expressed or spoken out, there is hidden a way in which the understanding of Dasein has been interpreted. This way of interpreting it is no more just present-at-hand than language is; on the contrary, its Being is itself of the character of Dasein. Proximally, and with certain limits, Dasein is constantly delivered over to this interpretedness, which controls and distributes the possibilities of average understanding and of the state-of-mind belonging to it. The way things have been expressed or spoken out is such that in the totality of contexts of signification into which it has been articulated, it preserves an understanding of the disclosed world and therewith, equiprimordially, an understanding of the Dasein-with of Others and of one's own Being-in. The understanding which has thus already been "deposited" in the way things have been expressed pertains just as much to any traditional discoveredness of entities which may have been reached, as it does to one's current understanding of Being and to whatever possibilities and horizons for fresh interpretation and conceptual Articulation may be available.[9]

The view of language being set forth by Heidegger is obviously contrary to that of traditional grammar. The Greeks, Heidegger asserts, took as their foundation for working out grammar the logic of a *logos* based on the ontology of the present-at-hand. The liberation of grammar from this logic cannot be accomplished merely by improving or modifying what has been handed down. Even the philosophical horizon of Humboldt is not adequate. The doctrine of signification and hence discourse and language must be "rooted in the ontology of Dasein." Heidegger asserts that prosperity or decay of the doctrine of signification will depend upon the fate of its ontology.[10]

LANGUAGE AFTER "BEING AND TIME"

In Heidegger's writings after *Being and Time,* language assumes more importance. This importance is seen in his description of the nature of language and his use of language, particularly poetry. Language becomes primary. In *Being and Time* discourse is the third of the *existentialia* and language is merely related in a derivative way to discourse. In later writing the other constituents give way to language. It is language which makes man what he is. But this language is no longer, as in *Being and Time,* merely the way in which discourse gets expressed. It is no longer simply a human activity. Language displaces or incorporates state-of-mind, understanding, and discourse. Moreover, "language is the language of Being as the clouds are the clouds of heaven."[11] "Language speaks" and "man speaks only as he responds to language."[12] Heidegger denies that language can finally be defined simply as "expression," "an activity of man," and "a presentation and representation of the real and unreal."[13] Even when the concept of language is expanded to include the "voicing of the inner man . . . the nature of language can never appear as anything but an expression and an activity of man" when attention is given exclusively to human speech. Human speech, however, "is not self-subsistent. The speech of mortals rests in its relation to the speaking of language."[14]

The profound view of language speaking instead of merely being spoken is found in *Being and Time,* expressed not in an explicit way, to be sure, but expressed in the relations set up by Heidegger among discourse, language, interpretation, and assertion. Understanding, mood, and discourse are existential components of *Dasein.* Interpretation and assertion are based on understanding and discourse. Interpretation is the appropriation of understanding, the "working-out of possibilities projected in understanding." It is the process of explicating *Dasein's* antecedent comprehension of meaningfulness. Assertion, moreover, presents a "derivative form in which an interpretation has been carried out." It is *"a pointing-out which gives something a definite character and which communicates."* Interpretation is an articulation before thematic assertion, an articulation of what has been understood, of meaning (*Sinn*). Assertion has an "ontological origin from an interpretation which understands." But it is also communication, language.[15]

Language, however, rests upon discourse as its existential-ontological foundation. Discourse, moreover, "is the Articulation of intelligibility" which "underlies both interpretation and assertion." Is there, then, an articulation of meaning in discourse which is prior to that articulation in interpretation? That there is such prior articulation is made clear when Heidegger speaks of the meaning "which can be Articulated in interpretation, and thus even more primordially in discourse."[16]

The totality-of-significations is articulated in discursive articulation. This must be explicated in concrete significations because of the constraints of the situations and these significations must be disengaged. These significations "always carry meaning (. . . *sind* . . . *sinnhaft*)" because they are "what has been Articulated from that which can be Articulated." In his discussion of assertion as a mode of interpretation, Heidegger emphasizes the "fore-having," "fore-sight," and "fore-conception" which form the existential foundations of assertion. Some inconspicuous fore-conception is always implied in assertion, "because the language already hides in itself a developed way of conceiving."[17]

John Sallis relates the ideas being expressed in a groping way at this point in *Being and Time* with the later view of language:

> Discourse is not . . . primarily an articulation of meaning which *we* perform but rather an articulation which is always already performed for us, and articulation which is, of necessity, already delivered over to us, which we have already taken over inadvertently, by virtue of our living in a language—by virtue of our having been thrown into a language with its concealed, yet already developed ways of conceiving.[18]

In the lecture of 1935 entitled "Introduction to Metaphysics" we observe the elevation of language to a more important place. (This lecture was not published until 1953.) The metaphysical concern of Heidegger is clear from the title and content. Being now takes the center of interest in the place of *Dasein*, and language is the means of Being: "The origin of language is in essence mysterious. And this means that language can only have arisen from the overpowering, the strange and terrible, through man's departure into being. In this departure language was being, embodied in the word: Poetry. Language is the primordial poetry in which a people speaks being."[19]

Seen in the correct view, prior to deformation and decay, "words and language are not wrappings in which things are packed for the commerce of those who write and speak. It is in words and language that things first come into being and are." Heidegger at times seems to equate

language with words and he sees language (words) as being used up.
The emptiness of the word "Being" is not only cited as "a particular
instance of the general exhaustion of language" but, more importantly,
"the destroyed relation to being as such is the actual reason for the
general misrelation to language." The word that expresses a Being is
not something given subsequent to the discovery of the Being. It is not a
purely arbitrary sign. The word is formed in the process of discovery
and that word preserves the Being in its discovered openness. Language
and *Dasein* arise together, and in both Being retains its primacy. Language seems to be at the disposition of *Dasein,* but actually the reverse
is true. *Dasein* discovers itself only in and with language.[20] The concept
of words in *Being and Time* is essentially the same as in later works.
Words are important because "the totality-of-significations of intelligibility is *put into words.*" But even here, at the deepest level, significations
do not come from the words: "To significations, words accrue, but word-
Things do not get supplied with significations." A clear statement of this
view of words is given in the earlier discussion of "reference and sign."
"A sign is not a Thing which stands to another Thing in the relationship
of indicating; it is rather *an item of equipment which explicitly raises a
totality of equipment into our circumspection so that together with it the
worldly character of the ready-to-hand announces itself.*"[21]

In a later statement, Heidegger uses the contrast between buckets of
water and wellsprings to express the difference between words as terms
and words as that which accrues to significations: "Words are not terms,
and thus are not like buckets and kegs from which we scoop a content
that is there. Words are wellsprings that are found and dug up in the
telling. . . ."[22]

The important consequence to which Heidegger is moving in his
later work is that *Dasein* may question Being itself by properly discovering the original sense of words. Also important is the fact that *Dasein's*
primordial "poetizing" with words enjoys a special affinity with Being.
Heidegger thus sees the original experience of Being as language coming
to pass for the Greeks in the poetry of Homer.[23] The new task of
Heidegger then is set forth in his "Introduction to Metaphysics."
Through poetry, and through a process of retrieving the primal fresh-
ness of words, Being will be interrogated. In "A Dialogue on Language"
(1953–54) Heidegger acknowledged that the relationship between Being
and language was a theme which became central for him in his earliest
years as a student.[24] William J. Richardson refers to this period as "Ur

Heidegger" and therefore concludes that "Heidegger II" was *more original than Heidegger I*, went with him along the way."[25]

DILTHEY AND HEIDEGGER

In Dilthey there is a broad conceptualization of language and literature involving the creativity of man and creativity as universal and historical reality; the text as an expression of the historical experiences of man and the structure of the mind; meaning as reference to things in the world, meaning as reference in terms of the course of life, meaning that belongs to life, and meaning as life itself. There are levels of creativity, text, and meaning; and there are relationships among these levels and the elements of the various levels. Dilthey was planning to unite the various elements and levels in a new edition of the *Poetik*, notes for which he sketched in 1908.[26]

The contribution of Heidegger is regularly placed in relationship to the traditional understanding of Dilthey. The latter is regarded as the " 'sensitive' interpreter of the history of the spirit, especially the history of literature, who 'also' endeavors to distinguish between the natural and the humane sciences, therefore assigning (*zuweist*) a distinctive role to the history of the latter group and likewise to 'psychology,' then allowing the whole to merge together in a relativistic 'philosophy.' "[27] Central in this interpretation of Dilthey is his search for the logic of the humane sciences. Heidegger, then, is seen as subsuming the search for the logic of the humane sciences, relocating the entire hermeneutical question with ontology. Dilthey, it is affirmed, contrasted the epistemology of the natural sciences with a hermeneutic which was an epistemology of the humane sciences. Heidegger questioned the basic presupposition of hermeneutics as epistemology. Instead of "how do we know?" the question is "what is the mode of being of that being who only exists through understanding?" When this approach is related to textual understanding, the result is that the understanding of the text does not involve the finding of an inner meaning contained in the text. To understand a text is to unfold the possibility of being which is indicated by that text.

The summary of the significance of the work of Heidegger given above is, of course, valid. However, I propose to examine the contribution of Heidegger in the light of the comprehensive poetics of Dilthey suggested in his outline for a revised *Poetik*. Considering the contribution of both the earlier and later periods of the work of Heidegger as a whole, one may argue that Heidegger deals with all the major elements with which Dilthey dealt: the creativity of the author, the text, and meaning. He deals with all of these on the one level of life or Being. In his treatment he extends and amplifies the concern of Dilthey with meaning as life. Heidegger's estimation of the philosophical importance of Dilthey gave a focus to the work of Heidegger, for Dilthey's importance was "in the fact that in all this [in his attempts to understand the experiences of life in their structural and developmental inner connections] he was, *above all*, on his way toward the question of 'life.' "[28]

Creative Capacity of Man

Heidegger correctly sees that for Dilthey the logic of the humane sciences was not the central concern as is so often asserted. While he did research on the humane sciences in distinction to the natural sciences and wrote on the history of the humane sciences, Dilthey was also concerned with a psychology in which the "whole fact of man" could be presented. All the areas of study permeate and intersect in the goal of understanding life philosophically and of securing a hermeneutical foundation for this understanding of life in terms of life itself. Man as the object of the humane sciences, and, especially the root of the sciences, is central, for everything centers in the way that man is.[29]

Heidegger himself is not primarily interested in man. His interest in man is as a means of questioning Being. "Understanding of Being belongs to the kind of Being which the entity called 'Dasein' possesses." The problem of fundamental ontology can be solved as *Dasein* is explicated. The investigation of *Dasein* by Heidegger is a philosophical and existential analysis. The existential analysis will make clear "that a priori basis which must be visible before the question of 'what man is' can be discussed philosophically." Heidegger moves directly to the ontological question and sees anthropological, psychological, and biological questions as questions to be handled subsequent to the existential questions.[30]

Heidegger sounds much like Dilthey when he speaks of a "totality of Dasein's structural whole" which is built upon the Being of *Dasein* and which gives access to the Being of *Dasein*. This is a unity which is not defined by the elements in its structure, by deduction from an idea of man, or even by "our immanent perception of experiences."[31]

Although *Dasein*, for Heidegger, is a means for questioning Being, and hence analysis is directed toward a more profound level than the analyses of Dilthey, he does attempt to show continuity between ordinary "talk" and discourse as an existential equiprimordial with state-of-mind and understanding. Discourse, state-of-mind, and understanding are fundamental *existentialia* which constitute the Being of the "there." Discourse is the articulation of intelligibility and underlies both interpretation and assertion. This articulation is the "totality-of-signification" which can be broken up into significations. But discourse has a kind of being which is specifically worldly. The intelligibility of Being-in-the-world expresses itself as discourse. "Discourse is existentially language, because that entity whose disclosedness it articulates according to significations, has, as its kind of Being, Being-in-the-world—a Being which has been thrown and submitted to the 'world.'"

> Discoursing or talking is the way in which we articulate "significantly" the intelligibility of Being-in-the-world. Being-with belongs to Being-in-the-world, which in every case maintains itself in some definite way of concernful Being-with-one-another. Such Being-with-one-another is discursive as assenting or refusing, as demanding or warning, as pronouncing, consulting, or interceding as "making assertions," and as talking in the way of "giving a talk."[32]

Heidegger does see that *Dasein's* understanding may be uprooted and that *Dasein* may keep "floating unattached." This does not amount to a " 'not-Being' of *Dasein*," for, indeed, this is "*Dasein's* most everyday and most stubborn 'Reality.'" Yet this uprooted understanding with *Dasein* "cut off from its primary and primordially genuine relationships-of-Being toward the world, toward *Dasein*-with, and toward its very Being-in," is not bereft of creative ability of a sort. Such an uprooted understanding produces "idle talk." The creativity of the "idle talk" is the "they," for it is the "they" which "prescribes one's state-of-mind, and determines what and how one 'sees.'" *Dasein* falls prey to the tradition which prevents it from providing its guidance. This tradition, however, operates on the understanding which is rooted in *Dasein's* own-most Being.[33]

In many ways the conceptualization of Dilthey can be seen in Heidegger with the important exception that Heidegger is concerned primarily with the creative aspects of man to show the nature of *Dasein's* expression of itself or really the communication of "the existential possibilities of one's state-of-mind" which amounts to a "disclosing of existence."[34]

The Text

Dilthey sees the text as an expression of the historical experiences of man and the structures of the mind. Heidegger, of course, sees the text in some fashion as a human product, but he is not concerned with the biological or psychological nature of the text. He denies that the ideas of "expression," "symbolic form," "communication as 'assertion,'" "the 'making known' of experiences," "the 'patterning' of life" allow us to grasp the "essence of language." Heidegger denies that these clues to conceptions of language could be united to achieve an adequate definition of "language." Heidegger is concerned with the "ontological 'locus'" of the phenomenon of language in "Dasein's state of Being." Yet, discourse does express itself and, for the most part, discourse expresses itself in language. Heidegger uses the term "assertion" as a general term for the phenomena which are "grounded on understanding." Such assertions present "us with a derivative form in which an interpretation has been carried out." "Assertion" means "pointing out," "prediction," and "communication." "Assertion" is then to be defined as "a pointing out which gives something a definite character and which communicates." An assertion, then, has an "ontological origin from an interpretation which understands." Heidegger acknowledges that there is a continuum of forms of assertion between "the kind of interpretation which is still wholly wrapped up in concernful understanding and the extreme opposite case of a theoretical assertion about something present-at-hand." These include "assertions about the happenings in the environment, accounts of the ready-to-hand, 'reports on the Situation,' the recording and fixing of the 'facts of the case,' the description of the state of affairs, the narration of something that has befallen." All of these "sentences" have their "source" in "circumspective interpretation."[35]

The previous discussion of "idle talk" and of the "they" introduces a problem: How can one distinguish from a given text whether or not it fails to go back to the ground of what is talked? More generally, how does one move back from discourse to language?

Heidegger makes an advance upon Dilthey in his observation that discourse, while it expresses itself for the most part in language, may express itself also in keeping silent and in hearing. Both keeping silent and hearing have the existential foundation of discourse, and both silence and hearing can "make one understand." Indeed Heidegger points out, "The person who keeps silent" can "make one understand . . . more authentically than the person who is never short of words."[36]

Meaning

Dilthey conceives of a continuity of meaning from the smallest elements of language to life itself. Heidegger extends the meaning of life to Being. The discussion of *Dasein's* discourse and the derivatives of discourse have already exposed the meaning with which Heidegger is concerned in *Being and Time.* Heidegger is interested in discourse's expression of itself. "In talking, Dasein expresses itself. . . ." It is in poetical discourse that the expression of *Dasein* may become the very aim of language. "In 'poetical' discourse, the communication of the existential possibilities of one's state-of-mind can become an aim in itself and this amounts to a disclosing of existence." Nevertheless, in all talking, discourse expresses itself. At times, the means of this expression are "intonation, modulation, the tempo of talk, 'the way of speaking.' " But in the thing said, discourse also communicates itself. In interpretation of things in general, Heidegger asserts, we do not "throw a 'signification' " over it; we do not "stick a value on it." When something is encountered, "the thing in question already has an involvement which is disclosed in our understanding of the world." What we interpret is this prior involvement. This is true with things in general; it is also true with talk. In the thing said in a talk or discourse, in the wishing, asking, or expression of one's self about something, "in this 'something said,' discourse communicates." The basis for this communication of discourse is essentially the same basis for the interpretation of things noted above. Communication is not simply the matter of conveying such things as opinions and wishes "from the interior of one subject into the interior of another." In communication, "Dasein-with is already essentially manifest in a co-state-of-mind and a co-understanding." What communication effects is the explicit sharing of Being with. Prior to communication, this Being with "*is* already, but it is unshared as something that has not been taken hold of and appropriated." In the section on "idle talk," Heidegger summarizes his conception:

> In language . . . there is hidden a way in which the understanding of Dasein has been interpreted. . . . The understanding which has thus already been "deposited" in the way things have been expressed pertains just as much to any traditional discoveredness of entities which may have been reached, as it does to one's current understanding of Being and to whatever possibilities and horizons for fresh interpretation and conceptual articulation may be available.[37]

In the period after *Being and Time,* Heidegger makes normative a relationship of *Dasein* to Being which is only suggested in *Being and*

Time. In the early work, "Being is always the Being of an entity." While "entities *are*" independently of their being discovered or disclosed, "Being 'is' only in the understanding of those entities to whose Being something like an understanding of Being belongs." ". . . only as long as Dasein *is* . . . 'is there' Being."[38]

Heidegger, apparently paradoxically, asserts, however, that Being "determines entities as entities," that Being is the basis on which "entities are already understood." While Being "pertains to every entity," "Being and the structure of Being lie beyond every entity and every possible character which an entity may possess." It is because Being "determines entities" that Being may be discovered by questioning *Dasein.* I indicated that this is apparently a paradox, because Heidegger, in *Being and Time,* is quite explicit that "we always conduct our activities in an understanding of Being." He is not in total darkness in questioning *Dasein* for Being. The meaning of Being is already available in some fashion, and it is out of this understanding that Heidegger develops the question of the meaning of Being.[39]

After *Being and Time,* the questioning of *Dasein* for the sake of Being is no longer the procedure. Rather, Being, in poetic terms to be sure, is the absolute. Language, moreover, in some sense is the equivalent of Being.

The ontological interest of Heidegger which became actively dominant in the period after *Being and Time* influences his conceptualization of the creative capacity of man and of text. *Dasein* is no longer the locus of discourse. Being itself is the explanation for language and the essence of language is Being's self-expression. Being is the creative explanation, Being is the text, Being is the meaning. Heidegger has taken Dilthey's view of meaning as life itself as far as it can be taken through existence into Being. In this we have been given no clear map of the movement forward, and there is certainly no way in the work of Heidegger back to other levels of language where the elements are not so closely identified.

John Macquarrie sees the ontological language of Heidegger as a "paradigm or prototype for the language of theology" and he sees the major problem as "the question of how one makes the transition from the language of existence to the language of being." Macquarrie's concern is not directly our concern at this point, but if we are able to throw light on the problem of the relationship of the different levels of language and the elements of the various levels, we should throw some light on the more specifically theological problem raised by Macquarrie.[40]

Heidegger may see no way back from Being. In the essay on "Language" in *Unterwegs zur Sprache* Heidegger says that the speaking of language should be sought in what is spoken purely, and he declares that "what is spoken purely is the poem." The basis of this assertion is not given in theoretical terms at all. The basis is experience. We may assert that "what is spoken purely is the poem" if "we succeed in hearing in a poem something that is spoken purely." While Heidegger in his interpretation overturns the "current view" of language that sees speech as "the activation of the organs for sounding and hearing" and "the audible expression and communication of human feelings" which are accompanied by thoughts, he does not wish to state in theoretical terms "a new view of language." "What is important is learning to live in the speaking of language." Man's speaking, indeed, is a response of hearing, so the way that man learns "to live in the speaking of language" is to "examine constantly whether and to what extent we are capable of what genuinely belongs to responding."[41]

GADAMER

Hans-Georg Gadamer, in his significant *Wahrheit und Methode,* comes back to the philosophical question: "How is understanding possible?"[42] He sees this as the same philosophical question that Kant asked about the condition and constraints of the knowledge through which modern science is possible and about the boundaries of modern science. Gadamer directs the question of understanding not only to science but to the entire range of human experience and practice in the world and life.

Gadamer accepts Heidegger's temporal analysis of *Dasein* as demonstrating that understanding is the way of being of *Dasein* itself. Understanding is "never a subjective relationship to a given object"; it is a relationship "to the being which belongs to that which is understood or to actively effective history (*Wirkungsgeschichte*)."[43] The thesis of *Wahrheit und Methode* is that ". . . the effective historical moment in all understanding of tradition is active and remains active, even where the method of modern historical science has taken its position and makes the historical event, historical tradition, into an 'object' which it establishes as an experimental finding—as if tradition were foreign and, humanly speaking, understood in the same way as the object of physics."[44]

The theory of historical consciousness, *wirkungsgeschichtliches Bewus-stein,* is the perspective from which we must see to what extent Gadamer has assisted in clarifying the levels of language and the elements within the various levels. The category of *wirkungsgeschlichtliches Bewusstein* is the consciousness of being acted upon by history so that this action upon us is not objectified but is part of the historical phenomenon itself. In *Kleine Schriften I* Gadamer explains what he means by the assertion that "all our historical understanding is defined through a *wirkungsge-schichtliches Bewusstein*":

> . . . we cannot lift ourselves out of the event and, so to say, confront it with the result that the past might become an object for us. If we think in this way we come much too late to receive the real experience of history. We are not only a part of this forward moving chain . . . but we also have the possibility of understanding that moment in the past which comes to us and transmits itself to us. I call this the *wirkungsgeschichtliches Bewusstein* because I wish to say, on the one hand, that our conscious-ness is defined by the effective working of history, that is, defined through an active element that does not allow our consciousness to be free in the sense of a confrontation with the past. On the other hand, I intend to say that it is possible for the consciousness of this action to be created in us —so that everything past which comes into our experience constrains us to become prepared with it to take over its truth in a certain way upon ourselves."[45]

The application of the theory of active historical consciousness is made by Gadamer in three areas of hermeneutics: aesthetics, history, and lan-guage. In each case the debate is between a method which studies an object and an experience of participation. In each area there is a legiti-mate application of criticism, but with criticism there is an experience of being grasped, being carried by tradition, participating with the creators of discourse.

In his discussion of aesthetics, Gadamer sees the artist as transforming his experience of being into an image, but the artist is not the major point of Gadamer's discussion of creativity. The viewer as the creator is Gadamer's concern. The idea of game (play) illuminates the action of the artist and viewer by showing the way of being of the work of art. A game (play) is a dynamic reality with goals independent of the player (or viewer). The game comes into existence as individuals participate, but while the game is being played it is master. A play, different from a game, does not exist primarily for the players but for the viewers who are caught up in the play. It is only through the transformation into images that the play gains its "ideality" and can be intended and understood as the same thing. But the play becomes detached from the act of the players who perform it and exists in the pure appearance of what the players perform.[46]

Translated into art, this means that the artist transforms his experience of being into images. This is not simply an alteration of materials whereby the actual materials remain and can be observed. An alteration would merely relate to the "accidence" of the substance. Transformation means that that into which the material is transformed is its true being. That which existed earlier is no more, but "that which now exists, which is presented in the play of art, is the truth that abides."[47]

The fact that in a play there is an underlying story and parts performed and in a work there is form and the use of raw materials, and the fact that (as the result of reflective thought, Gadamer says) "form" and "content" can be separated, brings Gadamer to stress what is implicit in his concept of "transformation into images," that in art "the mediation must be thought of as a whole." What is central in a work of art is neither content nor form but the "unity of truth which is recognized in the play of art." The genuine experience of a poem is missed when one considers the underlying plot and sees it in light of its origin. Also, the genuine experience of the play is missed when the spectator reflects on the conception which lies at the base of a performance or simply on the performance of the actor.[48]

The meaning of a material work of art, in the view of Gadamer, is not simply the enjoyment of sensuous form. This follows from the nature of the creation of the work and its abiding truth. Art is knowledge and to experience the work of art is to participate in this knowledge. Gadamer approaches the meaning of the material work not from an "artistic" but from an ontological perspective and deals with two questions: (1) the distinction between an image and a copy and (2) the way the image gives access to its world. A copy only has the function of identification (such as a passport photograph) but an image is defined ontologically as an emancipation of the archetype (*Urbild*). Gadamer chooses to characterize the way of being of an image in a sacramental fashion, through the idea of representation. The image possesses its own power of being and effects the original (*Urbild*). The image "can be grasped in its ontological structure. The image is a process of being—in it being comes to meaningful-observable appearance."[49]

The work of art allows a "world" to be encountered, but because of the nature of the work "this is not a foreign universe in which we are transformed in time and moment. Rather we learn to understand ourselves in it, and that means that we raise the discontinuity and punctuality of experience in the continuity of our *Dasein*." "All encounter with the language of art is an encounter with an open event and is even a part of this event."[50] The work of art questions us. The question is that question which called it into being. We do not question the work with our methods or merely see in the work what we bring; we come to the work participating in the same structure of being which is the basis for our understanding of what was intended in the work.

The principles which Gadamer gives for art in general are true also for literature and the understanding of literature. A text, as word, is not basically a mere instrument or sign of something. It is not symbolic form created by man. Just as words belong to the situation and are not constructed and endowed with meaning by man, a linguistic expression is an expression of situation and being. ". . . the word expresses not the mind but the thing which is intended. The point of departure for the formation of the word is the matter itself which the mind realizes." Gadamer, here, is not denying the process of mental activity; rather he is affirming such a process; but the word is not an expression of the mental process itself. The situation, the matter, is the starting point.[51]

Gadamer sees language as moving from situation or matter, through expression, to subjectivity. Language, then, discloses our world, not the scientific world, but the personal world. When we come to interpret a text, we do not merely repeat the text with other words. The logic of question and answer gives us insight into interpretation. That a text is the object of interpretation means that it presents a question to the interpreter. To understand the text is to understand the question of the text. Whoever wishes to understand the text must see it as the answer to the question. The meaning of a sentence is relative to the question to which the sentence is an answer. But the interpreter does not come as an empty vessel; he comes with a horizon of meaning which is broadened so as to become fused with that of the text. The possibility of a fusion of horizons is based on the grounding of text and interpreter in being.

The third part of *Wahrheit und Methode* establishes the foundation of hermeneutics by showing that language is the way of being of tradition and man. Such a view of language, declares Gadamer, is far superior to a limited view of language as form. "The language which lives in speech, which encompasses all understanding, even that of the interpretation of texts, is so fused with the process of thought and, therefore, interpretation, that we have too little in hand if we reject what language transmits to us in content and wish to think of language only as form."[52]

Gadamer affirms the ontological territory which Heidegger claimed, but, with that territory in possession, he wishes to deal with epistemology. The view of language in Gadamer, while not retreating from the ontological view of Heidegger, seems to be broader. Wilhelm von Humboldt's view of language as an unbordered creative power of thought and speech making unlimited use of limited materials is cited by Gadamer and is used to develop a hermeneutical principle: "Linguistic form and traditional content cannot be separated in the hermeneutical experience." Humboldt had said that the learning of a foreign language must be the winning of a new standpoint in a person's world view but that this achievement is not complete because one carries to the foreign language his own world view. Gadamer sees the carrying of one's world view to a language not as a limitation but as the means of the power of the hermeneutical experience, and he declares that Humboldt's meaning for hermeneutics is precisely his affirmation of the view of language as the view of the world (*Sprachansicht als Weltansicht*). "He recognized the vital power of speech, the linguistic energy as the essence of language. . . ."[53]

To be sure, the emphasis of Gadamer is "that language is a means in which 'I' and 'world' unite," or better that language is a means in which "I" and "world" have their original belongingness demonstrated. Language is "being which can be understood." The "universal ontological meaning" of language is its "speculative way of being," and "what comes to language is something other than the spoken word itself." "But the word is only word through that which comes to language in it. It is in its own meaningful being only there to be raised in what is said. Contrariwise, that which comes to language is no languageless pre-given thing, but it receives its precision (*Bestimmtheit*) in the word." Gadamer's view of language allows for, even demands, interpretation of tradition in texts in which the culture and tradition are made precise.[54]

That Gadamer wishes to find a way to move back to penultimate objective levels of language and elements of language and yet to hold onto an ontological level is evident in his treatment of history and philology. It could be thought, in light of his condemnation of the approach which makes objectivity its presupposition, that the disciplines of history and philology are anathema to Gadamer. It is true that "whoever seeks to understand a text as a philologist or a historian does not relate the speaking of a text to himself. He seeks to understand the intention of the author." Yet both actually do their work effectively for both come to the text with historically active consciousness. "In truth there is no reader at all before whose eyes the great book of world history lies closed." Readers do not simply read what is in the text. "Rather, in all readers, an application occurs so that whoever reads the text is himself involved in the meaning which is perceived." Moreover, while the reconstruction of the text historically and philologically in itself is not the work of hermeneutics, yet "the reestablishment of the conditions under which a work of tradition accomplished its original destiny is certainly an essential auxiliary operation for understanding." The result of the operation, however, is not the meaning of the work. "The reconstruction of the original condition . . . is a weak beginning in light of the historical nature of our being."[55]

The analogy of translation from one language into another in active conversation is used effectively by Gadamer to show that hermeneutics requires more than an objective method. The analogy, however, shows also that objective study is involved. Every translator has the task of bringing to recognition the meaning of the participant, "but he must bring out his meaning as it seems necessary to him in the genuine situation of conversation in which he is situated as one who knows both participants in the conversation." Hermeneutics has the task of suiting the meaning of a text to the concrete situation in which it speaks. Gadamer sees the task of historical study and hermeneutics not as two different efforts, however, but as one activity. In the case of texts, the text may bring a matter to language; it does this finally, however, only by means of the activity of the interpreter. Both text and interpreter must take part. Even when it is a matter of "lasting fixed expressions of life," the text and the interpreter are involved in bringing the text to language.[56]

In spite of the movement back from ontology to other levels of language, a vision of the interpreter involved in bringing a text to language, Gadamer seems not to combine effectively the ontological participation of belonging of the interpreter with the critical methodological attitude of the interpreter. Paul Ricoeur suggests that Gadamer's work results in an opposition between "alienating distanciation and participation." Ricoeur terms this opposition an antinomy because

it gives rise to an untenable alternative: on the one hand, alienating distanciation is the attitude that makes the objectification which reigns in the human sciences possible; on the other hand, this distanciation that is the very condition which accounts for the scientific status of the sciences is at the same time a break that destroys the fundamental and primordial relation by which we belong to and participate in the historical reality which we claim to construct as an object.[57]

Is there a way to maintain the methodological attitude and the attitude of truth?

Gadamer's concept of historical consciousness seems to offer a solution, but his view of a consciousness which is not fixed but which is influenced by history appears to me to reintroduce the very element in Dilthey's hermeneutics which is seen as questionable, the matter of the mental structure which man has or is and which operates in all linguistic activity, thinking, speaking, understanding, and interpreting. Gadamer acknowledged that Dilthey recognized the importance of the individual and general experiences of life in his hermeneutics but criticized Dilthey because he treated experiences purely on the private level. Can Gadamer move beyond that level?

Gadamer introduces historical consciousness into his hermeneutics explicitly in the discussion of the historical nature of understanding. The principle of actively effective history (*Wirkungsgeschichte*) is used to show the naiveté of a historicism which forgets its own historicality. A consciousness which is defined by actively effective history is a part of the process of understanding. This consciousness is first of all consciousness of the hermeneutical situation. Gadamer suggests that when one finds oneself in a new situation, one must orient oneself to the new situation even though this orientation is imperfect. In a hermeneutical situation involving tradition, one must also orient oneself. The orientation is not complete because of the "essence of the historical being which we are." Gadamer is not attempting to give a rule for interpretation; he is attempting to describe how in fact man interprets tradition whether he is conscious of it and controls it or not.[58]

In the specific analysis, Gadamer describes actively effective historical consciousness as appearing in the capacity man has to reflect upon that which is in consciousness. "The structure of reflectivity is fundamentally given with all consciousness. This must also be true for the consciousness of actively effective history." Such consciousness has the structure of experience. Gadamer does not dispense with Dilthey's concept of experience. He observes, however, that hermeneutics in the tradition of Dilthey has not given proper attention to the inner historicality of experience. "The hermeneutical experience has to do with tradition. It is tradition which is to come to experience. However, tradition is not simply an event which man recognizes through experience and learns to master; it is *language. . . ."* Experience speaks as a "you" (*Du*). One must experience tradition as one experiences a "you," not as one experiences an object. The tradition must be experienced as one who has something to say.[59]

Gadamer comes basically to the same dialetic of Dilthy when he speaks of the means of understanding. The means of understanding is the content of tradition, but "every meaning of tradition finds its reality (*Konkretion*) in relationship to the 'I' who is doing the understanding. . . ." Gadamer finds mediation of the two poles in language. Tradition brings itself to language and human consciousness is linguistic. In this mediation, human consciousness is not dissolved. Indeed, Gadamer emphasizes this when he strongly asserts that "there is no possible consciousness . . . in which the 'matter' which is passed down in tradition appears in the light of eternity." All meaning has a "relationship to an 'I.' "[60]

Gadamer, instead of solving Dilthey's problem of relating the linguistic ability of man to the text, drives us back forcefully to the problem of man's linguistic ability. When one attempts to do justice to the subject matter of a text, it is *man* who is doing this. The linguistic ability of man, the way man thinks in general and the way individual men doing the interpreting conceptualize in particular, is a part of the process of understanding. Certain cultural and historical elements in the formation of the linguistic ability of man in general and men in particular may be studied. Gadamer appears to be confident of the reflective ability of consciousness, but certain elements in the language ability of man may ultimately remain unconscious in their operation. The mental structure of Dilthey is at least one way of conceptualizing the linguistic ability of man which has certain universal elements and which has certain elements which are historically and culturally constrained.

NOTES

1. Martin Heidegger, *Being and Time,* trans. John Macquarrie and Edward Robinson (Oxford: Basil Blackwell, 1973), p. 230. Page numbers refer to original German.

2. Jan Aler, "Heidegger's Conception of Language in *Being and Time,*" *On Heidegger and Language,* ed. J. Kockelmans (Evanston: Northwestern University Press, 1972), pp. 36–38.

3. Heidegger, *Being and Time,* pp. 37, 25, 160.

4. *Ibid.,* pp. 25, 34, 160, 143, 148–49.

5. *Ibid.*, p. 150.

6. *Ibid.*, p. 161.

7. *Ibid.*, pp. 163–64.

8. *Ibid.*, pp. 162–63.

9. *Ibid.*, pp. 167–68.

10. *Ibid.*, p. 166.

11. Martin Heidegger, *Über den Humanismus* (Frankfurt: Vittorio Klostermann, 1949), p. 47: "Die Sprache ist so die Sprache des Seins, wie die Wolken die Wolken des Himmels sind."

12. Martin Heidegger, *Poetry, Language, Thought*, trans. Albert Hofstadter (New York: Harper, 1971), p. 210.

13. *Ibid.*, p. 192.

14. *Ibid.*, p. 208.

15. Heidegger, *Being and Time*, pp. 148, 154, 156, 158.

16. *Ibid.*, p. 161.

17. *Ibid.*, pp. 161, 157.

18. John Sallis, "Language and Reversal," *Martin Heidegger: In Europe and America*, ed. Edward G. Ballard and Charles E. Scott (The Hague: Martinus Nijhoff, 1973), p. 135.

19. Martin Heidegger, *An Introduction to Metaphysics*, trans. Ralph Manheim (London: Oxford University Press, 1959), p. 171.

20. *Ibid.*, pp. 13, 51, 171.

21. Heidegger, *Being and Time*, pp. 161, 80.

22. Martin Heidegger, *What Is Called Thinking*, trans. Fred D. Wieck and J. Glen Gray (New York: Harper, 1968), p. 130.

23. Heidegger, *An Introduction to Metaphysics*, p. 171.

24. Martin Heidegger, *On the Way to Language* (New York: Harper, 1971), pp. 1–54.

25. William J. Richardson, *Heidegger: Through Phenomenology to Thought* (The Hague: Martinus Nijhoff, 1963), p. 632.

26. *Gesammelte Schriften*, VI, 310–11

Erstes Buch. Der Dichter.

Erster Abschnitt. Das Erlebnis.

Erstes Kapitel. Allgemeine Beschreibung.

Zweites Kapitel. Unterschiede in den Erlebnissen. a) Erlebnislagen. b) Erlebnisrichtungen. c) Der Erlebnishorizont.

Drittes Kapitel. Erlebniskreise.

Zweiter Abschnitt. Die dichterische Phantasie.

Erstes Kapitel. Allgemeine Beschreibung der Phantasie.

Zweites Kapitel. Selbstzeugnisse der Dichter.

Drittes Kapitel. Analyse der dichterischen Phantasie.

1. Die Erlebnisphantasie. a) Ausdruck des Erlebnisses. b) Das Eingehen von Erlebnisausdrücken in die darstellende Dichtung.

2. Die dichterischen Phantasiebilder.

3. Sprachphantasie. Rhythmische und Klangphantasie.

27. Heidegger, *Being and Time*, pp. 397–98. See also Paul Ricoeur, "The Task of Hermeneutics," *Philosophy Today* 17 (1973), 120, 123.

28. Heidegger, *Being and Time*, p. 46.

29. *Ibid.*, p. 398.

30. *Ibid.*, pp. 200, 45, 16.

31. *Ibid.*, pp. 181–82.

32. *Ibid.*, p. 161.

33. *Ibid.*, pp. 167–70.

34. *Ibid.*, p. 162.

35. *Ibid.*, pp. 163, 166, 156, 158.

36. *Ibid.*, p. 164.

37. *Ibid.*, pp. 162, 150, 167–68.

38. *Ibid.*, pp. 9, 183, 212.

39. *Ibid.*, pp. 6, 38, 5.

40. John Macquarrie, *God-Talk: An Examination of the Language and Logic of Theology* (London: SCM, 1967), pp. 247, 239.

41. Heidegger, *Poetry, Language, Thought*, pp. 194, 192, 210.

42. Hans-Georg Gadamer, *Wahrheit und Methode* (3d ed.; Tübingen: J. C. B. Mohr, 1972), p. xvii: "Wie ist Verstehen möglich?"

43. *Ibid.*, p. xix: ". . . niemals ein subjektives Verhalten zu einem gegebenen 'Gegenstande' ist . . ." ". . . zur Wirkungsgeschichte, und das heisst: zum Sein dessen gehört, was verstanden wird."

44. *Ibid.*, p. xxi: ". . . das wirkungsgeschichtliche Moment in allem Verstehen

von Überlieferung wirksam ist und wirksam bleibt, auch wo die Methodik der modernen historischen Wissenschaften Platz gegriffen hat und das geschichtlich Gewordene, geschichtlich Überlieferte zum 'Objekt' macht, das es 'festzustellen' gilt wie einen experimentellen Befund—als wäre Überlieferung in dem selben Sinne fremd und, menschlich gesehen, unverständlich wie der Gegenstand der Physik."

45. Hans-Georg Gadamer, *Kleine Schriften I* (Tübingen: J. C. B. Mohr, 1967), 158: ". . . wir uns nicht aus dem Geschehen selber herausheben und sozusagen ihm gegenübertreten mit der Folge, dass etwa die Vergangenheit uns so zum Objekt würde. Wenn wir so denken, kommen wir viel zu spät, um die eigentliche Erfahrung der Geschichte überhaupt noch in den Blick zu bekommen. Wir sind immer schon mitten in der Geschichte darin. Wir sind selber nicht nur ein Glied dieser fortrollenden Kette . . . sondern wir sind in jedem Augenblick in der Möglichkeit, uns mit diesem aus der Vergangenheit zu uns Kommenden und Überlieferten zu verstehen. Ich nenne das 'wirkungsgeschichtliches Bewusstsein,' weil ich damit einerseits sagen will, dass unser Bewusstsein wirkungsgeschichtlich bestimmt ist, d.h. durch ein wirkliches Geschehen bestimmt ist, das unser Bewusstsein nicht frei sein lässt im Sinne eines Gegenübertretens gegenüber der Vergangenheit. Und ich meine andererseits auch, dass es gilt, ein Bewustein dieses Bewirktseins immer wieder in uns zu erzeugen—so wie ja alle Vergangenheit, die uns zur Erfahrung kommt, uns nötigt, mit ihr fertig zu werden, in gewisser Weise ihre Wahrheit auf uns zu übernehmen."

46. Gadamer, *Wahrheit und Methode*, pp. 106–7.

47. *Ibid.*, p. 106: ". . . das, was nun ist, was sich im Spiel der Kunst darstellt, das bleibende Wahre, ist."

48. *Ibid.*, p. 121: ". . . die Vermittlung als eine totale gedacht werden." P. 112: ". . . die Einheit der Wahrheit, die man im Spiel der Kunst erkennt."

49. *Ibid.*, p. 137: ". . . in seiner ontologischen Struktur erfassbar wird. Das Bild ist ein Seinsvorgang—in ihm kommt Sein zur sinnvoll-sichtbaren Erscheinung."

50. *Ibid.*, p. 92: ". . . bleibt dieses nicht ein fremdes Universum, in das wir auf Zeit und Augenblick hineinverzaubert sind. Vielmehr lernen wir uns in ihm verstehen, und das heisst, wir heben die Diskontinuität und Punktualität des Erlebnisses in der Kontinuität unseres Daseins auf." P. 94: ". . . alle Begegung mit einem unabgeschlossenen Geschehen und selbst ein Teil dieses Geschehens ist" (italics deleted).

51. *Ibid.*, p. 403: ". . . das Wort drükt gar nicht den Geist, sondern die gemeinte Sache aus. Ausgangspunkt der Bildung des Wortes ist der Sachgehalt selbst (die species), der den Geist erfüllt."

52. *Ibid.*, p. 382: "Die im Sprechen lebendige Sprache, die alles Verstehen, auch das des Interpreten von Texten, umgreift, ist so sehr in den Vollzug des Denkens bzw. Auslegens eingelegt, dass wir zu wenig in der Hand behalten, wenn wir von dem, was die Sprachen uns inhaltlich überliefern, absehen und nur die Sprache als Form denken wollten."

53. *Ibid.*, p. 417. "Sprachliche Form und überlieferter Inhalt lassen sich in

der hermeneutischen Erfahrung nicht trennen" (italics deleted). P. 419: "Er hat den lebendigen Vollzug des Sprechens, die sprachliche Energeia als das Wesen der Sprache erkannt. . . ."

54. *Ibid.*, p. 449: "Dass die Sprache eine Mitte ist, in der sich Ich und Welt zusammenschliessen. . . ." P. 450: "Sein, das verstanden werden kann. . . ." ". . . universelle ontologische Bedeutung . . ." ". . . spekulative Seinsart. . . ." "Was zur Sprache kommt, ist zwar ein anderes, als das gesprochene Wort selbst." "Aber das Wort ist nur Wort durch das, was in ihm zur Sprache kommt. Es ist in seinem eigenen sinnlichen Sein nur da, um sich in das Gesagte aufzuheben, umgekehrt ist auch das, was zur Sprache kommt, kein sprachlos Vorgegebenes, sondern empfängt im Wort die Bestimmtheit seiner selbst."

55. *Ibid.*, p. 318: "Wer als Philoge oder Historiker einen Text zu verstehen sucht, bezieht dessen Rede jedenfalls nicht auf sich selber. Er sucht nur die Meinung des Autors zu verstehen." P. 323: "Wahrlich gibt es niemals den Leser, vor dessen Auge das grosse Buch der Weltgeschichte einfach aufgeschlagen liegt." "In allem Lesen geschieht vielmehr eine Applikation, so dass, wer einen Text liest, selber noch in dem vernommenen Sinn darin ist." P. 159: ". . . ist die Wiederherstellung der Bedingungen, unter denen ein überliefertes Werk seine ursprüngliche Bestimmung erfüllte, für das Verständnis gewiss eine wesentliche Hilfsoperation." "Wiederherstellung ursprünglicher Bedingungen ist . . . angesichts der Geschichtlichkeit unseres Seins ein ohnmächtiges Beginnen."

56. *Ibid.*, p. 292: ". . . sondern er muss dessen Meinung so zur Geltung bringen, wie es ihm aus der echten Gesprächssituation nötig scheint, in der er sich als der Kenner beider Verhandlungssprachen allein befindet."

57. Paul Ricoeur, "The Hermeneutical Function of Distanciation," *Philosophy Today* 17 (1973), 129.

58. Gadamer, *Wahrheit und Methode*, p. 285: ". . . Wesen des geschichtlichen Seins, das wir sind."

59. *Ibid.*, p. 324: "Die Struktur der Reflexivität ist grundsätzlich mit allem Bewusstsein gegeben. Sie muss also auch für das Bewusstsein der Wirkungsgeschichte gelten." P. 340: "Die hermeneutische Erfahrung hat es mit der *Überlieferung* zu tun. Sie ist es, die zur Erfahrung kommen soll. |Überlieferung| ist aber nicht einfach ein Geschehen, das man durch Erfahrung erkennt und beherrschen lernt, sondern sie is *Sprache*. . . ."

60. *Ibid.*, p. 449: ". . . aller Sinn der |Überlieferung| in der Beziehung auf das verstehende Ich diejenige Konkretion findet. . . ." P. 448: ". . . es gibt kein mögliches Bewusstein . . . in dem die 'Sache,' die überliefert wird, im Lichte der Ewigkeit erschiene." "Ichbezogenheit."

CHAPTER THREE

New Testament Hermeneutics

This chapter is designed to examine developments in New Testament hermeneutics in light of Dilthey's broad poetic hermeneutics and Heidegger's ontological hermeneutics. To what extent are the contributions of Dilthey and Heidegger fruitful for New Testament study? What modifications are made in the views of Dilthey and Heidegger as they are applied to New Testament study? Does New Testament hermeneutics give a way to move from Being to *Dasein*, from a concept of language as Being to other levels of language with their elements? This chapter will focus on Rudolf Bultmann and the "New Hermeneutic" which derives in some measure from Bultmann.

RUDOLF BULTMANN

Bultmann's task as a New Testament theologian is not that of the philosopher Heidegger. Bultmann does not question language for Being nor does he analyze *Dasein* for philosophical ends. He sees his task as interpretation, *scientific* interpretation. He distinguishes between scientific interpretation and "paying simple heed to what the New Testament says" for which philosophical analysis is not necessary. He wishes "to make Scripture itself speak as a power which has something to say to the present, to present-day existence," not simply "to read the biblical writing as a compendium of dogmatic pronouncements, or as 'sources' for the reconstruction of a section of past history, or to study a religious phenomenon or the nature of religion in general, or to know the psychological course and theoretical objectivization of religious experiences."[1]

From the earliest days, Bultmann acknowledged that he was not simply interpreting a text in its historical and temporal context. Bultmann, like Heidegger, is interested in something more basic, the "central matter" which is not the text but which is expressed in the text.[2] He asks about the reality to which the text points, for this reality is the key to the question whether and in what way the New Testament writings have meaning for us, a meaning beyond sources for knowledge of a small area of first-century history.

The matter of the text relates Bultmann to theology as well as to philosophy, for Bultmann's theological work was done in the context of the dialectical theology of Karl Barth who declared that the identity of the subject matter (God, Christ, grace, etc.) of the text of the Bible with modern man solves the problem of distance and makes meaning possible in the present. For Barth, the method of Luther and Calvin was more proper than the method of such critical scholars of his era as Jülicher and Lietzmann.

> For example, place the work of Jülicher side by side with that of Calvin: how energetically Calvin, having first established what stands in the text, sets himself to re-think the whole material and to wrestle with it, till the walls which separate the sixteenth century from the first become transparent. . . . ! Paul speaks, and the man of the sixteenth century hears. The conversation between the original record and the reader moves round the subject-matter until a distinction between yesterday and to-day becomes impossible. . . . Taking Jülicher's work as typical of much modern exegesis, we observe how closely he keeps to the mere deciphering of words as though they were runes. But, when all is done, they still remain largely unintelligible. . . . The whole procedure assuredly achieves no more than the first draft of a paraphrase of the text and provides no more than a point of departure for genuine exegesis. The matter contained in the text cannot be released save by a creative straining of the sinews, by a relentless, elastic application of the "dialectical" method. . . . The Word ought to be exposed in the words. Intelligent comment means I am driven on till I stand with nothing before me but the enigma of the matter; till the document seems hardly to exist as a document; till I have almost forgotten that I am not its author; till I know the author so well that I allow him to speak in my name and am even able to speak in his name myself.[3]

Barth resolves the problem of the distance between the Bible and the modern period by recognition of the "infinite qualitative distinction" between time and eternity. Paul and Barth are both "confronted with the same unmistakable and unmeasurable significance of that relation," and so the tension between past and present is resolved by the theological category of "otherness."[4]

Bultmann agrees with Barth's attempts to go beyond the words of the text to the subject matter, and he agrees with Barth that the identity of subject matter solves the question of meaning. Some assumptions of Barth and Bultmann which may go somewhat unnoticed by the modern reader who shares these assumptions are important in light of modern discussions of language and should be noted before the disagreement of Barth and Bultmann on the subject matter of the New Testament is stressed. The assumption of Bultmann's theological tradition is that proper interpretation involves cognitive statements, statements which have a content which can be understood by contemporary people. That interpretation of the Bible involves statements of content is simply taken for granted. It is assumed that the purpose of biblical writings, the function of the Bible, is to impart a content, or at least that the function of the Bible with which scientific interpretation is involved is the communication of some content. The interpreter is to "make sense" of the Bible.

Bultmann also assumes that interpretation of the Bible results in statements that can be understood on the level of human existence. In "all interpretation which has comprehension as its basis," Bultmann affirms, *"the presupposition for understanding is the interpreter's relationship in his life to the subject which is directly expressed in the text."* This presupposition is true of the New Testament. For comprehension, there must be a "connection of text and interpreter, which is founded on the life relationship of the interpreter." Human existence is the connection between the interpreter and the New Testament text. The interpreter, in scientific interpretation, must concern himself "with the relevant concepts in which human existence may be spoken of" because interpretation "takes its orientation from the inquiry into the understanding of human existence which finds expression in the Scriptures."[5]

Bultmann answers the objection to his program which states that the subject of the New Testament is God by asserting that an *"existentiell* knowledge about God" is to be found in human existence "in the form of the inquiry about 'happiness,' 'salvation,' the meaning of the world and of history, and in the inquiry into the real nature of each person's particular 'being.'" "Inquiry into the reality of human existence," then, is "inquiry about God and the manifestation of God."[6] Bultmann sounds as if he could parallel Heidegger's movement from *Dasein* to Being—for Bultmann, from *Dasein* to the absolute, to God. But that is not the case. As early as 1925, Bultmann had declared that *"to talk 'about God'* . . . has no sense at all" because when talking *about* God the thought of

God as the absolute is lost. "For every 'talking *about*' presupposes a standpoint apart from that which is being talked *about*. But there can be no standpoint apart from God. . . ."[7] Bultmann chooses one side of the *Dasein*-Being dialetic of Heidegger. Being, for Heidegger, can be spoken of only from the reality of *Dasein*, but *Dasein* logically presupposes Being. For Bultmann, God can only be spoken of by speaking of man. God is not the necessary philosophical presupposition for man which can be reached through man. Bultmann, then, will utilize Heidegger for purposes which are only penultimate for Heidegger himself.

Bultmann's observation that the philosophy of existence is necessary for interpretation was made at the time he became aware of the possible use of the conceptualization and terminology of Heidegger for the relevant concepts for speaking of human existence. Bultmann denies that he is suggesting a "final philosophical system" or that exegesis is "to take over the actual answers that philosophy gives to the existential question of the meaning of my own particular existence." What is important is that Heidegger has "worked out an appropriate terminology for the understanding of existence, an understanding involved in human existence itself."[8]

The Bible as a whole, and its various parts, including the various literary forms, then, must be interpreted in terms of human existence. Myth, by whatever definition, as it occurs in the New Testament, must be interpreted existentially. What is the material means that allows the Bible to be interpreted in terms of human existence? Bultmann sees the importance of the author of the text for such interpretation. Interpretation is possible because author and interpreter "have the same relation in life to the subject which is under discussion." "Dilthey," Bultmann indicates, "maintained that the 'basis of human nature as a whole' is a condition for the possibility of understanding." Bultmann defines this further by saying that

> a condition for exposition is the fact that the expositor and author live as men in the same historical world, in which "human being" occurs as a "being" in an environment, in understanding intercourse with objects and our fellow-men. And, of course, an integral part of that understanding intercourse is to be found in our enquiries, our problems, our struggles and our sufferings—both in joy and in ascetic withdrawal from the world.

That such is true for biblical writings must be assumed from the principle of Bultmann that *"the interpretation of biblical writings is not subject to conditions different from those applying to all other kinds of literature."*[9]

Bultmann is convinced that existential interpretation is true to the nature of the biblical writings, but he is also aware that the purpose of a text does not always have to govern the direction of the investigation of a text. When the direction of the investigation is identified with the purpose of a text, the text "mediates the subject into which enquiry is made." But the direction of the investigation may "arise from interest in the circumstances which may become apparent in all possible phenomena of life and consequently in all possible texts." The object of interpretation can be supplied by "the interest in the *reconstruction of the context of past history . . . psychological interest . . . aesthetic interest . . ."* or *"interest in history as the sphere of life in which human existence moves."* The inquiry into "human being" as one's own "being" is a possibility for all texts, according to Bultmann.[10]

Bultmann's view of the Bible and the Word of God, of the church and proclamation, influenced his choice of the level of interpretation of the New Testament. Although he recognizes the possibility and legitimacy of using the Scriptures for historical and aesthetic purposes, the Bible, as Word of God, is to be interpreted so that it speaks as Word, for only in this way is faith and new understanding possible. To speak as Word to modern man is to speak in terms of human existence. "I think I may take for granted that the right question to frame with regard to the Bible—at any rate within the Church—is the question of human existence." Two reasons are given for this assumption: (1) "I am driven to that by the urge to inquire existentially about my own existence," (2) ". . . the Church's proclamation refers me to the Scriptures as the place where I shall hear things about my own existence which vitally concern me. . . ."[11]

Bultmann's theological task directs him to interpret the Bible in terms that modern man understands, in terms of human existence. The choice leads him to direct questions to the text which may not always be directly related to the purpose of the text. An important aspect of Bultmann's view of language is seen when the purpose of the text (and author) is not related to or is inconsistent with the subject matter. In Bultmann's criticism of Barth's work on Romans, he emphasizes the need to criticize the biblical text in terms of the "subject matter" because of the relativity of the word and the inability of any writer to speak only from the subject matter. "In terms of the subject matter one must . . . *measure* to what extent in all words and statements of the text the subject matter has really achieved adequate expression. . . . The subject matter is greater than the interpreting word."[12] It is in his treatment of myth that Bultmann comes to see not only the relativity of the word and the author but also the relativity of language as an objectifying of understanding, the objectification in myth being contrary to the understanding seeking expression in it. James M. Robinson calls attention to the contribution of Hans Jonas, a student of Heidegger and Bultmann, in this development in Bultmann's thought. In his preface to the first volume of Jonas's *Gnosis und spätantiker Geist,* Bultmann acknowledges: "The method of the author, of laying hold of the real meaning of a historical phenomenon by means of the principle of the analysis of existence, seems to me to have proven brilliantly its fruitfulness. I am certain that this work will fructify research in the history of ideas in many regards, and not least also the interpretation of the New Testament."[13]

Jonas saw myth as the problem of language and the human mind. In *Gnosis und spätantiker Geist* II, Part One, Jonas distinguishes between "inner concepts of *Dasein*" and "outward mythical objectification." He indicates that "because of their pervasive origin in a basic *objectification*," "the concepts of *Dasein*, with regard to their ontological structure, remain in a very broad sense 'mythical.' "[14] The need for moving from language back to meaning, according to Jonas, "derives from an unavoidable fundamental structure of the mind as such." "The innermost nature of the mind" is that it is "symbolistic," that is, "it interprets itself in objective formulae and symbols."

> In order to come to itself, it [the mind] necessarily takes this detour via the symbol, in whose enticing jungle of problems it tends to lose itself, far from the origin preserved symbolically in it, taking the substitute as ultimate. Only in a long procedure of working back, after an exhausting completion of that detour, is a demythologized consciousness able terminologically to approach directly the original phenomena hidden in this camouflage. . . .[15]

Bultmann, on the basis of his conclusion as to the subject matter of Scripture, must find that myth, instead of really intending to give an objective world view or to tell of divine powers, expresses the way man understands himself in his world,[16] and he can find justification for and a procedure for demythologizing in the work of Jonas.

Bultmann is conscious of various levels of language and the relationships of the elements on the various levels, but instead of dealing with all of the levels and elements he chooses deliberately in his hermeneutics to limit his interest to the existential level. In this existential questioning of the text from the past, Bultmann sees the necessity of a reversal whereby the question of the text confronts the interpreter. True understanding, in Bultmann's view, would be to listen to the *question* which is posed in the writing to be interpreted, to the claim which is met in that writing.[17] It seems possible from Bultmann's own discussion for the text to be questioned and to confront man on other levels, on any level, cognitive and non-cognitive, where human being may be confronted. Statements about God in the ancient text may not be interpreted directly by Bultmann because that is inconceivable for him (although it may not be inconceivable for others in the past or present—or future—time), but there are direct statements about the world, society, and history which could conceivably confront human being. The model of interpretation as a matter of being confronted by the text introduces non-cognitive functions of the text. Bultmann, however, chooses the existential level because he is convinced that this is in keeping with the nature of the biblical writings themselves. This choice influences his view of the other levels and the use he makes of the other levels of language. As indicated, he does not move beyond *Dasein* to the ground of *Dasein* as did Heidegger, so we have no guide from the existential to the ontological level. In his historical study, it seems clear that his existential interests influenced his historical and exegetical activities. Because of the nature of faith, for example, Bultmann declared the quest of the earthly Jesus as not only unnecessary but also illegitimate. He maintained this view even after the development of the "new quest" and the affirmation of the theological necessity for a new quest.

This analysis is not in the least intending to suggest that Bultmann's existential analysis of the New Testament is invalid. John Macquarrie has demonstrated the value of Bultmann's existential interpretation. Bultmann's approach is vindicated by its success in opening the New Testament for many for whom the New Testament was a closed ancient document. This analysis is designed simply to show that Bultmann's approach is a limited approach, that it does not deal with all of the possible levels of language and literature.[18]

THE NEW HERMENEUTIC

The "New Hermeneutic" is the name given to a movement associated with students of Bultmann, especially Ernst Fuchs and Gerhard Ebeling, which changes the hermeneutical dialectic from myth versus understanding of existence to language versus language-event. Ebeling, in the article "Hermeneutik" in *Die Religion in Geschichte und Gegenwart*, indicates that the new program is carried out "in the horizon of the problem of language" because "belief was and is a language-event."[19] It is clear that the New Hermeneutic is in a very real sense the transferring of the concern of Bultmann to another level in light of the hermeneutical insight of the later work of Heidegger. The terminology of the New Hermeneutic has been found difficult as have the philosophical and theological concepts. The following analysis makes no claim to completeness but is undertaken to contribute to the attempt to provide a more complete model of language and literature for New Testament hermeneutics.

The substantial dependence of Fuchs upon Heidegger is problematic. It is claimed that Fuchs was not dependent upon Heidegger for his understanding of language and that as early as 1932 Fuchs saw the need to go beyond Bultmann in a "new quest" in terms of Jesus and hermeneutics.[20] Nevertheless, the work of Heidegger did provide Fuchs with conceptual grounds on which to build his hermeneutics, and we understand the work of Fuchs against the background of the hermeneutical movement from Schleiermacher through Dilthey and Heidegger. But Fuchs, like Bultmann, comes to language as a theologian, not as a philosopher, and the contribution of Fuchs must also be seen in the light of dialectical theology and the question of how God is related to man.

Gerhard Ebeling entered the hermeneutical discussion from his discipline of church history with an essay on the history of the church as history of the interpretation of Holy Scripture.[21] But Fuchs and Ebeling were together at Tübingen after World War II and developed a somewhat common position on interpretation so that the New Hermeneutic is considered "a single school of thought with a shared leadership."[22]

The New Hermeneutic views the problem of "distance" in interpretation as in part the result of historical development, the development from Scripture "as the text of preaching carried out in the body of Christ" to Scripture "as the text of research, the historical 'source' for the reconstruction of period portraits of the past, in which Christology was relativized."[23] From the period of the Enlightenment after Luther, says Fuchs,

> the "text" was no longer primarily the text of proclamation, but rather at most its vehicle, even though in the practice of the church one did not like to admit it, owing to the fact that one had previously misused the text for creating doctrines. . . . Ebeling's and my own effort at hermeneutic reflection, materially speaking, is concerned with how the text, seen as a merely historical source, can again become the text of preaching—without our denying that the text is also a historical source, e.g., for the question as to the historical Jesus, a question that in view of Christology is not irrelevant.[24]

Language and the New Hermeneutic

The language which the New Hermeneutic sees as the key to the task of theology is not merely the creation of man. It includes what is normally called language but it goes beyond that which is spoken or written. "Language," Fuchs declares, "consists not only in a statement of meaning which is heard. Language is indeed not merely discourse. Language is rather primarily a sign or a letting see, a meaning in the active sense." He affirms that "where meaning is, there is also language."[25] But the meaning (*Sinn*) of something is "only an abbreviation of language."[26]

Fuchs seems to be utilizing the concepts of the later Heidegger, while at the same time maintaining continuity with insights in *Being and Time*. Like Heidegger in *Being and Time*, Fuchs sees understanding as an *existentiale*.[27] Also, as discourse and understanding are equiprimordial for Heidegger, so language and understanding for Fuchs belong together in an inseparable way.[28] Being and language are related not only in that Being is the condition of language but also in that language warrants Being. "Being is the ground of language," and "without Being language is groundless, absurd, imaginary, glossolalia, indeed impossible." But at the same time, language is "earlier" than its ground, earlier than Being, and "without language Being is also nothing." Although speech is not Being, only in speech is Being spoken out; so in language we must question for Being.[29] Being is not God. Being is not a "something" but a "how" which forms room for all beings, although beings are not created by Being and all beings as a totality are not equated with Being. Being is not reality although it is the possibility of responsiveness to an "ultimate" which is also "the first," man himself in the case of human beings.[30] In a less concealing but not less confounding fashion Ebeling also relates language to man and reality. Language is "the point at which all dimensions of our experience of reality intersect."[31]

Language, Theology, and the Bible

What is distinctive in the New Hermeneutic is the interpretation of biblical and theological ideas in terms of this overwhelming concept of language. Yet to be determined is the fruitfulness of such an interpretation. Language is the key not simply to Being but also to the Word of God. For Fuchs and Ebeling, as for the Old Testament writers, the spoken or acted Word is powerful. This Word in good Lutheran thought is not divorced from the Bible, Jesus Christ, or the proclamation of the church, but what is emphasized is the possibility of a "language-event" in the present which is the meeting place of man and Being. The Word of God, the New Hermeneutic affirms, has entered language and can do so anew.

Language-event and language-gain. Fuchs says that the language-event is a historical event which occurs in history and makes history. He uses an analogy: a war event is an event which occurs during war in which war appears as war. A language-event, then, is an event in the area of language and the expression of the event is itself linguistic. Language warrants Being and, as Being, allows and sets free. The essence of language is allowance (*Erlaubnis*). The true content of language, then, is Being itself and it not only exists in language but comes to expression as a language-event between men. Our being is expressed in language, historically, and so we ourselves must actively and passively "come to language (*zur Sprache kommen*)."[32] Jesus was language-event in that the proclamation of Jesus was a possibility for freedom and a freeing for this possibility.[33]

The language of faith, like every true language, is a "language-gain" (*Sprachgewinn*). That is, language not only creates "Being" but brings forth Being as an event which remains present, at least potentially, in language. Language-event extends the horizons of Being. A new reality is created in the present which allows new Being in the future. Fuchs cites Pauline theology as the master example that Christian faith has enriched language itself. The language-event in the theology of Paul was a word of possibility of faith for all,[34] and the language-gain which produced the literary style of the gospel is distinguished in the fact that "it made the language of the people serviceable for the highest, for the discourse of God."[35] Because of the language-event of Jesus, new Being before God is an actual and continuing possibility. The New Hermeneutic sees the vocation of the church as bringing to language once again the person and work of Jesus, and this is to be understood in terms of the challenge of freedom and love.

Ebeling, in perhaps an even more direct manner than Fuchs, declares the possibility of language-event today. "Only the Word by which God comes to man, and promises himself," is able to pledge one "and his future for the future of the other" and to give one "his word in the full sense of giving a share in himself." Some deny that the Word of God can enter language, but, Ebeling asserts, "that this Word has happened, and can therefore be spoken again and again, that a man can therefore promise God to another as the one who promises himself—this is the certainty of Christian faith." Ebeling says that "the event of the Word of God is necessarily bound up with the entire life of language," that "the happening of the Word of God has created a linguistic tradition of its own," and that "now the Word of God . . . wishes to aim at reality in present-day language, it wants to express it anew and so express itself anew." The task will not be accomplished simply by manipulating language, "by modernizing words and making use of fashionable jargon," but by hearing anew, "with tense attention to how the traditional Word manages to make itself understood in the real circumstances to which our lives are exposed." Ebeling concludes that "though this seems to be a linguistic problem for the Word of God, it is in truth our own linguistic dilemma."[36]

Language and the New Testament. Fuchs's view of language is so broad as to be necessarily the basis of all reality which man experiences. Language, for example, is not simply the objectification of self-understanding; it is also constitutive for self-understanding. The world, being, God, love, man are all linguistic by definition! The importance of the New Testament may be related to the concern of the New Hermeneutic for *authentic* language. Language for Fuchs, as for Heidegger, may be inauthentic, but in Jesus' language of love Fuchs finds authentic language and therefore moves from Heidegger's quest for Being to a "christological understanding of language."[37] Fuchs and Ebeling, then, are not philosophers dealing with literature in general but theologians concerned with the New Testament. The New Testament, not classical poetry, is the text to which the New Hermeneutic sets itself. It is concerned with the language of faith, but the language of faith must be made understandable in the language of unfaith.[38]

God who is found where faith, love, and hope are found, in Fuchs's theology, has involved himself in human language. In the Bible it is God who first grasps the Word. As language itself warrants Being and so is "allowance" (*Erlaubnis*), so when we speak of God's Word it is a matter of the allowance of grace and the allowance of freedom. As communication, the language of God makes the nearness of God an event, an allowness of faith.[39]

In a Heideggerian interpretation of the prologue of John, Fuchs gives a poetic statement of his understanding of language. He begins with Faust's translation "in the beginning was the deed." Then, on the basis of John 13:34, he revises the translation to, "in the beginning was love." In view of 1 John 4:15 ("God is Love"), "Love" becomes the translation for God rather than for Word. "In the beginning was the Word and the Word was with Love and the Word was Love." Then Fuchs gives his understanding of language.

> Yet what then does "word" mean? For we wish to achieve with the term word the expression that is able to grasp Christ once and for all. In the supplement to my *Hermeneutik* I made the attempt to understand word as that Yes that forestalls and precludes every No, as the Yes ultimately constitutive of every language event. The word is, after all, language; it speaks, as its very nature. In genuine language do we not, even before any affirmation, say this Yes, when we speak? And even more: With our language do we not correspond from the very first to a Yes that grants us entry, entry into the being in which we are with ourselves and yet precisely not left alone? Even though language usually alienates itself from the world, its ground, and builds all sorts of words that are only signs, does it not still in its own-most ground live from that Yes that is the word of all words? To be sure language would then be originally the language of God and its basic trait would then likely be named love.[40]

The primitive Christian community gives an example of how we can conceive the Word of God being communicated: Jesus Christ was identified as God's Word. The historically known human figure Jesus was proclaimed as means of God's revelation. Jesus did not speak for himself, but God came to language by him.[41] "Jesus himself is God's Word, but the New Testament is the Word of men even if it is full of the spirit of the first witnesses. . . . But God has made for us this language of Jesus and of his apostles powerful in that he disclosed Jesus as his

Word."[42] Nothing really new is given quantitatively but qualitatively something new occurs.[43] The Word has primacy over the text of the New Testament[44] but the New Testament is the means for the language-event.[45]

The goal of hermeneutics. The broad view of language allows a conceptualization of the task of hermeneutics which may best be seen in comparison with the hermeneutics of Bultmann. Bultmann desires to interpret the text of the New Testament scientifically, and chooses the existential level of questioning. For Fuchs, however, the text wishes to interpret man. "The text is therefore not just the servant that transmits kerygmatic formulations, but rather a master that directs us into the language-context of our existence, in which we exist 'before God.' "[46] Hermeneutics is concerned with what the texts themselves bring to the interpreter, what they change for the interpreter, simply because texts "live or are there."[47]

The goal of the hermeneutical process, therefore, is the interpreter and his need. In the work of Fuchs, the Bultmannian "preunderstanding" has been preempted to some extent by the "hermeneutical principle."[48] This principle shows how the process of understanding operates. In the *Hermeneutik* of 1954 Fuchs gives examples: "Whoever wants to learn to understand the cat can provide it with the mouse. He will then see the cat in the way it shows itself."[49] To understand man, give him freedom and in freedom he shows how he is defined. "A hermeneutical principle designates what bestows on understanding the power and truth of 'an occurrence.' It is the power of understanding in the birth of the language which names the truth. The hermeneutical principle points out the 'place' of truth." "It tells us where we must go if we will meet the truth."[50]

The place of our meeting with God is history because God's Word is mediated historically. The New Testament will confront its reader with the truth of faith and the assertion that man has a relationship to himself. The New Testament, then, orients its teachings concerning the Word of God and faith to the question as to ourselves. In practice the hermeneutical principle of the interpreter of the New Testament is simply the ethical earnestness of the interpreter. "The existential constraint for this interpretation is the question as to the ground of human existence."[51]

In Fuchs's treatment of translation and preaching[52] it becomes clearer in what way Fuchs's hermeneutics will transcend Bultmann's existential interpretation. Fuchs says that "translation" is the beginning point of every hermeneutic; at any rate every hermeneutic in exegetical theology.[53] Fuchs is not primarily interested in the translation of the New Testament text in a philological manner but in the translation of the language-event in these texts. The translator must form the room the text sought to form when the Spirit spoke in it. The content and form of the translation must unite to allow the life of the text to appear. Where is this room to be created? In the world? In existence? In the Word will the text create room, in language, in proclamation. Proclamation is the true translation of the text, not because the New Testament text was necessarily originally proclamation, but because of the nature of the Word itself.[54]

Fuchs, as seen earlier, uses the expression "language-event" to describe the occurrence of language, the event of Being which is the actual content of language. He strongly contrasts this "language-event" (*Sprachereignis*) with "language-experience" (*Spracherlebnis*). In a language-experience, a statement may become master so that subject and object may be changed in the process. But in a language-event, language appears as Word and the event produces "texts" which are not produced by language-experience alone. In language-event not only does object become subject but an answer is given to the call.[55]

The language-event is not basically a conveying of content; self-understanding results from language-event. The basic role of language in this sense is the stating and sharing of a new self-understanding. The Bible, correctly understood, brings us to this view, and this view is not in contradiction to historical analysis:

> . . . historical analysis can find precisely the language intent of its text, if it only proceeds in a sufficiently reliable way. Does not historical analysis come into its own precisely when it does *not* permit itself to exchange its concrete object, the text, for its metaphysical premise? It is a difference residing in the *subject matter*, whether the object of analysis brings one into dealings with the language-event or not. This is decided by the text. It is precisely the metaphysical premise of historical analysis, namely, the category "object," that drives us positively even to the discovery of the full function of the word as a language-event in the texts, and can and should serve to win from our tradition exactly that which can—and is intended to—unite us with people of long ago, overcoming the distance of time.[56]

Language and Theology in Gerhard Ebeling

Gerhard Ebeling, as indicated, began his contribution to the New Hermeneutic with a proposal for a new understanding of church history as "the history of the interpretation of Holy Scripture," and he has continued by recasting theology as a whole in terms of hermeneutic. Although much of the discussion so far has presented the New Hermeneutic as a unified program, Ebeling does make a contribution which moves away from Fuchs somewhat. "Dogmatics," says Ebeling, "resting on the exposition of Scripture and the history of theology, . . . has the task of bringing the church's teaching into contact and discussion with contemporary principles of thought, there to submit it to critical sifting and present it in its full inner coherence."[57]

Ebeling sees Holy Scripture, "the testimony to the provisional and the conclusive proclamation of God," as *the* absolute source of present proclamation" and "the authoritative text of theology." The historical-critical method itself leads to dogmatics and beyond the text of historical study. "Criticism is an element of integration in the effort to understand the text." But the ultimate purpose of the historical-critical method "is the interpreter's self-criticism in view of all of the conceivable possibilities of deceiving himself as to the aim of the biblical text," and "the question which is ultimately appropriate to the biblical text is how it affects the conscience." The biblical text, then, is not the Word of God in the strict sense. The proclamation is God's Word. "Insofar as the proclamation is dependent on the text, the exposition therefore serves toward the text proving itself a Bible text, i.e., becoming the source of God's Word."[58]

Ebeling sees that a turn from the historical to the dogmatic way of understanding is called for by the subject matter itself. So dogmatic theology does not compete with historical exegesis but completes it.

In dealing with a text there is a transition from an exposition *of* the text to an exposition *by* the text (i.e., that one is concerned to be taught the truth about oneself by the text). . . . For the text is not there for its own sake, but for the sake of the word-event which is the origin and also the future of the text. Word-event is the exposition-event which is carried out by the Word. . . . For the Word, which once happened and which has been recorded in the form of a text as an event which has occurred, must with the help of the text again become Word, and so come into being as the expounding Word. . . . The subject-matter of dogmatic theology is . . . the word-event itself, in which the reality of man is shown in its true light . . . which makes man true and so for the first time real. And so now we can say that the subject of dogmatic theology is the event, which occurs only in the Word, of the coming of God to man.[59]

In his *Introduction to a Theological Theory of Language* Ebeling sets the context for his interest in language. It is the "boredom with language," the "felt experience of the weakness and impotence of Christian language," the view of the "paradox of the Word of God in human language" as an impossibility, the failure to give assent "to the tradition of Christian language." He associates himself with the attempt of Wilhelm Herrmann and Schleiermacher "to break down a concept of the word which was stunted and set in a mold of orthodox rigidity." They and he would seek "the word as it were in the condition of flowing lava," where the links of the word with life do not need "to be restored retrospectively and with great trouble," but will well up with "elemental force, as the springing up of the word in the processes of life and the issuing forth of life from a living and life-giving word."[60]

The question, Ebeling says, is whether "it is possible for texts from a distant age and a strange context to utter this message in a new age and a new context, whether the words frozen in a text can ever become living words again and give power to say something relevant at the present day." He declares that the answer must be "yes" no matter what problems are raised. ". . . the spirit preserved in the letter can once again become spirit *through* the letter, and yet in a certain sense *against* the letter, by creating the presence of the spirit (for spirit by its very nature has the power of making present)."[61]

Ebeling's view of a language which can be of contemporary theological value goes far beyond the theories passed down from antiquity and becomes as broad as life itself. However, he does use the model of language as communication in which the basic structure can be expressed in the single formula: I am saying something to you. With such a model of language as the basis, Ebeling shows how a theological theory of language must deal with: (a) "The Speaker as the Subject of the Process of Language: The Authority to Speak," (b) "The Act of Utterance: Responsibility," (c) "The Object of the Statement: The Challenge to Understanding," (d) "The Person Addressed: Mutual Understanding," and (e) "Verification."[62]

Theology, as the theory of the language of faith, then, operates completely on the level of the language of the world. It "never ceases to exist in the form of an encounter in the midst of the confusion of languages present in the world. . . . Thus the language of faith is the dialogue of faith with the experience of the world." Ebeling's use of "language," certainly in *Introduction to a Theological Theory of Lan-*

guage, is analogical. Just as a sentence is a communication from one person to another, so theology is a "dialogue of faith with the experience of the world." With the use of "language" as an analogy, the reader is not at a loss as to the real subject under consideration. Yet Ebeling speaks of "processes deep down in life itself which are beyond control" which govern the fruitfulness of the thinking and learning with which he is concerned.[63]

Language in Fuchs and Its Relation to Other Views of Language

Fuchs's use of "language" generally expands the concept of language beyond what is commonly thought of as language. "Language" in Fuchs is not merely a metaphor or an analogy, although it is not "principally the means of expression for thoughts, concepts, or possibilities of understanding." Fuchs distinguishes between an "outer form of language" and the "spirit of the text." The formal aspect of language, such as the arrangement of words in the sentence, may be altered without causing "the spirit which characterizes the sentence" to disappear. "The spirit which characterizes the sentence does not necessarily disappear just because the sound, for example of Paul, no longer resounds in the same key in the translation. It may be sufficient if the translation simply creates the sphere which the text meant to create when the spirit spoke in it." The outer form of language is derivative and not basic. The outer form can be "struck dead" because it "makes no difference." It "can be repeated at will." The spirit of the text is what "creates the sphere which the text meant to create when the spirit spoke in it."[64]

The distinction between speaking-event and language-event shows Fuchs's broad concept of language. "Speaking-event" refers simply to the "brute fact" of spoken language, to the "outer form." Language-event is an event which we both "receive outwardly with the ear" and "grasp and receive inwardly, or else reject or ignore." Fuchs does not consider thought as the best way to consider the inward grasping. Thought itself is a word. Inner grasping is an event just as what is said is an event. This event of inward grasping takes place "both in our various moods and in our conscience. These two, mood and conscience, must be brought into harmony, if the word 'gets home.' "[65]

Fuchs himself declares that faith's "doctrine of language" is "not meant in the sense of linguistics."[66] Yet "language" is used not simply analogically or as a metaphor, and attempts have been made to enlist contemporary ideas of language to make Fuchs more understandable, to situate Fuchs's idea of language in relation to recognizable landmarks in general linguistic studies.

John Dillenberger sees the New Hermeneutic as taking "language too much at face value." That is, language for the New Hermeneutic expresses reality directly. It is objective, referring to certain objective realities. Of course, the language of the New Hermeneutic is not "the objective language of world and world picture." Rather it is "a kind of objective and objectifying language of the self." In light of this, Dillenberger criticizes the New Hermeneutic for reducing "the direct applicability to the human" of the avenues of language. He sees the task of the New Hermeneutic as impossible because of its limited view of language, its assumption that it can capture "the intentionality of a theological formulation" and simply translate it "into another form or universe of discourse."[67]

J. Verhaar criticizes the New Hermeneutic's concept of language in an opposite view. He says that, in hermeneutical theology, language is very nearly coextensive with the whole of reality and is dissatisfied with the failure of the New Hermeneutic to found its concept of language on an understandable theory of language. This failure opens the way for various understandings of the principles of hermeneutic theology and for interpretations which have no solid foundations.[68] John E. Zuck agrees with Verhaar that the New Hermeneutic's concept of language is implausible. Zuck admits that "it is and always will be logically conceivable that the real content of speech is being-itself, and that the essence of the New Testament message can be re-presented without remainder in a radically different conceptual and linguistic context." But, Zuck cautions, "language does not ordinarily seem to operate this way. . . ." Zuck's basic criticism is that the New Hermeneutic drives a wedge between the *meaning* of biblical language and the *words* in the text, and that one cannot retranslate or reformulate a conceptually inadequate piece of discourse into a satisfactory one and really have an equivalent meaning. The New Hermeneutic must import a theory of meaning to justify the translation of "an intentionality or meaning which once presented itself (but no longer does) through a particular set of words."[69]

Zuck uses the work of J. L. Austin and Gilbert Ryle to show that the New Hermeneutic's distinction between "the meaning of a text" and "the direct significance of the words through which the meaning comes to expression" is linguistically invalid. Fuchs sees the real content of speech as being-itself and "careful attention to the ways in which language is ordinarily made to operate" renders Fuchs's view implausible.[70]

A. C. Thiselton, however, utilizes the work of Austin to corroborate Fuchs's concept of language and language-event. In the language-event of Fuchs and the performative utterance of Austin, "the issuing of the utterance is the performing of an action."[71] Thiselton does criticize Fuchs for ignoring the function of language on the purely cognitive level and suggests that the work of the later Wittgenstein may help to bridge the gap between the function of language on the purely cognitive level and the function of language on the deeper level, the function of "exposing or reorienting attitudes and presuppositions."[72] Wittgenstein, according to Thiselton, is in accord with the view of the New Hermeneutic that "creative language requires a flexibility of usage or meaning which cannot be provided by completely 'closed' concepts or completely 'closed' assertions," but in contrast to the New Hermeneutic Wittgenstein assumes "that there are virtually endless *degrees of variation* between completely closed and completely open horizons of meaning."[73] Thiselton admits that Fuchs may press his ideas too far, but he declares that "the work of Wittgenstein and Austin has confirmed that, in general outline, Fuchs's understanding of the parable as language-event stresses, or at least gropes after, several important points in biblical hermeneutics."[74]

The two seemingly divergent attitudes toward the value of contemporary ordinary language analysis for unraveling the New Hermeneutic and for hermeneutics in general are both justified. Ordinary language analysis has expanded the view of the function of language beyond the model of ideal language of the logicians and allowed language to be seen as functioning legitimately in the area of human action and feeling. But this analysis, although it has taken language more seriously than has hermeneutics in an empirical-experiential sense, has not sought to move from the linguistic expression to the more basic level of the means of language. Ordinary language analysis has not been strongly involved in the linguistic sciences of the twentieth century.[75]

Ordinary language analysis does appear to be related to the project of the New Hermeneutic in that both are moving beyond the function of language as conveying information, and in this respect both approaches may be seen as paralleling aspects of the broad conceptualization of Dilthey and as correcting the limiting view of Bultmann. Paul Ricoeur has delineated the conditions of the functioning of language which have been uncovered by ordinary language analysis and which are "not provisory defects or diseases" to be eliminated by the reformation of language but are rather conditions which are "permanent and fruitful." These conditions are: "the variability of semantic values, their sensitivity to contexts, the irreducibly polysemic character of lexical terms in ordinary language. . . ." On the basis of the work of Wittgenstein and Austin, Ricoeur judges ordinary language "to be a kind of conservatory for expressions which have preserved the highest descriptive power as regards human experience, . . ." and he is convinced that hermeneutics will benefit from an inquiry into the functioning of ordinary language. "The whole problem of text-interpretation could be renewed by the recognition of its roots in the functioning of ordinary language itself."[76]

Yet the question of the relationship of the text itself and a meaning deeper than the text which is perhaps inadequately expressed in the words of the text is not illuminated by ordinary language analysis. Ordinary language analysis does not solve the problem consciously faced by Dilthey and inherent in hermeneutics in general: the way from the linguistic and literary expression by means of the linguistic sciences to the more basic ground of that expression—life and the mental structure (Dilthey), Being (Heidegger), the central matter (Bultmann), the Word (Fuchs). Can anything be said beyond more precise definitions of the problem? Are the processes involved in the movement genuine linguistic processes which can be studied by means of the linguistic sciences? If not, do the linguistic sciences provide an analogical model which helps us understand the processes?

NOTES

1. Rudolf Bultmann, "The Problem of Hermeneutics," *Essays Philosophical and Theological* (London: SCM, 1955), pp. 258–59.

2. Rudolf Bultmann, "Das Problem einer theologischen Exegese des Neuen Testaments," *Zwischen den Zeiten* 3 (1923). Cited in *Beginnings of Dialectical Theology*, I, ed. J. M. Robinson (Richmond: John Knox, 1968), 236–37.

3. Karl Barth, "The Preface to the Second Edition," *The Epistle to the Romans*, trans. from the 6th ed. by Edwyn C. Hoskyns (Oxford: Oxford University Press, 1933), pp. 7–8.

4. *Ibid.*

5. Bultmann, "The Problem of Hermeneutics," pp. 240–41, 256, 258.

6. *Ibid.*, pp. 257, 259.

7. Rudolf Bultmann, "What Sense Is There to Speak of God?" *Christian Scholar* 43 (1960), 213.

˜8. Rudolf Bultmann, "Bultmann Replies to His Critics," *Kerygma and Myth* I, ed. Hans Werner Bartsch (New York: Harper Torchbooks, 1961), 193.

9. Bultmann, "The Problem of Hermeneutics," pp. 243, 256.

10. *Ibid.*, pp. 252–53.

11. Bultmann, "Bultmann Replies to His Critics," pp. 191–92.

12. Cited in James M. Robinson, "Hermeneutics Since Barth," *The New Hermeneutic*, vol. 2 of *New Frontiers in Theology* (New York: Harper, 1964), p. 30, from *Christliche Welt* 36 (1922), 372–73.

13. Cited in Robinson, "Hermeneutics Since Barth," pp. 34–35, from Hans Jonas, *Gnosis und spätantiker Geist* I (Göttingen: Vandenhoeck & Ruprecht, 1934), xvii.

14. Hans Jonas, *Gnosis und spätantiker Geist* II, Part One (Göttingen: Vandenhoeck & Ruprecht, 1954). Printed in its relevant parts in 1934. See Robinson, "Hermeneutics Since Barth," pp. 36–37 n. 97.

15. Hans Jonas, *Augustin und das paulinische Freiheitsproblem* (Göttingen: Vandenhoeck & Ruprecht, 1930), p. 67. The translation is based on that in Robinson, "Hermeneutics Since Barth," p. 36.

16. Rudolf Bultmann, "New Testament and Mythology," in *Kerygma and Myth* I, 10.

17. Bultmann, "The Problem of Hermeneutics," p. 251.

18. See John Macquarrie, *An Existentialist Theology: A Comparison of Heidegger and Bultmann* (2d ed.; London: SCM, 1960); *Studies in Christian Existentialism* (Philadelphia: Westminster, 1965), pp. 153–57; *Existentialism* (London: Hutchinson, 1972), pp. 216–18. For a discussion of the theological limitation of Bultmann's approach, see Macquarrie, *God-Talk: An Examination of the Language and Logic of Theology* (London: SCM, 1967), pp. 34–41.

19. Gerhard Ebeling, "Hermeneutik," *Die Religion in Geschichte und Gegenwart*, vol. 3 (Tübingen: J. C. B. Mohr, 1959), pp. 257–58.

20. See Richard N. Soulen, "Ernst Fuchs: New Testament Theologian," *Journal of the American Academy of Religion* 39 (1971), 467–87.

21. Gerhard Ebeling, *Kirchengeschichte als Geschichte der Auslegung der Heiligen Schrift* (Tübingen: J. C. B. Mohr, 1947).

22. Robinson, "Hermeneutics Since Barth," p. 65.

23. Ernst Fuchs, "Response to the American Discussion," *The New Hermeneutic*, p. 235.

24. *Ibid.*, p. 236.

25. Ernst Fuchs, *Hermeneutik* (Bad Cannstatt: R. Müllerschön Verlag, 1954), p. 131. Hereafter abbreviated as *H*.

26. Ernst Fuchs, *Marburger Hermeneutik* (Tübingen: J. C. B. Mohr, 1968), pp. 177–78. Hereafter abbreviated as *MH*.

27. Ernst Fuchs, *Zum Hermeneutischen Problem in der Theologie*, vol. 1 of *Gesammelte Aufsätze* (Tübingen: J. C. B. Mohr, 1965), pp. 92–93. Hereafter referred to as *GA* I.

28. *MH*, p. 239.

29. *GA* I, 128: "Wohl ist das Sein der Grund der Sprache." Pp. 126–27: "Ohne das Sein ist die Sprache grundlos, absurd, phantastisch, Glossolalie, eigentlich unmöglich." ". . . ohne die Sprache ist auch das Sein nichts."

30. *GA* I, 124–25, 128.

31. Gerhard Ebeling, *God and Word*, trans. James W. Leitch (Philadelphia: Fortress, 1967), p. 1.

32. *MH*, p. 135; *GA* I, 24, 281–83; *Glaube und Erfahrung*, vol. 3 of *Gesammelte Aufsätze* (Tübingen: J. C. B. Mohr, 1965), pp. 12, 23, 131, 172, 212, 229, 308, 406, 427. Hereafter referred to as *GA* III.

33. *GA* I, 290–91.

34. *Ibid.*, pp. 113–15, 124–31, 296.

35. Ernst Fuchs, *Zur Frage nach dem historischen Jesus*, Volume II of *Gesammelte Aufsätze* (Tübingen: J. C. B. Mohr, 1960), p. 181 ". . . er sich die Sprache des Volks für das Höchste, für die Rede von Gott, dienstbar machte." Hereafter referred to as *GS* II.

36. Gerhard Ebeling, *The Nature of Faith*, trans. Ronald Gregory Smith (London: Collins, 1961), pp. 190–91.

37. *H*, pp. 78, 62–70.

38. *GA* I, 10.

39. *MH*, p. 2; *GA* I, 282–84, 304.

40. Ernst Fuchs, "Das Christus verstandnis bei Paulus und im Johannesevangelium," *Marburger Theologische Studien*, ed. H. Grass and W. G. Kümmel (Marburg: N. G. Elwert Verlag, 1963), pp. 11–20. Cited in *The New Hermeneutic*, pp. 60–61.

41. *GA* III, 426–27; *MH*, p. 22.

42. *GS* II, 61: "Jesus selbst ist Gottes Wort, aber das Neue Testament ist Menschenwort, wenn es auch vom Geist der ersten Zeugen erfüllt ist. . . . Aber Gott hat uns diese Sprache Jesu und seiner Apostel wichtig gemacht, indem er Jesus als sein Wort offenbarte."

43. *GA* III, 42.

44. Ernst Fuchs, *Studies of the Historical Jesus*, trans. Andrew Scobie (London: SCM, 1964), pp. 196–200. This is a translation of portions of *GA* II.

45. *Ibid.*, pp. 211–12; *GA* III, 173.

46. Fuchs, *Studies of the Historical Jesus*, p. 211.

47. *MH*, p. 31: "leben oder da sind."

48. *H*, pp. 103–18.

49. *Ibid.*, p. 109: "Wer z.B. die Katze verstehen lernen will, kann ihr eine Maus verschaffen. Er wird die Katze dann so sehen, wie sie sich selbst zeigt."

50. *Ibid.*, p. 111: ". . . ein hermeneutisches Prinzip nennt das, was dem Verstehen die Macht und Wahrheit eines *Vorgangs* verleiht. Es ist die *Kraft* des Verstehens in der Geburt *der die Wahrheit nennenden Sprache*. Das hermeneutische Prinzip zeigt den 'Ort' der Wahrheit."

51. *H*, pp. 114–17, 155: ". . . ist die frage nach dem Grunde der menschlichen Existenze *die existentiale Bedingung* dieser Auslegung."

52. Fuchs, *Studies of the Historical Jesus*, pp. 191–206.

53. *Ibid.*, p. 192.

54. *Ibid.*, pp. 192–96.

55. *MH*, pp. 11, 247–48.

56. Fuchs, "Response to the American Discussion," *The New Hermeneutic*, pp. 242–43.

57. Gerhard Ebeling, *Word and Faith* (London: SCM, 1963), p. 27.

58. *Ibid.*, pp. 427–29.

59. Gerhard Ebeling, *Theology and Proclamation* (London: Collins, 1966), pp. 28–29.

60. Gerhard Ebeling, *Introduction to a Theological Theory of Language* (London: Collins, 1973), pp. 15–16.

61. *Ibid.*, p. 22.

62. *Ibid.*, pp. 129–63, 166–80.

63. *Ibid.*, pp. 190–91.

64. Fuchs, *Studies of the Historical Jesus*, pp. 195, 194. Fuchs chooses to speak of the "live" part of the text or the "spirit" of the text instead of the "inner form" to contrast his approach with that of Humboldt. *Ibid.*, p. 194.

65. *Ibid.*, p. 196.

66. Fuchs, "Response to the American Discussion," *The New Hermeneutic*, p. 241.

67. John Dillenberger, "On Broadening the New Hermeneutic," *The New Hermeneutic*, pp. 151–54.

68. J. Verhaar, "Language and Theological Method," *Continuum* 7 (1969), 17.

69. John E. Zuck, "The New Hermeneutic on Language: A Critical Appraisal," *The Journal of Religion* 52 (1972), 411, 414.

70. *Ibid.*, pp. 407, 410.

71. J. L. Austin, *How to Do Things with Words* (Oxford, 1962), p. 6.

72. See L. Wittgenstein, *Philosophical Investigations* (Oxford: Blackwell, 1958), paragraphs 108, 316–94. David Pears points out that "it is Wittgenstein's later doctrine that outside human thought and speech there are no objective points of support, and meaning and necessity are present only in the linguistic practices which embody them." Pears, *Wittgenstein* (London: Fontana/Collins, 1971), p. 168. Associated with Wittgenstein's change in attitude to factual discourse, then, is a move to anthropocentrism which parallels Dilthey's relating of anthropology and the literary expression, poetics, and hermeneutics. See *ibid.*, pp. 168–86, for a discussion of the mediation of Wittgenstein's positivistic and anti-positivistic tendencies in "the true center" of man.

73. A. C. Thiselton, "The Parables as Language-Event: Some Comments on Fuchs's Hermeneutics in the Light of Linguistic Philosophy," *Scottish Journal of Theology* 23 (1970), 466.

74. *Ibid.*, p. 468.

75. Verhaar, "Language and Theological Method," pp. 8, 16; Paul Ricoeur, "From Existentialism to the Philosophy of Language, *Philosophy Today* 17 (1973), 95–96.

76. Ricoeur, "From Existentialism to the Philosophy of Language," pp. 95–96.

PART TWO

MEANING, LANGUAGE, AND STRUCTURE IN STRUCTURALISM

Introduction

Structuralism is most often seen as an approach which is diametrically opposed to hermeneutics. Hermeneutics is dialectical and moves back and forth from text to interpreter—from text to all possible contexts—into development of the present-day meaning of a text. Structuralism is most often seen as positivistic, rejecting the epistemological assumptions of hermeneutics and distancing the text from any subjective concerns of the critic. Structuralism conceives of structure as the prior abstract system of interrelationships from which the content and the function of the elements derive. Structuralism, then, would have methodological priority over hermeneutics. Part Two examines developments in structuralism to show that a severely structural approach to literature is impossible but that structural studies are nevertheless important for literary studies. Literature is neither a positivistic nor a totally subjective enterprise. The attempt to relate the text to human linguistic processes is taken as both the beginning point and the end of structural studies. Wilhelm Dilthey's unsuccessful efforts serve as a model for the present-day task. His concept of the developing mental structure of man is a key to the uniting of structuralism and hermeneutics in a comprehensive systems approach to interpretation.

Chapters Four and Five trace the developments in studies concerned with the text, the expression of the human mind. Ferdinand de Saussure, the Russian formalists, the Czechoslovakian structuralists, and the French structuralists may be thought of as pioneers in the development of the linguistic and literary tools which would accomplish what Dilthey, lacking such tools, could not in his day—the relating of the literary expression itself to human linguistic and literary processes. Saussure is generally regarded as the founder of structural linguistics which emphasizes the study of language as a living whole existing at a particular point in time instead of as an evolving reality. He stresses the language system (*langue*) behind the actual linguistic performance (*parole*), the view of meaning as a relationship between the objects and ideas on the one hand and the language which refers to the objects and ideas on the other hand, and the associative (or paradigmatic) relationship of signs as well as the syntagmatic relationship.

With the Russian formalists and the Czechoslovakian structuralists, literature is reduced to language; the literary work is conceived as a specific type of linguistic communication. Hence, linguistic communication is examined in the concrete appearance of the text of the work, and the literary communication is distinguished from practical language by the purpose for which the language is used. Practical language is that type in which linguistic resources have no autonomous value. Poetic language, however, is the language system in which the practical aim retreats to the background and the resources of language (sounds, morphological segments, etc.) acquire autonomous value. The concern in regard to literature changes from the questions "how did it appear?" "what is it about?" to "how is it made?"

The activities of Czechoslovakian structuralism in the areas of structure and the semiotic view of art are important for the study of narrative. In terms of structure, the following are stressed: meaning in literature is based on relationships in a structure; the aesthetic function is the dominant function of literary language; the literary work is relatively independent of non-literary structures; and the work of literature must be approached synchronically. Of continuing importance in the Czechoslovakian approach to art as semiotics are the emphases that the perception or the decoding of a work of art is a progressive activity which does not establish some final, unambiguous relationship to an external reality, that formal elements as well as elements of content are bearers of meaning, and that the viewer and the artist shape the work of art. The sign is not equal to the state of the author or the state of the receiver; however, both are important. The author and the viewer bring intentions to the work of art and complement one another in the development of meaning.

Roman Jakobson and Claude Lévi-Strauss are key figures in the development of a structuralism or a semiotics which eventually related the text and human creativity or competence. Jakobson maintained the structural tradition from Russian formalism through Czechoslovakian structuralism and mediated this viewpoint to Lévi-Strauss. By 1945, Lévi-Strauss was advocating the use of linguistics in anthropological study in particular and the social sciences in general. Lévi-Strauss claimed a formal relationship between anthropology and linguistics and is well known for his applications of structural linguistics in the study of myths.

The refinement of the tools to relate human competence and the literary text is due to the students of narrative in France who depend not only on the work of Russian formalism, Czechoslovakian structuralism, and the work of Lévi-Strauss on myth, but who also benefit from a complex of related activities. The adoption of a semiotic in place of a linguistic model brought a more inclusive approach and allowed for aspects of literature excluded by the purely linguistic approach. (The full impact of the difference between the semiotic model and the linguistic model may not yet have been felt.) French New Criticism created or was created by a new literary climate in France which allowed freer approaches to the literary work. The work of Propp on Russian folk tales (first published in Russia in 1928 but directly influential only since translation into English in 1958 and French in 1970) provides means for conceptualizing how a particular narrative is one instance of broader narrative structures by the detection of a limited number of functions (or moves) and actants (or character types). Noam Chomsky's work on generative grammar has helped students of narrative more easily conceive of a literary competence behind the specific literary performance.

The scholars working in a structural or semiotic framework have developed methods of moving from the level of manifestation of narrative to deeper levels which are related to human competence, to laws of a universal narrative grammar. Common to students of narrative, who include A. J. Greimas, Claude Bremond, Tzevan Todorov, and the early Roland Barthes, are three postulates: the definition of narrative as an autonomous level in the semantic organization of texts or an abstraction in relation to the "real" text, the distinction between different planes of narrative structures, and belief in the possibility of articulating the series of events in sequences of action and of developing a "lexicon" of narratives and rules of combination of such narrative units. However, important differences separate the researchers. Of significance for New Testament hermeneutics is the differing beginning point of analysis, ranging from the purely deductive logical approach to the more empirical approach concerned with the plurality of the texts. The scholars also differ in the "meanings" discerned in analysis, from purely non-historical formal patterns to a multiplicity of changing connotations.

The students of narrative from the structural perspective have advanced beyond the recording of phonological and morphological facts which may or may not be related to conventional meanings of the texts. The elements which are important in the structural study of narrative are semantical patterns which are related to the creator and reader of the narrative. There is basic agreement on the conceptualization of the analysis appropriate to such narrative in that analysis is related to human response in creation and in interpretation.

Chapter Six shows that the application of the insights of Dilthey to structuralism and hermeneutics results in an inclusive systems approach to interpretation involving all the levels of language, literature, and meaning which impinge upon a reader. Moreover, the integrated mental structure active in creation and interpretation is a developing capacity. The purposeful and dynamic nature of the mind, an active as well as reactive dynamism involved in understanding and interpretation, is a basic view of contemporary structural thought as it was of Dilthey. The view of this mental structure as a developing system is not so common. The process of formation of this structural system, for Dilthey, is both a process of learning, of internalizing social and cultural factors, and of physical and psychical development. The studies in modern structural psychology, especially the work of Jean Piaget, may be applied to the hermeneutical process. The structural psychology of Piaget denies that man is merely a passive reactor to the environment on the one hand, or the possessor of "innate ideas" which automatically unfold on the other hand. The insight of Piaget, brought into relationship with the hermeneutics of Dilthey, results in a view of competence which is dynamic, not only going through the stages from infancy to adolescence outlined by Piaget, but also continuing to interact with the forces impinging upon it and arriving at different levels of equilibrium, forming a "constantly increasing spiral."

CHAPTER FOUR

Structuralism and Literature: Background and Origins

INTRODUCTION

Wilhelm Dilthey saw clearly that human creativity must be considered in the interpretation of literature and he adopted and developed the idea of a mental structure responsible in part for literary expression. He saw this structure as more than a *model* for understanding literary processes in man; he conceived it as a real biological-psychological-historical structure in man. Toward the conclusion of his career, Dilthey attempted in vain to determine ways to move from the literary expression itself back to the linguistic and literary processes, but he recognized that the language sciences must be the means for such a study.

At the beginning of the twentieth century, studies of literary creativity from the perspective of the text itself were beginning to do what Dilthey envisioned. These studies dealt with the general questions of literary creativity not from the perspective of psychology but from the perspective of the work in itself. These poetic studies were based on linguistics, primarily the structural linguistics associated with the name of Ferdinand de Saussure. Early application of linguistics to literary study took place within Russian formalism and Czechoslovakian structuralism. Roman Jakobson was active in both of these groups and, through the influence of Jakobson, Claude Lévi-Strauss began to apply structural methods in anthropology in general and the study of myth in particular. A group of French scholars associated in a general way with the structuralism of Lévi-Strauss have, over the past decade, developed the field of the structural study of narrative, or "narrative semiotics," or (to use the term introduced by T. Todorov) "narratology." This narratology, however, has benefited from infusion from Russian formalism independent of Lévi-Strauss and, perhaps just as important, from developments in the generative grammar of Noam Chomsky and attempts to relate generative grammar to literature.

The present chapter and the one following trace the developments leading from Russian formalism to current work in narrative. These chapters, however, do not merely catalog the developments. They view the history from the perspective of Dilthey's attempt to relate the literary expression to human linguistic and literary capacity. The early formalists and structuralists attempted to deal with the text in isolation from all other factors. It is obvious to us today that this is impossible, for the reader brings to the text both content and a linguistic and literary capacity. Nevertheless, the ideal remained the analysis of linguistic elements independent of relationships with any external factors, including the creative capacity of the author or of man in general. The work of the linguist Roman Jakobson in particular shows the limitations as well as the fruitfulness of an approach that leaves human competence in writing and reading out of the analysis. Lévi-Strauss, however, comes to the text as an anthropologist and attempts to relate the text (myth) to the mind. His ingenious studies of myth, however, tend to reduce human creativity to transformations and mediations of binary oppositions and to reduce the mind to the reproduction of the world of nature of which the mind itself is a part.

With the second generation of French structuralists, the students of narrative, we return rather fully to both concerns of Dilthey—the text and human linguistic and literary capacity. The students of narrative are able to relate the two effectively because they draw upon advances in a number of disciplines which progressively emphasize the central importance of man. The students of narrative emphasize different aspects of narrative as human creation, or at least they begin at different points. Some begin with the abstract, logical level while others concentrate upon the actual level of manifestation of the narrative. To use Dilthey's conceptualization and terminology, some emphasize the universal while others emphasize the particular. Dilthey's appeal to both the universal and particular points us in the direction of accepting both emphases of narrative studies.

Chapter Six completes the specifically structural part of this work by dealing with two related subjects not explicitly treated by the narratologists themselves but which are essential for hermeneutics in general and New Testament interpretation in particular—the relationship of existential hermeneutics to structuralism and the nature of the competence of the interpreter, particularly the dynamic aspect of human competence. In these matters, the contributions of scholars outside the structural study of narrative are utilized, particularly the work of Paul Ricoeur and Jean Piaget. Ricoeur is a philosopher drawing upon existential hermeneutics but continuing to attempt to relate structural conceptualizations to his work. Piaget is a well-known psychologist who applies structuralist concepts in something of a different way from the approaches of Lévi-Strauss and the second-generation structuralists dependent upon him.

SAUSSURE AND STRUCTURAL LINGUISTICS

Theological scholars who use the biblical languages in their theological tasks are aware of the work done in grammar and philology in the past. Best known perhaps are the advances in comparative philology and the discovery of the papyri which brought studies in New Testament Greek to a high point in the nineteenth and the beginning of the twentieth centuries. These linguistic developments, however, do not suffice for the task of Dilthey and hermeneutics since his day. The linguistics in use today, indeed, is quite different from that known to most biblical scholars.

The key scholar in the movement from the historical linguistics of the nineteenth century to the linguistics of the twentieth century was a Swiss linguist, Ferdinand de Saussure. Through his lectures, published after his death by his students, Saussure's ideas became known and have continued to influence generation after generation of linguists. Publication of the lectures has been likened to a "Copernican revolution" in linguistics.[1] Saussure's contribution may be seen through four theoretical dichotomies from his work which continue to be important: synchronic/diachronic, language-system/language-in-use (*langue/parole*), that-which-is-signified/that-which-signifies (*signifié/signifiant*), and syntagmatic/associative (paradigmatic).[2]

The diachronic view of language emphasizes the evolution of a language, the changes of the language from one period to another. This was the type of linguistics which had been so influential in the comparative philology of the nineteenth century. Saussure emphasizes synchronic linguistics, the study of a language as a living whole, which exists at a particular point of time.[3]

Langue and *parole* are the two aspects of language in Saussure's analysis. *Parole* is the actual concrete act of speaking of an individual. This is the effect of language directly available to the linguist because it is a social activity which exists in a given situation. *Langue*, on the other hand, is the language system behind *parole*. *Langue* is the totality of a language deducible only from an examination of the experiences and memories of all the language users. Saussure felt strongly that *langue* is not simply an abstraction, that the characteristics of *langue* are actually present in the brain.[4]

In the dichotomy *signifié/signifiant*, Saussure gives his view of meaning. He insisted that meaning is a relationship between the objects and ideas on the one hand and the language which refers to the objects and ideas on the other hand. The relation of *signifié* to *signifiant* gives a linguistic sign, for Saussure the basic unit of communication, a unit within the *langue* of a community.[5] The signified is not a material thing; it is a concept. The signifier is not a material sound; it is a sound-image. Both the signified (concept) and signifier (sound-image), then, are psychological. They are united in the brain by an "associative bond."[6]

The sign is arbitrary in that (with some few exceptions, as in the case of onomatopoeia) there is no objective, natural, or inevitable link between the signifier and the signified. The signifier represented by *cat* may be used to talk of an animal of a certain species, but any other sequence of sounds could be used if they were accepted by the speech community. There is no fixed universal relation between signifier and signified. The signifier may be thought of as an arbitrary division of the sound spectrum (on an abstract level) and the signified as an arbitrary division of a conceptual field. In Saussure's linguistics, then, there are no positive self-defined elements with which to begin. Elements are defined by relationships, identities and differences.

Two major types of relationships exist, syntagmatic and associative (or paradigmatic).[7] The linear sequence of signs in actual discourse forms a syntagmatic relationship. In this relationship a term acquires value because it stands in opposition to other words in the discourse. There is a syntagmatic relationship between "James" and "runs" which allows the sentence "James runs." This relationship exists between any two words, the first of which can serve as subject to the second. Syntagmatic relationships serve to help define a word. The differences between a word and the other words in an acceptable sentence are crucial in the definition of the word.

The non-syntagmatic relationships of signs are also essential in the determination of meaning. Saussure uses the term "associative" to refer to one set of non-syntagmatic relationships. He says that words that have something in common are associated in memory. For example, the word "teaching" will unconsciously call to mind numerous other words: "teach," "acquaint," "education," "apprenticeship," and other terms related to these words. All of these relationships are essential in the sense that, if a word lost some such relationships and gained others, the word would lose its old identity. For example, if there were no word "education," the word "teaching" would change its identity in a subtle way. In his discussion of sentence construction and sentence interpretation, Saussure discusses non-syntagmatic relationships in a different fashion. Paradigmatic relationships of a word are those it has with words which may replace it in a sentence without making the sentence unacceptable. In the sentence "John runs," the verb "run" may be replaced by numerous other verbs such as "move," "flee," and "hasten." Again, all of the paradigmatic relationships of a word, all of the words which could be used in place of "runs," are essential in determining the formal identity of the word.

Syntagmatic and paradigmatic relations have been illustrated in terms of words and sentences, However, Saussure claims that the entire linguistic system can be reduced to a theory of syntagmatic and paradigmatic relations. This is the clearest assertion of the structuralist view of language: not merely that a language is a system of elements defined wholly by their relation to one another within a system but also that the linguistic system consists of different levels of structure, each level containing elements which contrast with one another and which combine with other elements to form units on a higher level. Structuralists, then, may work on the level of phoneme, morpheme, sentence, text, or even the total linguistic system. Theoretically, at any rate, results on any one level of research have implications for work on all other levels, for the principles of structure at each level are fundamentally the same.

"Structural linguistics" is the term used to describe schools of linguistics, especially in Prague, Copenhagen, and the United States, which were influenced directly by the ideas of Saussure and his Geneva school. Although different interpretations may be placed on the exact meaning of "structuralism," in part deriving from the different schools, no linguist today would deny the place of structural thinking in his work. This structuralism is grounded in Saussure's emphasis that *langue* is *forme*, not *substance*. It must be envisioned as a system of interrelated elements and not as a collection of self-sufficient entities.

The Prague school was constituted by a group of Czech and other scholars whose main interest was in phonological theory. Prince Nikolai

Troubetzkoy, a professor in Vienna 1923–39, was the person around whom the group centered doctrinally, and the most important work of the school was Trubetskay's *Grundzüge der Phonologie* completed just before his death in 1939. The major efforts of the Prague school were directed toward the application of Saussure's theory of *langue-parole* to the phoneme concept. The term "phoneme" had been used in the nineteenth century to refer to a unit of sound. In the Prague school, the phoneme was an abstract functional concept, a unit on the level of *langue*. The phoneme was the smallest distinctive unit in the network of structural relationships of the sound-system of a language. The phoneme was a complex unit. It was defined in terms of a set of distinctive features seen as oppositions, such as voiceless-voiced, aspirated-unaspirated, tense-lax. The /p/ phoneme, for example, is voiceless, aspirated, and tense as opposed to the /b/ phoneme which is voiced, unaspirated, and lax. The difference between /p/ and /b/ is in the *opposition* of voicing, aspiration, tension, and other such oppositions (regardless of the variation in *degree* of voicing and aspiration, etc.). Phonological systems were classified according to the features of the phonemes in the system. Phonemes in different positions enter into different systems of relationship.

Members of the Prague school made contributions to areas of linguistics other than phonological theory. Roman Jakobson, now of Harvard University, may be credited with greatest responsibility for extending theory and practice of the Prague school into new areas of research. He applied the analytic procedures used in phonology to study the Russian case system and to attempt to abstract a base semantic content for each case.[8]

The Copenhagen school was founded in 1933 under the influence of Louis Hjelmslev. This school was less "empirical" than the Prague and American schools. For Hjelmslev, *langue* was a deductive system, and its exposition involved numerous theoretical postulates and categories. The theme of Hjelmslev was Saussure's emphasis on form as against substance (*langue* versus *parole*) on the levels of content and expression and on the definition of form as the interrelationship of elements. Hjelmslev carried these ideas to a logical extreme unmatched until the work of Chomsky. Analysis is to be carried out by a linguistics which is operationally self-sufficient and self-contained. That is, analysis is to have no reference to meaning. The subject matter will be analyzed and will have an existence only in terms of the patterns arrived at by completely formal inherently determined procedures. Hjelmslev called his system "glossematics" and summarized the essence of his approach in these words:

> The linguist discovers certain properties in all those objects that people agree to call languages, in order then to generalize those properties and establish them by definition. From that moment the linguistic theoretician has—arbitrarily, but appropriately—himself decreed to which objects his theory can and cannot be applied. He then sets up, for all objects of the nature premised in the definition, a general calculus, in which all conceivable cases are foreseen. This calculus, which is deduced from the established definition independently of all experience, provides the tools for describing or comprehending a given text and the language on which it is constructed. Linguistic theory cannot be verified (confirmed or invalidated) by reference to such existing texts and language. It can be judged only with reference to the self-consistency and exhaustiveness of its calculus.[9]

Hjelmslev is attempting to construct a theory of language as a system without relying upon non-linguistic information—physical, physiological, psychological, or sociological data. The system is derived by a series of propositions which are logically verifiable and which yield a "text" when applied to a mass of material (human discourse). According to Hjelmslev, the basic requirements for logically sound theories or propositions are that they must exhibit self-sufficiency, exhaustiveness, and simplicity. When theories are applicable to a large number of experimental data, they are appropriate or useful.[10]

The work of Saussure was less important for American structural thought than for the Prague or Copenhagen schools. Rather, practical purposes of the linguistics, at first the study of the Indian languages, later the teaching of foreign languages and attempts at machine translation, served as an important impetus in American linguistic developments.[11] Franz Boas, a specialist in American Indian languages, saw that, since the Indian languages had no written tradition and no history in the true sense, they could not be studied by classical historical methods. Concentration had to be on the correct description of existing linguistic phenomena. That is, the approach had to be exclusively synchronic. Boas's disciple, Edward Sapir, was also concerned with Indian languages. Independently of Saussure, Sapir began to emphasize language as an organized system. Sapir founded the idea of linguistic patterns, the idea that every man carries in himself the basic patterns of his language and that he expresses his ideas according to these psychological language patterns. Sapir designated the phoneme as a set of psychological associations which merge into an "ideal sound" in the subconscious which serves as a pattern for the creation of concrete speech sounds. Sapir believed that a decisive factor in the determination of the nature of the phoneme was the possibility of combinations in the speech chain. Sapir's psychological conception of the phoneme was of no continuing immediate importance (although his approach is akin to that taken later by Chomsky), but his distributional criterion was important for future developments. A method of linguistics developed which was based on the notation and description of the positions which units of a language system could occupy.[12]

The key figure of the distributionalism that characterized American structuralism was Leonard Bloomfield. Indeed, linguistics in America into the 1950s can be called "Bloomfieldian" linguistics. After Bloomfield's early work in linguistics, but before the publication of *Language* in 1933, Bloomfield had become a behaviorist under the influence of the psychologist Albert Paul Weiss. There is no doubt that this movement toward behaviorism on the part of Bloomfield was influential for his later work in linguistics. Bernard Bloch, in a biographical sketch of Bloomfield after his death in 1949, has said that "there can be no doubt that Bloomfield's greatest contribution to the study of language was to make a science of it."

> In his long campaign to make a science of linguistics, the chief enemy that Bloomfield met was that habit of thought which is called mentalism: the habit of appealing to mind and will as ready-made explanations of all possible problems. Most men regard this habit as obvious common sense; but in Bloomfield's view, as in that of other scientists, it is mere superstition, unfruitful at best and deadly when carried over into scientific research. In the opposite approach—known as positivism, determinism, or mechanism—Bloomfield saw the main hope of the world. . . .[13]

Bloomfield and the linguists influenced by him concerned themselves with the aspects of language suited to scientific investigation—the physical aspect, sound. The category of meaning was not included in analysis because non-linguistic criteria must not enter into a grammatical description of a language.[14] Bloomfield recognized that speech-sounds without regard to meanings was an abstraction, but a necessary abstraction because of his desire for scientific accuracy.[15]

The central matter in Bloomfield's scientific method was the *distribution* of linguistic units—the phoneme and the morpheme. The method of study was that of substitution. If a unit under study could be replaced by another unit in the same context without an essential change in the context, both units have the same grammatical properties and belong to the same class.

Morphological research was the area in which Bloomfieldians had most success. A morpheme is the smallest language unit having a meaning. It can be a word or part of a word. For example, *reading* consists of two morphemes: *read* and *-ing*. In development of the study, it became necessary to distinguish various levels of linguistic structure, and to be simple, precise, and practical in grammatical definition. For example /s/ is a phoneme in the word *show* and a morpheme indicating the plural in *pages*. A flood of new terms ending in *eme* for language units higher than the phoneme poured out: tagmeme, grammememe, semanteme, etc. Examples follow of the type of precise definition which the Bloomfield scholars found helpful: the English adjective is a word which can stand between the definite article *the* and a noun and which never takes *s* in the plural; the sentence is a linguistic form which is not in a construction with any other linguistic form.

Syntactical studies developed from morphological research, and an important contribution to the theory of syntax was the analysis of *immediate constituents*, those parts of the utterance physically connected with each other. Analysis of immediate constituents helped to reveal the principles by which the structure of an utterance may be linguistically organized. It was in immediate constituent analysis that the charts and diagrams so familiar in contemporary linguistics began to be used more abundantly.[16]

Bloomfield used the sentence *Poor John ran away* to show how a sentence can be split up into its immediate constituents. Two immediate constituents are present: *poor John* and *ran away*. These can be further analyzed. In IC analysis (as it was called) the sentence was seen as made up of layers of constituents. In the diagramming, each cutting point or "node" was given an identifying label.

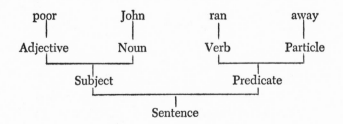

poor	John	ran	away
Adjective	Noun	Verb	Particle
Subject		Predicate	
Sentence			

Structural linguistics, especially in the Prague and Copenhagen forms, came to be important for literary study as literature was "reduced" to language. But the generative grammar of Noam Chomsky, which is also applied to literary study, developed out of the branch of the American variety of structuralism associated with the name of Z. S. Harris. So the insights of structural linguistics remain important in their own right and as they have been incorporated into other linguistic and literary approaches.

RUSSIAN FORMALISM AND
CZECHOSLOVAKIAN STRUCTURALISM

Early beginnings of the thrust of linguistics into other areas, particularly literature, may be seen in Russian formalism. The formalists stressed the autonomy of literary creation, the work itself, as over against external interpretations of the nineteenth century. The autonomy of literature and the intrinsic immanent laws of literature caused the literary work to be conceived as a specific type of linguistic communication and allowed the formalists to use linguistics as a tool to approach literature. The literary work, then, was viewed as linguistic communication to be examined in the concrete appearance of the text of the work. As language, the literary communication was distinguished, at least in the early stages of formalism, from practical language because of the postulated supremacy of sound over meaning in poetical works. This resulted from the work of scholars such as Baudouin de Courtenay, a representative of the Kazan school, and his students.[17] Lev Jakubinskij gave the formulation of the difference between practical language and poetic language, its key being the purpose for which the speaker uses his language resources: "If the speaker uses them for the purely practical purpose of communication, then we are dealing with the system of *practical language* (discursive thought), in which language resources (sounds, morphological segments, and so forth) have no autonomous value and are merely a *means* of communication. But it is possible to conceive and in fact to find language systems in which the practical aim retreats to the background (it does not necessarily disappear altogether), and language resources acquire autonomous value."[18]

The various individual components of the literary work, the means of the linguistic realization of the literary work with its poetic function, became central. B. Tomasevskij, who is important for the study of verse (as opposed to prose fiction), defined the relation of poetic and linguistics: "The object of poetics (in other words, the theory of verbal art of literature) is the doctrine of the ways of composing literary works. . . . Literature or verbal art, as the designation that has just been introduced indicates, is a component of man's verbal or linguistic activity. From this it follows that the theory of literature adheres to the doctrine dealing with language, that is, to linguistics."[19] The concern in regard to literature became not "How did it appear?" nor even "What is it about?" but "How is it made?" Roman Jakobson distinguished this concern from that of historians of literature. ". . . historians of literature act like nothing so much as policemen, who, out to arrest a certain culprit, take into custody (just in case) everything and everyone they find at the scene as well as any passers-by for good measure. The historians of literature have helped themselves to everything—environment, psychology, politics, philosophy. Instead of a science of literature they have worked up a concoction of homemade disciplines."[20] Jakobson and his colleagues sought for the features which make a work literature, and the very subject of literary studies was being redefined in terms of its construction and not in terms of its origin or subject matter.

For the purpose of understanding later application of linguistics, the work of Czechoslovak structuralism is vital. Similar concerns and approaches can be seen in Russian formalism, Czechoslovak structuralism, and later structural approaches such as that of Lévi-Strauss and other French structuralists. The key figure who insured continuity in all of these movements is Roman Jakobson,[21] who came to Prague in 1920 at a time when the Prague group was struggling to define the features of a literary work that distinguish it from other verbal messages. In 1923, in a study of Czech verse, Jakobson approached the work of literature as a system and applied to it the linguistic methodology. He compared the phonological systems of Russian and Czech and demonstrated that in large measure the differences in the systems of verse of Czech and Russian were determined by word stress and length which have different functions in the two language systems.[22]

The basic concepts of the early period of Czechoslovakian structuralism, when linguistics was being applied to literature and structural principles of literary study were being deduced, may be summarized in four points:[23] (1) meaning is based on relationships in a structure; (2) literary language has a dominant aesthetic function; (3) the literary work is (relatively) independent of non-literary structures; (4) the work of literature must be approached synchronically; diachrony exists in synchrony. The concept that meaning is based on relationships within a structure grows out of the linguistic postulate of the Prague school that phonemes have meaning because of their contrast to other phonemes, that phonemes have no intrinsic value in themselves. The principle is that the various components of the work of literature have their full meaning only in relation to all other component parts of the same work and, in a more comprehensive sense, in relation to the writings by the same author or of the same period, the same genre, etc.

The second concept grew out of the basic question of the unique nature of poetic language. Jakobson emphasized that poetic language has an aesthetic goal or function which dominates whatever other functions are present. The aesthetic function of poetic language causes that language to be oriented toward the poetic work itself. Poetic language calls attention to itself, its primary purpose is not that of providing referential information.

The attitude of the Czech structuralists toward the immanence of the literary work was the same as that of the formalists in the early period. Sklovskij has summarized the formalist view of immanence: "I am concerned in the theory of literature only with the examination of its inner laws. To use an industrial metaphor, when studying the art of weaving, I am not interested in the situation of the world cotton market, nor in the policy of the cotton trusts, but only in the count of yarn and the techniques of weaving."[24]

By the early 1930s, however, the leaders of Czechoslovak structuralism were taking issue with this thesis. Jan Mukarovsky agreed that the matter of weaving was of more concern to the structuralist than the conditions of the world market; but he declared that the cotton market could not be entirely ignored. The needs of the market have some relation to the development of the technique of weaving. The same is to be said for literature. Mukarovsky felt that the question of the immanence of the literary work could best be approached through the concept of aesthetic function. The aesthetic function is dominant in literary art but it exists throughout all human activity. Just so, the language of the work of literature forms a system which is related to the total system of the language in which it is written. And just as every level of language may have direct or indirect implications for the larger society, the linguistic system of a work of art may have relevance to the larger society in a complex and dialectical way.

Czechoslovak structuralism saw the importance of studying the history of a literature, and this history could be seen from the point of view of outside intervention or from the point of view of internal reordering of the component parts of the structure. Traditional literary historians may rely too heavily on external forces, but formalism can be criticized for placing literature in a vacuum. Mukarovsky mediated the two extremes with the view that the relation of literature to non-literary elements is essentially a relation between structures, each of the structures having autonomous evolutions but also interacting with one another.

ROMAN JAKOBSON

Roman Jakobson has been mentioned as the person responsible for the structural tradition from Russian formalism through French structuralism. Jakobson is best known as a linguist, but from the early years of formalism he had dealt with literature. Jakobson's concept of the nature of literature has governed his poetic approach. This concept, not just the invention of the formalists, but actually going back to the futurists and Mallarmé and the romantic tradition, emphasizes the autotelic nature of poetic language. As early as 1919, Jakobson gave his basic view of the essence of poetry, and he maintained continuity between this view and his latest pronouncement. The poetic function is "an element *sui generis.*" In poetry "the word is felt as word" and not simply as a substitute for another thing. The poetic function of language is characterized by "the aim of the message in itself, the emphasis upon the message for its own account."[25]

The relationship of the meaning of a work discovered through Jakobson's analysis of the means of production to the meaning of that same work obtained through traditional historical literary study is important in understanding the return to Dilthey's emphasis upon human creativity. Jakobson himself has modified his view of the relationship of the meaning of the various levels of the text and has carried out structural analyses of poetic works which involve traditional literary study. An examination of the development of Jakobson's own conceptualization, a description of his method, and the conclusions of literary critics as to the relations between linguistic facts and literary meaning may help us to see the possibility of successful and profitable movements from one level to another.[26]

An initial question is Jakobson's view of the function of a work and the relationship of the linguistic facts to the function. Does he totally equate a poetic work with an aesthetic or poetic function and the meaning with that which is associated with linguistic facts? In a 1935 lecture on the Russian formalist school, Jakobson admitted that such an equation could be seen in the early stages of Russian formalism. "However," Jakobson declared, "this equation is unquestionably erroneous: a poetic work is not confined to aesthetic function alone, but has in addition many other functions." A poetic work has non-aesthetic functions just as non-poetic works may have aesthetic functions. The address of an orator, normal conversation, newspaper articles, advertisements and scientific treatises, for example, may use words "in and for themselves, not merely as a referential device." Jakobson, however, is not willing to accept as the only alternative to the straight monistic point of view the mechanistic standpoint which judges a poetic work "as a mechanical agglomeration of functions." He acknowledges the multiple functions of a poetic work but maintains that the poetic work has integrity because of the dominant aesthetic function. "The definition of the aesthetic function as the dominant of a poetic work permits us to determine the hierarchy of diverse linguistic functions within the poetic work." Jakobson, then, allows for a referential function in elements of the poetic work. But if the aesthetic function is dominant, the referential components are subject to this decisive function.[27]

Another important question follows the acknowledgment that Jakobson does not totally equate the meaning of a work of literature with the meaning which may be obtained by an analysis of the linguistic facts: the relationship of meaning on the various levels. In 1921 in an article "Realism in Art," he spoke of the necessity of learning the "conventional language of painting in order to 'see' a picture" and the necessity of "knowing the language" to "understand what is spoken." It is true that innovation imposes new forms, but in the creation and interpretation of new forms with their aesthetic values, knowledge of the normative code is essential.[28] In an article "Linguistics and Poetics," in 1960, Jakobson affirms that "equivalence in sound, projected into the sequence as its constitutive principle, inevitably involves semantic equivalence, and on any linguistic level any constituent of such a sequence prompts one of the two correlative experiences which Hopkins neatly defines as 'comparison for likeness' sake' and 'comparison for unlikeliness' sake.' "[29]

It seems clear that Jakobson sees a definite relationship between conventional historical and literary meanings and the meaning uncovered by his analyses. Yet it also seems that Jakobson carries on his work with the assumption that linguistics alone provides a method for uncovering patterns which are present in the text itself.

> Any unbiased, attentive, exhaustive, total description of the selection, distribution, and interrelationship of diverse morphological classes and syntactic constructions in a given poem surprises the examiner himself by unexpected, striking symmetries and antisymmetries, balanced structures, efficient accumulation of equivalent forms and salient contrasts, finally by rigid restrictions in the repertory of morphological and syntactic constituents used in the poem, eliminations which, on the other hand, permit us to follow the masterly interplay of the actualized constituents."[30]

May an analysis of linguistic facts which are significant for aesthetic meaning be accomplished independent of literary meaning seen by the reader? Do the linguistic facts determine the semantics? In Jakobson's declaration there seem to be contradictions. Are these dialectical in nature, or are they genuine contradictions?

In 1962 Jakobson and Lévi-Strauss collaborated on an analysis of "Les Chats," a nineteenth-century sonnet by Charles Baudelaire (*Fleurs du Mal*, LXVI). The sonnet is reproduced below along with an English translation by Anthony Hecht.[31]

LES CHATS

Les amoureux fervents et les savants austères
Aiment également, dans leur mûre saison,
Les chats puissants et doux, orgueil de la maison,
Qui comme eux sont frileux et comme eux sédentaires.

Amis de la science et de la volupté,
Ils cherchant le silence et l'horreur des ténèbres;
L'Érèbe les eût pris pour ses coursiers funèbres,
S'ils pouvaient au servage incliner leur fierté.

Ils prennent en songeant les nobles attitudes
Des grands sphinx allongés au fond des solitudes
Qui semblent s'endormir dans un rêve sans fin;

Leurs reins féconds sont pleins d'étincelles magiques,
Et des parcelles d'or, ainsi qu'un sable fin,
Étoilent vaguement leurs prunelles mystiques.

CATS

Feverish lovers, scholars in their lofts,
Both come in their due time to love the cat;
Gentle but powerful, king of the parlor mat,
Lazy, like them, and sensitive to draughts.

Your cat, now, linked to learning and to love,
Exhibits a taste for silences and bloom—
Would make a splendid messenger of doom
If his fierce pride would condescend to serve.

Lost in his day-dream, he assumes the pose
Of sphinxes in the desert, languidly
Fixed in a reverie that has no end;

His loins are lit with the fires of alchemy,
And bits of gold, small as the finest sand,
Fleck, here and there, the mystery of his eyes.

The analysis deals with all types of morphological and syntactical elements and attempts to relate these elements to semantics. At the beginning of the analysis, the rhyme scheme is shown to be the product of three different rules which relate to grammatical categories of gender, number, and nature of the noun (substantival or adjectival); the authors suggest that "the close link between classification of rhyme and choice of grammatical category emphasizes the importance of the role of grammar . . . in the structure of this sonnet."[32]

The composition of the entire sonnet is seen as based on the tension between two modes of arrangement. One arrangement is that of three compound sentences which form a progression according to the number of independent clauses and the person of the verb forms in each clause. Each of the two quatrains and the two tercets taken together form the three sentences. The second mode of arrangement is that of two pairs of verses: one pair of quatrains and one pair of tercets.

Syntactic and semantic parallels are shown to exist between the pair of quatrains and the pair of tercets. For example: "Both the first quatrain and the first tercet consist of two clauses, of which the second is relative, and introduced in both cases by the same pronoun, *qui*"; and "The subjects in the first quatrain and the first tercet are all animate objects, whilst one of the two subjects in the second quatrain and all in the second tercet are inanimate substantives."[33] Striking relations are pointed out in the grammatical structure at the beginning and end of the sonnet. At the beginning and at the end, but nowhere else, are found two subjects with a single predicate and a single direct object.

Neither of the two modes of arrangement of the sonnet lead to a balance of isometric parts, according to the authors. A balanced arrangement can be discovered, however. The two middle lines of the sonnet "most clearly distinguish themselves by their grammatical construction from the rest of the poem," and when these lines are taken as a middle couplet, the poem falls into three parts: the couplet and two isometric groups. The authors note that "the tendency for the central couplet to stand out agrees with the idea of an asymmetric trichotomy, which puts the whole of the second quatrain in opposition to the first quatrain on the one hand and in opposition to the final sestet on the other, thus creating a central verse discrete in several respects from the verses on either side of it.[34]

In a summary of the analysis the authors show how the different levels blend and complement each other. Grammatical and semantic links are observed. From the perspective of the primary division of the three parts, each ending with a full stop, the first two sections allow the cats to be seen from the outside (in the first quatrain) then (in the second quatrain) through the activities seen in and by the power of Erebus. In the last part (the two tercets) the opposition is overcome by realizing in the cats an *actively assumed* passivity interpreted from *within* instead of from the outside.

The secondary division into two pairs of verses contrasts the two tercets with the two quatrains while at the same time revealing a connection between the first quatrain and the first tercet and between the second quatrain and the second tercet.

> 1. The sum of the two quatrains contrasts with the sum of the tercets in the sense that the latter dispenses with the point of the observer . . . and places the cats outside all spatial and temporal limits. 2. The first quatrain introduces these spatio-temporal limits . . . and the first tercet abolishes them. . . . 3. The second quatrain defines the cats in terms of the shades wherein they dwell and the second tercet in terms of the light they irradiate.[35]

A third structural form is discovered by the authors through regrouping the text into a chiasmus with the initial quatrain and the final tercet set over against the inside verses of the second quatrain and the first tercet. A semantic basis is given for these phenomena of distribution: "In the first group, the independent clauses assign to the cats the function of complement, whereas from the outset the other two stanzas assign to the cats the function of subject."[36]

When the sonnet is viewed from the perspective of the modes of arrangement of the three sentences, the two pairs of verses, or the chiasmus, the poem appears to be "relations of equivalence, which fit into one another like boxes and which form as a whole an apparently closed system." However, when the sonnet is viewed as two sestets separated by the couplet of lines 7 and 8, "the poem takes on the appearance of an open system in dynamic progression from start to finish," from the real order of the first sestet to the surreal order of the second sestet. Lines 7 and 8, then, make the important transition. The combination of semantics and form in these lines 7 and 8 "carries the reader for a brief moment into a doubly unreal universe, since, whilst sharing the characteristic exteriority of the first sestet, it still introduces the mythological tone of the second sestet." The authors compare this "sudden oscillation both of tone and theme" to "modulation in musical composition." This modulation resolves the conflict which is set up either implicitly or explicitly from the beginning of the poem.[37]

The movement of the poem indicated or supported by grammatical phenomena is from enclosure to spatial and temporal expansion, from seclusion to liberty. The final sestet transposes the conflict implicit in the first line of the poem onto a universal scale. ". . . the *reins féconds* recall the *volupté* of the *amoureux*, as do the *prunelles*, the *science* of the *savants*; *magiques* refers to the active fervor of the one, *mystiques* to the contemplative attitude of the other."[38]

In a brief final point, the authors use grammatical facts (the initial description of the cats as *puissants et doux* and the comparison in the final line of their *prunelles* to the stars; the fact that all beings in the sonnet are masculine while the cats, and their alter ego, *les grands sphinx*, are androgynous; and the paradoxical choice of feminine substantives for so-called masculine rhymes), other poems of Baudelaire, and judgments of literary critics to establish that "through the mediation of the cats, woman is eliminated from the poem's initial galaxy of *amoureux* and *savants*, leaving face to face, if not totally enmeshed, 'le poète des chats' freed from love 'bien restreint' and the universe, unfettered by the savants' austerity."[39]

Michael Riffaterre, whose evaluation of the analysis of *"Les Chats"* by Jakobson and Lévi-Strauss frequently serves as a starting point for the evaluation of structural methods in literature, concludes his description of the analysis of Jakobson and Lévi-Strauss with the confession of admiration: "The poem is like a microcosm, with its own system of references and analogies. We have an absolutely convincing demonstration of the extraordinary concatentation of correspondences that holds together the parts of speech." But immediately thereafter comes the major criticism and a statement of the problem of relating structuralism to literature: "But there is no telling which of these systems of correspondences contribute to the poetry of the text. And there is much to be said about the systems that do not."[40]

Riffaterre does not, as it first appears, deny that passage can be made from description to judgment, "from a study of the text to a study of its effect upon the reader." He simply denies that the categories used by Jakobson and Lévi-Strauss are capable of allowing movement to judgment. Riffaterre declares that the assumption in the analysis of Jakobson and Lévi-Strauss is that *any* structural system is necessarily a poetic structure, but he claims that their segmentation of the poem yields units which are not a part of poetic structure as well as units which do constitute a part of the poetic structure. The first organization of the poem (into three sentences) is accepted as beyond criticism and the second (the bipartite division) is well substantiated. The third structure (the chiasma-like division) seen by Jakobson and Lévi-Strauss is much more questionable and the fourth (two equal sestets separated by a distich) division uses constituents "that cannot possibly be perceived by the reader." Since these elements cannot be perceived by readers, Riffaterre concludes that these constituents must "remain alien to the poetic structure."[41]

Riffaterre, as indicated earlier, does not deny the relationship of the structural system and the description of the system to poetic judgment. He denies that grammatical categories, or any preconceived, aprioristic frame, are coextensive with "poetic actualization." Riffaterre is not simply negative. While emphasizing the limitation of the work of Jakobson and Lévi-Strauss, he indicates how he would determine the system which corresponds to the poetry of the text. The process of moving from description to judgment requires a proper consideration of the nature of poetry. The poetic phenomenon is the entire act of communication which involves the message (the poem) and the addressees (the readers). These are the only factors whose presence is necessary in poetic communication. All of the other factors—the language or code, the non-verbal context, the means of keeping open the channels—are selected from the message (the poem). The characteristic which Riffaterre sees as common to all of the various devices in the message is "that they are designed to draw responses from the reader." The devices are designed to draw these responses despite the wanderings of the reader's attention, despite the evolution of the code, and despite any changes in aesthetic fashion.[42]

Viewed from this perspective of poetic communication, the appropriate segmentation of the poem must be based on the responses of the reader. It could be thought that objective segmentation of the poem cannot be based on responses because a subjective circular relationship is inevitable. Riffaterre would guard against subjectivity in segmenting the poem through response by emptying the response of its content. "The response itself testifies objectively to the actuality of a contact."[43] All forms of reaction to the texts—reactions based on a reader's particular culture, era, aesthetics, and personality; responses based on the goal of the reader, whether literary or historical—all may be used to determine the pertinent segmentation of the poem. Riffaterre also would multiply the responses. This would guard against interference with contact such as the fatigue of the reader or the evolution of the language since the time of writing of the poem.

Riffaterre calls the tool of analysis made up of items which help trigger response a "superreader." The act of communication is performed over and over again and explored by means of the superreader. In distinction from the method of analysis of Jakobson and Lévi-Strauss, the superreader "has the enormous advantage of following exactly the normal reading process, of perceiving the poem as its linguistic shape dictates, along the sentence, starting at the beginning . . . ; it has the advantage of screening pertinent structures and only pertinent structures."[44]

Numerous questions are raised by the suggestion of Riffaterre. An important one is the matter of pertinence. The superreader screens pertinent structures. "Pertinent" to what? A fixed historical meaning? It could be thought that such is the case because of the emphasis of Riffaterre that the factors of language or code and non-verbal context come from the literary work itself. Yet the reader does the selection, and evolution of codes and changing of aesthetic fashion make a static meaning impossible. If a static meaning is not that to which structures are pertinent, cannot the linguistic approach of Jakobson provide a code to which a reader is sensitive?

Jonathan Culler has evaluated Jakobson's method of analysis and has found Jakobson's work to be an "important contribution to literary studies."[45] Culler recognizes that the meaning which Jakobson claims to derive from his analysis, the "message," is not propositional content but the utterance itself. It is only from this definition of meaning and message that Jakobson's global claim of the relevance of linguistics can make sense. Culler, however, attempts to leave aside for the moment the *relevance* of the patterns discovered through Jakobson's analysis to question the categories used. However, it is clear from Culler's criticism that he does not and perhaps cannot leave aside the *relevance* of the patterns (the meaning). He *assumes* the meaning or meanings tradition-ally found in poetry and judges that Jakobson's categories are not *directly* and *unambiguously* related to such meanings. According to Culler, the presence or absence of patterns found by Jakobson often has little relation to the effects of the poem (effects of meanings obtained by traditional methods of analysis), and categories of Jakobson are so flexible that practically any form of organization can be found.[46]

Culler comes closer to Jakobson's view of meaning when he attempts to salvage from Jakobson's theory something which will be helpful for literary criticism. He begins with the idea of Riffaterre that "patterns discovered are relevant only when they can be correlated with some experience that they explain." But he is not willing to adhere strictly to this narrow approach for a number of reasons: Riffaterre's "law of perceptibility" is not helpful in advancing the argument or providing a method of distinguishing between poetic and non-poetic structures "for the simple reason that it is an extremely awkward strategy to point to a particular pattern and then to claim that it cannot be perceived." What readers have actually perceived cannot be taken as a standard because (1) readers do not necessarily know the elements which con-tributed to the effects they experience, (2) the standard of readers' actual perceptions would eliminate on principle the possibility of a critic calling attention to something not observed but important, and (3) arbitrary rules would have to be set up to exclude Jakobson and similar critics from the company of those readers whose perceptions serve as the standard. In addition, Culler points out, Jakobson does not make the claim that his structures are *consciously* perceived. In Jakobson's view, they can function without conscious knowledge on the part of the reader or even the author.[47]

Culler does suggest that, instead of using Jakobson's analysis as a technique for discovering patterns in a text, one might begin at another pole with data about the effect of poetic language and "attempt to formulate hypotheses which would account for these effects." Jakobson's use of linguistics, his definition of the poetic function, would be thus "no longer the key to a method of analysis." Rather, "it becomes a hypothesis about the conventions of poetry as an institution and in particular about the kind of attention to language which poets and readers are allowed to assume." In Culler's view it is "as a theory of the operations which grammatical figures can induce readers to perform that Jakobson's account of poetic language is most usefully considered."[48] Culler still is tied to the more traditional meanings and effects of poetry as he tests the value of Jakobson's theory so redefined on Jakobson's analysis of Shakespeare's Sonnet 129.

Sonnet 129

I Th' expence of Spirit / in a waste of shame
    Is lust in action, / and till action, lust
    Is perjurd, murdrous, / blouddy full of blame,
    Savage, extreame, rude, / cruel, not to trust,

II Injoyd no sooner but dispised straight,
    Past reason huntd, / and no sooner had
    Past reason hated / as a swallowed bayt,
    On purpose layd / to make / the taker mad.

III Mad < e > In pursut / and in possession so,
    Had, having, and in quest, / to have extreame,
    A blisse in proofe / and provd / a < nd > very wo,
    Before a joy proposed / behind a dreame,

IV   All this the world / well knowes / yet none knowes well,
        To shun the heaven / that leads / men to this hell.

The analysis of Sonnet 129 by Jakobson and L. G. Jones attempts to relate theme to composition, meaning to structure; and the authors conclude that "an objective scrutiny of Shakespeare's language and verbal art, with particular reference to this poem, reveals a cogent and mandatory unity of its thematic and compositional framework."[49] The views of numerous critics (John Crowe Ransom, J. M. Robertson, Edward Hubler, C. W. M. Johnson, R. Levin, at one extreme, and Laura Riding and Robert Graves at the other extreme) are judged inadequate in light of the analysis. In particular, "the perspicuous confrontation of a joy proposed beforehand with a phantom lingering afterwards" seen by Jakobson in the interlaced structure and poetic texture of the sonnet "cannot be arbitraily recast to a joy 'to be desired through the dream by which lust leads itself on' or into such accessory 'legitimate' meanings as 'before a joy can be proposed there must be a dream behind, a joy lost by waking' or 'before a joy can be proposed it must be put behind as a dream.' "[50]

Culler chooses to evaluate Jakobson's analysis on the specific matter of Jakobson's connection of "on purpose layd" to "the heaven" and his suggestion "that heaven's sovereign is the culprit who has deliberately laid the bait."[51] Jakobson sees a division of the poem into the "first seven, *centripetal*, afferent lines, moving in a direction toward the center of the entire poem" and the "further seven, *centrifugal*, efferent lines proceeding in a direction away from the center,"[52] and he relates the first and last lines of the second division: "If the first centrifugal line of the sonnet introduces the hero, *the taker*, however, still not as an agent but as a victim, the final centrifugal line brings exposure of the malevolent culprit, *the heaven that leads men to this hell*, and thus discloses by what perjurer the joy was proposed and the lure laid."[53] This observation is made prior to Jakobson's notation of the specific grammatical parallelism cited by Culler:

> Only the even strophes display hypotaxis and end in multileveled "progressive" structures, i.e., constructions with several degrees of subordinates, each of them postponed to the subordinating constituent. . . .
>
> II   A) *hated* B) *as a swallowed bayt* C) *on purpose layd* D) *to make* E) *the taker* F) *mad.*
> IV   A) *none knowes well* B) *to shun* C) *the heaven* D) *that leads* E) *men* F) *to this hell.*
>
> The penultimate constituents of both progressive structures are the only animate nouns of the sonnet (II_4 the taker, IV_2 men), and both constructions finish with the only substantival tropes: *bayt* and *taker, heaven* and *hell* instead of heaven's sovereign and hellish torment.[54]

Culler sees Jakobson as deducing from structural parallels the equivalence of "heaven's sovereign" and the "one who deliberately laid the bait." Culler contrasts to this interpretation the "natural interpretation" of "heaven" as the vision of "bliss" and "joy proposed" which baits the taker.

Culler's criticism emphasizes the priority of logical and thematic relations:

> Jakobson, thinking in distributional terms, takes position to be the crucial factor: since "on purpose laid" directly precedes "to make" he relates it to "heaven" which directly precedes "that leads." But the reader would make this connection only if he approached the poem without paying any attention to logical and thematic relations. Position does play a role, but not in the way that Jakobson implies; it is subordinated to thematic considerations. The reader can notice that the phrase "on purpose laid," which appears between "bait" and "to make," has no constituent corresponding to it in the final line of the sonnet. The logical parallelism has been violated, and this has considerable significance: the vituperative and accusatory tone of "on purpose laid" has vanished by the time we reach the couplet. No longer is lust "past reason hated," with a passion that leads to random and undirected accusations. The fault lies, it is suggested, not with some unknown culprit who has deliberately laid this bait, but with men themselves who cannot move from one sort of knowledge to another— from *connaître* to *savoir*. The grammatical structure reinforces this effect by making one aware of the fact that a particular constituent has, by the time we reach the couplet, been repressed or overcome.[55]

The criticism of Culler shows the necessity of relating linguistic analysis to poetic effect, at least if the method of Jakobson is to assist in traditional literary criticism. The question remains, however, if the analysis of Jakobson is designed merely to assist traditional literary criticism or if it may not go beyond traditional literary criticism in terms of discovering meaning. The discussion at this point is not designed to question Culler's criticism of Jakobson. Indeed, Jakobson invited such criticism in his attempt to use linguistic analysis as a superior guide to traditional literary criticism. If traditional meaning is to be found, linguistic analysis can only be a help in something of the way that Culler proposes. "Stylistic preferences reflect cognitive preferences" is the way Richard Ohmann expresses the basic hypothesis.[56] Yet, is the meaning which Jakobson proposes identical with traditional meaning? Just as traditional poetic meaning uses regular language in a special way, may not linguistic poetic meaning use traditional poetic means in a special way?

Unless one is tied to the idea of a given meaning which is immutable in time and space, if one begins with Culler's starting point, the effects of a poem, one must ultimately deal with the effects of a poem upon a reader who has been sensitized to the possibility of a linguistic reading. The argument that different linguistic readings are possible is no real argument, again, unless one begins with the idea of a given meaning which does not become altered. The argument that such linguistic poetic meaning is not in the consciousness of the author does not seem to rule out the legitimacy of such meaning. Does interpretation end in complete anarchy? Should the threat of anarchy and purely private meanings cause us to eschew linguistic or syntactic poetic effect or meaning?

The relation of form and content in literature is a perennial issue. Some assistance may be given to the problem under discussion by introducing ideas from a discussion of the relationship of meaning to grammar in another context. Donald Davie's *Articulate Energy*[57] has a catalog of five "varieties of poetic syntax," through which he discusses arguments over the relationship of grammar, logic, and the poet. Suzanne Langer in particular is the theorist with whom Davie is in debate. Langer declared that the poet can use the forms of grammar for his own purposes. These purposes "are not, however, those of the grammarians." The poet "can make music out of them." Critics who begin with Langer's position, in the view of Davie, "assume that whenever traditional syntactical forms appear in poetry, they are *necessarily* emptied of their grammatical function, inevitably less than serious, a phantasmal play on the surface of the poem." Davie agrees that the poet can "make music" out of the forms of grammar, but he sees more uses of syntax: "More apposite to some kinds of poetry is Fenollosa's view that the syntax of the transitive sentence obeys a law of nature. Or again, in other kinds of poetry, syntax tenders a 'form of thought' more faithfully than the logician does and with a flexibility that Fenollosa did not dream of."[58]

The classification of Davie is accepted even by himself as tentative and open to modification, but clearly he has a view of language which has the potentiality of conveying meaning on a variety of levels, utilizing various elements of language in different ways appropriate to different meanings. The possible use of Davie's suggestions in the structural study of narrative in general is enhanced by his definition of "poetic syntax." Just as "poetic imagery" can appear in prose as well as in poetry, so also "poetic syntax" is applicable to prose as well as poetry. Moreover, all of the syntax in poetry is not "poetic syntax" for much of it is "unremarkable, like a human frame that is neither close-knit nor loose-limbed, neither well- nor ill-proportioned, but just normal." The "normal" syntax of poetry is not "poetic syntax" as understood by Davie. Poetic syntax, whether in poetry or prose, is that syntax which "can be itself a source of poetic pleasure." Davie, then, in much the same way as Riffaterre and Culler stress the effect of the poem, emphasizes the several pleasures which poetic syntax can give.[59]

Poetic syntax may be *subjective*. This is the case when the function of the syntax "is to please us by the fidelity with which it follows the 'form of thought' in the poet's mind." By "form of thought" Davie is not speaking of a logical reality. ". . . if we are to retain that expression—'form of thought'—at all, we must take 'thought' in the very loose sense it always has when we talk of 'poetic thought' in general; what is being rendered to us is a form of *experience*, from which 'thought' in the logician's sense is an abstraction." Yet, subjective syntax is not unrelated to the total meaning of the poetic work. "Every time it occurs, whether in a poem or . . . in a novel, it has to be shown to be in accord with the burden of the whole."[60]

Dramatic syntax is cited as a second kind of poetic syntax, but it is really a corollary of subjective syntax in that the function of dramatic syntax "is to please us by the fidelity with which it follows the 'form of thought' in some mind other than the poet's, which the poet imagines." *Objective syntax*, on the other hand, achieves quite different effects from the first two kinds of poetic syntax, in the judgment of Davie. "Poetic syntax is objective when its function is to please us by the fidelity with which it follows a form of action, a movement not through any mind, but in the world at large." The importance of syntactic features in objective syntax is that "they mime a pattern of action."[61]

The *syntax like music* is less related to a specific definition of the "form of thought" of the literary work. Davie uses the judgment of Suzanne Langer that in music "the actual function of meaning which calls for permanent contents is not fulfilled; for the *assignment* of one rather than another possible meaning to each form is never explicitly made." What sounds sad to one person may sound merry to another person. The sad feeling and the merry feeling, therefore, may have the same morphology. Davie concludes that "poetic syntax is like music when its function is to please us by the fidelity with which it follows a 'form of thought' through the poet's mind *but without defining that thought*." The distinction between *articulating* and *asserting* is used to describe the syntax like music. In music it is easy to "articulate without asserting." In poetry, however, it is difficult to "talk without saying what one is talking about"; it is difficult to "articulate without asserting." This difficulty in literature is circumvented by use of the "objective correlative, the invention of a fable or an 'unreal' landscape, or the arrangement of images, not for their own sakes, but to stand for a correlative for the experience that is thus the true subject of a poem in which it is never named."[62]

Nine lines of section two of "The Lost Son" by Theodore Roethke illustrate the syntax like music:[63]

> Where do the roots go?
>> Look down under the leaves.
> Who put the moss there?
>> These stones have been here too long.
> Who stunned the dirt into noise?
>> Ask the mole, he knows.
> I feel the slime of a wet nest.
>> Beward Mother Mildew.
> Nibble again, fish nerves.

Davie says that

> . . . the images serve to indicate roughly the area of experience that the poet is dealing with; they limit the number of possible answers to the question, "What is the poet talking about?" But a wide range of possible answers remains, and the poem does nothing to narrow this choice any further. Instead it defines, largely by syntactical arrangements and changes, the extent to which the nameless experience is a search, to what extent it is a surrender, to what extent an agony, to what extent a waiting, and so on. . . . But that experience is never defined, since we are never told to what it surrenders, what it seeks, what it is waiting *for*.[64]

Davie introduces his discussion of the *syntax like mathematics* with a statement of Valéry concerning Mallarmé's interest in syntax:

> In this—and I told him so one day—he approached the attitude of men who in algebra have examined the science of forms and the symbolical part of the art of mathematics. This type of attention makes the structure of expressions more felt and more interesting than their significance or value. Properties of transformations are worthier the mind's attention than what they transform; and I sometimes wonder if a more general notion can exist than the notion of a "proposition" or the consciousness of thinking no matter what.[65]

Poetic syntax is then described as being *like mathematics* "when its function is to please us in and for itself." All other forms of poetic syntax are mimetic, that is, they appeal for their justification to something outside themselves. The syntax to which Mallarmé and Davie refer "appeals to nothing but itself, to nothing outside the world of the poem." Davie indicates that this is one alternative "if the structures of expression are to be more interesting to the reader than the structures of experience behind them." Another alternative is "to have nothing behind them at all, that is, to have poems that are meaningless."[66]

Davie does not believe that the various types of poetic syntax are mutually exclusive. He does not think that a choice must be made between the "structures of expression" and "structures of experience." It is only as long as the poet is determined to make his poetry "pure" and "absolute" that he must either have nothing behind the poem at all or have poems that talk about themselves. In Valéry's formula, he notes, "it is not necessary that the structure of expressions should be *the only* source of interest in the poem, only that this should be more interesting than anything else." And Davie judges that even Valéry's formula is too narrow, "for there is no reason why this sort of syntax, any more than any of the other sorts, should be more than one source of pleasure among others." Davie asserts that, seen from this perspective, "any amount of older poetry can be seen to employ syntax-like-mathematics. . . ."[67]

When the conceptualization of Davie is accepted and applied to the analysis of Jakobson, it may be observed that the results of Jakobson's analysis need not be related directly to the content. The syntax of the text in and for itself may function as mathematics to bring pleasure to the reader. Yet Davie's conceptualization also allows the results of grammatical analysis to be related to content, to show us the undefined "form of thought" in the case of syntax like music or to mimic in a more defined way "the form of thought" in the poet's mind (his own mind or in one imagined by the poet). Davie's view of language and meaning will prove to be helpful in contemporary literary study in general, in part because of his definition of "poetic" and also because of his view of the "form of thought" of literature. Of course, the specific points of contact and relevance are altered as structural linguistics is supplemented by generative-transformational grammar in the study of literature, but in my estimation some comprehensive view such as that of Davie becomes inevitable.

The interesting point for me is that the conceptualization of Davie is in many ways precisely that of Dilthey. Indeed implicit in and necessary for some of Davie's classifications is the idea of a mental structure which operates along with various historical and cultural elements in the total linguistic and literary enterprise. A view of meaning extending to life itself may not be totally foreign to some of the classifications.[68] What is the relationship of meaning on the level of mathematical poetic syntax to meaning on the other levels? How can the meaning being expressed by the syntax-like-music and the syntax-like-mathematics be communicated other than through the original literary work? The answers to these questions are clearly related to psychological and anthropological facts and assumptions. The relationships of the various levels and meaning on the various levels alter, but the one constant factor is man. Davie distinguishes subjective and dramatic poetic syntax in that the function of objective poetic syntax "is to please us by the fidelity with which it follows a form of action, a movement not through any mind, but in the world at large." Immediately he notes that the difference is not really so complete, "for any form or movement observed in the external world is, in the process of observation, taken into the poet's mind and must dwell there until it is bodied forth in his writing." Davie does not follow up on his allusion to the poetics of creation, however, for he is interested in distinguishing between objective poetic syntax and subjective and dramatic poetic syntax. This in an "obvious distinction," says Davie, which is seen by "common sense."[69]

The importance of man, at least the importance of relating poetic effect upon man to the means of production of that effect, has been emphasized by almost all critics of Jakobson's analysis; many critics, such as Riffaterre and Culler, have attempted to relate description of the material means of the poem to poetic effect and judgment. A most interesting and instructive attempt to relate description of verbal patterns to interpretation is made by Stanley E. Fish. In his attempt he basically recreates the poetics of Dilthey (from the reader's perspective, at any rate) and restates the question of Dilthey as to how to relate the expression of human creativity to the source of that creativity through some "grammar" or "linguistics." Fish introduces the question of the significance of grammar in poetry by giving the two answers which are generally offered. First is the answer of Jakobson, or practically infinite analyses of the data. The description takes place in the "absence of that which marks out the field of description" and analysis goes on and on because "there is no way of deciding either where to begin or where to stop, because there is no way of deciding what counts."[70] The other option is to fit the accumulated data into a preconceived interpretive framework. Description, then, as Roger Fowler says, would be carried out under the influence of a prior literary hunch.[71]

Fish opts for a third way, making the descriptive and interpretive acts one act.

> In the kind of stylistics I propose, *interpretive acts are what is being described*; they, rather than verbal patterns arranging themselves in space, are the content of the analysis. This is more than a procedural distinction; for at its heart are different notions of what it is to read which are finally different notions of what it is to be human. Implicit in what the stylisticians do is the assumption that to read is to put together discrete bits of meaning until they form what a traditional grammar would call a complete thought. In this view, the world, or the world of the text, is already ordered and filled with significances and what the reader is required to do is get them out (hence the question, "What did you get out of that?). In short, the reader's job is to extract the meanings that formal patterns possess prior to, and independently of, his activities. In my view these same activities are constitutive of a structure of concerns which is necessarily itself the occasion of their coming into being. The stylisticians proceed as if there were observable facts that could first be described and then interpreted. What I am suggesting is that an interpreting entity, endowed with purposes and concerns, is, by virtue of its very operation, determining what counts as the facts to be observed; and moreover, that since this determining is not a neutral marking out of a valueless area, but the extension of an already existing field of interest, it is an interpretation.[72]

It might seem that Fish is substituting a completely wild impressionistic method for a precise and rigorous descriptive method. Indeed, Fish calls his stylistics "affective." In such an approach "the focus of attention is shifted from the spatial context of a page and its observable regularities to the temporal context of a mind and its experiences." However, it is not the intention of Fish to become more subjective. He really sees the practitioners of objective linguistic technique as more subjective than the impressionists. "For an open impressionism, they substitute the covert impressionism of anchorless statistics and self-referring categories. In the name of responsible procedures, they offer a methodized irresponsibility...."[73]

Fish clearly sees that his affective stylistics does not solve the problem of the relationship of the object of literature to the mind and both of these to meaning. He, however, is asking questions about formal characteristics from the perspective of the reader. In affective stylistics "it will be necessary to make use of all the information that formal characterizations of language can provide, although that information will be viewed from a different perspective. Rather than regarding it as directly translatable into what a word or a pattern *means*, it will be used more exactly to specify what a reader, as he comes upon that word or pattern, is *doing*, what assumptions he is making, what conclusions he is reaching, what expectations he is forming, what attitudes he is entertaining, in short, what acts he is being moved to perform."[74]

In the work of Fish we have a clear return to psychology or anthropology. Fish sees this and admits that the problems of making the descriptive and interpretative acts one "are for the most part a direct consequence of its assumption about what it means to be human." Rules in the sense of discovery procedures are impossible when interpretation is viewed from the human perspective, since "the contextualizing ability that characterizes being human is not circumscribed by its previous performances, performances which, while they constitute the history of that ability do not constitute its limits." From this human perspective, "all you have when you begin is a sense of this finite but infinitely flexible ability and a personal knowledge of what it means to have it. You then attempt to project the course that ability would take in its interaction with a specific text, using as the basis of your projection what you know, and at the same time adding to what you know by the very effort to make analytical use of it." Yet, there are some things that can help: formal linguistic characterization, literary history, other minds, analyses of perceptual strategy. But finally, "you are left only with yourself and with the impossible enterprise of understanding understanding." The enterprise is impossible because it is endless, an open system which is unable ever to prove anything. Fish declares that the impossibility of the enterprise makes rigor and precision more necessary, not less necessary, and he exalts the impossible nature of the enterprise by declaring that this is "the reverse side of its greatest virtue . . . : the recognition that meaning is human."[75]

The value of the work of Jakobson is enhanced as it is evaluated and, in some measure, redirected by critics such as Riffaterre, Culler, and Fish. Of course, presuppositions of traditionally oriented critics are also called into question and reoriented by the linguistic analysis of Jakobson. Seen from the broad conceptualization of Dilthey, the various perspectives are not mutually exclusive but unite to give a more satisfying comprehensive view of language, literature, and meaning. The work of Jakobson can be viewed as an expression of confidence that there is a relationship between the literary expression and human creativity. Jakobson's attempt to move from the expression to meaning restates in a concrete way the very problem of Dilthey: the way to move from expression to human creativity behind the expression by means of linguistic and literary sciences. The problem as it is re-raised by Jakobson is attacked by Lévi-Strauss, and in the work of Lévi-Strauss we come to a different method of relating the literary expression (myth) to the creative force behind the expression (human being, world), a method which most directly influences the development of narratology.

CLAUDE LÉVI-STRAUSS

Claude Lévi-Strauss is perhaps the best-known scholar who has attempted to apply linguistics to other human sciences. Lévi-Strauss in a sense continues the line from the Russian formalists and the Prague structuralists. This linguistic heritage was mediated through Roman Jakobson, who like Lévi-Strauss was exiled to the United States during the Second World War. Lévi-Strauss says, "My encounter with Roman Jakobson, in 1941, showed me that what I was trying to do in the field of kinship had been done successfully by linguists in their own field."[76] By 1945 Lévi-Strauss was advocating the use of linguistics in anthropological study in particular and the social sciences in general. The use advocated went beyond the occasional application of certain findings from linguistics in anthropology and the other social sciences. He claims a formal relationship between anthropology and linguistics. "Kinship phenomena," declares Lévi-Strauss, "are *of the same type* as linguistic phenomena." The phenomena in anthropology may be of *"another order of reality"* than linguistics, but since they are *"of the same type,"* the method of structural linguistics ought to achieve the same kind of progress in non-linguistic human sciences. Lévi-Strauss even prophesies that "structural linguistics will certainly play the same renovating role with respect to the social sciences that nuclear physics, for example, has played for the physical sciences."[77]

In articles in 1951 and 1953, Lévi-Strauss suggests not only that "the different aspects of social life . . . be studied by the methods of, and with the help of, concepts similar to those employed in linguistics," but also that the various aspects of social life "constitute phenomena whose inmost nature is the same as that of language." He suggests that language and other aspects of culture are due to nothing other than the human mind. The structural method advocated by Lévi-Strauss is that which had been given by N. Troubetzkoy of the Prague school. Lévi-Strauss lists four basic operations:

First structural linguistics shifts from the study of *conscious* linguistic phenomena to study of their unconscious infrastructure; second, it does not treat *terms* as independent entities, taking instead as its basis of analysis the relations between terms; third, it introduces the concept of *system* . . . ; finally, structural linguistics aims at discovering *general laws*, either by induction "or . . . by logical deduction, which would give them an absolute character."[78]

Lévi-Strauss is best known for application of the principles of structural linguistics in the analysis of myth. In his analysis, Lévi-Strauss finds and uses an innate tendency of the human mind to work by a process of binary analysis. Binary oppositions on all levels are utilized: nature versus culture, raw versus cooked, hard versus soft, fresh versus rotten, full versus empty, continuous versus discontinuous, up versus down. These are transformed by inversion, in metaphor, and other figures. Along with the oppositions, there is a tendency of the human mind toward mediation of the opposites. Polar extremes of life and death, for example, are mediated by an element such as hunting which is related to both life and death.

In his analyses of South American myths in particular, Lévi-Strauss shows that human relationships (kinship, friendship, sexual relationships, dependency) may be represented in myth as: relationships between different kinds of natural and supernatural beings, relations between kinds of foods, relations between categories of sound and silence, relations between categories of smell and taste, relations between plants and animals, and relationships between categories of geography, seasonal changes, climate, time changes, and the heavenly bodies. Lévi-Strauss moves from myth to myth, from layer of meaning to layer of meaning in what seems to be an endless cycle. Indeed "the layered structure of myth . . . allows us to look upon myth as a matrix of meanings which are arranged in lines or columns, but in which each level always refers to some other level, whichever way the myth is read. Similarly, each matrix of meanings refers to another matrix, each myth to other myths."[79]

The method of analysis of myth used by Lévi-Strauss gives evidence that the "meaning" with which Lévi-Strauss is primarily concerned is not the meaning that we usually associate with the interpretation of a literary text. Myth is a mode of language and the elements of myth (as elements of language) take on signification through their relationships with one another. The meaning with which Lévi-Strauss is concerned is the underlying structure of relationships of the elements of myth. In his analysis the individual elements of narrative—persons, animals, objects—are meaningless in themselves. As we shall observe in detail later, Lévi-Strauss acknowledges that myth may convey meanings distinct from their own structure, meanings related to the elements of myth and historical circumstances. But Lévi-Strauss's purpose is not primarily directed to the meanings in specific historical circumstances. The analyses of myth by Lévi-Strauss must be read in light of his primary purpose to discover principles of thought formation which are valid for all human beings.

A description of Lévi-Strauss's analysis of "The Story of Asdiwal"[80] will illuminate his method on a limited group of materials, one myth existing in four different versions. The Tsimshian Indians along with the Gitskan and Nisqa lived just south of Alaska in a region embracing the basins of the Nass and Skeena rivers. People in this region did not farm; they gathered wild foods, hunted, and fished. River fishing especially, with its complex pattern of movement, made the deepest impression on the tribe. The Nisqa Indians remained relatively settled, but the Tsimshian moved annually from their winter villages to the fishing places, first to the Nass for candlefish, then to the Skeena for the salmon. Lévi-Strauss sees marriage practices of the Indians as important. The Tsimshian were divided into four matrilineal clans and into three hereditary castes. Marriage took place within the caste but outside of the clan.

The four versions of the myth were collected from 1895 to 1916 by Franz Boas. The fullest version of the myth is summariezd by G. S. Kirk:

> . . . a mother and daughter, both widowed by famine as winter ends, leave their dead husbands' villages and move to meet each other, from downstream and upstream respectively, along the Skeena river. They have nothing to eat but a rotten berry, but then they are visited by a young stranger who is also a bird; he gives them food and marries the daughter. A child, Asdiwal, is born, and his supernatural father gives him magic weapons, snow-shoes, and a cloak, before he himself disappears. The child grows up and his grandmother dies; the survivors move downstream to the mother's birthplace. There Asdiwal captures a white bear and follows it up into the sky, where it turns into a beautiful maiden, daughter of the Sun. Asdiwal marries Evening Star, as she is called, after overcoming all sorts of trials sent him by his prospective father-in-law. He becomes homesick for his mother, and he and his wife descend to earth, where he deceives Evening Star with a mortal woman, is killed by her in retribution, but is revived by his father-in-law. A second time he returns to earth, where his divine wife finally leaves him. He takes up with another mortal woman, and in early spring moves up towards the Nass river with her and her four brothers. There he quarrels with the brothers about the relative merits of hunting by land and by sea (the Tsimshian do both at different times of the year), and infuriates them by making a good catch in his land hunting, with the help of his magical weapons, while they catch

nothing at sea. They take their sister and leave him, but he immediately meets another group of four brothers and a sister, and takes up with this sister as with the previous one. After a successful fishing season they return south for the late summer and winter. Now Asdiwal boasts that he can hunt seals better than his brothers-in-law. They go out to a reef, which is so sheer and slippery that only Asdiwal can climb up it by using his magic shoes. Rather justifiably by Tsimshian standards (for they are very susceptible to loss of face, as is shown in the extraordinary custom of the potlatch) they strand him there. He survives by various magical tricks, and then goes down to the home of the seals under water, heals the wounded ones, and begs from them a boat to take him back ashore; the boat is made out of the seal-king's stomach. His wife and new son are waiting for him, and the wife plots with him to destroy her brothers. In spite of this tie Asdiwal's wander-lust eventually reasserts itself, and he abandons his wife to return to his childhood haunts far up the Skeena river. His son joins him; during the winter Asdiwal goes hunting up a mountain, but leaves his magical implements behind. As a consequence he is stranded and turns into stone, where he and his dog can still be seen.[81]

After giving essential facts about the Tsimshian Indians and summarizing the 1912 version of the myth, Lévi-Strauss describes the essential points of the structure of the narrative: physical and political geography, economic life, social and family organization, and cosmology. The first two (geography and economy) are exact transcripts of reality, the fourth (cosmology) is unrelated to reality, but the third (social and family organization) has real and imaginary institutions interwoven. With the natives, however, the four levels are not separated out. "It is rather that everything happens as if the levels were provided with different codes, each being used according to the needs of the moment, and according to its particular capacity, to transmit the same message."[82]

The nature of the message of the levels is treated by Lévi-Strauss through retelling the story in a way to allow us to see the *sequences* and the *schemata*:

Winter famines are a recurrent event in the economic life of the Tsimshian. But the famine which starts the story off is also a cosmological theme. . . . the hunger of the two women in our myth has a cosmic significance; these heroines are not so much legendary persons as incarnations of principles which are at the origin of place-names.

One may schematize the initial situation as follows:

Mother	(is opposed to)	Daughter
Elder	(is opposed to)	Younger
Downstream	(is opposed to)	Upstream
West	(is opposed to)	East
South	(is opposed to)	North

The meeting takes place at the half-way point, a situation which, as we have seen, corresponds to a neutralization of patrilocal residence and to the fulfillment of the conditions for a matrilocal residence which is as yet only hinted at. . . .

Asdiwal's first adventure presents us with an opposition: heaven/earth which the hero is able to surmount by virtue of the intervention of his father, Hatsenas, the bird of good omen. . . . Even so, Asdiwal does not manage to overcome his earthly nature. . . . Thus there remains a series of unresolved oppositions:

Low	High
Earth	Heaven
Man	Woman
Endogamy	Exogamy

Pursuing his course westwards, Asdiwal contracts a second matrilocal marriage which generates a new series of oppositions:

Mountain-hunting	Sea-hunting
Land	Water

These oppositions too are insurmountable, and Asdiwal's earthly nature carries him away a third time, with the result that he is abandoned by his brothers-in-law.

Asdiwal contracts his last marriage not with the river-dwellers, but with islanders, and the same conflict is repeated. The opposition continues to be insurmountable, although at each stage the terms more [sic] closer together. This time it is in fact a question of a quarrel between Asdiwal and his brothers-in-law on the occasion of a hunt on a reef when the seas are running high; that is to say, on land and water at the same time. . . .

Asdiwal, the earth-born master of the hunt, finds himself abandoned on a reef in high seas; he has come to the furthest point of his westward journey; so much for the geographic and economic aspects. But, from a logical point of view, his adventures can be seen in a different form—that of a series of impossible mediations between oppositions which are ordered in a descending scale: high and low, water and earth, sea-hunting and mountain-hunting, etc.

Consequently, on the spatial plane, the hero is completely led off his course, and his failure is expressed in this *maximal separation* from his starting-point. On the logical plane, he has also failed because of his immoderate attitude towards his brothers-in-law, and by his inability to play the role of a mediator, even though the last of the oppositions which had to be overcome—between the types of life led by the land- and sea-hunters—is reduced to a *minimal separation*. There would seem to be a dead end at this point; but from neutral the myth goes into reverse and its machinery starts up again.

The king of the mountains . . . is caught on a mockery of a mountain. . . . The ruler of wild animals and killer of bears is to be saved by a she-mouse, a mockery of a wild animal. She makes him undertake a *subterranean journey*, just as the she-bear, the supreme wild animal, had imposed on Asdiwal a *celestial journey*. . . .

. . . The man who had killed animals in their hundreds goes this time to heal them and win their love. The bringer of food . . . becomes food, since he is transported in the sea-lion's stomach.

Finally, the visit to the subterranean world (which is also, in many respects, an "upside-down world") sets the course of the hero's return, for from then onwards he travels from West to East, from the sea towards the mainland, from the salt water of the ocean to the fresh water of the Skeena.

. . . When Asdiwal returns to his people and to the initial patrilocal situation, he takes up his favorite occupation again, helped by his magic objects. But he *forgets* one of them, and this mistake is fatal. After a successful hunt, he finds himself trapped half-way up the mountain-side. . . . And on the spot he is changed to stone, that is to say paralyzed, reduced to his earth-born nature in the stony and unchangeable form in which he has been seen "for generations."[83]

The sequences (such as the meeting of the two women, the intervention of the young stranger, and the birth of the child) make up the apparent content and are ordered chronologically. These sequences are organized in accordance with schemata "which exist simultaneously, superimposed upon another" and "on planes at different levels (of abstraction)." Lévi-Strauss compares the organization of sequences and schemata with a melody composed for several voices which is "held within bound by constraints in two dimensions, first by its own melodic line which is horizontal, and second by the contrapuntal schemata (settings) which are vertical." He catalogs the schemata: (1) *Geographic schema.* In the geographic schema "the hero goes from East to West, then he returns from West to East. This return journey is modulated by another one, from the South to the North, and then from the North to the South. . . ." The South and North journeys correspond to the seasonal migrations for fishing. (2) *Cosmological schema.* The cosmological schema consists of three supernatural visits which "establish a relationship between terms thought of respectively as 'below' and 'above.' " The fate of Asdiwal, in being trapped in the mountain, "then appears as a *neutralization* of the intermediate mediation (between atmospheric heaven and earth) established at his birth but which even so does not enable him to bring off two further extreme mediations." (3) *Integration.* Integration of the geographic and cosmological schemata takes place by a third schema "consisting of several binary oppositions, none of which the hero can resolve, although the distance separating the opposing terms gradually diminishes." (4) *Sociological schema.* The sociological schema involves a mother and her daughter at the beginning, a husband, his wife, and his brothers-in-law in the middle, and a father and his son at the end. At the beginning, patrilocal residence prevails, but this gives way progressively to matrilocal residence. This matrilocal residence "becomes murderous . . . then merely hostile . . . before weakening and finally reversing . . . to allow a return to patrilocal residence." (5) *Techno-economic schema.* Winter famine begins the myth and a successful hunt ends the myth. Between, the myth follows the factual economic cycle and migrations of the natives. (6) *Global integration.* The myth can be finally reduced to two extreme propositions: the initial state of affairs and the final state. Lévi-Strauss presents a diagram to illustrate this global integration:[84]

(Initial State)		(Final State)
Female		Male
East-West	axis	High-Low
Famine		Repletion
Movement		Immobility

The separation of the code and analysis of the structure of the message are preliminary to decipherment of the meaning. Before attempting to give a meaning of the myth, Lévi-Strauss introduces another version of the story which brings into play Waux, the son of Asdiwal's second marriage. Waux is a doublet of his father although his adventures take place after those of his father. Chronologically, then, the episodes concerning Waux form supplementary sequences of events, but when arranged in schemata, they are seen to be homologous to those of the first story, more explicit, and helpful in finding the meaning of the story. The most important transformation in the version introduced by Lévi-Strauss is that represented by the marriage of Waux. His father had contracted a number of marriages, all of which were unsuccessful. Waux, however, marries only once; but this marriage is fatal. The marriage of Waux was arranged by his mother and with a cousin, whereas the marriages of Asdiwal were adventurous marriages with strangers.

With this transformation as a clue, Lévi-Strauss examines the marriage practices of the Tsimshian Indians. A fundamental aspect of the social organizations of the Tsimshian is hostile equilibrium. In a system of exchange resulting from the preferential marriage with the daughter of the mother's brother, each family will occupy the position of "wife-giver" with respect to some other family, and "wife-taker" with respect to another. A certain equilibrium can be achieved in this type of exchange. One way to achieve equilibrium is by following the principle that all marriage exchanges are equivalent; another is to stipulate that one position (wife-giver or wife-taker) is superior to the other. Lévi-Strauss indicates that "the societies of the northwest Pacific Coast could not, or would not, choose one of these points of balance, and the respective superiority or inferiority of the group involved was openly contested on the occasion of each marriage."[85]

> In such circumstances, is there anything amazing about the horrid little story in which the natives see the origin of their marriage institutions? Is there anything surprising in the fact that the ceremony of marriage between first cousins takes the form of a bloody battle? When we believe that, in bringing to light these antagonisms which are inherent in the structure of Tsimshian society, we are "reaching rock bottom" (in the words of Marcel Mauss), we express in this geological metaphor an approach that has many points of comparison with that made by the myths of Asdiwal and Waux. All the paradoxes conceived by the native mind, on the most diverse planes: geographic, economic, sociological, and even cosmological, are, when all is said and done, assimulated to that less obvious yet so real paradox which marriage with the matrilateral cousin attempts but fails to resolve. But the failure is *admitted* in our myths, and there precisely lies their function.[86]

Lévi-Strauss sees that the marriage of Waux with his matrilateral cousin "symbolizes the futile last attempts of Tsimshian thought and Tsimshian society to overcome their inherent contradictions."[87]

After specifying the meaning of the story, Lévi-Strauss undertakes to use the results of his analysis to suggest the relationship of myth in general to empirical facts. The myth is not a representation of given facts, but the myth is certainly related to facts. "The relationship is of a dialectic kind, and the institutions described in the myth can be the very opposite of the real institutions." The myth, seen in this light, has a limited use as a documentary source. Its limitation as documentary source, however, opens the way for other possibilities. Lévi-Strauss suggests that "we gain, on occasions, a means of reaching unconscious categories."[88]

A final problem treated by Lévi-Strauss is that posed by the differences between the versions of the story. Lévi-Strauss sees the different versions resulting from the transmission of the myth from one population to another. A fundamental property of mythical thought as it is transmitted is defined by Lévi-Strauss as inversion: "When a mythical schema is transmitted from one population to another, and there exist differences of language, social organization, or way of life which make the myth difficult to communicate, it begins to become impoverished and confused. But one can find a limiting situation in which, instead of being finally obliterated by losing all its outlines, the myth is inverted and regains part of its precision."[89] An example from optics is used to explain this inversion. When observed through an adequately large aperture an image can be seen in full detail. As the aperture is narrowed, the image becomes blurred. When the aperture is further reduced, the image is inverted and becomes clear again. In the transmission of myth, when communication is about to vanish and the myth obliterated, inversion takes place and the myth regains part of its precision.

Lévi-Strauss's analysis of the story of Asdiwal appears to have been the work which convinced other anthropologists that there was some merit in his method of analysis,[90] but it is the four-volume *Mythologiques*[91] which must be used to gain a complete picture of Lévi-Strauss's method of analysis and view of the relationship of meaning and the means of composing myths.

In an interview concerning *Mythologiques*, Lévi-Strauss gave an indication of his method of analysis on a broad scale and the type of meaning he is seeking in the analyses. The work as a whole is to be seen as an anthropological study, an attempt to understand the way the Indians of the Americas conceived of and represented the transition from nature to culture. Lévi-Strauss indicates that his own conception has changed from one which sees the contrast nature versus culture as simply grounded in the order of things to a view of this contrast as an antimony of the human mind. "I believe that I have understood that with the South American Indians this contrast is generally expressed through the relationship of Raw and Cooked. . . ." That is the thesis of the first volume of *Mythologiques*. In the research on this volume, however, he discovered that the concepts of *less than raw* and *more than cooked* exist. *Honey* and *tobacco* were chosen to represent these dynamic contrasts. "The meaning of *honey* mediates a continual descent from nature while *tobacco* mediates ascent towards the supernatural." The contrast honey versus tobacco, then, is the theme of the second volume. In the second volume, also, myths are no longer defined through ideas of space, through the opposition of high and low, but through ideas of time. The third volume moves beyond aspects of cooking to good manners, and the fourth volume moves to myths from North America. But the myths from North America are the same as those dealt with in the first volumes, only transformed in the light of a different geography, economy, and technology.[92]

The meaning of myth for Lévi-Strauss may be situated at the level of anthropology but results at this level lead to a more ultimate significance of myth. Yet, Lévi-Strauss does not eschew meaning at the historical level, and he does not feel (as some do) that his method is a substitute for traditional literary study. The inclusive attitude toward meaning of Dilthey is also held by Lévi-Strauss—although he does not share Dilthey's concept of the meaning of life. Lévi-Strauss also sees the relationships between history-and-culture and the creative individual and between the literary expression and the process of creation which Dilthey saw, and his method of analysis can be seen as an attempt to answer the question raised by Dilthey and Jakobson as to how to move from the text to the deeper sources of the text by means of a "grammar" or "linguistics."

Since specific methods of structural analysis of narrative will be treated in a later chapter, the remainder of this chapter will treat the various views of meaning which Lévi-Strauss sees contained in the text. In an introductory statement in the first volume of his work on myth, Lévi-Strauss indicates that all of his work in anthropology and literature results from one aim: ". . . to reduce apparently arbitrary data to some kind of order, and to attain a level at which a kind of necessity becomes apparent, underlying the illusions of liberty." In his study of myth, he feels that if it is possible to prove "that the apparent arbitrariness of the mind, its supposedly spontaneous flow of inspiration, and its seemingly uncontrolled inventiveness imply the existence of laws operating at a deeper level," then "we would inevitably be forced to conclude that when the mind is left to commune with itself and no longer has to come to terms with objects, it is in a sense reduced to imitating itself as object . . . it shows itself to be of the nature of a thing among things."[93] It seems that Lévi-Strauss is inverting Dilthey's concept of the meaning of life. He extends meaning beyond the historical but he finds this meaning referring back to the world.

Lévi-Strauss believes that those who create and transmit myths are at best only partially and intermittently aware of their real structure and mode of operation. Mythological study, then, is not an attempt to show how men think. It is an attempt to show how myths operate in men's minds without their being aware of the fact. In myth, raw material is taken from nature. But the material in myth is the instrument of meaning, not its object. "Myths signify the mind that evolves them by making use of the world of which it is itself a part. Thus there is simultaneous production of myths themselves, by the mind that generates them and, by the myths, of an image of the world which is already inherent in the structure of the mind."[94]

In the process of analysis of specific myths, Lévi-Strauss points out two fundamental characteristics of mythic thought "which are at once complementary to each other and diametrically opposed." One characteristic is that "mythic thought seems to proceed as if the sign system had its own built-in resistance to the buffetings to which the things signified have to submit from without."[95] Analyses show "that the demarcative features exploited by the myths do not consist so much of things themselves as of a body of common properties, expressible in geometrical terms and transformable one into another by means of operations which constitute a sort of algebra." Mythic thought operates in a world of concepts which have been released from obligations of relationships with concrete experiences. The concepts "combine not with reference to any external reality but according to the affinities or incompatibilities existing between them in the architecture of the mind."[96]

Another fundamental characteristic of mythic thought, however, is that "the syntax of mythology is never absolutely free within the confines of its own rules. It is inevitably affected by the geographical and technological substructure."[97] Indeed, history and non-formal content and meaning are dealt with continually in the work of Lévi-Strauss. The message and the form are not unrelated. In his second volume, Lévi-Strauss deals with a group of myths from the northern Tupi, the Chaco tribes, and the central and eastern Ge: "We already know that, from the formal point of view, all the myths we have examined so far . . . form one group. But now we understand why. All these myths transmit the same message, without necessarily using the same vocabulary or the same grammatical constructions . . . all the myths deal with the question of bringing up young people. . . ."[98] The ultimate significance which Lévi-Strauss sees in myths may not be history or content, but there is penultimate significance.

Structural analysis is, therefore, not *necessarily* opposed to historical study. The ultimate goal of radically historical study is not the same as the ultimate goal of radically structural study, it is true, but historical study is necessary for structural analysis as carried on by many structuralists. Lévi-Strauss indicates this necessity when he sets forth his starting point in the study of myth:

> I shall take as my starting point *one* myth, originating from *one* community, and shall analyze it, referring first of all to the ethnographic context and then to other myths belonging to the same community. Gradually

broadening the field of inquiry, I shall then move on to myths from neigh-boring societies, after previously placing them, too, in their particular ethnographic context. Step by step, I shall proceed to more remote com-munities but only after authentic links of a historical or a geographic nature have been established with them or can reasonably be assumed to exist.[99]

The formal interpretation can be made only with the help of historical study. These two different perspectives must be maintained in analysis.

The historical perspective is absolute and independent of the observer, since we must accept as a fact that a cross-section made at any point in the material of the myths always has a certain degree of diachronic thick-ness because this material, a heterogeneous mass from the historical point of view, is a conglomeration of elements which have not evolved at the same rate and cannot therefore be said to come before or after. The other perspective is that of structural analysis, but the analyst knows that, wherever he starts from, he will, after a time, inevitably come up against a relationship of uncertainty as a result of which any myth examined at a late stage in the inquiry is at once a local transformation of the myths immediately preceding it and a complete totalization of all or part of the myths included in the field of investigation."[100]

Lévi-Strauss acknowledges that difficulty arises "from the necessity of taking two different perspectives simultaneously into account." He admits that it would seem "that we can never know the two things at once and that we have to be satisfied with collecting information related either to the general structure of the system or to the special links between certain of the elements, but never to both at once." Yet, Lévi-Strauss emphasizes that "one kind of knowledge necessarily precedes the other, since it is impossible to inquire directly into the structure without being previously acquainted with a sufficient number of relationships between the ele-ments. Consequently, whatever the starting-point chosen in practice, the nature of the results will change as the inquiry proceeds."[101]

Not only is historical investigation necessary for structural analysis in the view of Lévi-Strauss, but structural analysis may validate historical interpretation. An ethnographic conclusion from the first volume of his analyses of myth is that "the Ge, far from being the 'marginal' people they were supposed to be in 1942, when Volume 1 of *The Handbook of South American Indians* came out (I protested at the time against this assumption), represent a pivotal element in South America, whose func-tion is comparable to the part played in North America by the old settle-ments along the Fraser and Columbia rivers, and their survivors." Lévi-

Strauss concludes: "Therefore, in spite of its formal approach, structural analysis establishes the validity of ethnographic and historical interpretations that I put forward more than twenty years ago; at the time they were thought to be somewhat rash. . . ."[102]

In spite of the anthropological and philosophical levels of meanings of myth, Lévi-Strauss affirms the fact of meaning on other levels. Just as he is not opposed to historical study, he is not opposed to traditional methods of literary study. "The analysis of literary work is illuminated very much by the help of the structural method. But this method only renews and complements traditional means. It does not make traditional means superfluous." Indeed, as we have seen earlier, Lévi-Strauss does not conceive of the possibility of the study of structural aspects of a work without first "securing all information which history, biography, and philology can offer interpretation."[103]

In terms of the study of literary works, Lévi-Strauss is skeptical of much that goes under the title of structuralism. "Instead of searching methodologically for the real meaning behind consciously elaborated metaphors," Lévi-Strauss says, some believe that they can use structuralism "as a pretext for indefinitely substituting one set of metaphors for another." This, Lévi-Strauss calls a "structuralism-fiction."[104] Lévi-Strauss contrasts two conceptions. One sees the work as a giant organic molecule whose inner characteristics and structure form a very complex structuration. This is the structural view of Lévi-Strauss. The other conception sees the work as a kind of Rorschach test image which has only that meaning which is given to it by a reader in a particular context.[105]

CONCLUSION

The use of linguistics in the study of literature approaches the matter of literary creativity from the perspective of the literary expression of the text. As long as the method of analysis centers upon formal elements whose relationships may be purely fortuitous, the meanings may be purely private and accidental. The claim of Lévi-Strauss to use formal elements in his analyses which are not the result of fortuitous events but which result from the very nature of man himself, if true, would answer the objection of critics of Jakobson's structural analysis that inappropriate formal elements are used. Even if it is argued that meaning may be found in fortuitous structuring of elements, the meaning derived from elements which are based on the creative nature of man (conscious or unconscious) would be less individualistic and the meanings at the various levels would be homologous. Historical meaning would not be totally discontinuous from literary meaning; lexical meaning would not be divorced from syntactical meaning. Meaning on one level could, therefore, be a key to meaning on another level.

The value of the pioneering efforts of Lévi-Strauss, from the perspective of this work on the value of structural study of narrative for New Testament hermeneutics, is seen precisely in its pioneering character. The students of narrative are able to draw upon some specific elements from the work of Lévi-Strauss, but more importantly, they are able to take his broad conceptualization of a necessary relationship between the human mind and the expression of that mind and, with the help of advances in disciplines related to linguistics, arrive at fresh approaches to narrative which are perhaps less idiosyncratic and therefore more useful than that of Lévi-Strauss. The narratologists are inhabiting and cultivating the wilderness pioneered by Lévi-Strauss.

NOTES

1. P. A. Verburg, "The Background to the Linguistic Conception of Bopp," *Lingua* 2 (1950), 441.

2. David Crystal, *Linguistics* (Harmondsworth: Penguin, 1971), introduces the subject, giving attention to pragmatic, historical, and philosophical questions. A more complete work is Gerhard Helbig, *Geschichte der neueren Sprachwissenschaft* (Munich: Max Hueber Verlag, 1973). For treatments of the work of Saussure in light of most recent developments, see Jonathan Culler, *Saussure* (Glasgow: William Collins and Sons, 1976) and Philip Pettit, *The Concept of Structuralism: A Critical Analysis* (Dublin: Gill and Macmillan, 1975), pp. 1–29.

3. Ferdinand de Saussure, *Cours de Linguistique Générale*, published by Charles Bally and Albert Sechehaye, with the collaboration of Albert Riedlinger (3d ed.; Paris: Payot, 1949), pp. 114–40.

4. *Ibid.*, pp. 23–39.

5. *Ibid.*, pp. 97–103.

6. *Ibid.*, p. 66.

7. *Ibid.*, pp. 170–75.

8. See John T. Waterman, *Perspectives in Linguistics* (2d ed.; Chicago: The University of Chicago Press, 1970), p. 68; R. H. Robins, *A Short History of Linguistics* (London: Longmans, 1967), pp. 204–6; Helbig, *Geschichte der neueren Sprachwissenschaft*, pp. 48–60.

9. Louis Hjelmslev, *Prolegomena to a Theory of Language*, trans. Francis J. Whitfield (Madison: The University of Wisconsin Press, 1961), pp. 17–18.

10. Robins, *A Short History of Linguistics*, pp. 201–2; Waterman, *Perspectives in Linguistics*, pp. 83–86; Helbig, *Geschichte der neueren Sprachwissenschaft*, pp. 60–72.

11. Helbig, *Geschichte der neueren Sprachwissenschaft*, p. 91.

12. See Milka Iric, *Trends in Linguistics*, trans. M. Heppell (The Hague: Mouton, 1965), pp. 152–59.

13. Bernard Bloch, "Leonard Bloomfield," *Language* 25 (1949), 92–93.

14. Leonard Bloomfield, *Language* (New York: Holt, 1933), pp. 139–40.

15. See Waterman, *Perspectives in Linguistics*, pp. 94–96.

16. See Iric, *Trends in Linguistics*, pp. 156–61.

17. See Ladislav Matejka, "The Formal Method and Linguistics," *Readings in Russian Poetics: Formalist and Structuralist Views*, ed. Ladislav Matejka and Krystyna Pomorska (Cambridge, Mass.: The MIT Press, 1971), p. 281.

18. Lev Jakubinskij, "On Sounds in Verse Language," quoted in B. M. Ejxenbaum, "The Theory of the Formal Method," *Readings in Russian Poetics*, p. 9.

19. Quoted in F. Svejkovsky, "Theoretical Poetics in the Twentieth Century," *Current Trends in Linguistics*, XII/2 (The Hague: Mouton, 1974), 878–79.

20. Quoted in Ejxenbaum, "The Theory of the Formal Method," p. 8.

21. Russian formalism has been seen as the seminal agent for Czechoslovak structuralism, but a Czech scholar, Oleg Sus, has stressed the importance of the nineteenth century Prague school of aesthetics which based its work on the theories of Friedrich Herbert. See Thomas G. Winner, "The Aesthetics and Poetics of the Prague Linguistic Circle," *Poetics* 8 (1973), 80.

22. The study of Jakobson has been reprinted as Brown University *Slavic Reprint* VI (Providence, R.I., 1969).

23. See Winner, "The Aesthetics and Poetics of the Prague Linguistic Circle," pp. 81–89.

24. Viktor Sklovskij, *O teorii prozy* (Moscow: Federachnya, 1929), pp. 5–6. Quoted in Winner, "The Aesthetics and Poetics of the Prague Linguistic Circle," p. 86.

25. See Tzvetan Todorov, "Roman Jakobson poeticien," *Poetique* 7 (1971), 275.

26. Todorov traces the development of Jakobson's own concept of the relationship between words and what they designate. *Ibid.*, pp. 275–82.

27. Roman Jakobson, "The Dominant," *Readings in Russian Poetics*, pp. 83–84.

28. Roman Jakobson, "On Realism in Art," *Readings in Russian Poetics*, p. 39.

29. Roman Jakobson, "Linguistics and Poetics," *Style in Language*, ed. Thomas A. Sebeok (Cambridge, Mass.: The MIT Press, 1960), pp. 368–69.

30. Roman Jakobson, "Poetry of Grammar and Grammar of Poetry," *Lingua* 21 (1968), 603.

31. Charles Baudelaire, *The Flowers of Evil*, selected and edited by Marthiel and Jackson Mathews (New York: New Directions, 1962), pp. 83–84.

32. Roman Jakobson and Claude Lévi-Strauss, "Charles Baudelaire's 'Les Chats,'" Introduction to Structuralism, ed. M. Lane (New York: Basic Books, 1976), p. 205.

33. Ibid., p. 206.

34. Ibid., pp. 208–9.

35. Ibid., p. 217.

36. Ibid., p. 218.

37. Ibid., pp. 218–19.

38. Ibid., p. 220.

39. Ibid., p. 221.

40. Michael Riffaterre, "Describing Poetic Structures: Two Approaches to Baudelaire's Les Chats," Structuralism, ed. Jacques Ehrmann (New York: Doubleday, 1970), p. 195.

41. Ibid., pp. 190, 191, 195.

42. Ibid., pp. 201–3.

43. Ibid., p. 203.

44. Ibid., pp. 203–4.

45. Jonathan Culler, Structuralist Poetics: Structuralism, Linguistics and the Study of Literature (London: Routledge and Kegan Paul, 1975), p. 74.

46. Ibid., p. 62.

47. Ibid., pp. 66–67.

48. Ibid., pp. 69, 71.

49. Roman Jakobson and Lawrence G. Jones, Shakespeare's Verbal Art in "Th' Expence of Spirit" (The Hague: Mouton, 1970), p. 32.

50. Ibid.

51. Culler, Structuralist Poetics, p. 72.

52. Jakobson and Jones, Shakespeare's Verbal Art, pp. 10–11.

53. Ibid., p. 18.

54. Ibid., p. 21; Culler, Structuralist Poetics, p. 72.

55. Culler, Structuralist Poetics, p. 73.

56. Richard Ohmann, Shaw: The Style and the Man (Middletown, Conn.: The Wesleyan University Press, 1962), p. 22. Quoted in Donald C. Freeman, "The Strategy of Fusion: Dylan Thomas' Syntax," Style and Structure in Literature: Essays in the New Stylistics, ed. Roger Fowler (Oxford: Blackwell, 1975), p. 19.

57. Donald Davie, Articulate Energy: An Inquiry into the Syntax of English Poetry (London: Routledge and Kegan Paul, 1955).

58. Ibid., pp. 66–67. Also see Suzanne K. Langer, Philosophy in a New Key (Cambridge, Mass.: Harvard University Press, 1957) and A Theory of Art (New York: Charles Scribner's Sons, 1953).

59. Ibid., pp. 67–68.

60. Ibid., pp. 68–69, 74.

61. Ibid., pp. 76, 79–80.

62. Ibid., pp. 85–86.

63. Ibid., p. 87.

64. Ibid., pp. 87–88.

65. *Ibid.*, p. 91, from Variété III, p. 28.

66. Davie, *Articulate Energy*, pp. 92–93.

67. *Ibid.*, p. 94.

68. See discussions of the relationship of grammatical structures to meaning in *Approaches to Poetics*, ed. Seymour Chatman (New York and London: Columbia University Press, 1973) and *Style and Structure in Literature*, ed. Fowler.

69. Davie, *Articulate Energy*, p. 79.

70. Stanley E. Fish, "What Is Stylistics and Why Are They Saying Such Terrible Things About It?" *Approaches to Poetics*, p. 149.

71. *Ibid.*, p. 150. See Roger Fowler, *The Languages of Literature: Some Linguistic Contributions to Criticism* (London: Routledge and Kegan Paul, 1971), pp. 38–39.

72. Fish, "What Is Stylistics?" pp. 148–49.

73. *Ibid.*, pp. 144, 140.

74. *Ibid.*, p. 144.

75. *Ibid.*, pp. 150–52.

76. Claude Lévi-Strauss, "Interview," *Diacritics* 1 (1971), 47.

77. Claude Lévi-Strauss, *Structural Anthropology* (New York: Basic Books, 1963), pp. 34, 33.

78. *Ibid.*, pp. 62, 71, 33.

79. Claude Lévi-Strauss, *The Raw and the Cooked* (New York: Harper, 1969), pp. 340–41.

80. Claude Lévi-Strauss, "The Story of Asdiwal," *The Structural Study of Myth and Totemism*, ed. Edmund Leach (London: Tavistock, 1967), pp. 1–47.

81. G. S. Kirk, *Myth: Its Meaning and Functions in Ancient and Other Cultures* (Cambridge: Cambridge University Press, 1970), pp. 51–52.

82. Lévi-Strauss, "The Story of Asdiwal," p. 14.

83. *Ibid.*, pp. 14–17.

84. *Ibid.*, pp. 17–21.

85. *Ibid.*, p. 27.

86. *Ibid.*, pp. 27–28.

87. *Ibid.*, p. 29.

88. *Ibid.*, pp. 29–30.

89. *Ibid.*, p. 42.

90. See Mary Douglas, "The Meaning of Myth," *The Structural Study of Myth and Totemism*, pp. 49–69, and Kirk, *Myth*, pp. 50–58.

91. Claude Lévi-Strauss, *Le Cru et le Cuit* (Paris: Librairie Plon, 1964); *Du Miel aux Cendres* (Paris: Librairie Plon, 1966); *L'Origine des manières de table* (Paris: Librairie Plon, 1968); and *L'Homme nu* (Paris: Librairie Plon, 1971).

92. "Wie arbeitet der menschliche Geist?" *Antworten der Strukturalisten*, ed. Adelbert Reif (Hamburg: Huffman und Campe Verlag, 1973), pp. 79–81. First published in *Les Lettres françaises*, January 12, 1967.

93. Lévi-Strauss, *The Raw and the Cooked*, p. 10.

94. *Ibid.*, p. 341.

95. *Ibid.*, p. 245.
96. Lévi Strauss, *From Honey to Ashes* (New York: Harper, 1973), p. 473.
97. Lévi-Strauss, *The Raw and the Cooked*, p. 245.
98. Levi-Strauss, *From Honey to Ashes*, pp. 148–49.
99. Lévi-Strauss, *The Raw and the Cooked*, p. 1.
100. Lévi-Strauss, *From Honey to Ashes*, pp. 354–55.
101. *Ibid.*
102. Lévi-Strauss, *The Raw and the Cooked*, pp. 8–9.
103. "Wie arbeitet der menschliche Geist?" pp. 86, 85.
104. Lévi-Strauss, "Interview," p. 45. See also "Wie arbeitet der menschliche Geist?" p. 85.
105. "Wie arbeitet der menschliche Geist?" ed. Reif, p. 86. Interpretation, nevertheless, whether it is by scientific analysis or narration of tradition, varies according to the "temperament, talent, imagination environment, and personal experience" of the one doing the narration or analysis. *Ibid.*, p. 107.

CHAPTER FIVE

Structural
Study of Narrative

Contemporary study of narrative is interdisciplinary, involving notably the study of folklore, linguistics, anthropology, myth, stylistics, poetics, logic, and philosophy. The questions of the elements of analysis, the levels of analysis, and the meanings resulting from the structural analysis of narrative are constantly being approached from different vectors as advances are made in the various disciplines and as new disciplines are brought to bear upon the questions. The basic question of the nature of narrative and the appropriate model—linguistics or semiotics—to use in the study of narrative is revitalizing the discipline and giving a broader perspective from which to view the object of study; the literary questions of the new criticism and later approaches to literature associated particularly with the name of Roland Barthes have sensitized students of narrative to significations which are new and different from conventional meanings; the study of folklore has enabled students of narrative to deal more successfully with the elements of narrative on the abstract level; the generative grammar of Noam Chomsky has been applied to literature, and this further development of linguistics has produced a more satisfactory model for the study of literature in the opinion of many. All of these elements and many more are related in different ways as they are applied to the study of narrative. This chapter will identify and discuss the elements which have become important most recently for the study of narrative and outline the major approaches to the study developed by leading French scholars.

A common theme in the various movements influencing the students of narrative (particularly semiotics, French new criticism, and generative grammar) and the models for the study of narrative is anthropocentrism. Man and his semiotic, literary, and linguistic competence are seen to be factors which not only cannot be ignored but which are necessary for the understanding and appreciation of all cultural facts.

LINGUISTICS, SEMIOTICS, AND NARRATIVE

The treatment of linguistics and semiotics is an excellent example of the way different but related studies, each of which is consistently developing, have come to be applied to narrative study at various stages of development of each of the disciplines. Structural linguistics was the model for the structural analysis of literature of Jakobson and Lévi-Strauss. Some limitation of that specific approach to linguistics brought about developments in linguistics itself and caused students of narrative to find a broader basis for narrative study in semiotics. The developments in generative grammar will be discussed later, but at this point the movement from the linguistics of Saussure to the semiotics of C. S. Peirce will be discussed.

Semiotics[1] as a modern discipline was cofounded by Charles Sanders Peirce and Ferdinand de Saussure, and two different definitions of semiotics may be traced to these founders. Saussure, historically of greater importance for structural linguistics and the structural study of literature, defines semiotics (he uses the term "semiology") in reference to language.

> Language is a system of signs that express ideas, and is therefore comparable to a system of writing, the alphabet of deaf-mutes, symbolic rites, polite formulas, military signals, etc. But it is the most important of all these systems.
>
> A *science that studies the life of signs within society* is conceivable; it would be a part of social psychology and consequently of general psychology; I shall call it semiology (from Greek *sēmeîon*, "sign"). . . . Linguistics is only a part of the general science of semiology; the laws discovered by semiology will be applicable to linguistics, and the latter will circumscribe a well-defined area within the mass of anthropological facts.[2]

For Saussure language is the center of attention and the linguistic sign is the key to the relationship of language to other semiotic systems.

> Signs that are wholly arbitrary realize better than the others the ideals of the semiological process; that is why language, the most complex and universal of all systems of expression, is also the most characteristic; in this

sense linguistics can become the master-pattern for all branches of semio-logical system.[3]

For the early structuralists (as for other linguists, such as Bloomfield and Weinreich)[4] human language was the semiotic system par excellence. Roland Barthes, in an early period, declared it necessary to "face the possibility of inverting Saussure's declaration: linguistics is not a part of the general science of signs, even a privileged part; it is semiology which is a part of linguistics."[5] The problematic of the legitimacy of the direct application of linguistics to literature, however, brought about the desire for a broader scientific model which could be applied in more than an analogical fashion to literary works. The distinction between linguistics and semiotics, the development of several specific semiotics divorced from the linguistic model, and the application of semiotic as well as linguistic models to the study of narrative began in the 1960s.

The approach of Saussure, claims Julia Kristeva, is philosophically justified to the extent that sign is not possible without language, that the model of sign is given a priori in spoken language, and consequently that there can be no science of signs outside of linguistics. But two questions disturb the easy approach of Saussure: Are the available models of linguistics sufficient to construct a general semiotics by themselves? And how can account be given of the process of the production of meaning in the systems of signs, a task which linguistics with its concepts of communication has not accomplished? Kristeva declares that semiology must be broader than linguistics, borrowing its models from the formal sciences. Linguistics in turn can borrow from this new science for its own renewal.[6]

As structuralists recently came to seek a broader base for the construction of models to assist in analysis, the work of Peirce became more important. The definition of semiotics given by Peirce (independently of the work of Saussure) was broader than that of Saussure, for Peirce wrote as a philosopher within the tradition of the philosophical analysis of signs. Indeed, Peirce can be considered the founder of modern semiotics, for he aimed at systematic investigation as "a pioneer, or rather a backwoodsman, in the work of clearing and opening up . . . semiotics,"[7] while Saussure really limited his interest to linguistics.

Peirce distinguished triadic sign-processes from dynamical actions or actions of physical or psychical force between *two* subjects; ". . . by 'semiosis' I mean . . . an action, or influence, which is, or involves, a cooperation of *three* subjects, such as a sign, its object, and its inter-pretant, this tri-relative influence not being in any way resolvable into actions between pairs."[8] The definition of sign in semiosis is an original contribution of Peirce. A sign is a reality which is related to its object but which is also related to its interpretant, which the sign is capable of determining. In broad terms, the interpretant is the meaning of the sign. The interpretant, in turn, becomes a sign with its own interpretant.

A sign, for Peirce, is anything that acts in the process of "semiosis." All the universe "is perfused with signs."[9] Signs are not limited to "existents" (although the "universe of existents" forms a part of the universe of signs), for thought itself is "essentially of the nature of the sign." A sign which is really a sign must be translated into another more fully developed sign.[10] And, more obviously, in thinking "we have present to the consciousness some feeling, image, conception, or other representation, which serves as a sign."[11] The human being is himself a sign, "for, as the fact that every thought is a sign, taken in conjunction with the fact that life is a train of thought, proves that man is a sign; so, that every thought is an *external* sign proves that man is an external sign."[12] Moreover, "everything which is present to us is a phenomenal manifestation of ourselves."[13] Peirce is directly idealistic in his concept of the relation of the human and the sign. Although "things which are relative to the mind doubtless are, apart from that relation," it is also true that "there is no thing which is in-itself in the sense of not being relative to the mind."[14]

In 1867, in a paper "On a New List of Categories," Peirce gave a now famous triad of signs which proves to be important for modern semiotics.[15] He bases his suggestion on the theory that "the function of conceptions is to reduce the manifold of sensuous impressions to unity" and the idea that "the validity of a conception consists in the impossibility of reducing the content of consciousness to unity without the introduction of it."[16] He claims that the three fundamental conceptions, at least of logic, are reference to a ground, reference to an object, and reference to an interpretant. Three kinds of representation must therefore be distinguished: "First. Those whose relation to their objects is a mere community in some quality, and these representations may be termed *likenesses*."[17] The term "icon" is used for this type of representation. "Second. Those whose relation to their objects consists in a correspon-dence in fact, and these may be called *indices* or *signs*." (In later writings an index is taken to be but one of various kinds of signs.) "Third. Those the ground of whose relation to their objects is an imputed character, which are the same as *general signs*, and these may be termed *symbols*."[18]

The third type of representation involves the interpretant. "Interpretant" is often taken to mean the interpreter or the interpreter's reaction to a sign. Umberto Eco suggests that the idea of an interpretant "frightened many scholars who hastened to exorcise it by misunderstanding it," but Eco declares that the usefulness of the idea of an interpretant is due to "the very richness and vagueness" of the idea. The interpretant can assume different forms: the equivalent sign in another system of communication (a drawing of a dog corresponds to "dog"); the index directed to the single object implying an element of universal quantification ("all objects like this"); a scientific definition in terms of the same communicative system ("salt" signifies sodium chloride); an emotive association which gains an established connotation ("dog" signifies "fidelity"); or the simple translation of the term into a different language.[19]

The concept of art as a sign and the relating of semiotics to the study of art developed in Czechoslovak structuralism beginning in the 1930s, particularly in the work of Mukarovsky. The contribution of Mukarovsky is directly applicable to literary art and the study of narrative. In a short article published in 1934, Mukarovsky first suggested that art should be viewed as a sign in that it communicates between an artist and the viewer. As a sign, however, the work is autonomous in the sense that it does not relate directly and unambiguously to the distinguishable reality. The sign is "a perceptual reality which relates to another reality outside itself, to which it points and which it evokes." "Without a semiological orientation," Mukarovsky declared, "the theoretician of art will always be inclined to regard the work of art as a purely formal construction or as the direct reflection either of the psychic, even physiological dispositions of the author, or of the distinct reality expressed by the work or of the ideological, economic, social, or cultural situation of the given milieu."[20] Art as a sign cannot be limited to the material object. Nor can it be considered simply the psychological state of mind of its creator or the psychological state it evokes in the viewer.

In later articles, Mukarovsky clarifies somewhat the relationship of the aesthetic sign to realities outside of the work itself. In 1936, in "Aesthetic Function, Norm and Value as Social Facts," Mukarovsky suggests that the question of truth which accompanies the reception of the message in normal communication and which helps to determine response to the message is not the same in the communication of art. The work of art does not refer to a specific "truth" or reality but to a multitude of realities. The work of art is polysemantic. Yet, the reception of a specific work of art is not simply an individual matter. Art as a sign is social as well as individual. As a social reality, art must refer to some context and use a social code.

Winner suggests four points which are of continuing importance in the development of Mukarovsky's views of art as a sign.[21] First, the perception or the decoding of a work of art is a progressive process. It continues through time. Second, because perception is a linear process, the work of art does not emphasize some final, unambiguous relationship to an external reality, but it stresses the process by which such a relationship may arise. Meanings of parts of the work affect meanings of other parts and of the whole, and these meanings are arranged in a linear and in a hierarchical relationship. When literary art is considered, components will be seen as arranged in linear fashion (words following words and sentences following sentences, etc.), but components are also arranged vertically, from the lowest level of phoneme to higher lexical and thematic elements. A third point is the lack of dichotomy between form and content in the artistic sign. Formal elements are also bearers of meaning, and all elements of content have to do with the form of sign. In poetry, for example, euphony is both a formal and a semantic element. A fourth point emphasizes that the viewer and the artist shape the work of art. Although the sign does not equal the state of the author or of the receiver, both are important. The author and the viewer bring intentions to the work of art. Since these intentions are not identical, there is a complementary and active relationship between the artist and the viewer in the semiotic approach to art.

Saussure's approach to semiotics is today seen as a limiting approach in some respects because phenomena which today are considered "semiotic" would be read out by Saussure's notion that linguistics has a necessary relationship with semiotics—even if semiotics is superordinate.[22] Today, the subject matter of semiotics is considered "all cultural processes as communicative processes"[23] or "the exchange of any messages whatever and of signs which underlie them."[24] The attempt to distinguish between a "semiology" which has the work of Saussure in mind and a semiotics which calls upon Peirce as founder, however, is not completely successful *in practice*. Language is the vehicle by which meaning is expressed no matter which model is envisioned. Language is a semiotic system which is used to express meaning in other semiotic systems.[25] Linguistics has been profitably used in the study of literature, and such use is certainly legitimate because of the close relationship of language and literature. The important question is the appropriate application of linguistics. Instead of applying linguistics directly in literature, may linguistics be used in a broader study of semiotics and the broader study of semiotics then applied to literature?

The question as to the meaning of "language" in hermeneutics, particularly in the New Hermeneutic, may be clarified somewhat by the distinctions between linguistics and semiotics which are currently being made in the structural study of narrative as well as linguistics in general. At points, of course, linguistics may be applied directly to the text; at other times, linguistics becomes a heuristic, analogical model for the study of the text or of literature; at other times (depending upon the particular linguistics being used) linguistics must broaden into general semiotic studies before it can be useful in the study of literature. The appropriate use of linguistics depends upon the level of the text being studied and, of course, the level of meaning with which the interpreter is concerned. Here, again, the comprehensive view of Dilthey will serve to unite what often appear to be opposing and even mutually exclusive approaches to the text.

ROLAND BARTHES AND THE NEW CRITICISM IN FRANCE

The year 1966 can be taken as the date of birth of "narrative semiotics" of French structuralism for in that year a special number of the French journal *Communications* was devoted to the analysis of narrative structures. The birth, of course, had been preceded by a period of formation which included the change in the cultural environment of France in the 1960s, the questioning of traditional criticism, and the growth and diffusion of knowledge in linguistics. The work of Claude Lévi-Strauss formed a part of the background, although the aims and concerns of the later generation of French structuralists did not exactly coincide with those of the first generation. A most instructive argument about the function of criticism in the teaching of literature—instructive insofar as Parisian literary life and the theoretical background of the structural analysis of narrative are concerned—took place in the sixties. The debate involved Raymond Picard and Roland Barthes. In 1963 Barthes published *Sur Racine*, a volume of studies on Racine done in a new mode. The first study had appeared in *Théâtre Classique Français* in 1960 and dealt with the figures and functions in the tragedies in a structural manner. The second study was a review of a production of *Phèdre* which appeared in *Théâtre Populaire* in 1958. The third study "Historie ou Litterature?" had appeared in *Annales* in 1960 and dealt with the critical problem of literature. This essay is of particular importance for understanding the debate.[26] The mode of criticism in *Sur Racine* was not entirely new. In fact, one critic considers it legitimate to take the cosmogonic thematics of Gaston Bouchelard and the voluntarist thematics of Georges Poulet, both dating from the thirties and forties, as the ancestors of French new criticism. From 1955, moreover, literary criticism had been increasingly influenced by a method which was breaking away from literary history, the criticism of taste, and an older type of literary stylistics.[27] Neveitheless, Raymond Picard wisely chose Barthes as the representative of new criticism to attack because he was "without doubt the most distinctive representative of the movement and its most articulate spokesman."[28]

Picard first attacked Barthes in 1964 in articles in *Le Monde*, and in 1965 he leveled a full-scale attack by means of an extraordinarily passionate volume entitled *Nouvelle critique ou nouvelle imposture*.[29] The next year Barthes answered Picard in *Critique et vérité*. Picard characterizes new criticism as "intolerant, neo-magical nihilism, a parasite criticism which at best considers the literary work as a dunghill where flowers can be made to grow."[30] In order to appreciate the significance of the structural analysis of narrative and its importance for New Testament hermeneutics, the rhetoric must be eliminated and the real differences between the positions of Picard and Barthes clarified. Because of the almost inevitable tendency to equate French new criticism with the American new criticism, it might be more beneficial to contrast Barthes not only with historical criticism but also with American new criticism.

Edward Wasiolek, citing Doubrovsky's study of French new criticism, emphasizes that historical criticism and American new criticism agreed on the major point against which Barthes argued. Historical criticism and the American new criticism shared "the most fundamental of assumptions," the assumption of "the existence of an objective text, which could be elucidated by critical process."[31] The American new critics found fault with the historian of literature because of the desecration of the purely literary by a reduction of literature to biography, history, and human events—to facts of the environment. The American new criticism, opposing extrinsic and referential criticism, stressed intrinsic criticism and close reading; but it insisted on the objectivity of the text. Although American critics were careful to state that the commentary on the text "did not 'paraphrase' the text, nor did it state the meaning in some categorical and definitive way," supporters as well as antagonists of American new criticism "never questioned that criticism was an act of approximating in language a work that had objective status, and that its intelligibility and worth were measured by that objectivity."[32]

Barthes, and French new criticism, of course, clearly do not dispute that there is an objective text in the sense of the printed page and objective meaning in the sense of the normal public meanings of the words. But they see this conventional reading as a possible reading and not necessarily as the most important. There is no objective text, no "neutral" or "innocent" position from which to read the text. Barthes sees this fact as a positive factor in criticism and not as a liability to be overcome. "How can anyone believe that a given work is an *object* independent of the psyche and personal history of the critic studying it, with rights to which he enjoys a sort of extra-territorial status?"[33]

The reconstruction of the circumstances and the meanings of the words of past works, moreover, while a possibility, is not objective and impersonal. It is the result of a choice and is as subjective as criticism with avowed ideological positions. A total criticism does not claim universality for any position. "Racine," Barthes says, "lends himself to several languages: psychoanalytic, existential, tragic, psychological (others could be invented, others will be invented); none is innocent." Such a situation is not to be deplored but to be acknowledged and even cherished, for "to acknowledge this incapacity *to tell the truth* about Racine is precisely to acknowledge, at last, the special status of literature. It lies in a paradox: literature is that ensemble of objects and rules, techniques and works, whose function in the general economy of our society is precisely to institutionalize subjectivity."[34] Wasiolek conceptualizes Barthes's position for traditional readers as "a radical identification of sign and referent." The referent for Barthes "is as many things as there are ways of 'writing' about the sign."[35]

This description of Barthes's position makes clear that it is not one that is totally subjective in the sense that criticism is self-indulgent, allowing one to exercise his own peculiar whim and caprice. Barthes's criticism is subjective in that the work itself does not impose an absolute on criticism. Human choices are involved in the process of criticism, the choice of critical language, for example. But once the choice is made, constraints resulting from the choice come into play. One of the issues according to Picard was that of saying "anything" or saying something responsibly. But Barthes does not opt for saying anything. What he does opt for is "a human, ongoing, and unlimited objectivity, and truths created by human choice and intelligence, not truths existing somehow before them. . . . Barthes's position is an assertion of human right to create meaning in literature and a rejection of the view that such meaning lies ready-made."[36]

Serge Doubrovsky declares that Picard reached the real core of the argument with questions concerning the depth to which literature goes. Picard attacks the new critics for display of a total "indifference to literary structures" and a lack of belief in "the specificity of literature." They abolish or ignore literary structures and deal with psychological, sociological, or metaphysical structures. He asserts that the new critics "are like a man who is attracted to women but who by some strange perversion can only enjoy them when he sees them in X-ray."[37] For Picard, the classical tradition is self-evidently the correct position: the content signified by a literary work is completely exhausted by the work itself. The words of the work communicate the univocal meaning for writer and reader. An objective criticism is possible because of (1) agreement between what is said and intended by the work, (2) agreement between what the work says and what the author intended, and (3) agreement between what the work says and what the critic thinks it says—provided the reading is informed and intelligent.[38]

Barthes's answer to Picard is not only a challenge to the accusation brought against the new criticism but an accusation against Picard and his followers that they ignore the necessity for a symbolic reading in their insisting on considering language only according to its letter. The symbolic language has multiple meanings. Criticism may choose to deal with a single one of the meanings, but a science of literature would deal with all the meanings opened up by the symbolic language. The aim of the science of literature would not be to furnish the meanings themselves but to establish their intelligibility.[39] Barthes contrasts the language of science and the language of literature to clarify the need for a structural science. For science, language is "simply an instrument. . . . It is subordinate to the matter of science . . . which, so it is said, exists outside language and precedes it." For literature, however, language is not merely the "convenient instrument" or the "superfluous backcloth" of some "reality" which preexists it. "Language is literature's Being, its very world; the whole of literature is contained in the act of writing. . . ." Structuralism and literature are homogenous; so structuralism may be conceptualized as a science or as itself literature. Barthes sees a need for a science of literature which operates at the level of the content or the "form of the content," the level of the "forms of discourse," and the level of the words. But Barthes also sees the need for structuralism to "rejoin literature," and for the structuralist to move beyond science and become himself a "writer," but a writer who is not misled by the idea of a superior code of "scientific" discourse in the realm of literature, rather a writer who refuses "to be terror-stricken by what is wrongly thought of as the 'truth' of the content and of reasoning, and opens up all three dimensions of language to research, with its subversions of logic, its mixing of codes, its shifts of meaning, dialogues, and parodies."[40]

The background of the development of the structural study of narrative includes French new criticism of which Roland Barthes is a foremost representative. A structural study of narrative is not to be simply equated with new criticism, for the interests of Barthes and new criticism range wider than narrative, and the major theoreticians and practitioners of structural study of narrative do not all come to their task as literary figures in new criticism.

FOLKLORE AND NARRATIVE

The structures uncovered in folklore research have had an influence in the general study of narrative.[41] The work of Vladimir Propp can be considered the starting point of all structuralist activities in folklore. His work was first published in Russian in 1928; but it was a major exception to the prevailing atomistic trend in folklore, and general study in folklore did not immediately follow his example. Since the translation and publication of Propp's work in English and French, and in the new literary context, it has greatly influenced the field of folklore and narrative.

Propp calls his analytic approach "morphological," borrowing the term directly from biology. He intends to describe the tale according to its component parts and to show the relationship of these components to each other and to the whole. Propp analyzed a corpus of one hundred Russian fairy tales and discovered that there were only thirty-one functions in the tales. A function is an action of an actor that advances the plot, and therefore functions can only be defined in light of their place in the narrative. Propp indicates that a tale begins with some sort of initial situation. After the initial situation (enumeration of members of a family, introduction of the future hero, etc.) functions follow such as "absentation" ("one of the members of a family absents himself from home"), "interdiction" ("'an interdiction' is addressed to the hero"), or "violation" ("the interdiction is violated"), "reconnaissance" ("the villain makes an attempt at reconnaissance"), "delivery" ("the villain receives information about his victim").[42] While there are thirty-one functions, every tale does not consist of all of the functions. Some functions do not occur in a given tale, but the sequence of functions which do occur in tales is (with minor exceptions) always the same.

Propp also analyzed the character types which carry out the functions. There is evidence for seven character types or spheres of action: the villain, the donor, the helper, the princess and her father (a sought-for person), the dispatcher, the hero, and the false hero.[43] The thirty-one functions are distributed among the seven characters in such a way that the same functions are always carried out by the same characters.

Propp describes the tale as a whole:

> Morphologically, a tale . . . may be termed any development proceeding from villainy . . . or a lack . . . through intermediary functions to marriage . . . , or to other functions employed as a dénouement. Terminal functions are at times a reward . . . , a gain or in general the liquidation of misfortune . . . , an escape from pursuit . . . , etc. This type of development is termed by us a *move.* . . . Each new act of villainy, each new lack creates a new move.[44]

Alan R. Dundes used the work of Propp to study North American folk tales. Instead of "functions," however, Dundes borrowed the term "motifeme" from Kenneth Pike. "Propp's unit is the function, but he did not bother to standardize any term for the elements which fulfill the function, i.e., the constituents of the manifestation mode."[45] Pike, however, "labels the minimum unit of his feature mode as the *emic motif* or *motifeme.* This actually corresponds to Propp's function."[46]

On the basis of his research, Dundes concludes that "there are definite recurrent sequences of motifemes and these sequences constitute a limited number of distinct patterns which empirical observation reveals are the structural bases of the majority of North American folk tales."[47] A large number of the folk tales studied by Dundes consist of a move from disequilibrium. This is one example of the nuclear two motifeme sequence: lack/liquidation of lack. Other examples of the two motifeme sequence are task/accomplishment of task, interdiction/violation, and deceit/deception. Another widespread structural pattern cited by Dundes is a four motifeme sequence consisting of interdiction/violation/consequence/ attempted escape from the consequence. Another four motifeme pattern is lack/deceit/deception/liquidation of lack. Although simple tales can consist of just one of the motifeme patterns, a great many American Indian tales may best be defined structurally as combinations of motifemic patterns. The six motifeme pattern is a result of a combination. A common six motifeme combination consists of lack/liquidation of lack/ interdiction/violation/consequence/attempted escape.

Dundes belittles the idea that the uncovering of structural patterns serves no useful purpose. He declares that "accurate morphological analysis may prove an invaluable asset in the study of problems in such areas as typology, prediction, acculturation, content analysis, cross-genre comparison, function, and etiology." As far as typology is concerned, "the results of this study indicate that at least in American Indian folk tales, one may justifiably speak of structural patterns independently of specific content. That is to say, there is a six motifeme sequence which may be manifested by tales as diverse contentwise as Orpheus on the one hand and the story of The Girl and the Cricket on the other."[48]

The structural study as such will allow analysis of more than one tale at a time. A number of historically unrelated but structurally identical tales of a culture may be examined. Moreover, "if in content analysis it is important to study the deviations from structural norms, . . . then it is clear that the structural norms in folklore must be established. Without establishing structural norms, it is obviously impossible to study deviations from these norms."[49]

The structural method of Propp and Dundes has been termed "syntagmatic." In this type, the structure or formal organization of a folkloristic text is described following the chronological order or the linear sequence of elements in the tale as reported from an informant. Thus if a tale consists of elements from A to Z, the structure of the tale is delineated in terms of this same sequence. It is important to distinguish the Lévi-Strauss or the "paradigmatic" type of structural analysis from the "syntagmatic" type. "Paradigmatic" structural analysis in folklore "seeks to describe the pattern (usually based upon an a priori binary principle of opposition) which allegedly underlies the folkloristic text. This pattern is not the same as the sequential structure at all. Rather the elements are taken out of the 'given' order and are regrouped in one or more analytic schemes."[50]

A. J. Greimas, a leader in the structural study of narrative, has made some observations concerning narrative grammar which may harmonize the apparently divergent methods of analysis of Propp and Lévi-Strauss. Greimas sees that the message of narrative may be read on two distinctive "isotopes." "By isotopy we mean a redundant set of semantic categories which make a uniform reading of the narrative possible: the unique reading is reached through the identification of isomorphic levels."[51] The two levels are the discursive and the structural. The discursive level is the narrative isotopy. "The *narrative isotopy* is determined by a certain anthropomorphic perspective which means that the narrative is thought of as a succession of events in which the actors are living beings, acting or acted on."[52] The second isotopy is on the level of the structure of the components. "Here, the problem is to establish equivalence of the lexemes (and the sentences which constitute the narrative sequences), and of the articulations of the sememic content."[53] The narrative isotopy is to be considered the discursive manifestation of the structural isotopy. In the subclass myth there may, however, be "constant interplay of sequences situated alternately on one or another of the two isotopies within a single narration."[54]

GENERATIVE GRAMMAR AND NARRATIVE

In 1957, with the publication of *Syntactic Structures*, Noam Chomsky inaugurated a new era in the study of linguistics. Just as structural linguistics influenced the study of literature, Chomsky's generative grammar has engendered new models for literary study. It is difficult to comprehend how this brief monograph by a relatively unknown young scholar could produce such an immediate positive response around the world. Doubtless the reaction was due to the need at that particular time for some broad grammatical concept or theory which could serve as a model for further advances in linguistics, but it was also due to the particular model provided by Chomsky.

The grammar of Chomsky is termed "generative grammar" or "generative transformational grammar," and two different phases are to be distinguished in the development of Chomsky's theory: 1957, when he published *Syntactic Structures,* and 1965, when he published *Aspects of the Theory of Syntax.*

First phase. Chomsky sees the goal of linguistic analysis as the separation of grammatical sentences from ungrammatical sentences and the exhibition of the structure of grammatical sentences.

> From now on I will consider a *language* to be a set (finite or infinite) of sentences, each finite in length and constructed out of a finite set of elements. All natural languages in their spoken or written form are languages in this sense, since each natural language has a finite number of phonemes (or letters in its alphabet) and each sentence is representable as a finite sequence of these phonemes (or letters), though there are infinitely many sentences. Similarly, the set of "sentences" of some formalized system of mathematics can be considered a language. The fundamental aim in the linguistic analysis of a language L is to separate the *grammatical* sequences which are the sentences of L from the *ungrammatical* sequences which are not sentences of L and to study the structure of the grammatical sequences. The grammar of L will thus be a device that generates all of the grammatical sequences of L and none of the ungrammatical ones.[55]

In Chomsky's view, it is the grammar of a language which produces or generates all and only the grammatical sentences of a language. Chomsky uses "grammar" in an inclusive sense, covering the subject matter of phonology as well as morphology and syntax. The term "generative" is the precise term used to state the two main properties of grammar: its ability to account by its rules for all the sentences of a language and its ability to be explicit about the grammatical nature of sentences by defining the characteristics of their internal structure.

In *Syntactic Structure* Chomsky sees three components of a grammar which will be successful in carrying out the purpose of a grammar: phrase structure grammar, transformational rules, and morphophonemic rules. Phrase structure grammar is basically an immediate constituent analysis to provide information about the structure of a sentence. Instead of drawing a diagram as earlier linguists did to illustrate the structure, Chomsky gives a system of ordered rules. *The cat saw the rat* would have been analyzed as

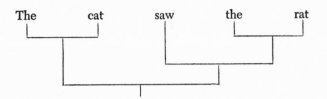

Chomsky, however, gives a notation which orders the analysis and relates the analytical decisions to each other by deriving each decision from some previous one. A simplified example follows:

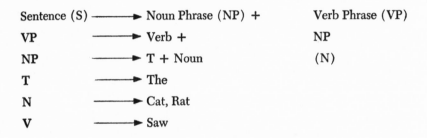

The arrow is an "instruction" to "rewrite" the element on the left into the "string" of elements on the right. The first rule makes an initial statement about the internal structure of a sentence. It says that sentences basically consist of two elements, noun phrases and verb phrases. The second and third rules tell what verb phrases and noun phrases are. A verb phrase is a verb plus a noun phrase; a noun phrase is an article (or determiner) and a noun. The underlying sentence has the form $T+N+V+T+N$. We can get *the cat saw the rat* or *the rat saw the cat*. By increasing the vocabulary items, the number of possible sentences increases. Other rules are added to introduce adjectives, auxiliary verbs, pronouns, etc., and to make the grammar more complex.[56]

Transformational rules operate on the strings produced by the phrase structure grammar and alter them in various ways. The way the transformations are understood and formalized is an important linguistic contribution of Chomsky, and a summary cannot do justice to the discussion in *Syntactic Structures*.[57] Two examples of transformations may prove helpful: transformations through use of conjunctions and transformations through change from active to passive or passive to active. "If we have two sentences $Z+X+W$ and $Z+Y+W$, and if X and Y are actually constituents of these sentences, we can generally form a new sentence $Z-X+$ and $+Y-W$." For example, from the two sentences *The scene - of the play - was in Chicago*, we get *The scene of the movie - and of the play - was in Chicago*.[58] "If X and Y are, however, not constituents, we cannot do this." For example, the sentences *The - liner sailed down the - river* and *The - tugboat chugged up the - river*, cannot be so transformed. Chomsky then derives the rule which he admits must be qualified: "If S_1 and S_2 are grammatical sentences, and S_1 differs from S_2 only in that X appears in S_1 where Y appears in S_2 (i.e., $S_1 = ..X..$ and $S_2 = ..Y..$), and X and Y are constituents of the same type in S_1 and S_2, respectively, then S_3 is a sentence, where S_3 is the result of replacing X by $Y+$ *and* $+Y$ in S_1 (i.e., $S_3 = ..X+$ *and* $+Y..$)."[59]

It is clear that in certain instances active sentences may be altered into passive sentences. *The boy will kick the ball* is the same as *the ball will be kicked by the boy*. Chomsky gives the rule for the passive transformation: "If S_1 is a grammatical sentence of the form NP_1 - Aux-V-NP_2, then the corresponding string of the form NP_2 - Aux+be+en - V - by +NP_1 is also a grammatical sentence." The rule says in effect: To form a passive sentence from an active sentence, reverse the position of NP_1 and NP_2, add the verb V in its proper form, a past participle affix, and the particle *by* between V and the NP.[60]

The final component is that of morphophonemics. Certain rules convert a string of words and morphemes produced by phrase structure grammar and transformations into a string of phonological units—the rules tell how the sentence as a whole is to be pronounced. For example, in the passive transformation, the exact form of *be* is not specified and how the affix gets transferred from its place in front of the verb to its place at the end of the verb is not stated. These and other matters are the subject matter of morphophonemic rules.

In *Syntactic Structures* a chapter is devoted to "Syntax and Semantics." Earlier in the book, Chomsky had stated that it was reasonable to expect grammars to provide explanations for some facts about language and linguistic behavior beyond the fact that a certain string is or is not a sentence.[61] Ambiguity should be dealt with. Such sentences as *the picture was painted by a new technique* and *the picture was painted by a real artist* are identically represented as $NP+was+Verb+en$ - by +NP on the phrase structure level. Their transformation history is quite different, however; and a generative transformational grammar shows the kernel sentences from which the sentences originate. Chomsky does not want to be misunderstood as supporting the notion "that grammar is based on meaning." His theory, he asserts, is "completely formal and non-semantic."[62]

In his summary,[63] Chomsky repeats that "grammar is best formulated as a self-contained study independent of semantics. In particular the notion of grammaticalness cannot be identified with meaningfulness. . . ."[64] He then summarizes his theory and its value:

> We can greatly simplify the description of English and gain new and important insight into its formal structure if we limit the direct description in terms of phrase structure to a kernel of basic sentences (simple, declarative, active, with no complex verb or noun phrases), deriving all other sentences from these (more properly, from the strings that underlie them) by transformation, possibly repeated. Conversely, having found a set of transformations that carry grammatical sentences into grammatical sentences, we can determine the constituent structure of particular sentences by investigating their behavior under these transformations with alternative constituent analyses.[65]

Second phase. In 1965 Chomsky published the *Aspects of the Theory of Syntax* which modified his earlier theory in important respects and which can be called the second phase of generative grammar. Two important ideas are developed in *Aspects*: the concept of linguistic competence and the place of semantics in grammar.[66]

The first phase of generative grammar was a break with the Bloomfieldian descriptive tradition.[67] Descriptive linguistics has stressed analyses of actual utterances. Theories and methods were devised for subjecting texts to a progressive analysis down to the basic units of phoneme and morpheme. Transformation, at the heart of Chomsky's work, played no part in Bloomfield's approach.[68] *Aspects* represents a further move from descriptive linguistics. Chomsky postulates that native speakers of a language master a system of rules which allows them to distinguish grammatical from ungrammatical sentences. Chomsky distinguishes between a person's knowledge of the system of rules and the actual use of the rules in discourse. The first Chomsky calls "competence," and the second "performance." This dichotomy is similar to that made by Saussure between *langue* and *parole*.[69] Chomsky says:

> The problem for the linguist, as well as for the child learning the language, is to determine from the data of performance the underlying system of rules that has been mastered by the speaker-hearer, and that he

puts to use in actual performance. Hence, in the technical sense, linguistic theory is mentalistic, since it is concerned with discovering a mental reality underlying actual behavior. Observed use of language or hypothesized dispositions to respond, habits, and so on, may provide evidence as to the nature of this mental reality, but surely cannot constitute the actual subject matter of linguistics, if this is to be a serious discipline.[70]

The implications of Chomsky's shift are far-reaching. In order to study competence, which is not directly observable, we must depend upon the "linguistic intuitions" of native speakers. "To maintain, on grounds of methodological purity, that introspective judgments of the informant (often, the linguist himself) should be disregarded is, for the present, to condemn the study of language to utter sterility."[71] Nevertheless, Chomsky says that hypotheses about language must be empirically testable.[72]

In *Syntactic Structures*, Chomsky reflects Bloomfield's emphasis when he indicates that semantic considerations are not directly relevant to syntactic description. In *Aspects*, however, meaning is given a much more central place. In order to introduce meaning, Chomsky revises the simple three-component grammar (phrase structure, transformational, and morphophonemic components). The new form of his grammar

> . . . contains a syntactic component, a semantic component, and a phonological component. The latter two are purely interpretive; they play no part in the recursive generation of sentence structures. The syntactic component consists of a base and a transformational component. The base, in turn, consists of a categorical subcomponent and a lexicon. The base generates deep structures. A deep structure enters the semantic component and receives a semantic interpretation; it is mapped by the transformational rules into a surface structure, which is then given a phonetic interpretation by the rules of the phonological component. Thus the grammar assigns semantic interpretations to signals, this association being mediated by the recursive rules of the syntactic component.[73]

The new grammar may be represented in a diagram:[74]

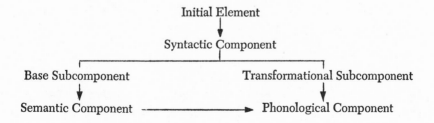

The base generates the underlying representations of sentences, the structural information. The deep structures are then (1) converted into pronounceable strings by the transformational subcomponent and the phonological component, and (2) their meaning is specified by the semantic component.

Chomsky states it this way:

> . . . the syntactic component consists of a base that generates deep structures and a transformational part that maps them into surface structures. The deep structure of a sentence is submitted to the semantic component for semantic interpretation, and its surface structure enters the phonological component and undergoes phonetic interpretation. The final effect of a grammar, then, is to relate a semantic interpretation to a phonetic representation—that is, to state how a sentence is interpreted. This relation is mediated by the syntactic component of the grammar, which constitutes its sole "creative" part.[75]

Expressed more simply, the syntax gives information about the structure of a sentence; the transformations and the phonology tell how the sentence is to be pronounced; and the semantics tell what the sentence means.

In the preface to *Aspects*, Chomsky cautions that his conclusions are tentative. His proposal is set forth positively, "but," Chomsky says, "I should like to reiterate that this can be only a highly tentative proposal."[76] In his conclusion to the chapter on the "Boundaries of Syntax and Semantics," he points out "that the syntactic and semantic structures of natural languages evidently offer many mysteries, both of fact and of principle, and that any attempt to delimit the boundaries of these domains must certainly be quite tentative."[77]

Nevertheless, Chomsky is convinced that it was a mistake to omit meaning so completely from his early work.

> In short, it has become clear that it was a mistake, in the first place, to suppose that the base component of a transformational grammar should be limited to a system of phrase structure rules, although such a system does play a fundamental role as a subpart of the base component. In fact, its role is that of defining the grammatical relations that are expressed in the deep structure and that therefore determine the semantic interpretation of a sentence.[78]

A third phase of generative transformation grammar is the movement beyond Chomsky insofar as semantic theory is concerned. "Generative semantics" is the name given to the work of linguists who are presently laboring on the question of meaning within the general framework and impetus of Chomsky's generative grammar.[79]

Text grammar. The application of Chomsky's generative grammar in literature has taken the form of an attempt to develop a text grammar; that is, to develop a grammar which deals with linguistic objects beyond the sentence. If textual structures could be defined as long sentences, generative grammar per se could be taken as a base for analyses of texts. This idea was put forward as literary theory by Katz and Fodor and others.[80] This method failed to produce the hoped-for result, however, and further systematic work has been done on textual structures in hopes of discovering some more suitable method of literary analysis. The hope is still to use Chomsky's generative grammar and the modifications made in recent generative semantics as a model if not as a base for a grammar of texts. It has been pointed out that even if generative grammar limits itself to a study of sentences, a grammar must be extended to a grammar of texts in order to account for some important linguistic relations in the utterances of native speakers.[81]

Tuen van Dijk has given his view of the theoretical framework within which grammar of literary texts would be developed.

A literary text may intuitively and very briefly be defined as a "specific" linguistic (i.e., lingual) object having some "specific" psycho-social functions. The task of a theory of literature can be described in that perspective as the explicit and systematic account of these "specific" aspects of the type of communication or semiotic process we conventionally call "literary." This task implies that we have to formulate the condition, the rules, and the functions that delimit the set of literary texts against other types of texts and the underlying system of "literary behavior" against other manifestations of linguistic, esthetic, etc., i.e., psycho-social behavior.[82]

In order to carry out this task, two different but complementary aims are formulated. The first aim is: "the construction of an explicit theory of the *formal* structure of literary texts, i.e., of the underlying system *abstractly* determining the generation of literary texts." The second aim is: "the construction of a more empirical theory of the *relations* between (1) this abstract system and its concrete manifestations in processes of communication [and] (2) texts and their psycho-social environment or context, i.e., the set of their conditions and functions."[83]

Using generative grammar as an analogical model for a grammar of literature, we must deduce and test the answers to certain questions.

As for the text itself we are confronted with questions that are similar to those raised in transformational linguistics: how is it possible that a writer/reader can produce/interpret an indefinite number of different literary texts by using only a limited (derived) competence, and how can these texts be differentiated from non-literary texts in order to be able to say that they can perform their specific function in the communication-process? Briefly: which system underlies the regularities of literary texts?[84]

Dijk deduces various levels of literary grammars: a grammar of texts in general (literary and non-literary), a grammar of literary texts, and grammars of types of literary texts such as a grammar of the novel and a grammar of poetry.[85] As with the generative grammar dealing with the sentence, Dijk is interested in universal literary structures, but he says that it might prove more helpful to begin with a type of literary text and construct a grammar of that type "just as in linguistics we first construct a grammar of language L^1 before we can proceed to considering more universal structures hoping that L^1 reflects at least some of them. A general theory of epic or folk-narrative has in this way been searched for. . . . Clearly such *sub-grammars* in literature can much more easily be tested on existing texts."[86]

NARRATOLOGY

A. J. Greimas is a leading figure among those who are engaged in the structural study of narrative, and a description of his conceptualization of the study will provide a concrete framework for discussing the various elements in narratology. Greimas quite consciously begins with the actual results achieved or theories formulated by scholars in other areas; but he questions, develops, and modifies the work of others to produce models for the study of narrative. Greimas's scholarly interests have evolved from lexicography to semantics and semiotics. The final chapters of *Sémantique structurale* (1966) contain reflections upon the actantial models of Propp and Souriau, a study of models of transformation which would account for the development of narrative situations, and an application of his "constitutional model" to the work of Bernanos. In *Du Sens* (1970) one of the four major parts is completely devoted to the narrative, and sections of the other part are related to the study of narrative.

In his works on narrative, Greimas attempts to uncover the elements which are essential for determining the meaning (*sens*) or the meaning-effect of the narrative by both deduction and induction, by theoretical studies, and by actual analyses of myth and folklore. The basic question dealt with in theory and analysis is how the anthropomorphic universe of narrative is constituted from the fundamental abstract structures. In order to appreciate the work of Greimas, careful and detailed attention must be given to the tedious and laborious process by which he traces the narrative from the level of manifestation through the intermediate anthropomorphic level to the most profound logical level and also expands the narrative structures from the basic "narrative statement" to the "performance," and the "performance series." The work of Greimas, as the semiotic study of narrative generally, is a work in progress, and the importance of the following description of his theories is the broad conceptualization, not primarily the multitude of specific details, many of which have been and will be altered in the process of Greimas's activities.

Greimas establishes his works in semantics and narratology on one preliminary epistemological choice. The choice is "to consider perception as the non-linguistic place where the apprehension of signification is situated."[87] This choice is provisional, he admits, but it is the epistemological attitude of the human sciences of the twentieth century in general and it appears acceptable to our historical epoch. Indeed, "it is difficult to imagine other pertinent criteria acceptable to all."[88] To affirm that significations are situated on the level of perception is to limit exploration to the sensible world, to the world of common sense.

Greimas establishes his works in semantics and narratology on one of the natural sciences and the qualitative approach of the humane sciences. A rigorous qualitative description, indeed, can do away with the hiatus between the natural and humane sciences; it can provide movement from the obscure world of meaning of the humane sciences to the world of the effect of meaning of the natural sciences, reconciling quantity and quality, nature and man. Greimas quotes an illustration from Lévi-Strauss to show how quantitative description aids the qualitative aspects of life.

> Modern chemistry reduces the variety of tastes and smells to different combinations of five elements: carbon, hydrogen, oxygen, sulphur, and nitrogen. By means of tables of the presence and absence of the elements and estimates of proportions and minimum amounts necessary for them to be perceptible, it succeeds in accounting for differences and resemblances which were previously excluded from its field on account of their "secondary" character.[89]

The initial operational concept of Greimas is borrowed from Hjelmslev:

the reciprocal relation of *signifiant* and *signifié*. *Signifiant* is the name given to "the element or the group of elements which make possible the appearance of signification on the level of perception and which are recognized at the same time as exterior to man." *Signifié*, on the other hand, designates "the significations which are recovered by the *signifiant* and manifested by means of its existence."[90] Greimas rejects the notion which defines *signifiant* as the relation between signs and things, and he also rejects the supplementary notion of referent which is often introduced as a compromise.[91]

The types of correlation between *signifiant* and *signifié* help us to understand the basic operational terminology of Greimas: (1) *Signifiants* belonging to the same order of the senses (sight, hearing, touch, etc.) can serve for the constitution of autonomous signifying units (union of *signifiant* and *signifié*). Natural languages and music are examples. (2) *Signifiants* of different orders of the senses can embrace an identical or equivalent *signifié*. An oral *signifiant* may have a written *signifié*. (3) Several *signifiants* can be combined in one simple global process of signification, as words and gestures.[92] Greimas concludes from these facts that a classification of *signifiés* is not possible from the status of *signifiants*, that signification is independent of the nature of the *signifiant* and the means by which it is manifested. It does not make sense to say that painting carries a painting signification or that music possesses a musical signification. Significations are ultimately simply human.[93]

The fact of different levels of signification is important for the study of narrative and is dealt with by Greimas early in *Sémantique structurale*. He points out that in natural languages different levels can be seen easily. German or English can be studied in a linguistic metalanguage using French, for example. Also, the words used in criticism of music or painting constitute a metalanguage. Greimas gives four different levels of language: (1) the object language, or the natural language; (2) the descriptive language—metalanguage to the natural language—or a translation language in which the signification contained in the object language may be formulated; (3) the methodological language which defines the descriptive concepts and verifies the internal cohesion; and (4) the epistemological language, capable of describing every signifying unit (*signifiant* and *signifié*) independently of the natural languages which serve for their description.

The levels must be studied inductively and deductively. For example, if description is a translation of an object language into a descriptive language, to be adequate it must adhere to reality, and inductive methods are valuable in determining the adherence or lack of adherence to reality.[94] But an inductive description cannot always encompass the limits of a given signifying unit; it does not attain the level of a general methodology. On the epistemological level of language, for example, deduction is absolutely necessary, for logic is the language of the postulates which are situated on this level.[95]

In Chapter Five of *Sémantique structurale*, "The Semiological Level," Greimas speaks of two autonomous levels of language prior to manifestation in discourse. The two levels are the semiological and semantic levels, and together they constitute the immanent universe of signification prior to manifestation in discourse. Greimas declares that, in order to do justice to structural semantics, the logical priority and autonomy of the semiological structure must be affirmed.[96] He compares symbolism and semiology to introduce some elements of a possible definition of the semiological level. One could say that semiology constitutes a kind of *signifiant* which articulates the symbolic *signifié* and constitutes it in a network of differential significations. Yet, semiology is indifferent to the symbolism with which it is involved. One and the same semiological level can serve to articulate different symbolism.[97] Yet, using the idea of symbolism, one could interpret the semiological level as "the form of content making possible the appearance of a particular symbolism."[98]

The principles outlined by Greimas are applied to lexemes as well as larger units in *Sémantique structurale*, but in recent work he devotes attention almost entirely to narrative. The deductions of Greimas and the application of the work of previous scholars, such as Propp, in the study of narrative are devoted to trying to conceptualize the course which the mind follows in constructing cultural objects. "Perhaps out of the desire for intelligibility," Greimas says, "we can imagine that the human mind, in order to achieve the construction of cultural objects (literary, mythical, pictural, etc.), starts with simple elements and follows a complex course, encountering on its way constraints to which it must submit, as well as choices which it can make."[99] Greimas sees the *level of appearance* of narration as the level where *language* exercises constraints. The linguistic project concerned with the surface level of appearance consists of setting up a mechanism of a unifying or generating character which accounts for the production of an unlimited number of sentences from simple elements and from original kernels. In their turn, the sentences are transformed and combined into discourse. Greimas is not concerned primarily with the linguistic surface level; he is concerned with the immanent level where narrativity is situated and organized prior to its manifestation, the semiotic level. *Narrative structures* are those units on the immanent level which utilize linguistic units on the surface level and correspond to linguistic structures of narrative on that level. It is the narrative structures on the immanent level which produce the meaningful discourse articulated in statements.[100]

Prior to the manifestation of signification on the level of surface in the various forms, Greimas sees two different but related events: the articulation of content (such content as can be imagined at this abstract level) and the manipulation and arrangement of the content leading toward manifestation. A semiotic theory which will attempt to account for the immanent level must have a place, therefore, for a fundamental semantics and a fundamental grammar. This semantics is not the same as the semantics on the level of linguistic manifestation. The fundamental semantics is seen by Greimas as "the elementary structure of signification," indeed as an axiomatic structure. "This elementary structure . . . may be conceived as logical development of a semic binary category, of the type white versus black, the terms of which are in a relation of contrariness, each being at the same time susceptible of projecting a new term which would be its contradictory, the contradictory terms in turn being able to contract a relation of presupposition with regard to opposite contrary terms."[101] The Square of Opposition used in deductive logic pictures the contradictory and contrary relationship. The first articulation of meaning in a semantic micro-universe is accounted for by this logical elementary structure of signification.

The elementary structure also manipulates the content without being identified with the content. That is, it is responsible for the fundamental grammar. Greimas indicates that as a grammar it presents a morphology and a syntax. The morphology has the character of a taxonomy in which the terms are defined in relation to one another. The syntax is a group of rules of operation or manipulation of the terms of the morphology. The taxonomic model, then, "is a structure of four terms which are mutually defined by a network of precise relations describable as the correlation between two schemes of two terms each."[102] The syntax is a series of operations effected upon the terms. The taxonomy may be considered the stable relations between terms, and syntax the operations upon these terms. So the relation of contradiction on the level of taxonomy serves to establish the binary schemes. On the level of syntax or operations it serves to deny one of the terms of the scheme and to affirm its contradictory term at the same time.[103]

From "the representation of syntax as a series of operations upon the defined terms of a taxonomic structure," Greimas is able to deduce a property of the grammar: "the syntactic operations are oriented." Moreover, "the recognition of the relationships of the elementary structure" means that "the syntactic operations are not only oriented, but they are also organized in logical series."[104]

Greimas summarizes the characteristics of a fundamental grammar:

1. The narrative grammar is composed of an elementary morphology furnished by the taxonomic model and of a *fundamental syntax which operates upon the taxonomic terms* defined in a preliminary way in relation to one another.

2. The narrative syntax consists of operations effected upon the terms susceptible of being invested with values of content; from this fact, it transforms and manipulates them in denying and affirming them, . . . in *disjoining* and *conjoining* them.

3. The syntactic operations, situated in the established taxonomic framework, are oriented and because of this fact they may be calculated beforehand.

4. These operations, moreover, are *ordered in series* and constitute processes which can be segmented in *operational syntactic units*.[105]

The level on which the fundamental semantics and grammar are located is not the level just prior to manifestation. Between the profound logical level and the surface level is an intermediate semiotic level.

. . . The fundamental grammar which is of a conceptual order receives an anthropomorphic representation (but nonfigurative) on an intermediate semiotic level in order to be able to produce narratives which are manifested in a figurative form (where human or personified actors accomplish the tasks, undergo the tests, attain the aims). It is this anthropomorphic level which is designed by the name of *superficial narrative grammar*, noting that the qualification "superficial" is not used in a pejorative sense but simply indicates that it is a question of semiotic level the grammatical definitions and rules of which are able to pass directly into discourse and linguistic statements with the aid of a final transcodage.[106]

Greimas, then, envisions two levels of grammar below the level of manifestation or two different metalanguages which account for the very same linguistic phenomena on the level of manifestation. The two metalanguages or grammars are equivalent or are isotopes of one another, but they are not of the same form. The fact that the grammars are equivalent means that a segment of one can be transcoded into a segment of the other. On the level of the fundamental grammar, logic prevails and syntactic operations on that level are of a logical character. To the logical syntactic operations on the fundamental level correspond anthropomorphic syntactic *productions* (*les faires*) on the superficial level. The logical operation on the fundamental level is seen as an autonomous metalinguistic process which brackets out any subject of the operation (the grammatical subject, the actor). The production, on the other hand, implies a human subject. Greimas cautions, however, that we must not think of a real performance on the level of the semiotics of the natural world but of a linguistic performance, a performance transcoded in a message.[107]

When the metasemiotic production relates to interpersonal relations or speaking in the superior semiotic system, the production in the interior of the process of communication is in fact an object/message which implies a sender/addresser (*destinateur*) and a receiver/addressee (*destinataire*). Hence, Greimas claims the production on the superficial level is doubly anthropomorphic. In that the production is an activity, it presupposes a subject (actor) and in that it is also a message, it is made into an object and implies the axis of transmission between the addresser and addressee.[108]

Greimas is interested in deducing a model which will explain narrative on the level of surface, and he gives the name *"simple narrative statement"* (*énoncé narratif simple*) to the result of the production on the superficial level. The simple narrative statement is composed of the production (*le faire*) which Greimas terms "function" (F) and the actant (A) (or the subject of the production). One can say, then, that every operation of the fundamental grammar can be converted into a narrative statement, the canonical form of which is F (A). Two points must be kept in mind: the narrative statements are syntactic statements which are independent of content; the two elements of the statement, function and actant, are isotopes of each other. "Every semantic restriction of F will necessarily reverberate upon A and inversely."[109]

Greimas, building upon his assumptions, and by means of a progressive introduction of semantic restrictions, develops a typology of narrative statements and actants. To add the qualification "to desire" to the narrative statement is to install the actant as a subject, as the eventual operator of the performance. It is also to introduce a new type of narrative statement—the modal statement. The statement which can be represented as (1) "Peter is departing" is a descriptive statement, while (2) "John desires that Peter depart" and (3) "Peter desires to depart" are modal statements. The second sentence is a modal statement with a descriptive statement as an object-actant, but the third sentence is the same except that the subject of both statements is identical, that is, "Peter desires that Peter depart." Greimas says, then, that "one can interpret the modal statement as 'the desire of realization' of a program which is present in the form of a descriptive statement but which is at the same time made a part of the modal statement in that it is the object of the modal statement."[110] He expands the typology through the addition of descriptive statements of the order of having and of the order of being along with those of the order of production (le faire); also, the qualifications "to know" (savoir) and "to be able" (pouvoir) along with that of "to desire" produce additional modalities.[111]

Greimas not only expands the typology of narrative statements; he also enlarges the unit on the superficial level. The initial means for constructing a larger unit is the observation that on the level of surface and of intermediate structures there is a polemic representation and a relation of contradiction. "If one admits that the anthropomorphic representation of the contradiction is of a polemic nature, the syntagmatic series—which corresponds to the transformation of content resulting from operations of negation and assertion on the level of fundamental grammar—will appear here as a series of narrative statements, the semantic restrictions of which have the task of conferring on it a character of confrontation and strife."[112]

Postulates necessary for the constitution of this syntagmatic series are:

(a) the existence of two subjects . . . (or of a subject and an antisubject) which correspond to the two contradictory productions, the relation of contradiction being a nonoriented relation;

(b) the semantic restriction of the syntactic production by the establishment of equivalence between the operation of negation and the function of domination resulting from the polemic antagonism;

(c) the recognition of the principle of orientation as valuable for the two levels of grammar: to an orientation of logical operations corresponds an arbitrary choice of the negator subject and of the domination of one of the subjects by the other;

(d) the admission that the dialectical procedure, according to which the negation of one term is at the same time the assertion of the contradictory term, is represented on the level of superficial syntax by two independent narrative statements, the first of which (with its function of domination) corresponds to the moment of negation, and the second of which (with the function of attribution) to the moment of assertion.[113]

Greimas gives the name *"performance"* to the simple syntagm: "If the functions and the actants are the constitutive *elements* of this narrative grammar, if the *narrative statements* are the elementary syntactic forms, the *narrative units*—the pattern of which is represented here by the *performance*—are syntagmatic series of narrative statements."[114]

Before expanding his treatment to include the *performance series*, Greimas makes two points concerning the performance. Performance is a narrative unit, and the statements which constitute it are equivalent to logical operations on the fundamental level. These operations are oriented; hence, there is orientation, or more properly, a relationship of implication, on the level of superficial grammar. If, for example, the orientation of the order of statements is: $EN_1 \rightarrow EN_2 \rightarrow EN_3$, the implication is simply orientation in an inverse sense: $EN_3 \supset EN_2 \supset EN_1$. This principle of implication is important for the level of manifestation with its rules of ellipsis and catalysis. The presence of the last unit in a series of implication is sufficient to reestablish the earlier units in the series.

Greimas applies the principle earlier established concerning modal statements to set up different types of performance. Statements characterized by "desire" install the subject as a potentiality of performance. Those characterized by "knowing" and "being able" determine the eventual performance in two different ways, as a performance issuing from knowledge or being founded upon ability. So, Greimas distinguishes between performances characterized by "knowing how," in which the subject acts on the level of manifestation by illusion and fraud, and performances characterized by "being able to," where the subject only uses his energy or power, real or magical.[115]

The unit of performance is enlarged by deducing a performance series. To this point, Greimas has emphasized the narrative statement on the superficial level (which corresponds to the logical assertion of the fundamental grammar) as a statement of attribution where an object is acquired by the subject. Greimas says that such an attributive statement is a reflexive performance in that the subject is attributed to himself when he is considered as the subject of the descriptive statement (an object of value). Such a reflexible attribution is a particular case of the general scheme of communication or, more general, of the structure of exchange. The structure of exchange can be represented as a statement with three actants—the addresser (sender), the addressee (receiver), and the object of communication. Such a formulation allows clear distinction between two syntactic levels: (1) the level on which the syntactic operator of the assertion is situated—in the surface grammar this is translated as the performer-subject of the attribution, and (2) the level where the transfers occur. The level of transfer is where, through anthropomorphic topological representation, the objects of value can be introduced or withdrawn. The transfer can be interpreted on the superficial level as privation or attribution and (at the same time) on the fundamental level as disjunction or conjunction. Replacing the attributive statement by translative statements means that one statement can represent two logical operations. An object of value is attributed to the dominant subject, but at the same time the dominated subject is deprived of the object of value.

Greimas identifies the topology of the circulation of the objects of value with the deixis of the transfer in terms of the taxonomic model. At this point, the logical elementary structure of signification must be reviewed. From any starting point, X_1 by use of formal logic, a value which is the contradiction of X_1 ($\bar{X}_1$) can be deduced. Then contrary values to each of these may be deduced, X_2 being the contrary value of X_1 and $\bar{X}_2$ being the contrary value of $\bar{X}_1$. These relationships can be presented in a diagram in which contradictory relations are shown by unbroken lines and contrary relations by broken lines:

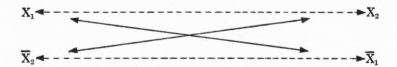

Greimas points out that on the superficial anthropomorphic level there are circulations of value-objects which represent the relationships of terms on the fundamental logical level. To the contradictory terms on the fundamental level are related those conjoined (but not conformed) relations (they correspond to the same axis of contradiction) on the superficial level. To the contrary terms on the fundamental level are related those disjoined but conformed relations of the superficial level (they have a relation of presupposition).

Two courses are possible, then, for the circulation of values interpreted as a series of transfers of objects of value. Greimas uses the functions of Propp to chart the two courses: (1) society suffers a loss, the villain ravishes the daughter of the king, and carries her away in order to hide her; (2) the hero finds in some way the daughter of the king and returns her to her parents. Using the logical square (small d equals deixis):

The first course would be: $F(d_1 \ O \ \bar{d}_1) \ F(d_1 \ O \ d_2)$: Society (d_1) suffers a loss, the villain $(\bar{d}_1)$ ravishes the daughter of the king (O) and carries her elsewhere in order to hide her (d_2). The second course would be $F(d_2 \ O \ \bar{d}_2) \ F(\bar{d}_2 \ O \ d_1)$. The hero $(\bar{d}_2)$ finds in some way (d_2) the daughter of the king (O) and returns her to her parents (d_1).

Greimas notes that the Russian tales manifest a circular system of values by using successively two performance subjects and by valuing one of the slots (that of the hero) to the detriment of the other (that of the villain). On the other hand, the myths of origin generally consider the absence of an object of value as an original situation and the gaining of the value is accomplished by one course—the second course above. Of course, the acquisition of value by d_1 is necessarily and simultaneously privation of value for d_2; so the same narrative is one of victory and defeat, depending on the viewpoint.

The logical operations of fundamental grammar are used by the syntax of transfers and, doubling the courses of the execution of meaning, organize the narrative as a process of creation of values. Therefore, it is the topological syntax of transfers which is charged with the administration of meaning in the narrative and therefore is the principal armature.

> So, from the formal point of view, as the translative statements are the terminal statements of performance and imply them logically, the syntactic courses, expressed in the form of transfers, really constitute syntagmatic series of performances: that is to say, they are syntactic units of a superior rank.[116]

The topological syntax of transfers is a purely descriptive syntax of operations, but another syntax of operators can also be constructed, a metasemiotic level which will explain the transfers of values. The syntactic operators will be subjects of a possibility of a particular production which would make them able to accomplish an operation of transfer. This potentiality is a modality, knowing how to, or being able to. So performances which are designed for the acquisition and transfer of modal values can be distinguished from those characterized by the acquisition and transfer of objective values. One series institutes subjects as operators and creates the potentiality, while the other effects the operations and actualizes the potentialities. So a syntagmatic series of performances having to do with the transfer of modal values parallels that having to do with the transfer of objective values.

The initial operator-actant which unfolds the entire syntactic course is created by a contract which institutes the subject by the attribution of the modality of wishing. ". . . it is the desire of the subject which makes him able to accomplish the first performance which is marked by the attribution of the modal value of knowing how to or being able to."[117] Hence, there is a hierarchy of modal values:

to desire → to know how to → to be able to → performance

which is basic for the syntagmatic series of performances.

Certain implications are pointed out by Greimas: (1) only the acquiring of the modal value of being-able-to enables the operator-actant to accomplish the performance which gives him the objective value; (2) the acquiring of the modal value of knowing-how-to results in the attribution of the being-able-to-perform which is necessary for accomplishing the production; (3) the mediation of knowing-how-to is not necessary for acquisition of the being-able-to-produce—some subjects are able by nature while others obtain power by an initial acquisition of knowing-how-to.[118]

Greimas applies the previously deduced polemic nature of narrative to establish that two courses for the transfer of modal values are to be conceived. In one the subject acquires power by means of a knowledge obtained, while another subject loses knowledge and power. In the other case, the subject acquires knowledge because of a recognized power while the other subject loses power and hence knowledge.

Greimas sees the unfolding of the narrative on the level of superficial narrative syntax (corresponding to the logical operation on the level of profound grammar) represented

. . . as the establishment of a conjunctive contractual relation between a sender and a subject-receiver, following a spatial disjunction *between* the two actants. The achievement of the narrative would be marked, on the contrary, by a spatial conjunction and a final transfer of values, instituting a new contract by a new distribution of values, objective as well as modal.[119]

After summarizing the elements of his syntactic organization of narrative, Greimas explains the value of such an achievement:

Such a narrative grammar . . . would have a deductive and analytical form at the same time. It would trace a group of courses for the manifestation of meaning: from elementary operations of fundamental grammar which constrain the routes of processes of actualization of signification to the combination of syntagmatic series of superficial grammar which are only anthropomorphic representations of these operations. The contents would be invested by the medium of performances in narrative statements which are organized in linear sequences of canonical statements related to one another, as links in a single chain, by a series of logical implications. Possessing such sequences of narrative statements, one will be able to imagine the linguistic manifestations of the narrativized signification with the aid of a rhetoric, stylistics, but also with the aid of a linguistic grammar.[120]

The quest of Greimas for laws of a universal narrative grammar unites the various students of narrative. Indeed, three postulates or principles seen in the work of Greimas are common to all students of narrative: the definition of narrative, the distinction between different planes of narrative structures, and belief in the possibility of articulating the series of events in sequences of action and of developing a "lexicon" of narratives and rules of combination of such narrative units.[121]

The unity and agreement of the narratologists must not be overstated or the productive differences will not be appreciated. The problem of Dilthey insofar as the general and particular, the universally valid and historically conditioned, is also the problem of students of narrative. Dilthey rejected any metaphysical or speculative approach which understands and interprets man and his cultural expressions apart from concrete historical experiences. Yet he wanted to define objective and universal principles for understanding. How would he react to the approach of Greimas, who deduces a system from a purely logical base? Would he agree with Bremond's criticism of Greimas's scheme as "a Platonic nostalgia"[122] or with Barthes's comparison of the attempt to develop a narrative structure with the activity of "Buddhists whose aesthetic practices enable them to see a whole landscape in a bean"?[123]

Claude Bremond believes that there is a logic in the development of the narrative, that the actions are not joined empirically according to chance.[124] But he disagrees that the logical constitutional model of Greimas can apply to narrative structure generally. His initial disagreement with Greimas is over Greimas's distinction between the fundamental and superficial levels. Bremond agrees with the distinction between a plane of immanent narrative structures and a plane of manifestation (linguistic and non-linguistic). He even agrees that some narration may be characterized by this bi-plane structure. "But the question is to know if this 'bi-plane' structure is essential to narrative in general."[125] Bremond feels that to explain the narrative as the result of a series of hypostases from the constitutional model is to deny real meaning to what the narrative form figures, what it represents. "It is true that the narrative form is particularly apt to figure, by comparison or by metaphor, the play of abstract ideas. But this is precisely the point: it *figures* that which it is not."[126]

One particular limitation of the constitutional model is that "the temporality characteristic of the superficial narrative is limited to the events of human interest."[127] Why must all narrative assume anthropomorphic character and the "operation" be characterized as a "production" (*le faire*) involving a subject (human or non-human)? Bremond denies that the narrative statement (EN) can be represented as F (A); he declares that "EN = E (event)."[128]

As far as the application of the constitutional model to narrative structure, Bremond (1) admits that the axis of contradictory terms can receive a narrative interpretation, but (2) doubts whether the axes of the contrary and subcontrary terms concern the narrative directly, and (3) sees no possibility of the relations of implication playing a determining role in the production of the events of the narrative. "This relation is non-temporal and cannot cease to be non-temporal: it would be absurd to give it a temporalized interpretation and to wish, for example, that the term 'implying' (rich) and the term 'implied' (not poor) succeed one another as two distinct chronological events, the first relating to the second as a cause producing its effect."[129]

In spite of some logical difficulties in the application of the constitutional model to narrative, Bremond judges that the major problem is not that the constitutional model is radically wrong or inoperative. The major problem is that the constitutional model does not allow the essential notion of narrative to be seen. "It fails to recognize a law of narrativity: the mental faculty, or rather the obligation of narrative being developed as a series of options to be chosen by the narrator, at each moment of the narrative, from among various ways of continuing his story."[130] For Greimas, "the essence of the narrative is concentrated upon a play (inter-action) of non-temporal concepts, transcending in the process the events which are recounted."[131] For Bremond, the essence of narrative is imma-nent in the process itself in which choices are made from several possi-bilities in order to continue and complete the narrative. "For us the impression of liberty, truth, and beauty . . . is not an illusion which marks 'the play of semiotic constraints.' If play there is, it is not imposed, it is a play *above* the constraints, a liberating experience which uses and moves beyond the constraints."[132]

With a view of the essence of narrative as a process involving choices from among a host of possibilities, Bremond develops the logic of narra-tive as the logic of choices which are possible. He maintains the notion of "functions" as actions and events which combine into sequences to form a narrative, and he sees the elementary sequence as: potentiality, actual-ization, and achievement. With each function, there is choice. The basic pattern can be diagrammed simply:[133]

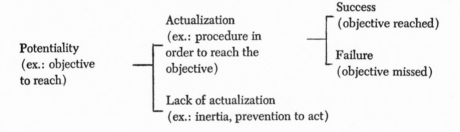

Bremond sees that the elementary sequences can be combined in dif-ferent ways to produce complex sequences, "kinds of 'archetypical' pat-terns reproducing the evolution of most frequent situations."[134] Bremond gives three typical patterns. The "end to end" sequence is simply one elementary sequence followed by another elementary sequence in which the final function of the first sequence becomes the opening function of the second sequence. The "enclave" sequence is the development of an elementary sequence in the interior of another elementary sequence which either mediates the movement in the first sequence from potentiality to actualization or from actualization to accomplishment. The "joining" sequence is the simultaneous development of two elementary sequences; the same material process, when viewed from two different perspectives, may be translated differently. The three figures below show the forms taken by the "end to end," "enclave," and "joining" sequences:

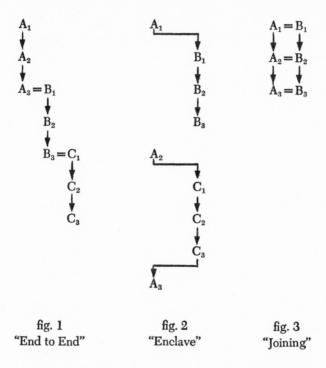

fig. 1   fig. 2   fig. 3
"End to End"   "Enclave"   "Joining"

In his early work, Bremond stressed simply the logical reconstruction of the potentialities of the story, considering the folk tale as a development of an action going through phases of degradation and improvement according to a continuous cycle. The narrator has the obligation of resolving the problems and releasing the tensions created by the narrative, but, except for this limitation, the narrator may go on and on, adding new incidents to the story.[135] In later work, Bremond defines the function not simply as an action or a process but also by the relationship of a subject to the process. The structure of the narrative rests not only upon the sequence of actions but also upon an agency of roles. In *Logique du récit*, Bremond catalogs the narrative roles, the major roles being patient (receiver of the action), agent, influencer, ameliorator and protector, degradator and frustrater, acquirer of merit, and retributor.

Bremond summarizes the results of his study of function and roles:

> We have decomposed the narrative into a complex of roles, simultaneous or successive; each role in turn is analyzed in combination with a process, each *process* can be viewed as having three stages of development: (potentiality, passage to action, and achievement) and moreover, the narrative can refer to a process not in order to signify its potentiality, passage to action, or achievement, but in order to deny these very matters; the processes which combine to define the roles maintain certain syntagmatic relations with one another (succession, simultaneity, causality, implication). Moreover, each process maintains a relation of predication to a subject with one or more *persons* which the narrative ordinarily designates by a proper name and which can be either *patients* or *agents* of the processes; the agents in their turn can be seen as either voluntary or involuntary initiators of processes.[136]

Bremond, then, sees the essential categories of an "elementary narrative proposition" to be: the syntactic relationship, the process, the phase of the process (potentiality, passage to action, or achievement), volitional quality (voluntary or involuntary), the name of the agent, and the name of the patient. For analysis each of these elements is to be identified, because together they produce the narrative proposition. The important point for Bremond is that the logic of the narrative be related to the possible choices and to the roles of persons involved in the actions in the choices made: "It is a question of the study of the principal narrative roles, that is to say, of the universes which appear in the tracking of the act of narration."[137]

Tzvetan Todorov has used the model of the sentence to develop a set of categories which can be used to analyze narrative. He uses the work of Propp on functions and the work of Greimas on actants. *Proper nouns* are agents which are subjects or objects of the action, verbs are actions which modify the situation; *adjectives* do not alter the situation in which they appear but correspond to the quality of the agents. Actions can be categorized as to *status* (negation is one possible status), *modality* (imperative and optative, for example), and *point of view*.[138]

A minimal narrative is a sequence of clauses perceived by the reader as a completed story. "This impression of completion is caused by a modified repetition of the initial clause; the first and the last clause will be identical but they will either have a different mood or status, for instance, or they will be seen from different points of view." Todorov sees different relationships between the clauses in the sequence, and on the basis of this relationship suggests different categories of narrative organization.[139] Causal and chronological relationships exist between the clauses of a narrative, but the only relationship between the units is not that of causal or chronological succession. The units must also have a relationship of transformation; hence, there are two principles of transformation.[140]

Simple transformations are those in which there is modification of a basic predicate (in its positive or negative form) with or without a modal component. Todorov illustrates this by a unit in a tale from the *Decameron*. In the particular unit, Todorov says, "Ricardo is unhappy in the beginning, happy at the end: thus negation. He wants to possess Catella, then he does possess her: thus, a modal transformation." Complex transformations are those in which "the initial predicate is accompanied by a second one, so that paradoxically, 'to plan' or 'to learn' designates an autonomous action, yet, at the same time, can never appear by itself: one always plans for *another* action." Units from the same tale from the *Decameron* illustrate the complex transformation. In the tale, "the very same action is presented three times: first, there is Ricardo's project of drawing Catella into the bathing establishment; then there is the erroneous perception of this scene by Catella, who thinks she is meeting her husband; finally, the real situation is revealed." The relationship between these propositions is more complex than in the first instance. The relationship between the first and third propositions is the relationship of a plan and its realization. In the second and third propositions, we see the relationship of opposition of an erroneous and a correct perception of an event.[141]

Todorov is able to catalog three types of narrative organization on the basis of the kind of transformation contained in the narrative. The mythological type organization is that which combines the principle of succession and simple transformation. The gnoseological type of narrative organization is that in which the principle of succession is assisted by the complex type of transformation. Gnoseological narratives are those "narratives in which the importance of the event is less than that of our perception of the event, of the degree of knowledge that we have about it."[142] A third type of narrative organization is proposed by Todorov which is not mythological or gnoseological. He calls this type of organization "ideological, insofar as it is an abstract rule, an idea, which produces the different adventure." Todorov illustrates the ideological organization by three episodes in a tale analyzed by Propp. On the way in search of her brother, a little girl requests information. The stove promises information to her on the condition that she eat some of its bread. The girl insolently refuses to meet the demand. Next she meets an apple tree, then a river. These propositions are analogous to the first in that there is the same insolence in the reply of the little girl. Todorov says that the relationship among these three episodes is not that of transformation. "Rather than transformations of one another, these propositions appear to be *variations* of a single situation, or paralleled applications of the same rule."[143]

Todorov's early work was an attempt to use the homological model of four classes to describe plot, but he felt that the arbitrariness necessary to force actions to fit the structure made that model questionable. In his *Grammaire du Decameron* he began to use a metalanguage based on the sentence because he felt it could be used on all levels and would not force actions into a particular structure. The sentence model does allow movement from the purely logical level to the more empirical level. Some of the categories of his metalanguage, however, seem to exceed the sentence model.[144]

Perhaps the approach *within* the broad structural school which is most in contrast with Greimas's is that of Barthes. Barthes is interested in the very opposite of a timeless meaning imposed by logical constraints. He opts for an unlimited plurality of meanings constrained only by readers who actively participate as structuring elements of the writing. S/Z, Barthes's dissection of *Sarrasine*, a little-known novella of Balzac, presents most vividly Barthes's view that "the goal of literary work (of literature as work) is to make the reader no longer a consumer, but a producer of the text." He contrasts the readerly text and the writerly text. The readerly text is negative, reactive; it gives the reader only the freedom to accept or reject the text. The writerly text is positive, open; it is *"ourselves writing*, before the infinite play of the world . . . is traversed, intersected, stopped, plasticized by some singular system . . . which reduces the plurality of entrances, the opening of networks, the infinity of languages."[145]

The explosion of meaning in S/Z was prepared for in Barthes's early writing. In *Essais* he declared, "Writing is but an open-ended proposition to which we will never know the answer."[146] The concept of an open work becomes a major motif in *Critique et vérité*: "The work is always in a prophetic situation . . . requiring the symbol to seek the symbol. . . . The symbol is not an image, but the plurality of meanings."[147] S/Z, however, is unique not only because it contains the essential points of Barthes's literary theories but also because it illustrates the very theoretical points which Barthes advocates; it is a detailed textual analysis showing how the text actually produces meanings.

Barthes posits for purposes of discussion and interpretation (by "interpretation" he does not mean giving a meaning but appreciating the "plural" which constitutes a text) an "ideal text," a "triumphant plural, unimpoverished by any constraint of representation (of imitation)."[148] The text is "a galaxy of signifiers" to which we gain access by numerous entrances. Even moderately plural texts can be appreciated by means of connotation. Connotation "is a determination, a relation, an anaphora, a feature which has the power to relate itself to anterior, ulterior, or exterior mentions, to other sites of the text (or of another text)." Connotation is not mere association of ideas, however. Association of ideas "refers to the system of a subject" while connotation is "a correlation immanent in the text, in the texts; or again, one may say that it is an association made by the text-as-subject within its own system."[149]

Denotation, in Barthes's view an illusion, "no more than the *last* of the connotations," is important also in the appreciation of the text.[150] Barthes describes connotation (and denotation) topically, analytically, topologically, semiologically, dynamically, historically, functionally, structurally, and ideologically. *Topically*, connotations are meanings, but meanings which are not in the conventional dictionary or grammar. *Structurally*, denotation and connotation, supposedly different systems, "enable the text to operate like a game, each system referring to the other according to the requirements of a certain illusion." This game has an ideological value in that it affords the classic text a certain innocence, for denotation appears "to be telling us something simple, literal, primitive; something *true*, in relation to which all the rest . . . is literature." Connotation *functions* to corrupt the "purity of communication." It is a "static" which is deliberately introduced into the "fictive dialogue between author and reader." It is a "painstakingly elaborated" countercommunication. *Historically*, connotation induces meanings (not just lexical meanings) that are apparently recoverable and, thereby, establishes a literature of the signified as over against the literature of the signifier. *Dynamically*, connotation "is a subjugation which the text must undergo." Meaning, then, is a force. From the *semiological* perspective, "each connotation is the starting point of a code" or "the articulation of a voice which is woven into the text." Connotation, *topologically*, is what makes possible a dissemination of meanings, "spread like gold dust on the apparent surface of the text."[151]

The description of connotation from an analytical point of view enables us to follow more intelligently the structural method of Barthes: "Analytically, connotation is determined by two spaces: a sequential space, a series of orders, a space subject to the successivity of sentences, in which meaning proliferates by layering; and an agglomerative space, certain areas of the text correlating other meanings outside the material text and, with them, forming 'nebulae' of signifieds."[152] Of course, all the while, the reader/writer of the text, the "I" approaching the text, "is already itself a plurality of other texts, of codes which are infinite or, more precisely, lost. . . . I am not hidden within the text, I am simply irrecoverable from it: my task is to move, to shift systems whose perspective ends neither at the text nor at the 'I.' "[153]

Barthes outlines a step-by-step method of analysis and commentary appropriate for the purpose of plural reading. The method is slow, dispersive, non-penetrating, moving to the last detail. Barthes indicates that the step-by-step method "is never anything but the *decomposition* (in the cinematographic sense) of the work of reading: a *slow motion*, so to speak, neither wholly image nor wholly analysis."[154] The text, or "the tutor signifier," is first of all cut up into a series of brief, contiguous fragments, which Barthes calls lexias, "since they are units of reading."[155] The cutting up is arbitrary and implies no methodological responsibility. It bears on the signifier, while the analysis itself bears totally on the signified. The lexia may include one word, a few words, or several sentences. Barthes simply says that a lexia is "the best possible space in which we can observe meanings," and the dimension of the lexia must be empirically determined, varying according to "the moments of the text." Across the lexia, the artificial articulations of signifiers, are shifts and repetitions of the signifieds. The systematic discernment of the signifieds is the object of analysis, but this does not have the purpose of establishing "the truth of the text" but aims at the purity of the text. All of the textual signifiers, lexias, can be grouped into five major codes. The codes are voices which together weave the text. Writing, then, is "a stereographic space where the five codes, the five voices, intersect."[156] What the reader inventories, then, is the units which result from the codes; the reader is able to do this because of the relationship of the unit to "the remainder of a catalog." We note the units resulting from the code because "they are so many fragments of something that has always been *already* read, seen, done, experienced; the code is the wake of that *already.*" "The Kidnapping," Barthes declares, "refers to every kidnapping ever written."[157]

Barthes uses analogies to help describe how the codes enter the text. One analogy is that of the production of lace:

> The text, while it is being produced, is like a piece of Valenciennes lace created before us under the lace-maker's fingers: each sequence undertaken hangs like the temporarily inactive bobbin waiting while its neighbor works; then, when its turn comes, the hand takes up the thread again, brings it back to the frame; and as the pattern is filled out, the progress of each thread is marked with a pen which holds it and is gradually moved forward: thus the terms of the sequence: they are positions held and then left behind in the course of a gradual invasion of meaning. This process is vital for the entire text.[158]

Each code, or voice, is a thread; the grouping of codes forms a braid. Alone, the thread (code, voice) does no labor; but when the inert threads are intertwined, "there is labor, there is transformation."[159]

Another analogy is that of a musical score. To appreciate this analogy, a closer look at the five codes is necessary. The code of actions (the proairetic code, the empiric voice) is a code related to acts which are of a sequential nature. In the reading, certain data are amassed under the generic titles for action such as *stroll, murder, rendezvous.* The basis for the code is strictly empirical. Barthes indicates that the reading results from "a patrimonial horde of human experiences," which can be either "a practical reservoir of trivial everyday acts" or "a written corpus of novelistic models."[160] The sequences of the code of actions "are generally open to catalysis, to branching, and can form 'trees'; . . . when subjected to a logico-temporal order, they constitute the strongest armature of the readerly; . . . by their typically sequential nature, simultaneously syntagmatic and organized, they can form the favored raw material for a certain structural analysis of narrative."[161]

The hermeneutic code is defined by Barthes as involving "all the units whose function it is to articulate in various ways a question, its response, and the variety of chance events which can either formulate the question or delay its answer; or even constitute an enigma and lead to its solution."[162] The function of the hermeneutic code is related by Barthes to the poetic code of Jakobson. He notes that rhyme "structures the poem according to the expectation and desire for recurrence," and suggests that "the hermeneutic terms structure the enigma according to the expectation and desire for its solution."[163] The hermeneutic code causes the dynamics of the text to have a paradoxical nature. It is a "static dynamics" in that the sentences unfold the story and help move it along, while the hermeneutic code delays the flow of the story. The hermeneutic code labors to arrest the enigma and to keep it open. Barthes compares the hermeneutic narrative with the conventional image of the sentence. To narrate is to raise the question as if it were a subject. The predication is delayed, but when the predicate comes, the sentence (the narrative) is complete.[164] Under the hermeneutic code can be listed the various terms by which an enigma can be "distinguished, suggested, formulated, held in suspense and finally disclosed."[165]

The code of actions and the hermeneutic code impose their terms according to an irreversible order. In comparison with the musical score, the code of actions, the sequence and cadence of familiar gestures, sustains the score, causing the regular flow and bringing everything together, like the strings. The hermeneutic code also sings and flows smoothly, moving "by accidentals, arabesques, and controlled ritardandos through an intelligible progression."[166] The series of enigmas of the hermeneutic code, their delayed resolution, is like the melody often given the woodwinds. Barthes likens the development of an enigma to that of a fugue: "both contain a *subject*, subject to an *exposition*, a *development* . . . , a *stretto* . . . , and a *conclusion*."[167]

The three remaining codes correspond to "what stands out, what flashes forth, what emphasizes and impresses" in the musical score.[168] These three codes establish connections outside the constraint of time, permutable, reversible connections. The cultural or referential codes (the voice of science) are "résumés of common knowledge."[169] All the citations of the cultural codes, taken together, form a "miniature version of encyclopedic knowledge." The cultural code is the code of the "everyday 'reality' in relation to which the subject adapts himself, lives."[170] When all the knowledge of the cultural code is collected, the monster of ideology is created which produces proverbial statements which never question their utterances and which provide an intolerant reading.[171] The semic code (the voice of the person) according to Barthes is "a connotator of persons, places, objects, of which the signified is a *character*." (A seme is the smallest possible semantic component of a word.) The person, from this perspective, is a collection of semes. Sarrasine, then, is the sum and point of convergence of: turbulence, artistic gift, independence, excess, femininity, ugliness, composite nature, impiety, love of whittling, will, etc.[172] The naming of the semes is the essence of the reader's activity: "to read is to struggle to name, to subject the sentences of a text to a semantic transformation."[173] Of course, this activity is erratic. Transformation will hesitate among several names: "If we are told that Sarrasine had *one of those strong wills that know no obstacle*,' what are we to read? *will, energy, obstinacy, stubbornness*, etc.?"

The symbolic field (the voice of symbol) "is the place for multivalence and for reversibility."[174] Antithesis is the formal device on which the symbolic code is based. If the text gives two items as oppositions, then the groundwork is laid for "a vast symbolic structure" which can "lend itself to many substitutions and variations. . . ."[175] The first manifestation of the symbolic code in *Sarrasine* is the lexia: "*I was deep in one of those daydreams.*" This finds the narrator seated in a window with an elegant party on one hand and the garden on the other. This opposition of garden/salon is developed in various ways through possible symbolic readings: dance of death/dance of life, nature/man, cold/hot, silence/noise. Barthes distinguishes between paradigmatic opposites, which differ merely by the presence or lack of a simple relationship, and antitheses which separate for eternity. "The antithesis is the battle between two plenitudes set ritually face to face like two fully armed warriors." The joining of two antithetical terms, a mixture or conciliation, constitutes a transgression, a "paradoxism," the code's "ultimate attempt to affect the inexpiable."[176] In *Sarrasine*, it is the narrator's position which mediates the two antitheses (outside and inside, cold and heat, death and life).

Each lexia has units of meaning (connotations) but simply to discern these signifieds is not to establish the truth of the text. The purpose of identifying the units is not to regroup them into some structure which is ultimate. Barthes's analysis proposes the semantic substance: it divides the substance of several kinds of criticism (psychological, psychoanalytical, thematic, historical, structural) but it does not distribute and reorganize the semantic substance so as to provide an ultimate construction or a metameaning. However, Barthes does not deny the privilege of each kind of criticism to come into play, "to make its voice heard, which is the hearing of one of the voices of the text."[177]

The approach of Barthes which emphasizes the reader's reaction to the text and a plurality of meanings seems to rule out any real relationship of the two approaches of Greimas and Barthes. The contrast of the two approaches is seen at the very beginning of S/Z:

> Precisely what the first analysts of narrative were attempting: to see all the world's stories . . . within a single structure: we shall, they thought,

extract from every tale its model, then out of these models we shall make a great narrative structure, which we shall reapply (for verification) to any one narrative: a task as exhausting . . . as it is ultimately undesirable, for the text thereby loses its difference.[178]

For the plural text, Barthes says, "there cannot be a narrative structure, a grammar, or a logic."[179] Yet, Barthes does acknowledge that the matter of narrative structure, grammar, and logic can come forward *"in proportion* (giving this expression its full quantitative value) as we are dealing with incomplete plural texts, texts whose plural is more or less parsimonious."[180] The plural text as presented by Barthes, however, is an ideal; the classic text, for example, is only "moderately plural"; it is "incompletely reversible."[181] The failure of texts to maintain the ideal, then, will allow the development of such things as a narrative structure, a grammar, and a logic. In the treatment of the various codes, it is evident that Barthes's approach allows, even demands, the structuring of the text. The two codes of action and hermeneutic cause a sustained flow of the text; and, while the remaining codes demand that the classic text be viewed as tabular and not linear, the text does follow a logico-temporal order.[182] The logic or generative impulse that explains narrative is suspense, according to Barthes. The narrative is read as a "dilatory area" existing from the question to the answer. In that area the text is preserved by various types of delays which heighten the suspense:

> The dynamics of the text (since it implies a truth to be deciphered) is thus paradoxical: it is a static dynamics; the problem is to maintain the enigma in the initial void of its answer; whereas the sentences quicken the story along, the hermeneutic code performs an opposite action: it must set up *delays* . . . in the flow of the discourse.[183]

Barthes's inclusive pluralistic approach allows for the various types of reading (methods of interpretation) conventional in literary biblical study. These interpretations (readings) are possible not only from the cultural, semic, and symbolic codes but by viewing the totality of these semantic substances uncovered from a particular vantage point. The structural approach remains a vital element in the interpretation proposed by Barthes, although it is not the final approach. In terms of the structural approach to plot as such, Jonathan Culler is convinced that there is no necessary essential contradiction between the approaches of Greimas and Barthes. Barthes focuses upon the reader and the process of organizing the text according to the basic principle of expectation. But the ultimate logic and form are due to the four-term homology emphasized by Greimas.[184]

The application of structural theories and methods to narrative has resulted in an advance beyond the recording of phonological and morphological facts which may or may not be related to conventional meanings of the text. The elements which are important in the structural study of narrative are semantical patterns which are related to the creator and the reader of the narrative. Although the beginning points of analysis differ among the narratologists (ranging from the purely deductive logical approach to the more empirical approach concerned with the plurality of the text) and the "meanings" discerned in analysis also vary (from purely non-historical formal patterns to a multiplicity of changing connotations), there is basic agreement on the definition of narrative as "a specific or autonomous level in the semantic organization of texts, as an *'abstraction par rapport au texte réel.'* "[185] The articulation of the elements is seen as obeying rules and involving invariant patterns. There is basic agreement on the conceptualization of the analysis appropriate to such a narrative in that analysis is related to human response in creation and interpretation. The different conceptualizations and approaches are not mutually exclusive.

Jonathan Culler, for example, mediates the different approaches. He refuses to accept either the view of narrative which begins from a purely logical position and determines from that beginning point the narrative sequence or the more empirical perspective which begins at the conclusion of the narrative process and judges that the end of the process determines the sequence. He opts for "reciprocal determination."[186] Culler postulates that "the hierarchy of kernels and sequences is governed by readers' desire to reach an ultimate summary in which the plot as a whole is grasped in a satisfying form," and he sees the "four-term homology" of Lévi-Strauss and Greimas, the "transformation" of Kristeva, and the "modification of a situation" of Todorov all as expressing that form.[187]

CONCLUSION

The developments in structuralism from the formalists to those engaged in narrative semiotics and the attempts to relate all of these works to the study of literature (discussed in Chapters Four and Five) may result in a new approach to literature, not one which displaces conventional literary criticism but one which supplements it. In such a new approach certain factors which have been touched upon in different contexts or which are implicit in the discussion need to be stressed.

1. An initial point is that the polemical relationship between literary structuralism and conventional literary criticism has faded. Many of the critics cited in the discussion are not linguists but literary critics who see the value of linguistics in the study of literature. Moreover, the literary scholars cited, such as Culler, Fish, and Riffaterre, are critics who direct their use of concepts and procedures from linguistics toward problems in literary criticism. They will not reduce literature to linguistics, but they find values in linguistics.

2. The variety within structural studies in general and the structural study of narrative in particular needs to be observed. While the present work speaks of *structuralism* and *the* structural study of narrative, to be precise we should speak of *structuralisms* and the structural *approaches* to narrative. There is unity within the variety, however, and when viewed within the unity all of the varieties of approaches can make a contribution to literary studies.

3. Meaning in the structural study of narrative is important. A popular view of structuralism in literature a decade ago saw the meaning of the literary work as limited to the relationships set up in the linguistic elements themselves. As we have seen, however, even Jakobson and Lévi-Strauss do not have such a limited view of meaning. However much structuralism calls attention to the meanings which are to be observed in the relationships of the grammatical elements, structuralists see conventional meanings—of words, sentences, and larger literary units.

4. The different levels of meaning and analysis must be observed. Saussure's dichotomy *langue/parole* has been repeated as competence/performance, deep level/surface level, etc., and proper use of linguistics in literary study must examine presuppositions about meaning and function before attention can be appropriately directed to the proper level. It seems to be clear that just as a sentence can be decomposed into its underlying sentence or strings and a story can be abstracted, a narrative can be decomposed into a more abstract form in accord with the human linguistic and literary competence active in creation. If the function of literature is seen as simply the affective appeal which is made by a particular genre, then attention may be directed to the deep structures. As Dilthey pointed out in his discussion of the "type" or the "typical," it is the type of work which makes it effective. For more complete appeal to all of the levels of response of which a reader is capable, however, the

surface level cannot be abandoned. Moreover, the type or genre is obtained only from the particular narrative on the surface level. The core of meaning, as Dilthey says, may be the same for all time, but man is a historical being and is spoken to only in the particular—in a dialectical relationship to the universal.

5. The relationship of history to structuralism is frequently misunderstood. In our study, we have not seen a complete separation of history and structure. Narrative structures cannot be properly identified apart from history. Indeed, from one perspective (that of Dilthey) they do not really exist apart from the historical manifestation. A minimum of historical study is necessary for structuralism. Does historical-critical study not need structural analysis? Or at least does structural analysis not assist historical study? Lévi-Strauss has asserted that his form of structural analysis has confirmed judgments about historical facts, but can structuralism help obtain the meaning of the text which conventional historical study seeks? Obviously, structural study is not aimed at some of the kinds of historical information of interest, for example, to students of the synoptic gospels. Structuralism, per se, is not designed to assist in source, form, and redaction study. It does not look at the material from the perspective of traditional material being modified by the community. Structuralism takes a synchronic approach. It is interested in a study of the material as it exists at a given moment, usually the material in its final literary form; and it looks at the material from the perspective of the creative and structuring ability of human being. It begins (from the surface text, of course) by moving to the more abstract structures which are not influenced by constraints of the material of the real world. To assist conventional historical study, it must move back from the ahistorical abstract level to the historical level. And this it *can* do. Whether or not it does depends upon the person using the structural method. At an early period in the history of structuralism, a great deal was made of the anti-historical ideology of structuralism. The autotelic nature of literary work was taken to mean not only that historical study was not a part of the structural approach but also that historical study was not legitimate for literary works. We have already indicated that the use by Jakobson, Lévi-Strauss, and others of the structural method did not abolish for them all referential and historical dimensions of the text.

The question of the significance or lack of significance of progression in a particular narrative is related to the broader question of history and structure. In the work of Roland Barthes, who prefers to remain close to the actual narrative in analysis, the narrative is seen as consisting of achronic and diachronic codes. Moreover, the different codes of Barthes may be isolated (as seen in S/Z) and different but related (isotopic) readings made. Even Greimas, who stresses the profound logical abstract level, does not completely eliminate diachronic elements. It is true that one possible reading of a narrative is non-temporal, beginning with the logical constitutional model. But another, diachronic, reading is possible. In this reading "the narrative is reduced, in effect, to the text-sequence which manifests the actantial model in discourse, in some way humanizes the significations, and is presented as a succession of human or para-human actions."[188] The very same narrative, then, can be seen as having an achronic structure and a diachronic structure.

> This possibility of a double interpretation only underlines the large num-
> ber of contradictions which the narrative can contain. At the same time, it
> is the affirmation of both permanence and the possibilities of change,
> affirmation of a necessary order and of a liberty which breaks or reestab-
> lishes that order. . . . It is in this perspective that it appears essentially in
> its role of mediation, or rather of multiple mediations: mediations between
> structure and actions, between permanence and history, between society
> and the individual.[189]

Instead of a concern for the achronic structures and the discovery of these structures by means of the diachronic, the procedure could be reversed: the diachronic would be disclosed by means of the achronic structures.

6. The relationship of existential hermeneutics to structuralism and the developing dynamic nature of human competence are matters which have not been of interest to the structuralists concerned with the study of narrative and, therefore, have not been considered in Chapters Four and Five. Nevertheless, these two matters are crucial when man is seen as the central fact in the study of literature. Chapter Six will treat these related matters.

NOTES

1. The term "semiotics" was adopted by the International Association for Semiotic Studies in 1969 to embrace "semiology" and "semiotics," and is in general usage today. See Umberto Eco, *Einführung in die Semiotik*, an author-ized translation of the Italian *La struttura Assente* (1968) by Jürgen Trabant (Munich: Wilhelm Fink Verlag, 1972), p. 17 n. 1. (The 1972 German edition is actually a completely revised form of the 1968 Italian edition. The English

translation, *A Theory of Semiotics* [Bloomington, Ind.: University of Indiana Press, 1976], was not available when the manuscript was prepared.) Some authors, notably Louis Hjelmslev, distinguish sharply and regularly between the two terms however. See Eco, pp. 41–44, and Thomas A. Sebeok, "Semiotics: A Survey of the State of the Art," *Current Trends in Linguistics* 12/1 (The Hague: Mouton, 1974), 211 n. 1.

2. Ferdinand de Saussure, *Course in General Linguistics*, ed. Charles Bally and Albert Sechehaye in collaboration with Albert Riedlinger, trans. Wade Baskin (rev. ed.; London: Peter Owen, 1974), p. 16.

3. *Ibid.*, p. 68.

4. Leonard Bloomfield, "Linguistic Aspects of Science," *International Encyclopedia of Unified Science* (Chicago: The University of Chicago Press, 1955), I, 55; Uriel Weinreich, "Semantics and Semiotics," *International Encyclopedia of Social Sciences* (New York: Macmillan, 1968), XIV, 164; Sebeok, "Semiotics," p. 220.

5. Roland Barthes, *Elements of Semiology*, trans. Annette Lavers and Colin Smith (London: Jonathan Cape, 1967), p. 11.

6. Julia Kristeva, *Le Texte du roman: Approche sémiologique d'une structure discursive transformationnelle* (The Hague: Mouton, 1970), p. 10.

7. Charles Sanders Peirce, *Collected Papers* (Cambridge, Mass.: Harvard University Press, 1931–35), V, 335.

8. *Ibid.*, p. 332.

9. *Ibid.*, p. 302.

10. *Ibid.*, p. 416.

11. *Ibid.*, p. 169.

12. *Ibid.*, p. 189.

13. *Ibid.*, p. 169; see also pp. 185–89; VI, 235.

14. *Ibid.*, V, 186.

15. *Ibid.*, I, 287–305.

16. *Ibid.*, p. 287.

17. *Ibid.*, p. 295.

18. *Ibid.*

19. Umberto Eco, "A Semiotic Approach to Semantics," *Versus* 1 (1971), 25.

20. Jan Mukarovsky, "L'Art Comme Fait Sémiologique," *Actes du huitième Congrès international de philosophie à Prague* (Prague: Comité d'organisation du Congrès, 1936), pp. 1067, 1070. ". . . le signe est une réalité sensible se rapportant à une autre réalité qu'il est destiné a évoquer." "Sans orientation sémiologique, le théoricien de l'art sera toujours enclin à regarder l'oeuvre d'art comme une construction purement formelle, ou même comme le reflet direct soit des dispositions psychiques, voire physiologiques de l'auteur, soit de la réalité distincte exprimée par l'oeuvre, soit de la situation idéologique, économique, sociale, ou culturelle de milieu donné."

21. Thomas G. Winner, "The Aesthetics and Poetics of the Prague Linguistic Circle," *Poetics* 8 (1973), 94–95.

22. See Eco, *Einführung*, pp. 28–29; Sebeok, "Semiotics," pp. 220–21.

23. Eco, *Einführung*, p. 38: ". . . alle kulturellen Prozesse als Kommunikationsprozesse."

24. Sebeok, "Semiotics," p. 211.

25. See Oswald Ducrot and Tzvetan Todorov, *Dictionnaire encyclopédique des sciences du langage* (Paris: Seuil, 1972), p. 17 n. 1.

26. Roland Barthes, *On Racine*, trans. Richard Howard (New York: Hill and Wang, 1964).

27. Gerald Antoine, "La Nouvelle Critique: How Far Has It Got?" *Style* 8 (1974), 18–19.

28. Edward Wasiolek, "Introduction," to Serge Doubrovsky, *The New Criticism in France*, trans. Derek Coltman (Chicago: The University of Chicago Press, 1973), p. 2.

29. Raymond Picard, *New Criticism or New Fraud*, trans. Frank Towne (Seattle: Washington State University Press, 1969).

30. *Ibid.*, p. 26.

31. Wasiolek, "Introduction," p. 9.

32. *Ibid.*, p. 6.

33. Roland Barthes, "Criticism as Language," *Times Literary Supplement* 27 (September 1963).

34. Barthes, *On Racine*, pp. 171–72.

35. Wasiolek, "Introduction," p. 9.

36. *Ibid.*, p. 32.

37. Doubrovsky, *The New Criticism in France*, p. 86. See Picard, *New Criticism*, pp. 119, 117, 128.

38. Doubrovsky, *The New Criticism in France*, p. 58.

39. See Yves Velan, "Barthes," *Modern French Criticism*, ed. John K. Simon (Chicago: The University of Chicago Press, 1972), pp. 336–37.

40. Roland Barthes, "Science versus Literature," *Structuralism: A Reader*, ed. Michael Lane (London: Jonathan Cape, 1970), pp. 411–15. This article originally appeared in the *Times Literary Supplement* of September 28, 1967.

41. In 1909 Axel Olrik published a short article "Epische Gesetze der Volksdichtung," *Zeitschrift für deutsches Altertum* 51 (1909), 1–12, which attempted to delineate principles which govern the composition of folk narrative in general. He calls these "the epic laws of folk narrative" and claims that they apply to all European folklore and to some extent beyond that. But he claims that these laws limit the freedom of composition of oral literature in a much different and more rigid way than in written literature. William O. Hendricks has examined Olrik's view and refuted it by showing parallels between Olrik's laws and observations of literary critics and by demonstrating that a literary work actually exemplifies some of Olrik's laws. See Hendricks, "Folklore and the Structural Analysis of Literary Texts," *Language and Style* 3 (1970), 83–121.

42. Vladimir Propp, *Morphology of the Folktale*, trans. Laurence Scott (2d ed.; rev. and ed. with a preface by Louis A. Wagner and a new introduction by Alan Dundes; Austin: University of Texas Press, 1968), pp. 19, 25–65. A. J. Greimas reduced the thirty-one functions of Propp by joining some as binary oppositions and by assimilating others. See Greimas, *Sémantique structurale* (Paris: Larousse, 1966), pp. 172–91.

43. Greimas was working with the character types of Propp when he developed his actantial model. The father of the princess and dispatcher of Propp become the *destinateur* of Greimas, the hero of Propp is the *sujet* and *destinataire* of Greimas, the princess is the *objet*, the villain and false hero are joined into the *opposant*, and the donor and helper into *adjuvant*. See Greimas, *Sémantique structurale*, pp. 176–80.

44. Propp, *Morphology*, p. 92.

45. Alan Dundes, *The Morphology of North America Indian Folktales*, Folklore Fellows Communications No. 195 (Helsinki: Suomalainen Tiedeakatemia, 1964), pp. 58–59.

46. *Ibid.*, p. 59.

47. *Ibid.*, p. 61.

48. *Ibid.*, pp. 97–98.

49. *Ibid.*, p. 104.

50. Alan Dundes, "Introduction to the Second Edition," Propp, *Morphology of the Folktale*, p. xi.

51. A. J. Greimas, "The Interpretation of Myth: Theory and Practice," *Structural Analysis of Oral Tradition*, ed. Pierre Maranda and Elli Kongas Maranda (Philadelphia: University of Pennsylvania Press, 1971), p. 84.

52. *Ibid.*

53. *Ibid.*

54. *Ibid.*

55. Noam Chomsky, *Syntactic Structures* (The Hague: Mouton, 1957), p. 13.

56. *Ibid.*, pp. 26–33.

57. *Ibid.*, pp. 36–45, 61–84.

58. *Ibid.*, pp. 35–36

59. *Ibid.*, p. 36.

60. *Ibid.*, p. 43.

61. *Ibid.*, p. 83.

62. *Ibid.*, p. 93.

63. *Ibid.*, pp. 106–8.

64. *Ibid.*, p. 106.

65. *Ibid.*, pp. 106–7.

66. Gerhard Helbig, *Geschichte der neueren Sprachwissenschaft* (Leipzig: Max Hueber Verlag, 1973), pp. 286–314, summarizes these and other developments of the second phase.

67. See R. B. Lee, "Review of *Syntactic Structures* by Noam Chomsky," *Language* 33 (1957), 375–408.

68. It is true that prior to the work of Chomsky, Harris had outlined the concept of a conversion relation or a transformation between two or more actual sentences in texts. See Z. S. Harris, "Discourse Analysis," *Language* 28 (1952), 1–30. See also Noam Chomsky, *Current Issues in Linguistic Theory* (The Hague: Mouton, 1964), pp. 62–63 n.2.

69. Chomsky notes this relationship but rejects the view of *langue* as merely a "systematic inventory of items" and returns to the Humboldtian conception of "underlying competence as a system of generative processes." Noam Chom-

sky, *Aspects of the Theory of Syntax* (Cambridge, Mass.: The MIT Press, 1965), p. 4.

70. *Ibid.*
71. *Ibid.*, p. 194 n.1.
72. *Ibid.*, p. 40.
73. *Ibid.*, p. 141.
74. David Crystal, *Linguistics* (Harmondsworth: Penguin, 1971), p. 230.
75. Chomsky, *Aspects*, pp. 135–36.
76. *Ibid.*, p. vi.
77. *Ibid.*, p. 163.
78. *Ibid.*, p. 99.
79. See articles on generative semantics in *Semantics: An Interdisciplinary Reader in Philosophy, Linguistics and Psychology*, ed. Danny D. Steinberg and Leon A. Jakobovits (Cambridge: Cambridge University Press, 1971).
80. Jerrold J. Katz and Jerry A. Fodor, "The Structure of a Semantic Theory," *The Structure of Language: Readings in the Philosophy of Language* (Englewood Cliffs, N.J.: Prentice-Hall, 1964), pp. 479–518.
81. Tuen A. van Dijk, "On the Foundation of Poetics: Methodological Prolegomena to a Generative Grammar of Literary Texts," *Poetics* 5 (1972), 111.
82. *Ibid.*, p. 90.
83. *Ibid.*
84. *Ibid.*, p. 112.
85. *Ibid.*, p. 91.
86. *Ibid.*, p. 104.
87. A. J. Greimas, *Sémantique structurale* (Paris: Larousse, 1966), p. 8: ". . . considérer le perception comme le lieu non linguistique où se situe l'appréhension de la signification."
88. *Ibid.*, p. 9: ". . . il est difficile d'imaginer d'autres critères de pertinence acceptables par tous." Greimas cites two striking illustrations of the influence of this twentieth-century epistemology: ". . . la psychologie de la forme et du comportement se substituer à la psychologie des 'facultés' et de l'introspection. On voit aussi que l'explication des faits esthétiques se situe actuellement davantage au niveau de la perception de l'oeuvre, et non plus à celui de l'exploration du génie ou de l'imagination."
89. Claude Lévi-Strauss, *The Savage Mind* (Chicago: The University of Chicago Press, 1966), p. 12.
90. Greimas, *Sémantique structurale*, p. 10. *Signifiants* are ". . . les éléments ou les groupements d'éléments qui rendent possible l'apparition de la signification au niveau de la perception, et qui sont reconnus, en ce moment même, comme extérieurs à l'homme." *Signifié* designates ". . . la signification ou les significations qui sont recouvertes par le signifiant et manifestées grâce à son existence."
91. *Ibid.*, p. 13.
92. *Ibid.*, p. 11.
93. *Ibid.*
94. *Ibid.*, p. 16.

95. *Ibid.*

96. *Ibid.*, p. 55.

97. *Ibid.*, p. 60.

98. *Ibid.*, p. 61: ". . . la forme du contenu rendant possible . . . l'apparition de tel ou tel symbolisme."

99. A. J. Greimas and F. Rastier, "The Interaction of Semiotic Constraints," *Yale French Studies* 41 (1968), 86–87. In French in A. J. Greimas, *Du Sens* (Paris: Seuil, 1970).

100. Greimas, *Du Sens*, pp. 158–59.

101. *Ibid.*, p. 160: "Cette structure élémentaire . . . , doit être conçue comme le développement logique d'une catégorie sémique binaire, du type *blanc* vs *noir*, dont les termes sont, entre eux, dans une relation de contrairiété, chacun étant en même temps susceptible de projeter un nouveau terme qui serait son contradictoire, les termes contradictoires pouvant, à leur tour, contracter une relation de présupposition à l'égard du terme contraire opposé."

102. *Ibid.*, p. 163: ". . . est *une structure à quatre termes* qui sont mutuellement interdéfinis par un réseau de relations précises descriptibles comme *la corrélation entre deux schémas.*"

103. *Ibid.*, p. 164.

104. *Ibid.*, p. 165: "La réprésentation de la syntaxe comme suite d'opérations effectuées sur les termes définis d'une structure taxinomique. . . ." "*Les opérations syntaxiques sont orientées.*" "La connaissance de propriétés relationnelles de la structure élémentaire." ". . . les opérations syntaxiques sont non seulement orientées, mais aussi organisées en séries logiques."

105. *Ibid.*, pp. 165–66.

"1. La grammaire narrative se compose d'une *morphologie élémentaire* fournie par le modèle taxinomique, et d'une *syntaxe fondamentale qui opère sur les termes* taxinomiques préalablement inter-définis.

2. La syntaxe narrative consiste en opérations effectuées sur les termes susceptibles d'être investis de valeurs de contenu; de ce fait, elle les transforme et les manipule, en les niant et en les affirmant . . . , en les *disjoignant* et *conjoignant.*

3. Les opérations syntaxiques, situées dans le cadre taxinomique établi, sont *orientées* et, de ce fait, prévisibles et calculables.

4. Ces opérations sont, de plus, *ordonnées en séries* et constituent des procès segmentables en *unités syntaxiques opérationnelles.*"

106. *Ibid.*, p. 166: ". . . la grammaire fondamentale, qui est d'ordre *conceptuel*, pour pouvoir produire des récits manifestés sous forme *figurative* (où des acteurs humains ou personnifiés accompliraient des tâches, subiraient des épreuves, atteindraient des buts), doit d'abord recevoir, à un niveau sémiotique intermédiaire, une représentation *anthropomorphe* mais non figurative. C'est ce niveau anthropomorphe que l'on désignera sous le nom de *grammaire narrative superficielle*, en précisant que le qualificatif "superficiel," n'ayant rien de péjoratif, indique seulement qu'il s'agit d'un palier sémiotique, dont les définitions et les règles grammaticales sons susceptibles, à l'aide d'un dernier transcodage, de passer directement dans les discours et les énoncés linguistiques."

107. *Ibid.*, p. 167.

108. *Ibid.*, p. 168.

109. *Ibid.*: ". . . toute restriction sémantique de F se répercutera nécessairement sur A, et inversement."

110. *Ibid.*, p. 169: ". . . on peut interpréter l'énoncé modal comme 'le désir de réalisation' d'un programme qui est présent sous forme d'énoncé descriptif et fait en même temps partie, en tant qu'objet, de l'énoncé modal."

111. *Ibid.*, p. 171.

112. *Ibid.*, p. 172: "Si l'on admet que la représentation anthropomorphe de la contradiction est de nature polémique, la suite syntagmatique—qui correspond à la transformation des valeurs de contenu résultant, au niveau de la grammaire fondamentale, des opérations de négation et d'assertion—devra apparaître ici comme une suite d'énoncés narratifs dont les restrictions sémantiques auront pour tâche de lui conférer un caractère d'affrontment et de lutte."

113. *Ibid.*:

"a) l'existence de *deux sujets* . . . (ou d'un Sujet et d'un Anti-Sujet) qui correspond aux deux *faire* contradictoires, la relation de contradiction étant, on le sait, une relation non orientée;

b) la restriction sémantique du faire syntaxique par l'etablissement de l'équivalence entre l'opération de *négation* et la fonction de *domination*, résultant de l'antagonisme polémique;

c) la reconnaissance du principe d'orientation valable pour les deux niveaux de la grammaire: à telle orientation d'opérations logiques correspond tel choix arbitraire du sujet négateur et de la domination de l'un des sujets sur l'autre;

d) l'admission que la procédure dialectique, selon laquelle la négation d'un terme est *en même temps* l'assertion du terme contradictoire, se trouve représentée, au niveau de la syntaxe superficielle, par deux énoncés narratifs indépendants, dont le premier, avec sa fonction de domination, correspond à l'instance de négation, et le second, avec la fonction d'attribution, à l'instance d'assertion."

114. *Ibid.*, p. 174: "Si les fonctions et les actants sont les *éléments* constitutif de cette grammaire narrative, si les *énoncés narratifs* en sont les formes syntaxiques élémentaires, les unités narratives—dont l'échantillon est représenté ici par la *performance*—sont des suites syntagmatiques d'énoncés narratifs."

115. *Ibid.*, p. 175.

116. *Ibid.*, p. 178: "Ainsi, du point de vue formel, comme les énoncés translatifs sont les énoncés terminaux des performances et les impliquent logiquement, les parcours syntaxiques exprimés sous forme de transferts constituent en fait des *suites syntagmatiques de performances*: c'est-à-dire des unités syntaxiques d'un rang supérieur."

117. *Ibid.*, p. 179: ". . . c'est le vouloir du sujet qui le rend apte à accomplir la première performance, marquée par l'attribution de la valeur modale du savoir ou du pouvoir."

118. *Ibid.*, pp. 179–80.

119. *Ibid.*, p. 182: ". . . comme l'établissement d'une relation contractuelle *conjonctive* entre un destinateur et un destinataire-sujet, suivie d'une *disjonc-*

tion spatiale entre les deux actants. L'achèvement du récit serait marqué, au contraire, par une conjonction spatiale et un dernier transfert des valeurs, instituant un nouveau contrat par une nouvelle distribution de valeurs, aussi bien objectives que modales." Greimas finds not only the idea of "contract" but also the idea of "test" helpful in the representation of a narrative. The narrative is conceptualized as the organization of sequences from a broken contract and aborted communication between a sender and receiver to the reestablishment of communication and contract. Applying this abstract conceptualization to a social order: the initial situation is characterized by the existence of order; because of disobedience, the order is disrupted and misfortune or lack occurs; a hero comes from the group with the charge of suppressing alienation and reestablishing communication; initial lack of contract and lack of communication eventually result in final establishment of communication and contract. Between the initial and final sequences, the narrative organizes the transformations resulting in the inversion of the initial situation. Within the relation of contract (broken in the beginning and reestablished at the end) is a series of tests, each of which is a partial reestablishment of the broken global contract. The tests end with the total liquidation of the lack. The first test is called by Greimas the "qualifying test": A sender charges a hero with a certain mission, and by a test the hero is qualified as the subject of the quest. In terms of this initial test, the hero receives a helper who assists in the accomplishment of the principal test which ends in the reception of an object which will assure the liquidation of the lack, the reestablishment of the broken global contract. The glorifying test is the recognition of the subject as victor by the social body. The scheme of the tests maintains a parallelism with that of actants. The (nonglobal) contract is established between the sender and the receiver; the battle to meet the tests confronts the helper and the opponent; the consequence of winning the battle is the acquisition of the object by the subject. See *Sémantique structurale*, pp. 195–98, and *Du Sens*, pp. 185–230.

120. Greimas, *Du Sens*, pp. 182–83: "Une telle grammaire narrative, . . . aurait une forme déductive et analytique à la fois. Elle tracerait un ensemble de parcours pour la manifestation du sens: à partir des opérations élémentaires de la grammaire fondamentale qui empruntent les voies du processus d'actualisation de la signification, à travers les combinaisons des suites syntagmatiques de la grammaire superficielle qui ne sont que des représentations anthropomorphes de ces opérations, les contenus s'investissent, par l'intermédiaire des performances, dans les énoncés narratifs, organisés en séquences linéaires d'énoncés canoniques reliés entre eux, comme des chaînons d'une seule chaîne, par une série d'implications logiques. Quand on possédera de telles séquences d'énoncés narratifs, on pourra imaginer—à l'aide d'une rhétorique, d'une stylistique, mais aussi d'une grammaire linguistique—la manifestation linguistique de la signification narrativisée."

121. See Claude Bremond, *Logique du récit* (Paris: Seuil, 1973), pp. 101–2.

122. *Ibid.*, p. 89.

123. Roland Barthes, *S/Z*, trans. Richard Miller (London: Jonathan Cape, 1975), p. 3.

124. Bremond, *Logique du récit*, p. 333.

125. *Ibid.*, p. 89: "Mais la question est de savoir si cette structure 'biplane' est essentielle à la narrativité."

126. *Ibid.*, p. 90: "Il est vrai que la forme narrative est particulièrement apte à figurer par comparison ou métaphore, le jeu des idées abstraites. Mais précisement, elle *figure* ce qu'elle n'est pas."

127. *Ibid.*: ". . . la temporalité caractéristique de la narrativité superficielle se limite d'abord aux événements d'intérêt humain. . . ."

128. *Ibid.*, p. 92.

129. *Ibid.*, p. 93: "Cette relation est achronique et ne peut cesser de l'être: il serait absurde de lui donner une interprétation temporalisée et de vouloir, par exemple, que le terme 'impliquant' (*riche*) et le terme 'impliqué' (*non pauvre*) se succèdent comme deux événements chronologiquement distincts, le premier entraînant le second comme une cause produit son effet."

130. *Ibid.*, p. 99: "Elle méconnait une loi de la narrativité: la faculté, ou plutôt l'obligation de se développer comme une suite d'options opérées par le narrateur, à chaque instant du récit, entre plusieurs façons de continuer son histoire."

131. *Ibid.*, p. 101: "L'essentiel du récit se concentre pour lui dans un jeu de concepts intemporels, transcendant au devenir des événements racontés. . . ."

132. *Ibid.*: "Pour nous l'impression de liberté, de vérité, de beauté, . . . n'est pas une illusion qui masque le 'jeu des contraintes sémiotiques.' Si jeu il y a, celui-ci, n'est pas subi, c'est un jeu *sur* les contraintes, l'expérience libératrice qui les exploite et les surmonte."

133. Claude Bremond, "Morphology of the French Folktale," *Semiotica* 2 (1970), 249. See *Logique du récit*, p. 131.

134. Bremond, "Morphology," p. 249.

135. *Ibid.*, pp. 247–76.

136. Bremond, *Logique du récit*, p. 309: "Nous avons décomposé le récit en un complexe de *rôles*, simultanés ou successifs; chaque rôle s'analyse luimême en une combinaison de *processus*; chaque processus est susceptible d'être saisi à trois stades de son développement (*éventualité, passage à l'acte, achèvement*) et, en outre, le récit peut faire référence à un processus, non pour signifier son éventualité, son passage à l'acte, son achèvement, mais pour les nier; les processus qui se combinent pour définir le rôle entretiennent les uns avec les autres certaines relations *syntaxiques* (succession, simultanéité, causalité, implication). Par ailleurs, chaque processus entretient un rapport de prédicat à sujet avec une ou plusieurs *personnes*, que le récit désigne ordinairement par un nom propre, et qui peuvent être soit les *patients* soit les *agents* de ce processus; les agents à leur tour peuvent se comporter en initiateurs *volontaires* ou *involontaires* du processus."

137. *Ibid.*, p. 333: "Il s'agit bien d'une étude des rôles narratifs principaux, c'est-à-dire des universaux qui apparaissent dans le sillage de l'acte de narrer."

138. "When we write 'Y believes that X is not violating the law,' we have an example of a verb ('believe') which differs from the others. It is not a question of a different action here but of a different perception of the same action. We

could, therefore, speak of a kind of 'point of view' which refers not only to the relation between reader and narrator, but also to the characters." T. Todorov, "Structural Analysis of Narrative," *Novel* 3 (1969–70), 74.

139. *Ibid.*

140. Todorov acknowledges that marginal narratives exist which embody only one of the principles, but "ordinarily, even the simplest, least developed narrative simultaneously incorporates the two principles." "The Two Principles of Narrative," *Diacritics* 1 (1971), 39.

141. *Ibid.* Todorov catalogs simple transformations as those of mode, intention, result, manner, aspect, and status. Complex transformations are those of appearance, recognition, description, supposition, subjectivization, and attitude. O. Ducrot and T. Todorov, *Dictionnaire encyclopédique des sciences du language*, pp. 368–74.

142. Todorov, "The Two Principles of Narrative," p. 40.

143. *Ibid.*, p. 42.

144. See Culler, *Structuralist Poetics*, pp. 214–17.

145. Barthes, S/Z, p. 4.

146. Roland Barthes, *Essais critiques* (Paris: Seuil, 1964), p. 176.

147. Roland Barthes, *Critique et vérité* (Paris: Seuil, 1966), pp. 54–73. Note, however, the change in the perspective of S/Z. See "A Conversation with Roland Barthes," *Signs of the Times* (Cambridge: Granta, 1971), p. 44.

148. Barthes, S/Z, p. 5.

149. *Ibid.*, p. 8.

150. *Ibid.*, p. 9.

151. *Ibid.*, pp. 8–9.

152. *Ibid.*, p. 8.

153. *Ibid.*, p. 10.

154. *Ibid.*, pp. 12–13.

155. *Ibid.*, p. 13.

156. *Ibid.*, p. 21.

157. *Ibid.*, p. 20.

158. *Ibid.*, p. 160.

159. *Ibid.*

160. *Ibid.*, p. 204.

161. *Ibid.*

162. *Ibid.*, p. 17.

163. *Ibid.*, p. 75.

164. *Ibid.*, p. 76.

165. *Ibid.*, p. 19.

166. *Ibid.*, p. 29.

167. *Ibid.*

168. *Ibid.*

169. *Ibid.*, p. 184.

170. *Ibid.*, p. 185.

171. *Ibid.*, pp. 97–98.

172. *Ibid.*, p. 191.

173. *Ibid.*, p. 92.

174. *Ibid.*, p. 19.

175. *Ibid.*, p. 17.

176. *Ibid.*, p. 27.

177. *Ibid.*, p. 15.

178. *Ibid.*, p. 3.

179. *Ibid.*, p. 6.

180. *Ibid.*

181. *Ibid.*, p. 13.

182. *Ibid.*, p. 30.

183. *Ibid.*, p. 75.

184. Jonathan Culler, "Defining Narrative Units," *Style and Structure in Literature*, p. 139.

185. Philippe Hamon, "Narrative Semiotics in France," *Style* 8 (1974), 36.

186. Culler, *Structuralist Poetics*, p. 209.

187. Culler, "Defining Narrative Units," p. 139. The narratologies discussed in this chapter may be viewed as a more detailed treatment of the vision of Dilthey. See above, pp. 23–24, for a description of the importance of plot for Dilthey. In his view both characters and actions are central in the movement from the mind of the creator to the actual composition. Dilthey's "type" is the plot of narrative literature, or what is termed genre today. See above, pp. 21–22.

188. Greimas, *Sémantique structurale*, p. 211.

189. *Ibid.*, p. 213.

CHAPTER SIX

Man, Hermeneutics, and Structuralism

Proponents of existential hermeneutics in general see in structuralism an alternative approach to the text which can have nothing to do with hermeneutics.[1] And a structuralism that reduces literature to linguistics and does not consider human linguistic and literary competence may, at least theoretically, be divorced from existential hermeneutics. But *man* unites the two. The inclusive approach to interpretation advocated in this work demands a relationship between the existential and the structural. The structural study of narrative cannot be carried out apart from existential hermeneutics. Nor can existential hermeneutics apart from structuralism utilize the literary text as effectively as possible. In the initial part of this chapter we will examine the relationship of structuralism and hermeneutics, in large measure through a look at the work of Paul Ricoeur, and the final part will present a view of man and his developing mental structure which is informed by the work of both Wilhelm Dilthey and Jean Piaget.

HERMENEUTICS AND STRUCTURE

The relationship of hermeneutics to structuralism may be mediated by the historical. Logically, if historical study is impossible apart from existential meaning and if structuralism assists historical study, then hermeneutics and structural analysis must be related.[2] Paul Ricoeur's involvement in structuralism from a hermeneutical stance may help us to see the implications of each of these studies for the other. Ricoeur sees his work from 1950 to the present as a project on the "Philosophy of the Will" which includes an eidetics, an empirics, and a poetics of the will. The 1950 volume, *The Voluntary and the Involuntary*, was the eidetics;

Fallible Man (1960) and *The Symbolism of Evil* (1960) form the empirics, and the poetics is the focus of Ricoeur's present work.[3] In the process of his work on the philosophy of the will, Ricoeur has moved from existential phenomenology, to a hermeneutics of symbol, to a more general hermeneutics of written language and texts.[4]

Although he did not use the term "phenomenology" at the time of *The Voluntary and the Involuntary*, Ricoeur indicates that the book can be described as existential phenomenology: phenomenology, "in the sense that it tried to extract from lived experiences the essential meanings and structures of purpose, project, motive, wanting, trying, and so on";[5] existential phenomenology, "in the sense that these essential structures implied the recognition of the central problem of embodiment, of *le corps propre*."[6] The work was an attempt at a pure phenomenology of will, excluding the problems of bad will and evil. In this work, the problem of language did not arise, for, as Ricoeur says, "a direct language was thought to be available."[7]

The work on the two volumes *Fallible Man* and *The Symbolism of Evil* raised the problem of the introduction of sin (speaking in religious terms), guilt, bondage, and alienation into the framework of the philosophy of the will. Ricoeur distinguished between finitude and guilt, and this distinction created a language problem: "Why symbolic language when we pass from a philosophy of finitude to a philosophy of guilt?"[8] Purpose, motive, and ability can be spoken of in direct language, but evil is spoken of by metaphors such as estrangement, errancy, burden, and bondage; these symbols are embedded in mythical narratives which tell the story of how evil began. In an attempt to answer the question of the necessity of an indirect approach Ricoeur applied hermeneutics to the interpretation of symbolic language.

> I tried to limit the definition of hermeneutics to the specific problem of the interpretation of symbolic language. . . . I defined symbolism and hermeneutics in terms of each other. On the one hand, a symbolism requires an interpretation because it is based upon a specific semantic structure of double meaning expressions. Reciprocally, there is a hermeneutical problem because there is an indirect language. Therefore, I identified hermeneutics with the art of deciphering indirect meanings.[9]

In his later work, Ricoeur has moved from the problem of the will to the problem of language and has broadened his definition of hermeneutics. Psychoanalysis, structuralism, the post-Bultmannian "theologies of the Word," and ordinary language philosophy were factors compelling

Ricoeur's movement in hermeneutics. Psychoanalysis reduces symbols, explaining them as the results of unconscious factors; but an opposing hermeneutic moves toward the recovery of the original meaning of the symbol. Ricoeur's problem of uniting the two approaches broadened his view of hermeneutics:

> My problem was to link these two approaches and to understand their relation as dynamic and as moving from first *naiveté* through a critique toward what I called at the time a second *naiveté*. Therefore, without giving up my earlier definition of hermeneutics as the general theory of symbolic language, I had to introduce into the theory the polarity between these two hermeneutical demands and to link philosophical reflection not only to a semantics of indirect language, but to the conflictual structure of the hermeneutical task.[10]

Structuralism is cited by Ricoeur as a reason for his shifting to a "more linguistically concerned kind of philosophizing."[11] The structuralism confronted by Ricoeur was not just a method of analysis based on an epistemological model; it was also a philosophy which drew "radical consequences from this epistemological model which directly affect the presuppositions of existentialism." Existentialism and hermeneutics, therefore, are called into question by the philosophy of structuralism. Structuralism's "displacement of analysis from the level of the subject's intentions to the level of linguistic and semiotic structures" overthrows the primacy of subjectivity strongly emphasized by existentialism. Also, since language for structuralism "does not refer to anything outside of itself" but "constitutes a world for itself," the claim of hermeneutics to reach beyond the "sense" to the "reference" of a text, to what the text says about the world, is excluded.[12] Ricoeur, however, is not willing to follow the lead of those existential thinkers who simply turn their backs on structural analysis because they see in it an alternative approach to texts which is not reconcilable with the hermeneutical approach.[13] He does deny that the literary work may have meaning which is expressed in its structure or its codes apart from reference to some extra-linguistic reality. Or, at any rate, he insists that existential interpretation cannot be related to a view of meaning or message which results from the structures or codes.[14] His relation of structural analysis and hermeneutics will not, then, be done by investigating the relationships of the meaning or meaning effect uncovered by structuralism and existential content. Rather, he defines the task and object of hermeneutics as built upon and moving beyond structural modes and analysis.

Hermeneutics has to do with text as work. Discourse is defined by Ricoeur as "the actualization of language in a speech-act based on a kind of unit irreducible to the constituents of language as 'code.' This basic unit of language as speech or discourse is the sentence."[15] Because text is discourse, the questions of "the *reference forward* to an extra-linguistic reality, the *reference backward* to a speaker, and the *communication* with an audience" are raised. The triple-event character of discourse is not abolished by the fact that discourse becomes actualized as text. Distanciation of all sorts may take place (between text and author, the initial situation, and the initial audience) but this "cannot abolish the dimension of *discourse* which still holds texts within the sphere of language."[16]

The task of hermeneutics is "to bring back to discourse the written text, if not as spoken discourse, at least as speech-act actualized in the act of reading." The object of hermeneutics, then, is not the text but "the *text as discourse* or *discourse as the text*."[17] How is structural analysis related to the task and object of hermeneutics? Discourse appears as a *work* because of modes of discourse or literary genres which impose a form upon discourse.

> The concept of work must be taken literally. It implies the extension to discourse of categories proper to the world of production and labor. To impose a form upon a material, to subject a production to specific codes, to produce those unique configurations which assimilate a work to an individual and which we call style, these are ways of considering language as a material to be worked and formed. They are ways in which discourse becomes the object of a praxis and a technique.[18]

Literary genres, as Ricoeur sees them, are means of production, but they also function in communication to: (1) provide a common ground of understanding and of interpretation because of the contrast between the traditional genre and the novel message; (2) preserve the message from distortion because of the anatomy of the form; and (3) secure the survival of the meaning after the disappearance of its primitive *Sitz im Leben*. The form or genre, then, may start the process of " 'decontextualization' which opens the message to fresh reinterpretation according to new contexts of discourse and of life." The form, then, not only establishes communication and preserves the message from distortion but it also opens the text to a history of interpretation.[19]

Hermeneutics has the task of using the dialectics of discourse and work, but for the reconstitution of discourse, for the message. It aims at the message by means of the codes: "It is the task of hermeneutics to identify the individual discourse (the 'message') through the modes of discourse (the 'codes') which generate it as a work of discourse."[20] In terms of narrative, Ricoeur finds the sense of the narrative only in the narrational communications, the use of the narrative.

Is the model of discourse an appropriate model for written texts which, if they ever did, now have no relationship to an original act of communication? How can proper attention be given to the text as work when the end in mind is the text as discourse? Is the text as work communication? In his treatment of distanciation resulting from the text as work, Ricoeur is eager to maintain the model of hermeneutics as the "art of discerning the discourse in a work," in which the discourse is "constituted by an ensemble of sentences where someone says something to someone about something." The redefinition of author, audience, and situation of discourse makes it possible for a work "to transcend its psycho-sociological conditions of production and to be open to an unlimited series of readings, themselves situated within different socio-cultural contexts."[21] The distanciation of the text, however, does not merely affect "the relation of the discourse to its speaker, of the writing to the writer, of the work to its author," for the distanciation is one "which crosses the very world of the work."[22]

Conventionally, discourse maintains a reference or a denotation; discourse maintains a relationship with reality; discourse "intends things, is applied to reality, expresses the world."[23] When discourse becomes a text, however, "the structure of the work alters the reference to the point of making it entirely problematic."[24] In oral discourse, the reference is determined by the situation of discourse which furnishes the reference. In literature, this denotative character of discourse is lost because "the concrete conditions for the act of pointing something out no longer exist." The abolition of reference to the given world is true of poetic literature "where the language seems to glorify itself without depending on the referential function of ordinary discourse."[25] Ricoeur, however, is not willing to abolish the role of reference in his model of communications: "The objectification of discourse in a structured work does not suppress the fundamental and first trait of discourse, namely, that discourse is constituted by an ensemble of sentences where someone says something to someone about something."[26] The abolition of "first order reference" in poetic literature is "the condition of possibility for the liberation of a second order of reference which reaches the world not only at the level of manipulative objects, but at the level Husserl designated by the expression *Lebenswelt* and Heidegger by 'being-in-the-world.' "[27] Ricoeur can no longer define hermeneutics as "the search for another person and his psychological intentions that hide behind the text." Yet he is not willing to "reduce interpretation to the identification of structures." Ricoeur sees his remaining option to be interpretation as the explication of "a sort of being-in-the-world unfolded in front of the text."[28]

For Ricoeur the key to the movement from structure to the existential interpretation he envisions is the semantics of metaphor, the metaphorical process (not simply rhetoric) which reinterprets reality by abolishing the literal reference and illuminating the "life-world" and "non-manipulable being-in-the-world."[29] Ricoeur's semantics of metaphor denies that metaphor is simply a rhetorical figure in which a figurative word is substituted for a literal word on the basis of resemblance. Metaphor has to do with the function of predication at the level of statement and the strategy by which metaphor gains its meaning is absurdity. Metaphor, on the level of words, consists of a shift of meaning. But this shift of meaning on the level of word produces another shift at the level of the entire statement. This shift "consists in the mutual unsuitability of the terms when interpreted literally."[30] The notion of resemblance in metaphor, when the whole statement is considered in the process, results in tension not between words (a literal word and a figurative word) but in tension between two interpretations in the whole statement, one literal and one metaphorical; this tension "gives rise to a veritable creation of meaning of which rhetoric perceived only the end result."[31] Metaphor, then, "includes *new information*"; it "says something new about reality."[32]

Ricoeur sees the abolition of reference (using Gottlob Frege's distinction between meaning [*Sinn*] as what a statement says and reference [*Bedeutung*] as that about which a statement speaks) in poetic language as "related to the self-destruction of meaning for a literal interpretation of metaphorical statements." The self-destruction of meaning in poetic language is the reverse side of an innovation of meaning: ". . . the metaphorical interpretation gives rise to a re-interpretation of reality itself, in spite of, and thanks to, the abolition of the reference which corresponds to the literal interpretation of the statement."[33]

> Poetic language also speaks of reality, but it does so at another level than does scientific language. It does not show us a world already there, as does descriptive or didactic language. In effect . . . the ordinary reference of language is abolished by the natural strategy of poetic discourse. But in the very measure that this first-order reference is abolished, another

power of speaking the world is liberated, although at another level of reality. This level is that which Husserlian phenomenology has designated as the *Lebenswelt* and which Heidegger has called "being-in-the-world." It is an eclipsing of the objective manipulable world, an illuminating of the life-world, of non-manipulable being-in-the-world, which seems to me to be the fundamental ontological import of poetic language.[34]

This poetic language must not be confused with scientific language, for "poetic language does not say literally what things are, but what they are like. It is in this oblique fashion that it says what they are."[35]

Ricoeur, in his treatment of parable, suggests how the "sense" (*Sinn*) of narrative implies its metaphorical "referent" (*Bedeutung*). He indicates that the beginning point is not structure itself, but a conviction that the narrative has a referent or even a "participation in the referent."[36] This is possible because "the narrative stands metaphorically for the poetic experience which comes to language."[37] Yet a narrative structure must provide clues—even apart from the explicit and more important clues given by the context. The plot of the narrative must contain the signs of metaphoricity—the plot as the dramatic structure. Structural analysis of the narrative will help in understanding the plot, and, therefore, the crisis at the surface structure. Ricoeur sees "existential transparencies" of the narrative as rooted in the dramatic structure, and structuralism is, then, merely an aid in understanding this surface structure "plot," "crisis," and "answer."

What is it that compels us to take the elements within the narrative as referring to some similar structures of human experiences outside the narrative?[38] Ricoeur indicates two complementary factors: the normalcy of the story and, more importantly, the element of extravagance which makes the "oddness" of the narrative, by mixing the "extraordinary" with the "ordinary."[39]

Structural analysis in itself, according to Ricoeur, emphasizes the closure of the narrative form. It has to do with literary genre which provides distanciation, autonomy, and form. What opens the narrative "toward the outside, namely, toward both the infinity of life and the infinity of interpretation" is the metaphorical process.[40] Structural analysis is seen as preliminary and secondary to hermeneutics for which metaphor is the key. Ricoeur's treatment of the use of structural analysis in *Semeia*, number 4 (1975), is set in the context of a larger concern, the application to biblical hermeneutics of insights gained from his work on metaphor. Metaphor is the perspective from which he sees both structuralism and biblical hermeneutics. Religious language is a variety of poetic language where the poetic function is seen as "the power of making the redescription of reality correspond with the power of bringing the fictions of the imagination to speech."[41] Structuralism, in the articles of 1975, is a service to the more important existential interpretation. It serves because the structures of literature are only related to literature as a work. In communication, the structures seen as literary genres do assist by providing a basis for understanding and interpretation: ". . . the 'form' not only establishes communication, thanks to its *common* character, but it preserves the message from distortion, thanks to the *circumspection* which it imposes upon the work of art, and it *opens* it to the history of its interpretation."[42]

Ricoeur's failure to emphasize the meaning of form as form results from his concern to discover the reference and meaning of poetic works from the perspective of his postulates concerning metaphor. May not the redescription of reality which the poetic work accomplishes as a heuristic fiction, however, be accomplished by the structure of discourse as work as well as by the second order reference of fictional discourse? An inclusive model of interpretation should be able to incorporate and relate meanings on the levels of work and of event. For Ricoeur, the text has meaning only as it is seen on the surface level. He does suggest that a depth-semantics may exist, but it exists not in the achronic structures emphasized by structuralism but in the diachronic structures.[43]

The cautious estimation of the value of structural analysis is justified for Ricoeur (and perhaps encouraged) by Louis Marin's analysis of Matt. 13:1–23. Marin's approach is achronic with the understanding that the "inventory of the codes is the only important thing" and that "ultimately, a narrative is the manifestation of its own codes in the form of quotation."[44] In the view of Ricoeur, this approach not only "leaves no room for an interpretation of the parable in terms of metaphorical transposition" but it offers an alternative interpretation which results in "the dissolution of all *referential* values in the interplay of correlations."[45] There is nothing of existential meaningfulness to inquire about in the parable because the text is a "communication of a message concerning communication."[46] In his analysis of the narrative of "The Women at the Tomb," Marin claims to have hit upon the specificity of the Christian text: "a surface narrative about a supernatural event tells of another narrative, which tells the communication itself of the message."[47]

In earlier treatments of structuralism, in the Warfield lectures at Princeton Theological Seminary in 1973, for example, Ricoeur views the possibility of structuralism from a slightly different perspective. In these lectures, Ricoeur expresses his view of the possibility of interpretation as the explication of "being-in-the-world unfolded in front of the text" in place of the "search for another person and his psychological intentions that hide behind the text" or the "identification of structures."[48] (The possibility of explication of the "being-in-the-world unfolded in front of the text" is carried further in the *Semeia* articles in terms of metaphor.) However, in the Warfield lectures, Ricoeur suggests that the mediation of speaker and hearer, of creation and understanding, by the generative function of literary genres itself has hermeneutical consequence. ". . . the dynamics of form is at the same time a dynamics of thought. . . . The theological content itself is produced in harmony with the rule of the corresponding literary genre."[49] Ricoeur stresses that his view of literary genres is not taxonomic but genetic, that literary genre is a means of production. "To master a genre is to master a 'competence' which offers practical guidelines for 'performing' an individual work. . . . The same competence in the reader helps him to perform the corresponding operations of interpretation according to the rules prescribed by the 'genre' for both *sending* and *receiving* a certain type of message."[50]

In his treatment of genre as a means of production, however, Ricoeur seems to be limited by the traditional classification of genre. He distinguishes various forms as "prophecy," "hymn," "proclamation saying," "proverbial saying," and "parable," and judges that the meanings of religious language "are ruled and guided by the modes of articulation specific to each mode of discourse."[51] The "confession of faith" expressed in biblical documents and the form of discourse in which it is expressed are inseparable. Each form of discourse gives rise to a particular style of confession of faith, and the confrontation of the various forms gives rise to tensions and contrasts, which are theologically significant.[52] Ricoeur stresses the opposition between narration and prophecy as one of the pairs of structures whose opposition "contributes to engendering the global shape of its meaning," but he feels that oppositions between other forms give rise to theological significations.

Ricoeur may be criticized both for going too far and for not going far enough. In his use of metaphor he forsakes the primitive discourse event in order to open the way for new significations. Must the original discourse event be abolished for new signification to be obtained? Does not the original event, even if it is ultimately an illusion, give direction to the search for new significations? To deny the meaning of structures themselves, on the other hand, is to fail to appreciate the relationships of the meaning or the meaning effect of structures to life. Ricoeur does see a possible implication of structuralism for hermeneutics when he emphasizes the generative nature of genre, but he does not go far enough when he (perhaps constrained by a traditional view of genre) conceives of genre simply in broad terms of narrative, prophecy, etc. If genre is a means of production, cannot the *variety* of narrative structures being uncovered by the application of the structural method, as well as the narrative form in general, be applied to meaning on the historical and existential levels, and indeed on the structural level?

Ricoeur sets up a model of interpretation which contrasts event with work and hermeneutics with structuralism. This model will not contain all of the insights of Ricoeur. The model must be expanded into something of a "systems" approach. The approach could acknowledge a variety of levels of language, not just morphemes, words, sentences, and texts, but also the levels of manifestation and deep structure. Such a system would acknowledge numerous meanings: references, historical meanings, structural meanings, existential meanings, extending on to life itself. Meaning on no level, at least theoretically, could be dealt with apart from meaning on all the other levels. Such a systems approach is really an expansion of the dialectical models set up in the various hermeneutical systems. The inclusive model of interpretation will give proper attention to every level of language, literature, and meaning to which the interpreter is sensitive. No one level will necessarily be the final level, and each level will be related to every other level. The careful work done by scholars isolated by time, geography, and ideology all belong to and contribute to this approach. The only limiting factor is the claim to superiority of some approaches or the view that one approach necessarily excludes other approaches. The historical meaning, however, cannot be discerned apart from the existential perspective, but the structural meaning or meaning effect—even if unconscious—is giving clues at both of these points. The structure and its meaning or meaning effect will be homologous with both the historical and existential, and can provide, if the interpreter is so minded, the broadest backdrop for the focusing of the various meanings.

Structural meaning may be the most difficult to distinguish from the historical and existential. The interpreter may keep the structural method as a helping method. He may see the analysis of the structures as analysis of the means of production (much as the analysis of a sentence into noun, verb, and modifiers helps us to discover the meaning of the sentence). But once initial prejudices are overcome, and the interpreter appreciates the possibilities of language and literature, he may make structural meaning the focus and rely upon historical and existential meaning as helps.

STRUCTURAL PSYCHOLOGY AND INTERPRETATION

The consideration of interpretation as a harmonious enterprise involving multiple interacting levels of language, literature, and meaning inevitably involves the nature of the interpreter. Is man merely to act as a simple calculator, consciously and unconsciously reacting to the literary expression in light of the various possibilities of meaning, ruling out certain options and accepting others? Or is man himself more actively involved in the process? The focusing of horizons emphasized by Gadamer, as we saw earlier, involves an "I" which is not simply a neutral static object upon which history and the text impinge. Structuralism also emphasizes the active capacity of the author and the reader, not merely the reactive. This capacity is illuminated by the generative grammar of Noam Chomsky, but an even more suggestive model for interpretation of literary texts was provided by the work of Dilthey.

As early as 1860, Dilthey declared that the "I" is productive in the sense that every influence from the outside is at the same time an activity of the subject: "The conceptions which are urged from without are created and made definite only through the production of the active 'I.' "[53] The concept of a complex static-dynamic mental structure active in interpretation goes back to the early days of Dilthey's dissatisfaction with the idea of a transcendental-subjective, a priori, ahistorical, asocial, and acultural pure reason. In *Grundriss* Dilthey sees the classical mental capacities as forming a dynamic Gestalt, a totality which is a synthesis of various relationships.[54] The *Braslauer Ausarbeitung* of 1880 related the mental structure of Dilthey and the central question of reason, the question of truth. How is it possible for knowledge to be justified? What is the final basis for knowledge? Dilthey affirms the finite, questionable, and historical nature of all human knowledge on the basis of the dynamic system of interpretation and study. In place of absolute sources or an absolute ground of knowledge, Dilthey sets man in the context of a dynamic system of mankind and his physical and cultural environment. Instead of man being an isolated reality with individual isolated mental capacities, man is a highly complex integrated part of a larger system involving his total environment.[55]

After 1880, Dilthey broadened his conception of the mental structure. He saw it as having a fundamental capacity of regulating all of the single elements in the basic structural system and adapting the organism to the environment in both an active and passive way. In addition, he regarded the behavior of the dynamic system as teleological with the capacity for development.[56] Peter Krausser says that Dilthey made virtue out of necessity. The necessity (which is the necessity for every non-naive modern reflective theory of knowledge) is the impossibility of discovering a final ground for knowledge, the impossibility of ultimately proving the validity of propositions. This necessity is imposed by the fallibility of logic and the historical nature of experience; consequently there is no absolutely foolproof way to verify truth. Dilthey made a virtue out of this necessity by his system which unites all factors together as variables in such a way that "the dynamic totality of this unification forms an open, self-controlling, and self-correcting system, in short, a 'learning' system."[57]

The purposeful and dynamic nature of the mind, an active as well as reactive dynamism, which is involved in understanding and interpreting, is a basic view of contemporary structural thought as it was of Dilthey. The view of this mental structural system as a developing system is not so common.[58] The process of formation of the acquired system (der erworbene Zusammenhang) is both a process of learning, of internalizing social and cultural factors and procedures of conduct, and of physical and psychical development. There is a fundamentally qualified inner capacity for adaptation and learning on the basis of which a structural system is formed through personal individualization, socialization, and acculturation, and the transmission of social and cultural traditions.[59]

In 1883 Dilthey spoke of the social and cultural systems of a society. They

. . . secure a general adaptation of their mutual functions and actions in society by virtue of the permanent adaptation of an individual activity in them as well as by virtue of the unified purposeful activity of the association which belongs to them. This general adaptation gives particular characteristics of organization to their inner relationship.[60]

When this is applied to the individual human being, what is seen is "relatively stable subsystems in a complex, adaptable system being related to all other subsystems of the system with which they stand in communication as a total system is to the environment: dynamically adaptive."[61]

In 1888, Dilthey made a statement directly related to the development of the individual's mental structural system:

> At the beginning, the mental development has not unified the different ways that the emotions and impulses relate to conceptions. Each of them acts purposefully even if it is in a crude and limited way. But the development of the life of the mind establishes relationships through a stable coordination between them, through which a more complete teleological system of the life of the mind in the individual and in the growing development of the realm of the mind and of history takes place.
>
> One observes a child! The drive for food, the reaction to injuries, the tender submission appear in him yet isolated, without a relationship to the totality of his needs and without, thereby, an evaluation of their worth and claim. As sunshine, affection rushes over his face and makes way for other emotions and impulses.[62]

José Ortega y Gasset's image of "an idea carrying water to its 'source' "[63] may be apt for the application of developments in structural psychology to hermeneutics. Dilthey is doubtless a source if not the source for the structural psychology associated with the name of Jean Piaget. Piaget began his work as a biologist influenced by evolutionary theory, but his view that processes and states are to be understood in terms of their developmental course was not simply Darwinian theory. An early experiment with aquatic mollusks caused him to see that Darwin's account of natural selection was too simple. Piaget transported aquatic mollusks from the calm marshes of Europe and Asia into the great lakes of Switzerland with their more turbulent waters. The growth of the mollusks in the rough movement of the waters created a new breed of mollusk, a globular-shaped mollusk more responsive to the currents of the water. When returned to calmer waters, the mollusk retained its new shape instead of taking the more elongated shape of the mollusk from the calmer waters. The conclusion of Piaget directed his later work: the structure of an organism has potential to develop in various ways depending on the environment. The organism adapts to a new condition by an active restructuring and accommodation. Intelligence is embodied in an organism in structures with potential for development which takes places in interaction with the environment. The essential capacity of the organism is action, and the development in an organism involves the mastery of a current group of actions and the coordination of actions into more complex actions. The order and pace of development depend upon the organism's own equilibrating processes and the organism's interaction with its environment.[64]

Thinking, for Piaget, is a series of mental operations or internal actions and sequences of action. But the intellectual capacity of the human is not a static given; it is subject to the developmental scheme outlined above. Piaget has concentrated his work on children, and, through observation and experimentation, he has deduced three principal stages of intellectual development for the children with whom he has dealt: the sensorimotor stage is the stage of infancy during which the child increasingly masters his actions in a world of objects. The next stage can be called the preoperational, intuitive, semiotic, or representational stage. During this stage the development of the child is toward processes of concrete operations. "Concrete" indicates that the child continues to deal with objects, physical states, persons and so on. But "operations" indicates that the action may be carried out on an implicit plane; mental manipulation rather than the physical manipulation is the key. The final stage is that of formal operations and involves the use of deduction, the term "formal" referring to logical, linguistic, or abstract compositions.[65]

 The structural psychology of Piaget denies that man is merely a passive reactor to the environment or, on the other hand, the possessor of "innate ideas" which will automatically unfold. The structural psychology of Piaget can be seen as basically the conception of Dilthey, although Piaget supports his view by careful observation and experimentation and numerous scholars have used Piaget's deductions as the basis for further work. The view of Piaget, supplemented by the work of his followers, when brought into relationship with the hermeneutics of Dilthey, will result not only in a view of interpretation as a systems approach with different levels of language, literature, and meaning, but also a view of competence which is dynamic, not only going through the stages from infancy to adolescence outlined by Piaget, but also continuing to interact with the forces impinging upon it and arriving at different levels of equilibrium, forming a "constantly increasing spiral."[66]

Before we suggest some possible implications of structural psychology for interpretation, we should observe some distinctions made by Piaget among intelligence, thought, and language.

Intelligence for the child is the solution of a new problem, the coordination of the means to reach a certain goal which is not accessible in an immediate manner; whereas thought is interiorized intelligence no longer based on direct action but on a symbolism, the symbolic evocation by speech, by mental pictures, and other means, which makes it possible to represent what the sensorimotor intelligence, on the contrary, is going to grasp directly.[67]

Intelligence exists, then, before thought and language. Piaget gives an example. A child is offered a blanket beneath which a beret has been slipped without the child's knowledge. Then the child is offered an object which is new to him, an object which he wants to grasp. The object is then hidden under the blanket. The child will raise the blanket in order to find the object. When he fails to see the object, but sees only the beret, he will raise the beret in order to find the object. Piaget indicates that this is a very complex act of intelligence. The act supposes the permanence of the object, the localization of the object, individual above-below relations, etc. "But an act of intelligence of this kind can be constructed before speech and does not necessarily suppose representa- tion or thought."[68] The formation of thought and the acquisition of language are correlative but are not related in a simple causal way. Both thought and language are "bound up with a still more general operation which is the constitution of the symbolical function," which may be termed semiotic.[69] It is important to note the distinctions made by Piaget for purposes of his study, for unless it is noted that hermeneutics and structuralism often do not make these distinctions, a difference of termi- nology could be taken to be a more basic contradiction.

Clearly the developmental scheme of Piaget would apply to the matter of interpretation in cases where an individual or a whole group is moored at the concrete-operational level, where the cultural environ- ment discourages the use of formal operations, or where the application of formal operations in particular realms would lead to results which are considered undesirable. It would be fairly easy to equate the under- standing and use of the Bible on the part of some individuals and groups with the preliminary stages in the development scheme of Piaget, if not in the sensorimotor stage, certainly in the stage of concrete operations. The immediate religious environment and training of the individual simply will not allow him to progress beyond this stage, at least in the use of the Bible.

In any application of structural psychology to interpretation, the matter of lag must be considered. There are horizontal lags and vertical lags. These lags "characterize the repetition or the reproduction of the same formative operations at various levels."[70] Horizontal lag refers to the situation in which the mastery of a certain stage in one content area is only later able to be applied to another content area. Piaget gives an example from the field of concrete operations. A child aged seven or eight will know how to seriate quantities of material, lengths, etc. He will be able to classify, count, and measure them. He will also acquire notions of conservation relative to the contents. However, at seven or eight, the child will be incapable of all these operations in the field of weights. About two years later, he will apply the concrete operations mastered in the one content area in the other content area; he will generalize the concrete operations. Vertical lag refers to the reconstruction of a structure by means of other operations. At the close of the sensorimotor period, for example, an infant will have mastered a practical "group of displacements" in terms of his immediate environment. He will know how to orient himself in his apartment. "But this *group* is only practical and by no means representative." Several years later the same displacements are discovered on the level of representation.[71]

In the application of structural psychology to interpretation, the question arises if one particular approach to the text must be incorporated before another particular approach can be appropriated (historical-literary → phenomenological-hermeneutical → structural), or if there are necessary stages in the appropriation of each particular approach— or even if there are subsystems of the various approaches (perhaps associated with different levels of language, literature, and meaning) which must be appropriated before subsections of various other approaches can be appropriated.

Is it possible that the fullest appropriation of structuralism (not merely as a method to help uncover conventional meaning but also as an independent but related medium of meaning or meaning-effect) is impossible before the mental structure accommodates the hermeneutical approach along with the historical-literary? If so, some of the bitter opposition and total indifference toward structural methods on the one hand and the "domestication" of structuralism as a servant of conventional approaches on the other hand would be explained. This hypothesis would not only help in the history of structural analysis, but it would give a clue as to the proper incorporation of structural analysis. (I am not suggesting that interpreters who have incorporated historical-literary and hermeneutical approaches will automatically accommodate structural insights. There are still problems associated particularly with the "philosophy" of structuralism.) The structuralism which I have suggested as properly being built upon hermeneutics is the structuralism not merely of external linguistic forms but the structuralism which relates those forms to production, to linguistic and literary competence.

The hermeneutics upon which such a structuralism is to be founded, moreover, is phenomenological hermeneutics as exemplified in the work of Merleau-Ponty. Jonathan Culler judges that the view of structuralism and phenomenology as radical opposites results from a structuralism which excludes concerns with the perspective of the actor or speaker. As we have seen, a complete theory of structuralism does not simply establish inventories of elements, oppositions between those elements, and a calculus of possible accommodations; a coherent theory of structuralism includes the speaker. Culler concludes that "it is only possible to determine elements and oppositions and to set up a calculus of possible combinations if one takes as the object of one's analysis the system which speakers have assimilated and tacitly know. Structural analysis must take place within phenomenology in that its goal must be that of explicating and formalizing what is phenomenally given in the subject's relation to his cultural objects."[72] Culler surveys the attempt of Merleau-Ponty to overcome the dualism of subject and object and his reluctance to dispense with subject or with man. In notes for his unfinished work *Le visible et l'invisible*, Merleau-Ponty charted the movement from a criticism of subject and object to a criticism of meaning, and it appears to Culler "that Merleau-Ponty would have attempted in his last work to ground structural linguistics and a structuralist vocabulary of configurations and articulations on a phenomenological ontology." The phenomenologist must become a structuralist when he considers the implications of his theory.[73]

It is illuminating to relate Merleau-Ponty's developing relationship with structuralism to the stages of development of structural psychology. In an initial period, language for Merleau-Ponty had an adjunct relationship to the development of his thesis of the primacy of perception, the thesis that among the various modes of experience the structures of perception are the most fundamental and serve as the paradigm for analogs at all the other levels. Language enables a speaker to fix a new meaning in the mental space of his linguistic community, and Merleau-Ponty's concern is to analyze the structuration and restructuration which language brings into experience of the world. As with Heidegger, the emphasis is on the emergence, properties, institution, and meaning-structures of words. He leaves questions of syntax and semantics out of consideration and is hardly aware of the unconscious syntactic systems behind the act of speaking.[74]

In a second period, language begins to become more essential. Influenced by the linguistics of Saussure, Merleau-Ponty sees language as the privileged model for the experience of meaning. The relation of *parole* to *langue*, of word to syntax, and the problem of linguistic universals are important matters which are treated in an attempt to reconcile phenomenology and structuralism. Again, the concern of Merleau-Ponty (as with Heidegger) is with the level of word. Merleau-Ponty sees the crowning achievement of structuralism as the discovery of the phonological level of meaning in language. This meaning is independent of questions of reference or semantics. It is immanent to the linguistic system itself. In *The Phenomenology of Perception*, Merleau-Ponty declares that there is a phonological level of meaning "whose very existence intellectualism does not suspect."[75] The third period of development in Merleau-Ponty's relations to structuralism is really a further development of the second period. It is an attempt to integrate structuralism into a broader framework of a phenomenology of experience as a whole. In *Signs* we come to a final step, a use of structural insights to understand the relationships between "fact" and "essence," the instance and the type. In the essay "From Mauss to Claude Lévi-Strauss" Merleau-Ponty affirms the meaning of structure. "Structure . . . organizes its constituent parts according to an internal principle: it is meaning. But this meaning it bears is, so to speak, a clumsy meaning."[76] On the other hand, structuralism is no Platonic idea, no imperishable archetype which dominates the life of all possible societies, although there is nothing to limit structural research in the direction of universals. The relationship between the particular and the universal is the key:

Thus there appears at the base of social systems a formal infrastructure (one is tempted to say an unconscious thought), an anticipation of the human mind, as if our science were already completed in events, and the human order of culture a second order of nature dominated by other invariants. But even if these invariants exist, even if social science were to find beneath structures a metastructure to which they conformed (as phonology does beneath phonemes), the universal we would thus arrive at could no more be substituted for the particular than general geometry annuls the local truth of Euclidean spatial relations.[77]

Merleau-Ponty sees that the opposition of induction to deduction is

simply an ancient prejudice and is not productive in the "method of convergence." Actual thinking for Merleau-Ponty "moves back and forth
between experience and intellectual construction or reconstruction."[78]

> Now experience in anthropology is our insertion as social subjects into a
> whole in which the synthesis our intelligence laboriously looks for has
> already been effected, since we live in the unity of one single life all the
> systems our culture is composed of. We can gain some knowledge from
> this synthesis which is ourselves. Furthermore, the equipment of our
> social being can be dismantled and reconstructed by the voyage, as we
> are able to learn to speak other languages. This provides a second way to
> the universal: no longer the overarching universal of a strictly objective
> method, but a sort of lateral universal which we acquired through ethno-
> logical experience and its incessant testing of the self through the other
> person and the other person through the self.[79]

James N. Edie sees structuralism as opening the door for Merleau-
Ponty's task of formulating "essential" or structural laws that still participate in the historicity, contingency, and open-endedness of the primary
data being dealt with.

> It showed how essential laws, which ordinarily lie beneath the threshold
> of experience, can nevertheless be shown to be the necessary structural
> conditions of the experience of which they are the laws. It gave him one
> of the clearest illustrations of the correlativity of fact and essence in experi-
> ence and thus the means of bringing structuralism and phenomenology
> together and of reconciling them in a higher synthesis. All the phonologi-
> cal, morphological, syntactic, and other laws that govern the speech act
> and make it possible can clearly be shown to be *necessary* (and "invari-
> ant") laws, i.e., insofar as they thematize conditions without which speak-
> ing would be impossible, and yet these laws are themselves generated by
> historical, contingent acts of speech, which they serve and which they are
> *of*. They have no "substantiality" in themselves. . . . The ultimate unity of
> *la langue* and *la parole*, that is, of the structural conditions and of their
> actualizations in the experiences that confer on them their ontological
> validity, is what Merleau-Ponty was striving to understand and account
> for on the structuralist basis provided by Saussure.[80]

Peter Homans, building upon the work of Matthew Ikeda, has attempted to relate the stages of development of structural psychology to
Ricoeur's three levels of the creativity of symbols. Instead of drawing
directly from the conceptualization of Piaget, he uses the works of
Kohlberg and Loevinger concerning moral development and ego development.[81] The Kohlberg-Loevinger approach posits stages in the development of otherness in which there is increasing concern on the part of

individuals with the otherness of people, ideas, and ideals. The last three stages, as summarized by Ikeda, are:

> stage 4, *conscientious*—presence of self-evaluating standards; capacity for self-criticism; guilt for consequences of breaking the law; long-term goals and ideals; law-and-order orientation; stage 5, *autonomous*—capacity to cope with inner needs; ability to tolerate differences among groups of people; democratic frame of reference; and stage 6, *integrated*—reconciling inner conflicts; universal ethical orientation; renunciation of the unattainable; concern with universals and with essences.[82]

Ricoeur's levels of the creativity of symbols are: (1) The level of sedimented symbolism where stereotyped and fragmented remains of symbols are used. At this level, the work of symbolization is no longer operative. (2) The level of the useful functioning of symbols in everyday life. (3) The level of prospective symbols. At this level traditional symbols serve as the vehicles of new meanings.[83] Homans sees Ricoeur's first level of creativity of symbols (sedimented symbolism) as related to the first three stages of Kohlberg-Loevinger. This is the level at which symbols are not yet used in everyday life. The individual has not developed to the point where he enters into his own socialization in an active and direct way. Ricoeur's second and third levels of creativity of symbols relate to stages four, five, and six of the Kohlberg-Loevinger conceptualization. Stage four is a key stage for hermeneutics. This is the stage of conscientiousness where there is a capacity for self-criticism and a feeling of guilt for breaking laws. In this stage, corresponding to Ricoeur's second level, little awareness of myths and symbols outside of one's own culture exists, but there is great awareness of myths and symbols within one's culture. In stage five of the development of otherness, distance is placed between consciousness and myth. Stage six, the most advanced stage of development, is associated by Homans with the most inclusive hermeneutical style. Myth reemerges as a genuine possibility; there is a dialectic between human consciousness and the reappropriation of myth.

In the appropriation of structural psychology for development in the hermeneutics of symbols, there is really no need to depart from Piaget; Ricoeur's three levels of the creativity of symbols correspond directly to the three stages of Piaget. The recapitulation of these stages in the hermeneutical development of an adult could be interpreted as a lag in which the operations mastered on one particular content are repeated on another different content. Moreover, the three stages in the development of the use of symbols or cognitive development can be seen as also re-

capitulated in three stages of development in the creative use of structuralism. Let us use the term *genre* as the means of production which
results in a particular form on the surface level. The first stage of the
development of creativity of structures (of genre) would be the historical
or taxonomic level. On this level, the particular genres are simply seen
from a descriptive perspective. The second stage of the creativity of genres
is the level at which genres function in communication. They are useful in
interpretation on the conventional literary level. The third stage of the
creativity of genres is the level at which they serve as vehicles of new
meaning, no longer simply serving conventional historical-literary interpretation, but allowing a meaning or meaning-effect-like-mathematics.

Regardless of the specific ordering of different systems and subsystems
of interpretation, the application of structural psychology to interpretation reinforces the theory of the existence of a harmonious systems
approach. In the development of the mental structure, the various stages
are accommodated. They are not temporary stopping places; they remain
as part of the capacity of the individual. The sensorimotor competence of
the child is not given up when the stage of concrete operations is reached.
Nor are the possibilities of concrete operations lost when the period of
formal operations is achieved. "The moment the equilibrium is reached
on a point, the structure is integrated into a new system being formed,
until there is a new equilibrium ever more stable and of an ever more
extending field."[84] In terms of the systems approach to interpretation
(assuming a degree of equilibrium having been achieved in respect to
the different approaches and levels of language, literature, and meaning)
any one approach and any one level may be the center of attention. The
capacity of other approaches and levels is operative but "tuned down" or
directed toward the signification on the level which is the center of attention. Methodologically and consciously, all possible levels and all possible
approaches cannot be utilized at the same time. Unconsciously, of course,
whenever one approach is used, all of the other approaches which have
been mastered are involved because they are in equilibrium in a total system. Methodologically, particular approaches and levels will be the center
of attention at a particular moment.

NOTES

1. Paul Ricoeur, "Biblical Hermeneutics," *Semeia* 4 (1975), 63–65.
2. It will be observed that man is the necessary mediator in these relationships.

3. Loretta Dornisch indicates that "Ricoeur's present work is projected as Volume III of *The Philosophy of the Will* which will perhaps unfold in three parts: (1) the creative dimension of language, including metaphor; (2) the creative dimension of action, starting from freedom and including the invention of institutions; and (3) imagination, which is perhaps the heart of the process." Dornisch, "Paul Ricoeur and Biblical Interpretation: A Selected Bibliography," *Semeia* 4 (1975), 24.

4. See Ricoeur's own description of his pilgrimage, "From Existentialism to the Philosophy of Language," *Philosophy Today* 17 (1973), 88–96.

5. *Ibid.*, pp. 89–90.

6. *Ibid.*, p. 90.

7. *Ibid.*

8. *Ibid.*

9. *Ibid.*, p. 91.

10. *Ibid.*, p. 92. The first naiveté is an uncritical consciousness dismissing myth and symbol because of a supposed incompatibility with modern science and history. The second naiveté is a critical consciousness purging symbols and myths of literalism but listening to their message.

11. *Ibid.*

12. *Ibid.*, pp. 92–93.

13. Ricoeur, "Biblical Hermeneutics," pp. 63–65.

14. *Ibid.*, p. 65.

15. *Ibid.*, p. 66.

16. *Ibid.*, p. 67.

17. *Ibid.*

18. *Ibid.*, p. 68.

19. *Ibid.*, p. 71.

20. *Ibid.*, p. 70.

21. Ricoeur, "The Hermeneutical Function of Distanciation," *Philosophy Today* 17 (1973), 139, 133.

22. *Ibid.*, p. 139.

23. *Ibid.*

24. *Ibid.*, p. 140.

25. *Ibid.*

26. *Ibid.*, p. 139.

27. *Ibid.*, p. 140.

28. *Ibid.*

29. Ricoeur, "Biblical Hermeneutics," p. 87. See Paul Ricoeur, *La métaphore vive* (Paris: Seuil, 1975), pp. 273–321, "Métaphore et référence," for the fullest discussion of metaphorical reference in poetic works.

30. Ricoeur, "Biblical Hermeneutics," p. 78.

31. *Ibid.*, p. 79.

32. *Ibid.*, p. 80.

33. *Ibid.*, p. 84.

34. *Ibid.*, p. 87.

35. *Ibid.*, p. 88.

36. *Ibid.*, p. 96.
37. *Ibid.*
38. *Ibid.*, p. 98.
39. *Ibid.*, p. 99.
40. *Ibid.*
41. *Ibid.*, p. 107. Ricoeur indicates that religious language modifies poetic language by various procedures such as "intensification," "transgression," and "going to the limit." The limit-experiences of man (as well as the peak experiences of creation and joy and the tragic boundary experiences of suffering, death, struggling, and guilt) are the ultimate referent of religious language, and to these limit-experiences of man correspond the limit-expressions of religious language. Religious language itself, however, must be transposed from "images" or "figurative modes" to "conceptual modes" of expression. In the past, philosophical conception has mediated such a transposition. Today, however, we have only the wreckage of philosophical systems with which to do our conceptualization. In the task of conceptualization "in the space of confrontation of our present culture," nevertheless, the conceptual must remain "under the control of the hermeneutical potential of the metaphor." Ricoeur would parallel limit-concepts, limit-expressions, and limit-experiences. These limit-concepts must not become idols; they must remain on the boundary line of rational philosophy; they must "preserve the tension of the symbol within the clarity of the concept." The conceptualizations must continually be seen "as an 'approximation' of the 'sense' and 'reference' of religious symbols, with the acknowledgment of the *inadequacy* of these concepts." *Ibid.*, pp. 133, 135, 136.
42. *Ibid.*, p. 71. Ricoeur earlier had emphasized that a hermeneutical consequence of the generative function of genre was that "the dynamics of form is at the same time a dynamics of thought. . . . The theological content itself is produced in harmony with the rule of the corresponding literary genre." "The Hermeneutical Function of Distanciation," p. 136.
43. Ricoeur does suggest the possibility of a structural analysis assisting on the deep level if the function of structural analysis be seen as disclosing "the diachronic kernel by means of the achronic structure." In this case, the "diachronic kernel would constitute the *depth-semantics* of the narrative on which an existential interpretation could readily be grafted." "Biblical Hermeneutics," p. 50.
44. *Ibid.*, p. 56.
45. *Ibid.*, pp. 61–63.
46. *Ibid.*, p. 61.
47. *Ibid.*, p. 62. Ricoeur does see Marin's remarks concerning the "empty" place, the "other voice," as a possible way of relating the notion of communication to Fuchs's concept of language-event. The residues of the system of interplay and interaction may designate the "other" as an extra-linguistic being. If so, "the structural analysis has to open itself to another kind of interpretation which takes seriously the movement of transcendence of the text beyond itself." *Ibid.*, p. 63.

48. Ricoeur, "The Hermeneutical Function of Distanciation," p. 140.

49. *Ibid.*, p. 136.

50. *Ibid.*, pp. 135–36.

51. Paul Ricoeur, "Philosophy and Religious Language," *Journal of Religion* 54 (1974), 74.

52. *Ibid.*, p. 76.

53. Wilhelm Dilthey, *Die Hermeneutik Schleiermachers*, G.S. XIV/2, 661. Quoted in Peter Krausser, *Kritik der endlichen Vernunft* (Frankfurt: Suhrkamp Verlag, 1968), p. 29.

54. See Krausser, *Kritik der endlichen Vernunft*, pp. 47–48.

55. *Ibid.*, pp. 84–92.

56. *Ibid.*, pp. 109–10.

57. *Ibid.*, p. 210.

58. It should be noted that Dilthey speaks of various structural systems, the social system, the cultural system, the psycho-physical system of higher animals, the biological-physical system of all life generally, as well as the mental, cultural, linguistic, dynamic system of scholarly activity. The *erworbenen Zusammenhang*, however, is only spoken of in relation to individual human beings. *Ibid.*, pp. 143, 145.

59. *Ibid.*, pp. 149–51. Krausser indicates that in *Aufbau der geschichtlichen Welt* Dilthey answers the question of what binds together the different activities of a nation by a circular answer which ignores completely earlier superior insights into the question of the mental capacity of an individual. *Ibid.*, p. 152.

60. Dilthey, *Einleitung in die Geisteswissenschaften*, G.S. I, 64. Quoted in Krausser, *Kritik der endlichen Vernunft*, p. 151.

61. Krausser, *Kritik der endlichen Vernunft*, p. 152.

62. Dilthey, *Über die Möglichkeit einer allgemeingültigen pädagogischen Wissenschaft*, G.S. VI, p. 65. Quoted in Krausser, *Kritik der endlichen Vernunft*, pp. 158–59.

63. José Ortega y Gasset, *Concord and Liberty* (New York: Norton, 1946), p. 134.

64. See Howard Gardner, *The Quest for Mind: Piaget, Lévi-Strauss, and the Structuralist Movement* (New York: Knopf, 1973), pp. 51–110, for a summary of the thought of Piaget.

65. Jean Piaget, *The Child and Reality: Problems of Genetic Psychology* (New York: Grossman, 1973); pp. 49–61.

66. *Ibid.*, p. 172.

67. *Ibid.*, p. 11.

68. *Ibid.*, p. 12.

69. *Ibid.*, p. 117.

70. *Ibid.*, p. 53.

71. *Ibid.*, pp. 53–54.

72. Jonathan Culler, "Phenomenology and Structuralism," *The Human Context* 5 (1973), 37–38.

73. Culler is interested in the inverse proposition, namely, that "the struc-

turalist must become a phenomenologist if he scrutinizes the foundations of his method." *Ibid.*, p. 35.

74. The analysis of James M. Edie is used in this section. Edie organizes Merleau-Ponty's writings on language into three periods. See "Was Merleau-Ponty a Structuralist?" *Semiotica* 4 (1971), 297–323. See also Philip E. Lewis, "Merleau-Ponty and the Phenomenology of Language," *Structuralism*, ed. Jacques Ehrmann (New York: Doubleday, 1970), pp. 9–31.

75. Cited in Edie, "Was Merleau-Ponty a Structuralist?" p. 312.

76. Maurice Merleau-Ponty, *Signs* (Evanston: Northwestern University Press, 1964), p. 117.

77. *Ibid.*, pp. 118–19.

78. *Ibid.*, p. 119.

79. *Ibid.*, pp. 119–20.

80. Edie, "Was Merleau-Ponty a Structuralist?" pp. 322–23.

81. Lawrence Kohlberg, "From Is to Ought: How to Commit the Naturalistic Fallacy and Get Away with It in the Study of Moral Development," in *Cognitive Development and Epistemology*, ed. Theodore Mishel (New York: Academic Press, 1971); Jean Loevinger and Ruth Wessler, *Measuring Ego Development*, vol. I (San Francisco: Jossey-Bass, 1970).

82. Peter Homans, "Psychology and Hermeneutics: An Exploration of Basic Issues and Resources," *Journal of Religion* 55 (1975), 342.

83. Paul Ricoeur, *Freud and Philosophy* (New Haven, Conn.: Yale University Press, 1970), pp. 504–5. Quoted in Homans, "Psychology and Hermeneutics," p. 342.

84. Piaget, *The Child and Reality*, p. 60.

PART THREE

STRUCTURES AND MEANINGS IN NEW TESTAMENT NARRATIVE

Introduction

The narrative hermeneutics which results from the wedding of the hermeneutical and structural traditions attempts to do justice to both hermeneutics and the structural study of narrative. Narrative hermeneutics recapitulates the efforts of Dilthey to resolve the problem of universality and historicality without reducing one to the other. More importantly, narrative hermeneutics utilizes the fact of universality and historicality, the fact of the fundamental structure of the mind and the historicality of man, the fact of the generality and necessity of narrative and the singularity of narrative.

An illustration of the fact that narrative hermeneutics is not a simple adoption of structuralism or a reduction of hermeneutics to structuralism is the variety of ways in which the term "structure" is used in narrative hermeneutics. For the structuralist as such, concern is with a transtextual reality, the theoretical or abstract model or system of relationships which determine the narrative on the level of manifestation. In narrative hermeneutics, the term "structure" is used in this way. But no hesitation is made in using "structure" for the grammatical patterns in a particular text. "Structure" is used also as a verb to describe the activity of the structure of the mind as it is involved in both the abstract universal level and the concrete particular narrative.

Chapter Seven compares contemporary New Testament interpretation and the structural approach and gives an apology for a narrative hermeneutics which involves various critical approaches. New Testament study has virtually become historical study attempting to refer elements of the text to real, verifiable historical factors, to trace elements and forms of discourse and narrative from one period to another, and to refer literary texts to given problems in the history of the church so that the texts are seen as "answers" to particular historical problems. A radically histori-

233

cal approach, however, is inadequate to accomplish the purposes of the text, and the historical approach itself leads to literary approaches. The chapter proposes a method of analysis which maintains contact with the various levels of text and meaning and applies the method in a limited and illustrative way to Luke 5:1–11. Luke 5:1–11 is seen in narrative hermeneutics as a "performative utterance" which creates its object by the reader's participation. The text involves familiar elements, but these elements are put together in a way that the intention of the text can never be completely defined as the identification of elements with factors in the real world. The text presents and invites reactions to and attitudes toward the world of the reader, which may include versions of the world of Jesus, the tradition, and the church, and it is these reactions and attitudes that constitute the reality of Luke 5:1–11.

A modified structural approach to Luke 5:1–11 sensitizes the reader to elements of signification and opens up the possibility of affective interpretation, which yet remains related to the interpretation of the "material" of the text. The ontological and theological meanings cannot be ignored in interpretation. Certainly the theological and ontological level of meaning was operative in the mind of the writer when he created Luke 5:1–11.

The approach of "narrative hermeneutics," of course, does not prove the Reality of God, but it may give grounds for affirming that our existential language is based on Reality. Structuralism, then, may add a dimension to philosophy and theology as well as to literature.

CHAPTER SEVEN

Structuralism and
New Testament Interpretation

BACKGROUND: PHILOSOPHICAL AND THEOLOGICAL FACTORS

The significance which a New Testament interpreter will find in the structural study of narrative will depend upon a number of factors.[1] Two factors are of crucial importance: the broad philosophical and theological base on which New Testament theology is done and the critically "orthodox" method of historical criticism. A survey of these areas will show the need for further advances in interpretation which may be assisted by structuralism.

The Philosophical Situation

Theology in all of its forms, consciously or unconsciously, has been influenced by philosophy or philosophical conceptions. In a sense, the initial development of a theology took place because of the movement of Christian thought into the Greco-Roman world. The church both needed to elaborate a theological discourse and was able to do so because of Greek conceptuality. On the basis of theology from the earliest period, it seems that the only way to do away with philosophy in biblical study, whether it is Greek or modern, would be to do away with developed thought, not just to do away with formal theology.[2] Krister Stendahl, aware of the historical relationship between philosophy and theology, noted that "we can smile when we see how an earlier generation of biblical scholars peddled Kantian, Hegelian, or Ritschlian ideas, all the time subjectively convinced that they were objective scholars who only stated 'facts.' "[3] Stendahl, however, was writing in a period when adherents of a "Biblical Theology" in general felt that theology could be done not in terms of philosophy but in terms of biblical categories, and he declared that objectivity was possible. Although certainty in the enterprise is not possible, he felt that a "mature fruit of the historical method," "a new feature in biblical studies," was the descriptive task of discovering what the words of the Bible "meant when uttered or written by the prophet, the priest, the evangelist, or the apostle—and regardless of their meaning in later stages of religious history, our own included."[4] Once that objective scholarship was done, the question as to the meaning of the text in the present became necessary. Stendahl felt that even here the question of present relevance was not to be answered by modifications of a philosophical nature, "with Augustine correcting the earlier fathers, Thomas Aquinas correcting Augustine, Luther refuting Thomas, Schleiermacher touching up Luther, and Barth and Tillich carrying the traditional discussion up to our own time."[5] The possibility of descriptive study made possible a theology not in terms of philosophical and theological tradition but in terms of the original. Descriptive biblical theology "gives the systematic theologian a live option to attempt a direct translation of the biblical material, not a revision of a translation of a revision of a translation. . . ." "The ideal of an empathetic understanding of the first century without borrowing categories from later times has never been an ideal before, nor have the comparative sources for such an adventure been as close at hand and as well analyzed."[6]

Ironically, the very year that the important article by Krister Stendahl was published in *The Interpreter's Dictionary of the Bible,* what Brevard S. Childs considers the "final blow"[7] to Biblical Theology was delivered by James Barr. "Revelation through History in the Old Testament and in Modern Theology" is the title of Barr's inaugural lecture in which he outlined a series of arguments against the presuppositions of Biblical Theology.[8] The basic criticism of Barr is that Biblical Theology does not take seriously the biblical text itself, that the emphasis on history distorts the biblical narrative by formulating an abstraction which works on only a small portion of the Bible.

The failure of Biblical Theology to develop a theology from and *only* from *all* of the Bible would seem to demand that some conscious accommodation of biblical studies and philosophical conceptualizations continue to take place. A modern theology, as every theology, would state biblical truths in terms of some compelling comprehensive philosophy. The truths would have meaning, and indeed validity, to the extent that they cohered with the philosophical conception.

Peter Berger, in a brief volume dealing with "the possibility of theological thinking in our present situation," points out that all human societies are based on what is taken to be or believed to be "knowledge." "Most of what we 'know' we have taken on the authority of others, and it is only as others continue to confirm this 'knowledge' that it continues to be plausible to us. It is such socially shared, socially taken-for-granted 'knowledge' that allows us to move with a measure of confidence through everyday life."[9] The theologian, Berger points out, is not different from every other human being. The theologian exists in a social milieu. "His 'knowledge' has been socially acquired, is in need of social support, and is thus vulnerable to social pressures."[10]

Using the sociological interpretation of Berger, we see that the problem of a neo-liberal *theology* is that there is no longer any philosophical support, no "knowledge," which can be used as the basis for genuine theology—except in a descriptive, historical sense. Paul Ricoeur presents the same view from a philosophical perspective and points out that with the blows of the Kantian critique, Marxist metacritique, nihilism in the Nietzschean sense, psychoanalysis, and the human sciences, "it is now with an anti-ontological conceptuality that theology has to come to grips."[11] Peter Berger says that, at least traditionally, the meaningfulness of the term "supernatural" has been a necessary condition of the theological enterprise. "It follows that, in a situation where one may speak of a demise of the supernatural, and *where the theologian himself does so* when he describes the situation, the theological enterprise is confronted with truly formidable difficulties." Berger says that the theologian "more and more resembles a witch doctor stranded among logical positivists. . . ."[12]

Berger and Ricoeur do not advocate a return to an earlier situation in philosophy and theology. However, both are convinced that theology can be done today. Berger says that, whether we like it or not, we are in a situation in which transcendence "has been reduced to a rumor." This situation cannot be escaped with "one magical jump"; nor should we wish to return to some earlier situation. "We must begin in the situation in which we find ourselves, but we must not submit to it as to an irresistible tyranny." Secularized society is not the absolute, and although the signals of transcendence have become rumors in our day, "we can set out to explore these rumors—and perhaps to follow them up to their source." Berger suggests that the exploration will not simply be an overcoming of tragedy (as existential theologians have emphasized) but also, and perhaps more importantly, "it will be an overcoming of triviality, . . . the most careful attention to each human gesture that we encounter or that we may be called upon to perform in the everyday dramas of human life . . . just because . . . it is in the midst of these affairs that 'some have entertained angels unawares.' "[13]

Ricoeur declares that, although theology confronts an anti-ontological conceptuality, *formally* the task of theology is the same. Theology has to interpret its own meaning today in face of the problematic of the theology of secularization and the death of God. "It is the task of theology to coordinate the experience articulated by the biblical text with human experience at large and as a whole."[14]

In the contemporary philosophical and theological context, it seems only proper to investigate the potential of structural presuppositions for theological conceptualization as well as structural methods for biblical interpretation. The same defense which John Macquarrie gave for his existential approach to theology is valid for an evaluation of structuralism for theology:[15] (1) Structuralism is a pervasive way of looking at reality, and theology has a right, even an obligation, to use philosophical concepts in its apologetic task. In using structuralism, Christian theology cannot ignore that structuralism often becomes much more than a method. It has become the basis for the construction of world views. With Lévi-Strauss, for example, the structuralist method becomes a philosophy which sees the human mind as mere expression of the material world of which it is a part. Human freedom, therefore, becomes an illusion. But structuralism can lead in other directions and support theistic philosophies. The structural method and Christian theology are not inherently in opposition or in agreement, but, in fact, structuralism has an attraction for modern Christians because, as Günther Schiwy says, "it takes up and vigorously pursues theoretical questions which today in the sciences of nature and of man indicate the most progressive positions, such as analysis of language, critique of ideology, the objectification, functionalization and decentralization of man, and sociologization."[16] (2) A close relationship may be shown between structural concepts and theology. Structuralism begins with language and semiotics as the model of the world which can help us discover and explore other signs. Christian theology is also concerned with signs and with language, words, and *the word.* On the basis of the prologue of the Fourth Gospel, Schiwy asks,

> Isn't language for the Christian, on theological grounds, the primordial form of revelation, even as for the structuralist it is the primordial form of world-view and world-model? What would any other "sign from heaven" —such as the beauty of the world or its catastrophes, "wonderful events"

and even the astounding deeds of a Jesus of Nazareth—be without language? What would it be if it were not interpreted, explained, signified by a word and therefore incorporated into an already existing system of meaning, a "world-view"?[17]

(3) Biblical thought may be shown to have an affinity for structural conceptualization. The place of the Bible in Christianity, the appeal of the New Testament to the Old, the appeal of Christian theology to the Scriptures are easily understood from the point of view of structuralism.

The philosophical and theological situation of our day demands that all resources be used to develop a theology which can speak meaningfully to man in the philosophical anti-ontological conceptuality.

The Historical-Critical Approach

The critically orthodox approach to the Bible is the historical-critical approach. The approach is so ingrained in biblical scholars that it is almost impossible to be properly critical about this approach. Yet, the history of historical criticism points to weaknesses which demand strengthening by supplementation from other approaches. Numerous historical and cultural factors were involved in the movement toward historical criticism. The Renaissance and the Reformation liberated men from authority and tradition and favored the eventual development of a view of the Bible which could be approached with reason instead of as a supernaturally guaranteed revelation outside the scope of reason. The rationalism of Pierre Bayle (1647–1707) and John Locke (1632–1704), as a "habit of thought ruling all minds, under the conditions of which all alike tried to make good the peculiar opinions they might happen to cherish,"[18] became acceptable to churchmen. This type of rationalism was quite different from that of the later nineteenth century. In eighteenth-century English theology, then, "rationalism" was not a system which was antagonistic to Christianity. It was an attitude which assumed that reason is involved in religion. As Mark Pattison pointed out in the mid-nineteenth century, "The Churchman differed from the Socinian, and the Socinian from the Deist, as to the number of articles in his creed: but all alike consented to test their belief by the rational evidence for it."[19]

The Deist controversy, the discoveries of geology, the Darwinian evolutionary ideas were all important elements in the intellectual struggle leading to a new view of Scripture. It probably is not too much to say that the historical-critical approach to the Bible developed because the socially held "knowledge" would not allow older dogmatic approaches. The unquestioned postulates of society no longer legitimized the methods which once were dictated by and supported by those presuppositions. The new views of man and his world inevitably dictated methods which could be legitimized in light of the new views. The challenge of deism, rationalism, and evolution was met by Christian scholars who saw that in a scientific age biblical records had to be subjected to scientific study in order to retain their authority.[20]

Slowly but no less surely historical criticism became the orthodox method of Bible study. Unconsciously and consciously the socially held "knowledge" influenced Christians in general and theologians in particular. Today, two parallel movements seem to be modifying the reign of the historical approach. The socially held "knowledge" has changed radically since the beginning of historical criticism; and views of the world, of man, of meaning are no longer legitimizing the critical approach developed in the eighteenth and nineteenth centuries. Along with this is the gradual discovery on the part of biblical scholarship itself that the historical approach does not simply grow out of the nature of the Bible and in and of itself is not capable of accomplishing the purposes of the Scriptures.

Of crucial importance was the early association of the historical critical approach with an evolutionary conceptualization. As W. Neil says, ". . . under the influence of the evolutionary principle, the religion of the Bible came to be seen as part of the sweep of history, and the concept of progressive revelation became a yardstick for evaluating its claims."[21] For a time, the developmental approach solved the problem of the "primitive" ideas of God, man, society, etc. in the Bible, and it is impossible to deny that there are different levels of insight in the biblical material and even historical development in certain theological conceptualizations. But the question arises: Does the category of progress (nineteenth-century universal evolution) apply in the area of religious truth? Language and conceptualization may change, but, as Alan Richardson declares, "The truth would seem to be rather that insights into God's character and into man's relationship with God are independent of relative priority or lateness in an evolutionary series."[22]

Important also is the assumption in historical studies that human actions rather than an a priori divine plan is the basis for history. Christian historiography of the medieval period emphasized divine influence on human affairs, but the idea of cause and effect on the human historical level became the presupposition of later philosophies of history. The locus of meaning was in history; therefore the meaning of documents was tied up with the historical context out of which they arose. The Bible came to be treated, therefore, as a historical document whose truth could not be understood apart from such matters as authorship, dating, circumstance of writing, and relationship with previous oral and written material. Earlier readers of the Bible were aware of historical factors, but the assumption that the Holy Spirit was the real author made close attention to the historical factors unnecessary. Biblical scholars, of course, maintained that historical criticism was preliminary. As Richardson puts it,

> Before we can determine the meaning of any given passage of Scripture we must first ascertain with the aid of every scientific skill at our disposal what its original meaning was for those who first formulated it and first received it. Then we must understand its significance in relation to its place in the development of the biblical revelation as a whole. Only then shall we be in a position to comprehend its meaning for us in the changed situation of today. . . .[23]

It may be argued that, in practice, the acceptance of the presupposition of the historical approach precluded the accomplishment of the task of discovering anything but historical meaning, or the original meaning. If the historical method could uncover an absolute divine revelation in history separable from the relativity of history, then the historical method could well be shown to undergird biblical faith.[24] But how, on the basis of historical-critical presuppositions, can "a revelation which is thus immersed in the relativities of history be said to be a finally authoritative revelation? How, if we begin from the scientific investigation of historical events and utterances, are we to reach the absolute truth of God?"[25]

Historical studies may bring us face to face with the conviction of men that God has spoken to and through them. But historical study does not bring us to a historical event which can be ascertained by historical method to be God's eternal revelation of himself to man. A consequence of the historical-critical method, therefore, was the rise of a biblical criticism which dealt with historical problems on a scientific basis. Richardson says that historical theology as opposed to systematic theology "did not concern itself with ultimate questions or 'live' convictions. Its outlook was strictly scientific, and science does not deal with ultimate or existential questions and conviction."[26]

Walter Wink describes what happened in biblical studies:

> In this case the carrying over of methods from the natural sciences has led to a situation where we no longer ask what we would like to know and

what will be of decisive significance for the next step in personal or social development. Rather, we attempt to deal only with those complexes of facts which are amenable to historical method. We ask only those questions which the method can answer. We internalize the method's questions and permit a self-censorship of the questions intrinsic to our lives. Puffy with pretensions to "pure scholarship," this blinkered approach fails to be scholarly enough, precisely because it refuses to examine so much that is essential to understanding the intention of the text and our interest in reading it.

The conclusion of Wink that "historical biblical criticism is bankrupt" may be a rhetorical overstatement, but there is ample evidence that historical criticism as such "is incapable of achieving what most of its practitioners considered its purpose to be: so to interpret the Scriptures that the past becomes alive and illumines our present with new possibilities for personal and social transformation."[27]

Structuralism takes an approach which may be seen as the direct opposite of the historical approach. It is synchronic instead of diachronic; it emphasizes the text, not as the completion of earlier oral and written material, but as a work in and of itself. Structuralism does not attempt to discuss meaning on the basis of cause and effect on the level of history. Deeper atemporal factors are emphasized. The failure of historical study to accomplish the intention of the biblical text opens the way for the structural approach, not to supplant the historical-critical approach but to supplement it, guide and modify it, and in turn to be guided and modified by the historical approach.

STRUCTURALISM AND CONVENTIONAL
NEW TESTAMENT INTERPRETATION

The presuppositions and purposes of structural analysis would seem to preclude a relationship with conventional New Testament study. In order to determine whether this is true, we will compare conventional and structural approaches to the gospel narratives. It appears that structural study of narrative has been able to solve some of the problems which faced earlier structural approaches to literature in general. For that reason, and because source, form, and redaction study of the gospel narratives presents a clearly opposite approach to structuralism, the gospel tradition has been chosen as the basis for comparison. If structural study is helpful at any point, it should be helpful in the study of gospel material. Before we make a comparison of the structural and historical-critical approaches to gospel narrative, it should be noted that historians themselves have not ruled out literary approaches to historical writings per se. A structural approach to historical narrative, in fact, fits very closely with the views of historical theorists who emphasize a "literary" view of historical narrative. Hayden White describes this group as insisting that "historians explain the events that make up their narratives by specifically narrative means of encodation, that is to say, by finding the story which lies buried within or behind the events and telling it in a way that an ordinarily educated man would understand."[28]

Historical narrative may be thought of as composed of a plot, or a chronicle of events, and a story, or a presentation of the plot according to rules or logic of narrative. In this view, every historical narrative would have at least two levels of interpretation. The structure of the narrative would be related to basic logical principles of narration as well as to the objective facts in the narration.[29]

The nature of the study of the gospels has grown out of the nature of the gospel material itself and the use of the gospels by the church. All four of the gospels have amazing similarities in spite of their differences, and the synoptic gospels in particular contain a great number of narratives and discourses which exist in more than one gospel. There are agreements as well as differences in outline, and agreements in the specific narratives extending beyond subject matter to details of style and language.

The church has used the gospels to enlighten and reinforce its understanding and presentation of Jesus Christ, and the study of the gospels in the early periods of the critical approach concerned the historical questions of Jesus Christ—either to refute dogmatic conclusions, to confirm the teachings, or to rediscover the "historical" Jesus Christ. The assumption in early source analysis was that the uncovering of the earliest documents would carry us back to Jesus Christ because the gospels resulted from historical factors going back to Jesus and his disciples. By the early part of the twentieth century, the conclusions of source criticism were that Mark and Q served as sources for Matthew and Luke, that the earliest form of the "triple tradition" was that of Mark, and that the earliest form of the "double tradition" could be obtained by a study of the Matthean and Lukan forms of Q. Source criticism had also concluded that not only Matthew and Luke but also Mark and Q were influenced by theological views of the early church. The earliest documents contained not only early "authentic" materials but also materials of a later date. The discipline of source criticism, therefore, did not bring scholars to pure historical sources which allowed them to arrive at an unbiased primitive view of the earthly Jesus. To get behind the documents of a relatively late date, the discipline of form criticism developed. The same historical assumptions dominated form criticism, that is, that the narratives and discourses of the gospels resulted from historical factors in the life of the church.

Karl Ludwig Schmidt made a careful study of the synoptic tradition and showed that, with the exception of the passion narrative, the tradition of Mark consists of an abundance of individual stories which have been united by early Christians with various interests.[30] Martin Dibelius was the first actually to apply form criticism to the synoptic tradition. His purpose was to explain by reconstruction and analysis "the origin of the tradition about Jesus, and thus to penetrate into a period previous to that in which our Gospels and their written sources were recorded" and "to make clear the intention and real interest of the earliest tradition."[31] Rudolf Bultmann's volume on form criticism appeared in 1921, two years after that of Dibelius, with the purpose of "discovering what the original units of the synoptics were, both sayings and stories, to try to establish what their historical setting was, whether they belonged to a primary or secondary tradition or whether they were products of editorial activity."[32] The historical nature of the work of form criticism is seen clearly in the postulates which make the discipline possible. The "fundamental assumption" is that the tradition consists basically of individual sayings and narratives joined together in the gospels by the work of editors. Both Dibelius and Bultmann see this as a result of historical factors. They see movement toward uniting of the traditions in the oral period. Dibelius says, "That narratives were united even in the old tradition is seen most clearly in the interweaving of the story of Jairus with the healing of the woman with the issue. The union is so close here that we cannot regard it as originating in the evangelist as editor."[33] Bultmann stresses that "there is a natural limit to such groupings in the oral period, even if it cannot be precisely defined, a limit which can be exceeded for the first time in the written tradition."[34]

The purpose of the tradition is to serve the needs and purposes of the church. Dibelius must make some assumptions about these needs and purposes, for he follows a constructive method and reconstructs the history of the synoptic tradition from a study of the early Christian community. However, Bultmann, who follows an analytical method which begins with the text instead of the church, admits that he cannot "dispense with a provisional picture of the primitive community and its history, which has to be turned into a clear and articulated picture in the course of my inquiries."[35] A picture of the history of the early church is presented by Dibelius and Bultmann so that the particular traditions can be situated historically.

The assumptions of Dibelius and Bultmann regarding the "form" of the tradition show most clearly the historical nature of their concern. Dibelius and Bultmann assume that the narratives and sayings can be classified as to form and that the form enables the history of the tradition to be reconstructed. Dibelius indicates that a careful critical reading of the gospels gives evidence that the gospel writers took over units of material which already possessed a form of their own. Dibelius is not speaking of aesthetic standards created by a gifted individual when he speaks of "form." He is speaking of a style or form which has been created by its use among early Christians. The specific use to which a unit is put determines its form. In the church, the forms developed out of primitive Christian life itself. Bultmann is in complete accord with the assumption of Dibelius. "The proper understanding of form-criticism rests upon the judgment that the literature . . . springs out of quite definite conditions and wants of life from which grows up a quite definite style and quite specific forms and categories."[36] Every literary category then will have its own "life situation" which is a typical situation in the life of the early Christian community.

If New Testament criticism had been less historically oriented at the beginning of the twentieth century, form criticism could have moved in the direction of an understanding of form as it is understood in structural study today. Dibelius emphasizes the historical occasion for the development of the form but the reason for materials "automatically" taking on a definite form is that "it is only when such matters have received a form that they are able to bring about repentance and gain converts."[37] He emphasizes the paradigm because it constitutes the oldest Christian narrative style. The purpose of the paradigm is as an example in a sermon, and there is little artistic coloring and style. Yet Dibelius sees in the tales the regular appearance of literary style due to story-tellers and teachers "who understand their art and who love to exercise it."[38] In spite of the potential for development of form criticism in the direction of structural study, historical concerns dominated.

Redaction criticism, no less than source and form criticism, assumes that the gospels are a product of the historical process. The term "redaction" indicates the assumption and method by which the study takes place. "Editors" edited earlier materials to form gospels with unique purposes. The purposes can be ascertained by studying the ways that the gospel writer handles the traditional material. R. H. Lightfoot of the University of Oxford was one of the early scholars who saw in the fact that the tradition had virtually no order and arrangement before being set down in the gospels implications that the gospel writers were seeking to convey something by their selection and arrangement of the material. Lightfoot placed more emphasis upon the personality and intention of the individual evangelist than had earlier form critics. The purpose of Mark, according to Lightfoot, is not simply or chiefly biographical—it is doctrinal. Lightfoot, therefore, does not emphasize the life of Jesus as the history with which Mark is concerned, but he still emphasizes history. The chief purpose of Mark is "to show the history in the light in which he himself sees it, and wishes his readers also to regard it . . . to interpret the history and to set forth . . . its meaning and significance."[39]

Structural analysis looks at the materials being studied as the result of non-historical factors. Lévi-Strauss uses the work of the *"bricoleur"* to illustrate the way that myths use historical materials for construction of non-historical structures. It will be instructive to look at the materials of gospel criticism (whether at the level of individual narratives of the oral period, the documents of the written period, or the completed gospels) from the perspective of *"bricolage."*

The *bricoleur* is a jack-of-all-trades who uses various methods and whatever materials are at hand for the project. He is to be distinguished from the craftsman or engineer who has tools and raw materials for the precise purpose of the project. The *bricoleur*, when faced by a project, considers the tools and materials at hand in light of the problem. "A particular cube of oak could be a wedge to make up for the inadequate length of a plank of pine or it could be a pedestal—which would allow the grain and polish of the old wood to show to advantage."[40] The engineer, when faced with a project, "questions the universe" to find the precise tools and materials needed, while the *bricoleur* "addresses himself to a collection of oddments left over from human endeavors, that is, only a subset of the culture."[41] In terms of semiotics, for the *bricoleur*, "the signified changes into the signifying and vice versa." Reconstruction is continually taking place from the same materials. ". . . it is always earlier ends which are called upon to play the part of means."[42]

When the units of the gospel are studied structurally, then, the material of the units will not be evaluated in terms of their origins and earlier significations. The material will be judged in terms of their use in the units being analyzed. The sharp distinction between the historical and the structural cannot be maintained, however. As we have seen, Jakobson allows a referential function for a poetic work (although the referential function does not make the work a "straightforward document of cultural history, social relations, or biography").[43] He also affirms that synchrony does not deny the fact of diachrony. The concept of system or structure in synchronic study replaces the idea of "the mechanical agglomeration of material," but "pure synchronism now proves to be an illusion: every synchronic system has its past and its future as inseparable structural elements of the system."[44]

Using the analogy of the *bricoleur*, we observe that the elements in the constitution of the new structure are "preconstrained." There are limits on the freedom of the *bricoleur* to use the materials, depending upon their nature and previous function. The elements of the gospel tradition are not completely free; the uses to which they may be put are restricted by their nature and signification in previous structures.

The major factor uniting the historical and structural, however, is man himself. There is continuity because the meanings which are transmitted by means of historical elements and the structuring of those elements by and into forms or genres are transmitted only by man who perceives the meaning in the elements and forms and reformulates the traditional materials for new meanings.

An extremely historical approach leaves man out of account. He is simply a vehicle for reception and transmission of the material. An extremely structural approach makes the competence of man and the forms or genres associated with this competence the total focus, ignoring the meaning of the elements and the contribution that these meanings make to the significance of the gospel narrative. An extremely historical approach seems to be a figment of the imagination which totally ignores all of the data which historical criticism uses. If the presuppositions of source, form, and redaction criticism alone explain the gospels as they now exist, why such radical reformulation and radically different uses of the same elements in the four gospels? A severely structural approach is impossible. Even if reference is ruled out as finally an illusion, reference must be used to determine the surface structure from which deeper structures will be discerned. Again, radical structuralism really leaves man out of account, assuming that the deep structures exist prior to and independent of their manifestation and that they may have signification on a non-historical level, before they confront man simultaneously as a genre and as historical elements able to form the genre because of their referential value.

The severely structural approach to which I refer is not the structural approach of Dilthey or that of contemporary narratologists. It is perhaps that which can be attributed to Jakobson at some point. A contemporary and informed structural study of the gospel narratives must recognize that the creator and the interpreter of the narratives write and read on the basis of a competence (mental structure) which is a combination of innate and historical factors maintained in equilibrium. Mankind and his history and individual man and his cultural and historical experiences, then, are involved in the creation and interpretation of the New Testament narratives. But, also, the tradition, the historical elements embedded in forms, impinge upon man and have signification. In the interplay of man with his "horizon" and the "horizon" of the narrative, signification is achieved.

ANALYSIS OF NARRATIVE: DEVELOPMENT OF A METHOD

Introduction: Comprehensive Approach

The focus of this work is the significance of structural analysis of narrative for New Testament hermeneutics. In contrast to limited and limiting hermeneutical approaches to the New Testament text (Bultmann) and to hermeneutical approaches which are not related to recognizable linguistic landmarks (Fuchs) and in opposition to structural approaches which attempt to find conventional meanings in all discernible patterns of grammatical elements (Jakobson) and to structural approaches which reduce the narrative to a predetermined pattern, a comprehensive systematic approach has been suggested which considers the developing mental structure of man and the various levels of language, literature, and meaning as they are related to man. The principles which must guide any method based on the history of hermeneutics and structuralism include: (1) the primacy of the human in the activity of composition and interpretation; (2) the necessary relationship of the elements and patterns of analysis to human competence; (3) the different levels of meaning or meaning-effects; and (4) the interplay of the different levels of meaning.

In the study of narrative, a basic poetic meaning or meaning-effect may be taken to be that poetic meaning which is accomplished by the particular organization of the narrative (genre). But since our approach does not posit universal or ideal genres apart from particular expressions of the genre, the universal is seen only in the particular narrative with its historical or particular ideational content. This basic postulate of the unity of the affective and cognitive aspects of narrative allows the relating of all meanings which impinge upon a reader and interpreter of narrative.

Two ways of envisioning the reading and interpretation of a text will show the necessity of a comprehensive method incorporating different approaches and will help the formation of a method which is appropriate in light of the structures of narrative. Murray Krieger pictures the process of reading a poetic work in an allegory of a wanderer who comes upon a glass house filled with interesting objects. Initially, the wanderer looks into the house from without. Then he enters to examine the attractive objects he has seen. As he examines the objects, he first compares them with objects in the "real" world by glancing out through the glass walls, but then he becomes totally absorbed with the objects themselves and ceases glancing outside. Then the windows become mirrors which no longer look out but which reflect the objects in a multitude of ways and in various lights. The objects no longer appear as replicas of things outside, but take on an independent meaning. Eventually, the mirrors become windows again, and the wanderer now compares the objects outside with the vision of the objects in the glass house.[45] The allegory is the result of seeing that poetic language functions in three ways: "(1) As windows to the world, (2) as an enclosed set of endlessly faceted mirrors ever multiplying its maze of reflections but finally shut up within itself, and (3) as this same set of mirrors that miraculously become windows again."[46] Because the words or "raw material" of the poem seem to function as ordinary discourse they allow the reader to approach the poem. The interaction of each of the parts of the poem then allows it to become an independent organic unity and hence a window back to the world of the reader.

Norman H. Holland has viewed the "indeterminacy" of the reader's response or the differences among readings from the perspective of psychology and has carried out experiments to determine how people react to literary texts. He finds four principles of literary experience. The first is the overarching idea that a positive response on the part of a reader results from the ability of the reader "to put elements of the work together so that they act out his own lifestyle."[47] A reader approaches a text as he approaches a new experience, with a group of hopes, fears, and needs.

Readers want these expectancies to be met by the literary work in such a way that the readers are given "pleasure." The second related principle is that a reader has a favorable response if he is able to synthesize from the work "all or part of his characteristic structure of defense or adaptation." "For a reader to match his defenses by means of elements in the story, he must be able to satisfy his ego with them at all levels, including his 'higher' intellectual functions. Thus, it is the matching of defenses that draws on a reader's concern with language, his experience of prior works, his critical acumen, his taste and all the things people bring to bear when they deliberately evaluate literary works."[48] A third principle is that readers use materials "to create a wish-fulfilling fantasy" which is "characteristic" of themselves. The fantasy is not in the work itself but in the creative relationship between the reader and the text. Holland indicates that fantasy and defense "are intimately interlocked in literary response because of their deep relation in the mind."[49] Once the reader has achieved the matching of his defensive structure and the adaptation of this to suit his fantasies, the fourth principle comes into play: the reader will "make sense" of the text. The fantasy content will be transformed into some "literary point or theme of interpretation." The reader will use his "higher" ego functions (his interpretative skills, his literary experience, his experience of human character, and his sensitivity) and his social, moral, or political ideas in this task. "He will, finally, render the fantasy he has synthesized as an intellectual content that is characteristic —and pleasing—for him."[50]

The text is initially approachable only as a particular text whose elements relate to the historical world of the readers. For the reader to discern meaning and move toward interpretation *and* for the structuring of the text (the type, the typical, or the genre) to affect the reader, a particular text with elements relating to a world outside of the text is necessary. Personal meanings are also inevitably involved in the reading. Not only are these readings situated on levels determined by the level of development of the mental structure of the reader; the meanings are also influenced by the "cluster of wishes," the group of hopes, fears, and needs of the reader. A theologically or historically oriented reader may consciously and appropriately conclude the reading by making theological or historical sense or interpretation of the text, but involved in the interpretation is the reader's own level of development and previous experience. Structural analysis cannot be done apart from historical and existential consideration. In summary, the reader cannot discern elements and structures of meaning apart from the particular manifestation of those elements and structures and relationships of those elements and structures to other particular historical phenomena. Also, the reader cannot come to the text except with the cluster of wishes which make the text relevant for him. The human is not a neutral calculator merely reacting to the data in the reading process.

Preliminary Questions

The two conceptualizations of the process of reading and interpretation not only show the inevitability of a comprehensive approach to the text; they also allow us to picture more clearly the importance of the narrative structures for meaning and an appropriate method for analysis of narrative in a way which enhances the various meanings and meaning-effects. Two questions which have been broached in the description of the work of students of narrative must be faced in the process of outlining a specific method of analysis. Should analysis proceed from the completed narrative or should it proceed in a linear fashion corresponding to the reading process. Also, should analysis proceed as quickly as possible to the deep abstract level or should analysis remain at the surface level?

The process of analysis. Structural analysis will finally deal with the text as a totality from the perspective of the conclusion. The entire narrative is the result essentially (although not absolutely) of an individual coming to a satisfactory conclusion, finding meanings, making sense. There is some end position from which the creation is made. The completed narrative answers questions or brings a focus from all of the levels of meaning to which the individual is sensitive. The basic assumption which can direct the search for narrative developments, in fact, is that the creator of the narrative desires to reach the end position from which the plot of the total narrative may be grasped in a satisfying way.

But are there not some values to be gained from an approach which recapitulates the process of reading in that it moves from unit to unit in a linear fashion? Saussure emphasized that the meaning of units is determined by their syntagmatic and paradigmatic relationships and an analysis which moves from unit to unit from beginning to end will make more visible the process by which the mind actively anticipates *possible* syntagmatic and paradigmatic elements as well as considers the *actual* elements in the development of meaning. An application of the structural distinctions between syntagmatic and paradigmatic relationships on the level of narrative may be accomplished by considering a particular narrative as a genre of narrative. As the meaning of a sentence is determined by the relationship of the parts to one another in the totality of the sentence, so the narrative genre is determined by the relationships of the units of narrative. In analysis, the meaning of the narrative may be understood by comparing the actual moves with the potential moves. The model of Bremond will be helpful here, but it will soon be seen as a fairly reduced abstraction and must be supplemented by a larger catalog of functions such as those discovered by Propp and modified by Greimas. Paradigmatic relationships of a unit help determine the meaning of the unit. The question to ask here is what units could have occurred in place of the particular unit without changing the genre. Here the possibilities to be suggested depend not upon a logical limited catalog of moves but upon the particular moves which could appropriately express the underlying abstract function. The experience and imagination of the reader will in practice be the limiting factors in terms of the consideration of paradigmatic possibilities.

The structural approach of Saussure emphasized that the meaning of elements is *determined* by syntagmatic and paradigmatic relationships. In the study of more basic linguistic units, objectivity may at least be approached in defining a unit by determining the combinations into which it can enter and the elements which can replace it. The English phoneme /p/ may be defined by its possible combination with other phonemes: it can combine with any vowel, either preceding or following that vowel; the liquids /l/ and /r/ are the only consonants which can follow it within a syllable; /s/ is the only consonant that can precede it. But /p/ is also defined by its opposition to other phonemes which could replace it in a given context: in the context /-et/, it can be replaced by b, l, m, n, and s (bet, let, met, net, set). How can the same insights help in the larger units of narrative? When the postulates are accepted that the critical and interpretative acts are one (that the proper structuring of the unit and the interpretation of meaning move together) and that a narrative is polysemic, the objectivity of the structural study of paradigmatic and syntagmatic relationships is modified. The possibility of a variety of meanings, however, does not do away with the truth that meaning is related to paradigmatic and syntagmatic relationships.

The principle may be restated: the meaning which a person will assign to a particular unit will be related to those units he sees as having paradigmatic and syntagmatic relationships with that unit. The reader, then, will make conclusions as to thematic meaning and genre (and the narrative will be able to sustain affective meaning-effect) only on the basis of the reader's possession of some knowledge of the syntagmatic and paradigmatic possibilities of the units of narrative. This knowledge need not be brought to consciousness for meaning to be assigned to narrative and for the narrative to work its effect. But a critical reader may heighten the meaning and expand the possibilities of meaning by conscious consideration of syntagmatic and paradigmatic relationships.

An appropriate method of analysis will be the consideration of the narrative from unit to unit with a comprehensive review of the structures of the entire narrative after the linear analysis is complete. Of course, no analysis will really be made without some preliminary survey of the narrative which accomplishes in a provisional way what will be accomplished by the slower and more complete linear analysis.

The level of analysis. The question of the level of analysis is related to the larger question of the appropriate use of structuralism as a method. Philip Pettit has distinguished among "straight analysis," "systematic theory," and "systematic analysis," and he concludes that systematic analysis alone is both interesting and legitimate although he sees this as a reduction of the structuralist program.[51] The straight analysis in which patterns or devices are discovered in relatively unsystematic ways must be criticized because of the lack of control. There is no control because the elements which are used in the analysis may or may not have any relationships to the human capacity for creating and perceiving narrative. The structural analysis advocated here, therefore, will not be modeled upon the work of Jakobson or even Lévi-Strauss. (However, once a model has been set up which relates linguistic patterns and devices to human narrative competence, the patterns discerned by the method of Jakobson and Lévi-Strauss may be related to the more central method.)

The work of the second-generation structuralists who attempt to uncover the elements related to human narrative competence is the basis for the method to be suggested. In the work of these narratologists, however, we have seen two different emphases: on the deeper more logical or abstract structures and on those structures closer to the surface level. *Systematic theory* centers on the attempt to ascertain a system of rules which underlies narrative texts (generative theory) or the attempt to ascertain abstract elements which combine to form narratives (descriptive theory). The work of Greimas, for example, is theoretical and deals with both the rules and the elements and events in narration. Systematic theory often seeks to formulate narrative elements and rules in such a fashion that one abstract formula or pattern is seen as the pattern for all narratives. If a particular narrative does not contain all of the elements, it is seen as incomplete. The functions of Propp, for example, may be seen as constitutive for all Russian tales even though every tale will not have all functions. Greimas has suggested a form which all narratives follow, and doubtless other patterns could be suggested. Systematic theory, however, may also deal with elements and rules in a way that emphasizes not only the continuity but also the discontinuity among various narrative types. The use of systematic theory envisioned here is parallel to that used by Alan R. Dundes in the study of North American folk tales. Dundes distinguishes a limited number of distinct patterns in the tales and declares that morphological analysis assists in the study and comparison of types, content analysis, and in other historical and literary areas.[52]

Systematic analysis may be distinguished from systematic theory. Although analysis uses categories derived from the theoretical work, it concerns itself with the actual narrative. The later work of Barthes in S/Z is an example of such analysis. The distinction between the study of the abstract formal level of narrative and the analysis of actual narratives is logically possible, particularly when the formal study is done by purely logical means, such as the logical square, in total disregard of actual narratives. However, the narratologists do not ignore actual narratives in their formal study. Theory and analysis go hand in hand. The inability of the logical square to explain the variety of narrative types, for example, has led to the expansion of the logical square to the logical hexagon and the logical octagon by some students,[53] and to the abandonment of the logical square by other students such as Todorov. The study of the abstract and actual levels cannot be really divorced for several reasons. First, the abstract (or universal) structures exist only in terms of the surface (or particular) structures of the narrative. Although narratives are expressions of a narrative system, the narrative structures only exist in the narrative, and then only insofar as author and reader are influenced by them in creation and reading. We see competence only in the performance; we see power only in the action. Then, the perception of meaning on the surface level and the effective operation of the type or the typical (to use the terms of Dilthey) take place simultaneously in the same human being. Mediation of systematic theory and systematic analysis takes place as the reader approaches an actual narrative.[54]

The constant interpenetration of the different levels of the text and the various levels of meaning makes it vital for the level of manifestation to remain visible in analysis. Figurative language, for example, may operate on the cognitive level in terms of the literal reference of the figure. The figure itself, however, may be necessary for non-cognitive meaning-effects. Assume, for the sake of illustration, that one of the meaning-effects of Jesus' statement in the narrative of Luke 5:1–11, "You shall become fishers of men," is to mediate the two different spheres of land and water and what they represent in the narrative. The literal meaning of "fishers of men" can be taken to be "missionaries" or "evangelists" or some other similar term. This literal expression gives the proper cognitive force and must be used as the basis for the abstract structuring of the narrative. However, it is only the metaphor "fishers of men" that accomplishes the non-cognitive meaning-effect of mediating land and water. To move directly to the deep level and leave the surface completely would lose an important meaning or meaning-effect of the narrative.

The relationship envisioned between meaning and the structure of narrative will help to determine the level of structures used. If the presupposition is that by linguistics or linguistic-like transformations a hitherto undiscovered meaning will be achieved, the deep structure will be primary and analysis will proceed as quickly as possible to that level. The narrative begins, however, with non-narrative meaning and is often transformed into non-narrative meaning which is appropriate and relevant to the reader. Critics will be able to develop no scientific methodology to allow movement directly from the most profound structures to all of the possible significations. The human reader or interpreter and the actual level of manifestation of narrative always will remain vital. The most appropriate step, then, is to invent or devise, or adopt a flexible morphology and syntax capable of relating surface level to deep level, which yet remains related to readers' perceptions of meanings (semantics).

The best supposition seems to be that as the reader progresses through the narrative, the meanings (the identification of elements, the meaning of the related elements on the cognitive level, and the aesthetic and affective meaning-effects) are simultaneously perceived and/or affect the reader. A structural hermeneutics will not attempt to choose between systematic theory and systematic analysis, between generative and descriptive theory, between material and formal description. All of the factors which may be related to human narrative competence, whether viewed by a logical abstract approach or a descriptive historical approach, will be involved. What structures allow the narrative to be understood and to carry out the meaning-effects on the reader? What elements work within the structures to effect these meanings? What paradigmatic and syntagmatic relationships give the elements this significance?

The Structures of Structural Analysis

Introduction. The structures which will be determined in structural analysis have a variety of meanings or meaning-effects. The pleasure of satisfaction or completion accompanies the reading of a narrative in which there is some resolution. In itself, this pleasure of completion is further undefined. But, of course, it could not exist independent of the successful completion on the ideational level. The genre, the type, or the typical, also has an affective meaning-effect. The structures on the level of surface which can be thought of as the result of the genre on the abstract level constitute the basis also for cognitive meanings normally arrived at through development of the theme and/or character. Within the narrative is a variety of patterns which can be uncovered by a Jakobsonian-like straight analysis. Structuralists also see certain patterns which all narratives possess in some fashion. Greimas sees narratives as following a set pattern in terms of "contracts" and "tests," for example.

A basic question in the development of a method of analysis is the relationship and priority of the various systems with their meanings and meaning-effects. An appropriate arrangement of structural systems may be developed by taking as basic those structures which operate simultaneously in the development of some content used by the reader as the basis of some interpretation and in the development of a mood or tone. These meanings or meaning-effects may be used to strengthen one another, while other meanings or meaning-effects resulting from the same or other structures in the narrative will contribute to or coexist with the more basic meanings. They will not (normally) be opposed to the more basic meanings.

Plot. Plot is a concern of students of narrative in both traditional and structural or semiotic terms for plot allows a reader to assign thematic value to the passage and allows the narrative to be seen as a composition involving elements which can be analyzed from a structuralist perspective. The matter of plot is not new, of course, for more than two thousand years ago Aristotle pointed to the importance of plot for the author and his audience. Readers try to find unity, some central theme or idea around which the various details can be focused. When such a unity is discovered, each function, each episode can be related to one another and to the entire plot. Plot is to be seen in narrative semiotics from the point of view of creation or production. Just as Dilthey saw all of the results of literary criticism as valuable when once related to his view of the mental structure of man, all of the work on plot from a historical descriptive perspective may be accepted as valid when the plot (myth, fable) is seen as more than the result of historical factors. Plot, as Dilthey saw long before the narratologists, is related to the competence of man.

The work of Northrop Frye on genre and narrative categories of literature broader than or logically prior to genre may inform and complement contemporary work in narrative semiotics. In his work on genre and broader narrative categories, Frye declares that "it must happen very rarely that a writer sits down to write without *any* notion of what he proposes to produce." Frye sees "some kind of controlling and coordinating power" in the mind of the poet which is established very early and "gradually assimilates everything to itself, and finally reveals itself to be the containing form of the work." Coleridge called this the "initiative." And Frye indicates that the action of the poet relates to a variety of poetic elements, or "a group of initiatives." Prior to the ordinary literary genres (which are generally defined in descriptive terms rather than in structural-generative terms), then, Frye sees four narrative categories or "pre-generic elements of literature," "*mythoi*" or "generic plots": comedy (the mythos of spring), romance (the mythos of summer), tragedy (the mythos of autumn), and irony and satire (the mythos of winter).[55] The characterizations of generic plots must be viewed as a division into four somewhat arbitrary categories of what is actually a continuum—just as the division of the year into four seasons is somewhat arbitrary. Also, although the generic plots focus on moods, the plot must eventually take an ideational form, and it is only through the material of the narrative, the ideational contents, that the genre both carries out its affective function and can be dealt with in analysis.

The language of the narrative mediates the material and attitude. Finally, language "derives from and sacrifices itself to the possibilities of material and attitude," and becomes the only reality. As Wesley A. Kort expresses it, tone is "the element of narrative which is the image of that creative moment when choice of material, attitude toward it, and the use of language dance as one. . . ."[56] Holland admits that the principles which he has uncovered simply do not tell very much about the emotions or affects people have in their experience in literary works. A major difficulty of affective interpretation is that interpretation is given in words, and language is not a very precise instrument to describe emotions or affects. Yet, as we see it, the meaning conveyed in the ideational content of language and the meaning or meaning-effects conveyed in the structures as a type or as a genre are isotopes of one another. Indeed, in semiotic terms, one of the meanings might be seen as the interpretant of the other. As the reader makes sense of the narrative he consciously or unconsciously makes decisions which are related to both the development of the ideas of the narrative and to his emotional response.

The basic assumption which can direct the search for narrative elements is that the creator of narratives (original author *and* reader) desires "to reach an ultimate summary in which the plot as a whole is grasped in a satisfying form."[57] Roland Barthes sees this expectation and desire for solution as the basis for the action of his hermeneutic code.[58] The function of Barthes's hermeneutic code is the same as Jakobson's poetic code: "Just as rhyme (notably) structures the poem according to the expectation and desire for recurrence, so the hermeneutic terms structure the enigma according to the expectation and desire for its solution. . . . Expectation thus becomes the basic condition for truth: truth, these narratives tell us, is what is *at the end* of expectation."[59] The sentence is used as the image for construction of hermeneutic narrative. "To narrate (in the classic fashion) is to raise the question as if it were a subject which one delays predicting; and when the predicate (truth) arrives, the sentence, the narrative, are over, the world is adjectivized (after we had feared it would not be)."[60]

Analysis must begin with some end point which is related to the reader. (I am not attempting to set rules, I am describing what actually happens.) The reader comes with his horizon, with a multiplicity of texts already incorporated; he can no more begin at the beginning of the narrative and objectively analyze the units—either the surface or the deep level—than a scientist can put a thermometer into a test tube without affecting the temperature of that which is being measured. The necessity of personal involvement can be turned into virtue. The attempt to make sense can be recognized as a recapitulation of the author's attempt to make sense. The end point, however, should be as closely identified with the end point of the author as possible—in the initial stages of analysis.

An attempt should be made to discover the end from the narrative itself, from the relationship of the units to the total narrative and particularly from the capstone of the narrative. What happens in the narrative itself? A preliminary scanning of the surface level and a preliminary decomposition will assist the critical reader. The preliminary decomposition should consider both the surface level of the narrative and the abstract level which is one of the aims of the analysis. The preliminary scanning is comparable to immediate constituent analysis in sentence grammar, but the unit is not necessarily the sentence and its elements. It may be several sentences, or part of a sentence. Roland Barthes's "lexia" is the concern of this preliminary reading, and Barthes admits that the cutting up will be arbitrary and not the result of a careful methodology. ". . . it will suffice that the lexia be the best possible space in which we can observe meaning."[61]

Plot and lexia may be related if a lexia is thought of as some advance of the plot and the actor is thought of as the person, object, or quality which is involved in the action. The narrative then will begin to be organized into units which do justice to both the surface and deep levels. The first reading is an intuitive "making sense," but even involved in this reading are all levels of meaning impinging upon the reader. (With many narratives it is necessary to involve more than the narrative consciously because the narratives are elliptical or ambiguous.) The first reading may then result in a plot in the form of a series of sentences with an active verb and a subject in a nominal form (rather than pronominal). The order of the plot need not follow the surface level; it should be as logical as possible.

The next step is the investigation of the plot, so set up, by means of narrative grammars proposed by narratologists. The method of analysis advocated here maintains the surface level while using the more abstract levels. If interest is in opening up signification from the signifiers of an individual text, the particular signifiers must be considered. All possibility for signification is lost if relationship to the signifiers is lost, if the analysis becomes totally abstract. If, to use semiotic language, readers are interested in the interpretants and in the endless play of signs, readers must remain with a level which signifies. An extremely structural approach which is directed toward deep-abstract-logical structures is as unproductive as or even more unproductive than an extremely historical approach which seeks some objective original meaning independent of personal significance. Both perhaps are theoretically possible, but both ignore the purpose of biblical narrative. The abstract level helps, however, when it is used in relation to an actual narrative.

Greimas's model may be applied to the biblical texts to sensitize readers more completely to the signifiers of the biblical texts and to open them for significations on the level of both author and reader. For this to be done the principles of the narratologists, derived theoretically from the logical four-term homology, should be viewed and stated in terms of the way the human being creates meaning in narrative. This will keep attention on the actual text and allow use of the abstract model. The basic elements by which the mind organizes the actions can be considered "narrative statements," composed of specific types of actors and actions. (The lexias of the surface are already close to being translated into "canonical" narrative statements, and this process can be completed by making the subject and the verb more abstract, forcing them into one or another of a very limited number of categories.) The mind sees the meaning of the narrative statements only as they are joined together into chains. These are logical chains or "canonical" syntagms. Demand and accept (contractual syntagm); come and go (disjunctual syntagm); confront, dominate, and acquire (performance syntagm) are ways of conceiving these small chains of narrative statements. The syntagms themselves join into a larger sequence: the human mind conceives of and composes meaning in narrative by a logical arrangement of the syntagms. There must be some sort of demand and acceptance (contract) before there is a setting out to meet the demand and a carrying out of the demand of the contract. The sequence or set involves contract, disjunction, performance. Such a set may be conceived of both as related to human narrative competence producing the narrative and as an abstract structure which can be discerned or invented from the surface text. Such sequences can be repeated in the same or different modes.[62]

The work of Greimas emphasizes the constraints of the logical and anthropomorphic levels. Analysis will be concerned with these constraints, but especially with the choices within the constraints which allow for the variety of narrative forms and the variety of affective meanings. At this point all of the work of narrative genres from Aristotle through Frye can be utilized. As the term "genre" is used here, it has reference to the type or category into which narratives may be placed on the basis of both formal characteristics and emotional or affective meaning-effects. Genre is seen from a generative-structural perspective, not from a historical-descriptive perspective, but the work on genre from the historical-descriptive perspective may be "translated" into generative-structural perspectives and found helpful. The classification by Frye can serve at least as a beginning point. Frye sees the four mythoi or generic plots as four aspects of a central unifying myth. Each of the myths has an archetypal theme. The basis of romance is conflict and the narrative will contain a sequence of marvelous adventures. The archetypal theme of tragedy is pathos or catastrophe, whether in triumph or in defeat. Irony and satire are based on the sense that heroism and effective action are absent, disorganized, or doomed to defeat, and that reigning over the world are confusion and anarchy. The archetypal theme of comedy is recognition of a newborn society rising in triumph with a yet somewhat mysterious hero and his bride.[63]

The normal pattern of action for comedy is the desire of a young man for a young woman, the resistance of this desire by some opposition, usually paternal, and a twist near the end of the plot which enables the hero to have his will. Romance is the successful quest, and the complete form of the romance has a preliminary stage of a perilous journey and minor adventures, a crucial struggle in which either the hero or his foe or both must die, and the exaltation of the hero who has proved himself to be a hero even if he does not survive the conflict. Frye accepts Aristotle's definition of tragedy as an account of the events in the life of a person of significance which culminate in an unhappy catastrophe. Tragedy is a mimesis of sacrifice in that it is "a paradoxical combination of a fearful sense of rightness (the hero must fall) and pitying sense of wrongness (it is too bad that he falls)." Irony and satire are mythical patterns of experience, "the attempts to give form to the shifting ambiguities and complexities of unidealized existence." The central principle of ironic myth, in the opinion of Frye, is best approached as a parody of romance. The main difference between irony and satire is that "satire is militant irony."[64]

As suggested, the four generic plots of Frye serve only as a beginning point, even for the work of Frye himself. Each myth is shown to have different phases and certain of the phases are parallel to the phases of the neighboring myths. So the application of structural insights to genre must be done as a skillful art, not as an exact science.

The catalog of functions which Propp developed from the Russian tales and which has been revised by Greimas can serve at least in a preliminary way for the abstract categories of action. And the abstract category of actors (actants) as revised by Greimas can serve both for action and for the human and non-human factors involved in bringing about the action.

THE FUNCTIONS OF PROPP

1. absence	11. departure	23. unrecognized
2. interdiction	12. the first function	22. rescue
3. violation	of the donor	arrival
4. reconnaissance	13. the hero's reaction	24. see 8a
5. delivery	14. the provision	25. the difficult task
6. fraud	15. spatial translocation	26. task accomplished
7. complicity	16. struggle	27. recognition
8. villainy	17. marking	28. exposure
8a. lack	18. victory	29. transfiguration
9. mediation	19. lack liquidated	30. punishment
10. beginning counter	20. return	31. wedding
action	21. pursuit	

Propp suggested the possibility of pairing the functions according to their interdependence; that is, interdiction is implied by violation. Greimas combined functions two and three, four and five, six and seven, nine and ten, twelve and thirteen, sixteen and eighteen, twenty-one and twenty-two, twenty-five and twenty-six, twenty-eight and twenty-nine, and thirty and thirty-one.[65] Clearly all of Propp's functions are not of equal importance and their use in structural hermeneutics should be heuristic. When other categories are more helpful in determining the actual movement of the plot, they should be introduced. The important matter is to maintain categories which allow a distinction to be made between the course which all narrative theoretically must take and the different courses taken by narrative of different genres.

Actantial Model of Greimas

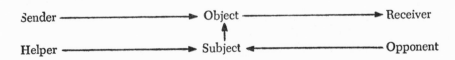

The definition of actants must be made in light of the three axes along which the actants lie. In the axis of communication, the *sender* determines that something (*object*) is to be communicated to someone else (*receiver*). The *sender* gives a mandate to a *subject*. On the axis of volition, the *subject* facilitates communication of the *object* by suppressing the obstacles which hinder it. On the axis of power, the *helper* is the power necessary for passage from desire to action. The *helper* may be qualities, information, knowledge, or inanimate objects as well as personages. The *opponent* is the power opposing the move to action. Actantial analysis regularly begins with the abstract categories and relates the human and non-human elements of the narrative to the categories. This model of analysis may be reversed when attention is on the level of manifestation by centering upon the actual persons or actors in the narrative and asking which of the character types they represent in the development of the plot.

In the determination of the genre, the type of action and the identification of the "sphere of action" of a character are not sufficient. The nature or quality of the individual carrying out the action is important. In broad terms, romance depicts the hero as superior in degree to other men and to his environment; tragedy shows the hero superior in degree to other men but not to his natural environment; comedy portrays the hero as "one of us," superior neither to other men nor to his environment; and irony has a hero inferior in power and intelligence to ourselves.[66] The importance of giving attention to the quality of the characters as well as to the sphere of action is one rationale for maintaining the surface level in structural hermeneutics. A method of study which gives attention to the quality of the character is semic analysis. The character in a narrative is made up of the totality of the attributes which may be assigned to him directly or indirectly from the various lexias. When there is no development in character in the narrative, the person will be considered as the collection of all of the semes in the narrative. However, there may be development in terms of character, and semic analysis will highlight this development.

Another choice to be made in analysis is between the elements which are essential for the action and those which are not essential. The nonessential elements are to be seen as Barthes's "hermeneutic code" and as highlighting the meaning of the essential elements and the meaning-effect of the total narrative.[67]

Structures unrelated to plot. The structural hermeneutics advocated here begins with those elements recognized by scholars in the descriptive tradition of Aristotle and by those who use a generative-structural approach. The question of the existence and significance of structures other than those related to plot must be taken seriously. That a straight analysis such as that of Jakobson uncovers a multitude of relationships cannot be ignored. A principle may be suggested to cover such patterns: the mind in creation and interpretation finds pleasure and satisfaction in grammatical patterns not necessarily related to the major narrative structures. The existence and discovery of these structures may be seen as depending upon the symbolic capacity of the author and reader. Such patterns, because the mind seeks satisfaction and pleasure of itself, need not be conscious literary devices, but may be patterns created quite unconsciously. Many, if not all, of these structures have been seen by literary critics; the major step in structural hermeneutics will be to see such devices in a generative-structural framework and to relate the structures to the basic narrative meanings and meaning-effects. Many patterns may be seen as reflecting the type of binary opposition emphasized by Lévi-Strauss in his study of myth, particularly when the type of relationship between the two elements is not limited to logical opposition. The parallelism of Hebrew poetry in which the second line parallels the first in one of a number of ways is an example. Many of the parallels and contrasts in Luke-Acts to which scholars have called attention since at least the early nineteenth century may result from natural rather than conscious art. Henry J. Cadbury cites the Lukan fondness for pairing of words, doubling of vocatives, paralleling of birth stories, parables, and miracles as well as wide paralleling of the careers of Jesus, Peter, Paul, and Stephen.[68]

Binary oppositions and transformations and mediations of binary oppositions are the basis for the symbolic code of Barthes, and doubtless the reader is affected by such relationships even if he is unaware of the reasons. A principle to be followed in the analysis of such grammatical patterns may be that the pleasure or satisfaction from the patterns is not to be at variance with the affective meaning created by the genre or with the cognitive meaning or interpretation of the reader. Moreover, due to the more subjective nature of the discernment of such elements, the meaning derived from the patterns of relationships of elements should not direct the search for the total meaning or meaning-effect. It may enhance the meaning at the cognitive level or merely accompany that meaning, but it will not be the major bearer of meaning in narrative. In the parallelism of Hebrew poetry, for example, it is evident that parallelism in and of itself is not the basis for interpretation. However, interpretation which ignores the existence of parallelism is bound to result in an inappropriate interpretation.

The mind may be seen as structuring the elements of the narrative not related to thematic development and, therefore, not related to plot in a different manner from the structuring that involves plot. All the aspects of narrative which can be related to plot, such as theme and character development, will be related to plot which has been presented in generative-structure terms, although the plot is discerned by the reader as interpretation is made of the narrative theme. Elements unrelated to thematic interpretation and plot may be discerned by the reader. Many of the patterns of elements and relationships discussed by Jakobson and Lévi-Strauss are of this nature. When such patterns comprehend the entire narrative, the patterns may be seen as perceived in accord with the law of *Prägnanz* of Gestalt psychology. This law dictates that the mind will see a good form in any set of data, a form that is simple, continuous, and bounded, and a form which accounts for the high proportion of the data. Philip Pettit views the assignment of all structures in the narrative text as based on Gestalt and not generative grounds.[69] I agree that the reader is always involved in the perception of structure, but it seems that the perception of structure in plot (involving ideational content and genre as defined here) is not purely idiosyncratic or simply dependent upon transitory conventions as perceptions of other structure *may* be. However, because of the more subjective nature of the perception of patterns outside of plot, attention given to such patterns will vary in accord with the purpose of the reader as well as his symbolic ability. The reader more concerned with an original meaning related to the author will be very cautious about finding significance in such patterns. Nevertheless, the reader who is open to new significations will be ready to find meaning in all of the various patterns perceived in the text as long as they are in continuity with the meanings ascertained by the plot.

It may be observed that this section on the development of a method is a contradicton in that the principles delineated at the beginning preclude a method which results in *the* truth. In the process of reading and interpretation the reader with his mental structure and "texts" previously assimilated comes to the text with its structures and contents resulting from the creation and experience of the author, and the reader creates meaning for himself. The "method" outlined is an attempt to make more explicit some of the factors in the process of interpretation and may be useful in organizing and testing the interpretation no matter how the interpretation actually arises to begin with. It is also possible that the method will sensitize readers to the creative possibilities of reading and interpretation of literature. The statement of the method is necessarily partial and tentative, but it does provide a framework for a comprehensive interpretation in which the structures uncovered by semiotic analysis are utilized.

NEW TESTAMENT STUDY AND
STRUCTURAL ANALYSIS

The method of narrative hermeneutics sketched above is an attempt to make use of the fact that critical analysis of the structures of narrative inevitably involves the interpretation with which hermeneutics is concerned. The process of reading unites criticism and interpretation. The hermeneutic use of structural analysis is not the only use, however, and a delineation of the various uses of structural analysis and the values of the hermeneutic use of analysis will help give direction to the application of the method in New Testament hermeneutics.

Uses of Structural Analysis

Structuralism in general and the structural study of narrative in particular are finding a place both in literary criticism[70] and in biblical studies.[71] The question of the proper use of structural analysis is vital. The structural study of narrative or, as it has come to be known, narrative semiotics, and New Testament study may be related in different ways. The emphasis may be on narrative semiotics with the New Testament narratives forming the corpus for study. The aim, then, is the development of an abstract "grammar" which in some sense is "before" or "deeper" than the narrative and which can be discovered from the narrative. This study is legitimate. The conceptual framework for such a study may be provided by the work of Tuen A. van Dijk (see pp. 165–66).

The "grammar" of narrative in its most inclusive definition as deduced by the students of narrative would serve as the background against which a "sub-grammar" of New Testament narrative would be deduced. Study would be directed to the formal structures of New Testament narrative. But, according to the conceptualization developed in this work, this would be at the same time a study of the deep structures abstractly determining the generation of New Testament narrative. Doubtless the fact that the Christian myth is comedy would influence the nature of the grammar of New Testament narrative. Study of the deep structures involves study of surface structures and the process of communication. So the study of the grammar of New Testament narrative will ultimately involve hermeneutics, just as narrative hermeneutics will ultimately involve the grammar of New Testament narrative. The focus of the study, nevertheless, would be upon the formal or abstract structures.

The emphasis in analysis may be on conventional New Testament study, with an attempt being made to answer historical-critical questions by means of structural analysis. Historical study, at least at a basic level, is clearly necessary for structural analysis. The models of reading of Krieger and Holland show that some awareness of the relationship of the elements of the narrative to the real world makes a beginning reading possible. The greater the knowledge of the denotation of the elements, of the actual uses of the elements in previous narrative, and of the possible metaphorical uses, the greater the possible use of the elements in the process of making sense of the text as literature. Also, the observation of literary relationships of the elements of narrative involves application to the real world once more. The sense or interpretation of narrative given by the reader during and after the reading process may be historical, and historical study may be carried out as a secondary task built upon the primary work of structural analysis. (Theological sense or interpretation may also be a conscious secondary task built upon structural analysis.) Continuity between the meaning and the meaning-effect of the narrative for the modern reader and for the author may be assumed and, hence, some guide for determining the "original meaning" or historical meaning may result from structural analysis.

In spite of the necessity of preliminary historical study and the possibility of later historical interpretation, it is difficult to see how structural analysis can make a direct positive contribution to traditional historical questions; but it is clear that structural study may be a corrective to historical study. An example may be given from the study of Luke-Acts. The parallels in Luke-Acts have been taken by some scholars to be a result of the conscious theological work of the author. F. C. Baur, for example, explains the parallels between Peter and Paul in Acts as a conscious attempt to reconcile hostile Jewish and Gentile wings of the church.[72] M. D. Goulder explains parallels between Acts and Luke by supposing that the life of Jesus provides the *type* of life of the church. The Pauline doctrine of the body of Christ is then expressed formally in the parallels between the two works.[73] If the parallels in Luke-Acts result from human and cultural constraints or conventions rather than from conscious theological motivation of the author, such parallels cannot be used directly to reconstruct the theological message of the author. The primary use of the grammatical patterns will be in narrative hermeneutics, the determination of the literary meanings and poetic meaning-effects of the patterns. From this, theological and historical studies may be done as a secondary activity.

An obvious point of contact between structural study of narrative and historical study is form criticism. Form critics have traditionally seen the formation of the material of the tradition as the result of social and historical factors and have reconstructed the history of the tradition on that basis. Early critics of form criticism called attention to the more or less natural form of the miracle stories. The form is explained as the way storytellers relate miracles, and it is evident that the form *per se* does not really help the reconstruction of the history of the miracle stories. It is only as the form takes concrete expression in a particular miracle story that historical study can be done, and this is on the basis of the material and not the form. Other forms which have been uncovered by form criticism must be examined to determine to what extent they may be the result of the narrative competence of man rather than of historical factors. The history of the synoptic tradition will need to be revised as a result of the introduction of human linguistic and literary competence to complement historical factors.

A way of combining narrative semiotics and New Testament study may be to forsake the aims of traditional New Testament study and replace them with a "meaning" which may be obtained only in the discovery of a narrative grammar. It appears that this enterprise is the most ambitious use of analysis. The postulate which would guide this application of structural study is that the meaning is grammar or that syntax is semantics. The reduction of meaning which Lévi-Strauss attempts in his study of myth would be the model for the study, although the reduction need not be in anthropological terms as it is with Lévi-Strauss. The work of

Erhardt Güttgemanns may be taken as an example of an application of generative-structural insights to the New Testament which forsakes conventional meanings.[74]

As early as 1970, Güttgemanns had conceived of a program of "generative poetics" of the New Testament. From his use of the expression "generative poetics," it is clear that Güttgemanns's program envisioned research on the deeper or generative level of language from the very inception, but the development of a specific method came in stages. In his early scholarly career, he did his work as a faithful exponent of Bultmann's hermeneutic as modified by Fuchs, but in the late 1960s a perception of stagnation in this approach brought Güttgemanns to consider a linguistic thrust, which, however, he sees as continuous with his earliest work.[75] The basic principles and early standard of the program appear in the first three issues of *Linguistica Biblica*.[76] In Güttgemanns's original "Theses" published in the first issue, he uses the vocabulary of form criticism to present theses fundamentally different from traditional form criticism. Instead of viewing the units of the gospel in an evolutionary framework, Güttgemanns regards them as "performance" texts resulting from a more basic "competence."[77] In an analysis of the parable of the begging friend in Luke 11:5-8 and in an article on semiotics, Güttgemanns stresses the functional derivation of the semantics from the syntax of the text, and states that text syntagmatics is the condition for the possibility of text semantics. That is, the macro-syntax of the text constitutes the meaning of the text.[78]

A major statement of the principle of generative poetics was given in a conference at Loccum Academy in February of 1971. Güttgemanns defends theology as a "science," the subject of which is the biblical text, and the task of which is the methodological penetration of the discourse concerning God (*die Rede von Gott*). Contemporary linguistics is the only legitimate method of this science and provides the language as well as method. The language of the science of theology, then, is a syntax or a metalanguage. "It speaks as science of the discourse of God concerning this discourse. As discourse theology is always metatext to a text. Therefore the so-called syntactic questions are its major questions; one must only correctly understand all that belongs to syntax."[79]

Güttgemanns directs his attention to the deep level of the narrative, and it is from this that the "meaning" of the text is derived. The question of the relationship of historical factors to meaning—indeed the relationship of anything external to the text to meaning—leads to Güttgemanns's concept of meaning which is a reduction of meaning in terms of conventional New Testament study. He is quite clear on the point that a concrete text is not the result of historical forces and its meaning is not governed by historical realities. A text is the result of grammatical forces and its meaning is governed by grammatical realities.[80] Meaning for Güttgemanns, then, eventually comes to be limited to the affective area of man's life, at least meaning of narrative material. This insight is arrived at gradually. In his early works, he treats the various functions of language in light of the work of Bühler, who suggested that language functions as symbol, symptom, and signal, and Jakobson, who suggested the emotive, conative, referential, phatic, metalinguistic, and poetic functions.[81] In the early treatment of the functions, a linguistic sign and its function are not differentiated from a text and its function; the functions discussed by Bühler and Jakobson are functions of texts. By the end of the second year of publication of *Linguistica Biblica*, however, Güttgemanns distinguished between the functional character of a sign and sentence and the functional character of a text, making it conceivable for a sentence to have one function and a text a different function. In May 1973, Güttgemanns concluded that a narrative text is directed to the affect as a rhetorical or persuasive communication. This appeal to the affect, then, becomes the overarching function of the synoptic texts as narratives.[82]

Applying structural analysis to synoptic narrative in the reductive fashion he follows, Güttgemanns concludes that whoever wants to learn the production of gospel narratives does not need to learn the performance phenomena but simply the abstract categories and the possibilities of the combinations of the abstract categories as determined by the logical square. Man is "capable in the present day and in modern verbalization of narrating stories of God through which he carries on generatively the synoptic stories so that the present proclamation represents a generative expansion of the canonical synoptic gospels."[83]

The relationship of analysis and New Testament study envisioned in this work is not reductionist. Justice must be done to semiotics and to New Testament narrative as both literary text and religious literature. The semiotic approach advocated is one which relates hermeneutics and structuralism in a way envisioned by Wilhelm Dilthey, in a way which comprehends all possible levels of text and meaning. Dilthey was concerned with creation and interpretation, with human capacity or competence composed of innate ability and historical and cultural elements equilibrated into an integrated mental structure, and text which is the expression of such human competence.[84] Unfortunately, Dilthey was unable to find a tool in his linguistic and grammatical tradition to unite the two poles, and his comprehensive vision was not incorporated into the continuing hermeneutical tradition; but the attempt to apply Chomsky's generative grammar in literature may be considered a return to Dilthey, although Dilthey's view of the teleological and developing nature of the mental structure is a more helpful model than that of a static competence.

What Dilthey could not do with the linguistic and grammatical tools at his disposal, formalism and structuralism began to do by means of structural linguistics. What really caused the two poles of Dilthey's concern to be reconciled, however, was the work of the structuralists on narrative. To the extent that narrative semiotics uncovers generative forms which direct the formation of the narrative, narrative semiotics weds the two poles of Dilthey's concern.

When one pole is excluded—for example, when analysis proceeds by dividing and subdividing categories on bases which have nothing to do with human linguistic or narrative competence, or when the concern is on purely psychological states or processes independent of the text or related to the text by devious idiosyncratic postulates and means which cannot be evaluated by anyone other than the analyst, when any one pole is excluded—one may get a mass of quantified data, on the one hand, or a collection of appealing personal testimony of meaning (existential, theological, etc.) on the other hand, but one is at sea, in my estimation, with no star visible to guide, no compass, no relationships, nothing to give control and direction.

Values of Narrative Hermeneutics

Narrative hermeneutics views the structures of narrative from the perspective of hermeneutics because the structures came into being originally because of the meanings and meaning-effects impinging upon the creator and because the structures inevitably are the vehicles for personal meaning for the reader (consciously or unconsciously) before they become the means for the other types of study listed above. Structural analysis which centers upon hermeneutics has several values, and the desire to realize these values will guide the application of analysis.

1. A value of the application of modern linguistics and semiotics to

New Testament study is the possibility of reading the New Testament narratives as literature. The application of the structural method presupposes and confirms that New Testament narratives are poetic literature or can be considered as such, that *literary* values are to be gained from the narratives. If New Testament material is approached primarily as simple historical or theological material, as direct conceptual language, then the investment of time in structuralism seems unwarranted. The New Testament is religious literature in the first instance, and it can be used for historical and theological conceptualization only in a secondary way. This view of the New Testament as literature should free readers from the necessity for a method of developing systematic theological or other doctrine directly from the text. The text is freed as literature.

2. A value of the structural method, therefore, is the benefit gained by looking at texts as the literary creation of individual early Christians. The material for creation is historically created and conditioned but the material does not totally constrain the creation. The text is the expression of a human who, beginning with certain innate linguistic capacity, has accommodated to his mental system symbolic capacity and historical and existential levels of meaning, extending on to life and to God.

All of the levels of meaning and capacity equilibrated in the individual are operative in the production of the text. The narrative may be viewed as the result of a focusing of various rays of language and meaning in the narrative space itself. The completed narrative is evidence of the successful focusing. With the proper "instrument" the various elements and relations of signification may be identified, the meanings of the author may be approached, and appropriate meanings for the modern reader may be suggested.

3. A value of structuralism paralleling the previous benefit is that of making modern readers more sensitive, aware of the levels of creativity, and aware of the fact that they not only discover some measure of the original meanings, but that they also invent meanings for themselves.

An assumption is that the author is creator at one point and that the reader is creator at another. Author and reader share innate linguistic and narrative capacities even if cultural aspects of their mental systems are different. The text is an expression of signification for the creator and becomes the means for signification for the reader.

The written text unites author and reader and insures continuity of meaning while allowing creativity on the part of the reader. The process of reading, of course, does not demand that a reader be creative. A text, say a legal or scientific writing, may refer solely to the real world, and the reader may refuse to see any significance beyond the specific occasion of the writing. The text may, however, refer to other than the real world, as in the case of a literary text. In such a case, however, the reader is not *forced* to refer the text to other than the real world. As Wolfgang Iser says (referring to indeterminancy of a reader's response to a literary text), a reader may refer "the text to real, verifiable factors in such a way that it appears to be nothing more than a mirror reflection of these factors. In this case it loses its literary quality in the reflection."[85]

If the text is viewed as real literature, reference will not be made to real, verifiable historical factors, but to something else, to perspectives on the world, to various poetic experiences or effects, to life, and to God. The reader is still involved, of course, and the perspective of the text can be reduced to that of the reader. Here the text also becomes a mirror reflection, not of facts but of perspective. On the other hand, a text may help the reader to develop perspectives and meanings which, while not mirror images of the reader, are more than restatements of the text.

Structural analysis will uncover the abstract narrative structures which may be conceived of as standing behind the surface structures and which are operative in the production of the narrative and in the reading process. Analysis will at the same time give insight into the affective poetic-effect of the narrative accompanying the ideational content. The meaning-effect at the affective level is isotopic with, or indeed may be the basis of, the meanings that can be expressed in terms of intellectual content; hence the possibility of narrative hermeneutics.

The meaning of the structure uncovered by analysis (as opposed to the elements as vehicles for meaning or to ideational content) may be conceived of as the "form of thought" or "poetic thought" or form of "experience" which Donald Davie sees expressed in "poetic syntax." Mood, intuition, tone, affective emotional experiences are involved. Instead of thinking of the meaning conveyed in the ideational content of language and the meaning or meaning-effect conveyed in the structures as isotopes of one another, it might be profitable to think of one of the meanings as the interpretant of the other. In this way, semiotic insights would become more useful in the movement among the various levels of meaning.

4. Narrative hermeneutics stresses the involvement of the reader in the creation of meaning and allows the text to be the vehicle for "language-

event" in the present time. Meanings at all levels are related to the structures of structuralism. All levels of language and meanings are equilibrated in a "mature" author and reader: the word, phrase, sentence, text; linguistic, cultural, emotive, and conative meanings of words; literal historical references, world view, personal and social existence; life, reality, God. All of these and whatever other levels may exist are related in the author and reader. The structures of the mind utilize all of these at various unconscious and conscious levels. There is no simple movement from purely logical and formal relationships and "meaning" to the surface level. As Greimas points out in his discussion of the interaction of semiotic constraints, the potentiality of deeper levels is governed by the actuality of other levels.[86] Systems on one level interact with systems on other levels.

History provides the elements of narrative, but worlds of personal meaning—social, religious, theological—help create and structure the text and may be discerned in the text. Historical criticism of the tradition itself forces us to view the narrative as something other than historical sources for Jesus, the oral period, or the church of the evangelists' time. This movement beyond history on the basis of history cannot be emphasized too much, for approaching the narrative from a literary or poetic perspective necessarily involves tools and approaches other than historical tools and perspectives. To read the narrative as literary art is to become involved. As we have seen, involvement of the reader as accomplice and collaborator is essential in artistic communication.[87]

In Austin's terms, then, a literary narrative is a "performance utterance" which creates its object by the reader's participation. The gospel narratives involve familiar elements but these elements are put together in a way that the intention of the text can never be completely defined as the identification of its elements with factors in the real world. The text presents and invites reactions to and attitudes toward the real world of the reader, which may include versions of the world of Jesus, the tradition, and the church, and it is these reactions and attitudes that constitute the meaning and reality of the text for the reader.

Since the meaning-object of the text cannot be determined by the text alone but must involve the reader, the discovery of the structures is a dialectical process—that is, if the structures have anything to do with meaning. Description and interpretation are one act, as Fish says. The involvement of the reader in the creation of meaning is not a minor factor which can be ignored in structural analysis. The involvement of the reader, the phenomenology of reading, may be used as a key to help keep structural study from becoming as arid as some claim historical criticism has become in New Testament studies.

5. Narrative hermeneutics can help resolve the aporia in New Testament hermeneutics by resolving the problem of distance between the first-century author with his situation in which the text was a living reality and modern man for whom the text is a dated historical object. The attempt of Bultmann to resolve the problem of distance by existential interpretation has been seen as a limited and limiting hermeneutical approach. It defines the meanings which may be found in the New Testament in terms of only one important area. Narrative hermeneutics sets no limit on the meaning, for the reader is involved with the text in the development of meaning. No area of man's concern is left out. The approach of Fuchs has also been questioned because of the inability to locate the "language" of "language-event" in the concepts of language in linguistics. When narrative semiotics is viewed as "language" which can express meaning only as the reader comes to the text and establishes meaning in terms of his circle of wishes, "language" is sufficiently wide enough to comprehend the conceptualization of Fuchs. Language-event for an individual, in view of the approach advocated, would take place when the various levels of language and meaning come to a focus for the reader as for the author, when the text as a "performance utterance" causes the reader to create meaning for himself which is as compelling as the meaning which inspired the author. The reader would not, then, merely restate the original historical meaning of the text. He would, rather, participate in the meaning so that interpretation would not be mental assent to a tradition but creative, perspective-changing, faith-producing activity involving all of the levels of meaning to which the interpreter is sensitive.

STRUCTURES AND MEANINGS IN LUKE 5:1–11

The goal and the extent of analysis in narrative hermeneutics are important factors which must be clearly understood for the operation to be successful. The final goal of analysis in narrative hermeneutics is the discovery or invention of personal meaning and meaning-effect from the basic narrative structures which serve as the vehicle for both cognitive meanings and affective meaning-effects and from the structures which reinforce or even merely accompany the basic narrative structures. It is assumed that use of the basic narrative structures will assure continuity between the original author and the present reader. But since the narrative structures are viewed in light of semiotics, the meanings or meaning-effects (and hence structures) must also be related to the modern reader.

Analysis of any particular narrative theoretically involves all other narratives when the structuralist perspective is taken. That is, if the meaning of the units of narrative and, therefore, the meaning of the entire narrative is related to all other units which could be used in their stead (paradigmatic relationships) and to the units with which they are in a relationship in the narrative (syntagmatic relationships), all narratives are related to meaning in any one narrative. The recognition of the central place of the reader in the process of analysis and interpretation causes some modification of this theoretical statement. That is, all narratives which are known to the reader are significant in the production of meaning for that reader. This is true for ideational meaning and affective meaning. For example, the meaning-effect of the comic genre is possible because other genres are known to the reader. It should be observed that the narratives which are most important in the development of meaning for the reader need not be literary or even written texts as such, and the reader's knowledge of the genres need not be self-conscious knowledge. So long as narratives are in the experience of the reader as genres and as material contents of genres, their units help determine the meaning and meaning-effect for the reader of a particular narrative. The present analysis will attempt to place most emphasis upon the syntagmatic relationships of the narrative structures, but at places paradigmatic relationships will be brought to light in order to stress the meaning or meaning-effect of the actual unit in the narrative being analyzed.

An analysis of Luke 5:1–11 will show how the basic structures of narrative and the accompanying structures may be useful for hermeneutics.[88] The basic premise on which the analysis proceeds is that the program of the structural study of narrative may be taken as a view of the process by which meaning and meaning-effect are created in and from narrative by author and reader. Analysis, therefore, is a "slow motion" recapitulation of the process of reading in which the structures responsible for the various meanings are brought to a conscious level and used for hermeneutical purposes.[89]

The Elements

The narrative divides itself initially into a series of episodes which can be distinguished by the major concerns: (1) to teach the people the word of God (5:1–3); (2) to catch fish (5:4–7); and (3) to call Simon to discipleship (5:8–11). The elements in the narrative are the characters (Jesus, Simon, James, and John), the lake of Gennesaret, two boats, nets, and fish. All of these elements had been used prior to the Lukan composition in various ways.

Jesus is the personal name of Jesus of Nazareth (Luke 24:19), the son of Mary (Luke 1:31), the prophet (Luke 7:39; 24:19), who is "a Savior . . . Christ the Lord" (Luke 2:11). The name is identical with Joshua and means "Yahweh is salvation" or ". . . Savior," or ". . . will save." The name was fairly common in the first century; nineteen persons called Jesus are cited in the writings of Josephus. The popularity of the name could be explained by the nationalism of the period following the Maccabean Revolt.[90] The uses of "Jesus" available to the author of the narrative range from the divinely appointed Messiah to the divine-human Savior.

Simon is the name for Peter, the most prominent of the Apostles of Jesus. While Peter (the name given by Jesus meaning rock, Cephas being the Aramaic equivalent) is dominant in the New Testament, Simon occurs often (five times in Matthew, six times in Mark, eleven times in Luke, and twenty-two times in John). Not only was the character of Simon Peter an element available to the author; so also was an account of Peter's call to become a disciple. Mark's account (Mark 1:16–20) followed by Matthew (4:18–22) has Jesus walking along the Sea of Galilee and calling Simon and Andrew and James and John to follow him. Jesus said to Simon and to Andrew, "Follow me and I will make you become fishers of men." Upon the call, the four left the fishing and followed Jesus.

An account of Jesus' teaching from a boat because of the pressure of a crowd along the shore (Mark 4:1) was also a part of the store of materials available to the author. Apparently, there was also available a story of a miraculous catch of fish, a variant form of which is found in John 21. In addition, the historical and chronological nature of the gospel framework within which the elements used by Luke existed may be considered as an element which directs and constrains the meaning of the narrative.

The meaning or denotation of the elements of the narrative and their uses in other creations do not *determine* the function and meaning of the elements in the literary narrative of Luke 5:1–11. For example, the meaning of "Jesus" in Luke 5:1–11 cannot be determined by discovering the nature of the hypothetical source common to Luke 5:1–11 and John 21:1–14—either a pre- or a post-Easter source. The denotations and early uses of the elements of the narrative, however, not only allow entry into the narrative, but also direct and constrain the meaning of the narrative although they do not dictate the meaning of the narrative. The historical study of the sources of Luke 5:1–11, then, does have some bearing on the meaning of Jesus in Luke 5:1–11. The possible use by Luke of a post-Easter narrative concerning the resurrected Christ broadens the perimeters of meaning. The question of the source of the statement ". . . henceforth you will be catching men" (Mark 1:17 or the source common to Luke and John 21), and the relationship of this statement to the catch of fish, again, is not determinative of the meaning but helps set the direction and the perimeters of meaning. The catch of fish as a figure of the mission of the church and as an epiphany of Jesus must be included as a possibility of meaning with which Luke is working.

Narrative hermeneutics is not solely interested in discovering an original historical meaning. It is interested in enabling the modern reader to create meaning in the present which is not discontinuous with the original meaning. So, the meanings of Jesus and Peter to the modern reader will play a part in the development of meaning in the present. To use the conceptualization of Gadamer, the horizon of the reader as well as the horizon of the text (and author) is effective in the determination of present significance. The theological discussion concerning the nature of Jesus Christ, and perhaps more importantly, the ways that modern man finds it conceivable to think of Jesus in his relationship to God the Father will be a part of the horizon of the reader of the narrative. In the case of Simon Peter, the intellectual, emotional, and volitional attitude of the reader toward the interpretation of Peter and his successors in the church color the character of Simon in the narrative and help direct and set the perimeters of present-day meaning.

Plot

The plot is seen in narrative hermeneutics as the basic concern of analysis. It is to be conceived of in generative terms as both the affective and material basis for the narrative. In analysis it is to be reconstituted by a process of abstraction and elimination of elements which are not essential to the plot. The insight that critical analysis involves hermeneutical interpretation and vice versa is a key to narrative hermeneutics. The assignment of abstract categories cannot be accomplished apart from perception of meaning; the designation of variable and invariable elements involves a total meaning of the narrative. The process of analysis and hermeneutical interpretation must go hand in hand with dialectical movement from one emphasis to the other, all the while recognizing the central importance of the nature and development of the structure of the mind which carries out analysis and interpretation. To guard against premature and inflexible analysis and interpretation and to allow for development of meanings differing from—though not discontinuous with —original meaning, analysis must maintain contact with the level of manifestation. An initial reading or analysis/interpretation may then result in a plot in the form of a series of sentences.

In Luke 5:1–11 the narrative can be reorganized into the following sentences: Jesus preached the word of God/People pressed and hindered the preaching/Jesus saw two boats/Jesus got into Simon's boat/ Jesus requested Simon to put out a little from land/Simon obeyed Jesus/ Jesus taught the people/Jesus accomplished the preaching of the word/ Jesus commanded Simon to put out into the deep/Jesus commanded Simon to let down the nets for a catch/Simon protested/Simon obeyed/ Simon and his companions enclosed a great shoal of fish/The nets were breaking/Simon and his companions beckoned to their partners/The partners came/Simon became aware of the power of the Master/Simon became aware of his sin/Simon requested Jesus to depart/Jesus refused to depart/Jesus told Simon not to be afraid/Jesus told Simon that he will catch men/Simon and his companions brought the boats to land/Simon and his companions left everything and followed Jesus.

The next step is the investigation of the plot, so set up, by means of narrative grammars proposed by narratologists. The use of the narrative grammars is not for the purpose of developing algebraic-type formulas[91] but for the purpose of sensitizing readers to the significance of the biblical text. Significations on the level of both author and reader may result from such an application.

The basic model of Bremond emphasizes the sequence of functions from potentiality to either success or failure. With each function there is choice:[92]

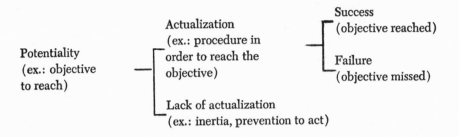

The model serves well to show the alternative choices in the episode of Luke 5:1–3:

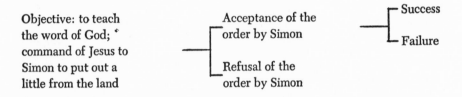

It is clear, however, that this sequence is embedded in a more important sequence:

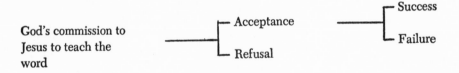

The initial function of Luke 5:1–3 may be seen as Jesus' request of Simon to put out a little from the land followed by Simon's acceptance of the request and the success of the teaching of Jesus. However, this organization of functions misses the major point of the entire narrative, and a more inclusive analysis would begin with the function (implied by the succeeding functions) of the sending of Jesus by God for the purpose of teaching the word of God. This function is obtained from Luke 5:1–11 itself, although it is clearly stated in the material immediately preceding the narrative (Luke 4:43).

A logical analysis (using the principle that the existence of a later function in a logical series presupposes the existence of the early functions in the series even if they are not actually stated) of Luke 5:1-11 would have the sequence of the sending of Jesus as the major sequence with the sequence of the order by Jesus to Simon to move from the shore as an embedded sequence. Bremond calls this an enclave sequence:

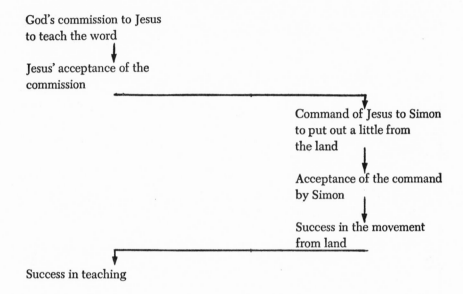

God's commission to Jesus
to teach the word

Jesus' acceptance of the
commission

Command of Jesus to Simon
to put out a little from
the land

Acceptance of the command
by Simon

Success in the movement
from land

Success in teaching

The episode in Luke 5:4-6 may be analyzed as an elementary sequence:

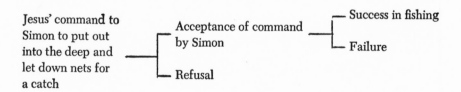

Jesus' command to
Simon to put out
into the deep and
let down nets for
a catch

Acceptance of command
by Simon

Refusal

Success in fishing

Failure

To this elementary sequence may be added another elementary sequence in an "end to end" manner, since the successful catch of fish creates another problem which makes the success problematic. The nets are breaking:

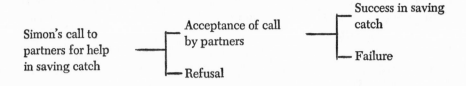

The episode of Luke 5:8–11 may be analyzed as another end-to-end sequence following the problematic success of the catch due to the sinking of the boat.

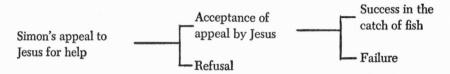

This episode cannot be so simply analyzed by a Christian sensitive to the question of the nature of the Lord and to the matter of the mission of Jesus and his followers. The form which Simon's appeal to Jesus takes is a confession of sin, a confession of the lordship of Jesus Christ. The response of Jesus (which obviously is a positive response to the plea for help because of the successful completion of the fishing mission) is an acceptance of Simon as a follower rather than a shunning of Simon as a sinner. This is logically necessary for the commissioning of Simon. The commissioning of Simon transforms the positive response of Jesus to Simon's request (although in a form which is appropriate to the subject matter on the surface level) into an initial function of another elementary sequence. The response of Simon and his partners to this commission is found in the final verse where they follow Jesus, but the final function of the sequence—successful completion of the mission—is not given, for it is still not successfully completed.

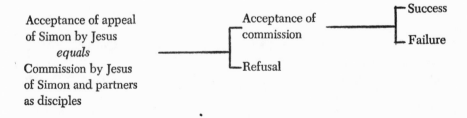

The final sequence of functions and the christological and ecclesiastical import of the words "... henceforth you will be catching men" allows a rereading of all of the previous sequences from the perspective of the initial commission of Jesus and the commissioning by Jesus of Simon. The sequences of the successful fishing expedition with the successive threats of failure by the breaking of nets and sinking boats become symbolic in accord with the final sequence.

An important analysis and interpretation results from viewing the narrative from the perspective of the initial function of the commissioning of Jesus by God:

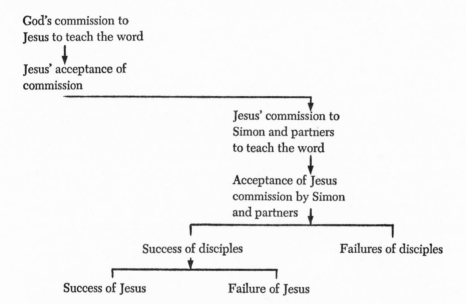

God's commission to
Jesus to teach the word

Jesus' acceptance of
commission

Jesus' commission to
Simon and partners
to teach the word

Acceptance of Jesus
commission by Simon
and partners

Success of disciples   Failures of disciples

Success of Jesus   Failure of Jesus

The completion of the mission of Jesus, the elementary sequence in which the other sequences are embedded, is dependent upon the successful completion of the commission given by Jesus to his followers. The embedded sequence of the catch of fish, then, as it is reinterpreted by the christological and ecclesiastical interpretation, serves as the model for the promise of the successful completion of both the commission given to Jesus by God and the commission given to his followers by Jesus.

Does the model of Greimas help us see Luke 5:1–11 differently than does the model of Bremond? According to Greimas, a narrative may be conceived of abstractly as an organization of sequences from a broken contract and aborted communication between a sender and receiver to the reestablishment of communication and contract (see Chapter Five, note 119). Three sequences may be differentiated: (1) an initial correlated sequence; (2) one or more topical sequences; (3) a final correlated sequence.

In an application of the model of Greimas to Luke 5:1–11 the initial situation may be seen as Jesus carrying out the mandate of God to teach the word. This order is disrupted by the press of the crowd which prevents Jesus from teaching. The reestablishment of the original order is carried out by a topical sequence in which the possibility of carrying out the original order is established. Simon is mandated to put out a little from the land. Successful completion of the topical sequences introduces a final correlated sequence in which the order of the initial sequence is reestablished. Jesus preaches to the crowd.

The episode of Luke 5:4–11 concerns a successful catch of fish. An initial situation must be presupposed in which there is successful fishing. This, however, is broken, evidence of which is found in the statement of Simon: ". . . we toiled all night and took nothing!" A topical sequence which reestablishes the original order—even improving the order by an exceptional catch of fish—begins with the order of Jesus to put out into the deep and let down the nets for a catch. When this is done, the original order of success in fishing is reestablished. Another sequence is necessary when the extraordinary success of fishing causes the nets to break. Simon calls for help from his partners. This ends in success, but when the boats begin to sink another sequence is necessary. Simon's appeal to Jesus results in return to land with the net, boats, and catch of fish.

The final episode, however, contains elements which cannot be ignored as variables unimportant for the narrative but which demand a more profound reading and structuring. The key element is the statement of Jesus ". . . henceforth, you will be catching men." This forces the analysis of Luke 5:4–11 to begin with Luke 5:1–3 or even with the social order prior to that of Jesus preaching freely—a social order the breaking of which brought about the mandate God gave to Jesus to teach the word. When the narrative of Luke 5:1–11 is put into this broad framework we get an initial correlated sequence (presupposed by the topical sequences designed to reestablish the order) involving God and man. The topical sequences are designed to reestablish this order. When the major part of Luke 5:1–11 is seen as consisting of topical sequences, the emphasis of Propp and Greimas on tests and contracts becomes important and may be used in a heuristic way to open up new insights. When one views narrative from the perspective of contracts and tests, there is an initial mandate or contract which is disrupted and cannot be carried out. By means of a qualifying test, a hero acquires some type of helper to assist in carrying out a secondary or topical mandate or contract to neutralize whatever has disrupted the original order. The main test is the attempt to carry out the secondary mandate. When this is achieved, another mandate or contract is carried out to provide some type of glorification for the hero—the glorifying test. A final correlated sequence takes place when there is a successful topical sequence.

In the narrative of Luke 5:1–11, the initial contract is disrupted. God sends Jesus with a communication to the people. An initial test enables Jesus to carry out the mandate in principle or in part and secures Peter as a helper. The main test in the narrative appears to be that of catching fish, but in reality this is symbolic of evangelizing mankind. The success of the fishing expedition is effective in securing the helpers for the real mandate with which the narrative is concerned and serves as a symbol for the ultimate success of the main test and hence the reestablishment of the original order.

In the application of the models of Greimas and Bremond to the narrative of Luke 5:1–11 for hermeneutical purposes (not to test the models but as heuristic devices) no real differences are seen.

Semic and Actantial Analyses

In the analysis to this point, an implicit analysis of the characters of Jesus and Peter and discernment of the character types has taken place. Explicit and detailed analyses may contribute to the development of meaning.

Semic analysis presupposes that a reader unconsciously develops a view of a character by observing the attributes of that character as he reads the narrative. The totality of the attributes *is* the character in the narrative insofar as the narrative is considered as literature and not as an objective statement about some historical figure. The attributes of Jesus from the perspective of the reader, although not from the perspective of Peter, are all of one piece; there is no critical change. From Luke 5:1 the reader concludes that Jesus is popular and is speaker of the word of God. The ingenuity of Jesus, his compelling authority, and his forgiveness and acceptance are seen clearly in the remainder of the narrative. The *level* of Jesus' compelling authority progresses in the narrative from authority concerning movement of the boat and the catch of fish to authority concerning catching men.

Peter, in contrast to Jesus, exhibits different attributes in different parts of the narrative. Obedience—even in the face of doubt—and authority are seen throughout. But at the catch of fish and danger of loss of nets, boats, and fish, Simon's impetuousness, sense of sin, and awareness of the true nature of Jesus (explaining the confession of Simon) come to the fore.

The application of the actantial model to Luke 5:1–11 helps relationships to be seen more closely and also makes plain some important changes of relationships. The narrative begins with God understood as the sender because God's word and/or Jesus is the object. Mankind is the receiver. The subject who will suppress obstacles and facilitate the communication is Jesus. The helper is Simon, a boat, and distance. The opponent is the press of the crowd. In the sequence beginning with verse 4, Jesus is the sender, the object is a catch of fish, the receiver is assumed to be the Simon and his companions and ultimately the people. The subject is Simon. The helper is faith in Jesus' word; the opponent is doubt and previous failure. The third person plural subject of the action may be taken to include Simon's companions as subject or helper.

Another sequence begins with the successful catch and the breaking of the nets in verse 6. This narrative may be considered as an enclave to complete the previous sequence but the sender is definitely plural, Simon and his companions, later named as James and John. The object is help. The receiver is also the sender. The subject is the partners in the other boat.

The successful assistance of verse 7 changes the locus of danger from the nets to the boat. Simon is the sender, the object is deliverance, the receiver is Simon and his companions. The subject is Jesus, the helper is the word of faith and the promise that Simon will in the future be catching men.

The statement of Jesus about catching men has the effect of instructing the reader to repeat all previous operations, at least from verse 4, with "men" replacing "fish." Jesus becomes the sender of the word in place of God, the object is the word (which is equated with catching men), the receiver is mankind. Simon in place of Jesus is the subject.

With success nearly creating failure in verse 4, Simon becomes the sender, the object is help, the receiver is people. The subject is the companions of Peter. The success again becomes the possibility of failure in verse 7. Again, Peter is the sender, the object is deliverance, the receiver is Peter and his companions, the subject is Jesus, the helper is the word of Jesus.

When the rereading is done, the initial sequence is also transformed. It becomes a pattern for the series of sequences with the interesting change of actants. The object, the receiver, and the opponent remain basically the same. The sender changes from God to Jesus to Peter. The helper becomes the sender, or the word of the sender.

From the word of Jesus, "Do not be afraid, henceforth you will be catching men," there is not only a backward reference giving additional significance but a forward thrust; readers of the gospel are recipients of the word by means of the success of the sender and the subjects. They are also subjects, and must they not become senders? The forward thrust again forces a rereading of the earlier narrative segments with the readers involved.

The process of reidentifying actants is not simply a result of structural analysis, although structural analysis makes clearer what is happening in the reading and rereading of the narrative. The process of the shifts and multiplication of significations is a result of the reading process itself. Wolfgang Iser (whose contribution on the phenomenology of reading supports the basic hypothesis about the necessity for a systems approach to interpretation) notes that not only is anticipation operative in the reading process but also retrospection. One statement opens up a horizon which is modified or completely changed by successive statements. "While these expectations arouse interest in what is to come, the subsequent modification of them will also have a retrospective effect on what has already been read. This may now take on a different significance from that which it had at the moment of reading."[93] Iser correctly complicates the process by speaking of an advanced retrospection in a second reading which modifies or changes the significations.

Affective Interpretation

What affective communication is involved? What feeling, mood, tone is involved for the creator? Again, a beginning can be made with the content, or the material of the narrative, for, as Wesley A. Kort expressed it, tone is "the element of narrative which is the image of that creative moment when choice of material, attitude toward it, and the use of language dance as one. . . ." Language mediates material and attitude. It "derives from and sacrifices itself to the possibilities of material and attitude," and becomes the only reality.[94] With the type of poetic work involved in Luke 5:1–11, structural analysis may allow another effective entry into the affective arena, for the fable, myth, or plot which is a means of production is also a communication of meaning. In fact, with ancient texts using materials which do not have connotations which they "naturally" had for the creator and first readers, one might do a better job of determining feeling, mood, and tone from plot than from content. Then, ideational content can be interpreted in relation to such affective meaning. That is, there is a dialectical relationship between meaning on the affective level and the meaning on the ideational level.

Just as the reader moves through a series of meanings on the thematic level and structures the narrative accordingly, so the narrative creates different affective meaning-effects. The genre of the narrative is interpreted variously, and eventually mood and tone are accomplished by effects on the level of the will. In the initial episode of Luke 5:1–3, the reader sees Jesus with a mission which is thwarted by the pressure of the crowd—the very ones to whom Jesus is to teach the word of God. The obstacle to the completion of the task is effectively removed with the help of Simon and his boat, and the mission is completed. The narrative creates an expectation for the reader which is met effectively by the successful conclusion. But the very completion of the narrative, the fact that the narrative has a denouement of any sort, brings a degree of satisfaction to the reader.

The episode not only has a comic successful ending but it also has earlier humorous touches. The *lack* is created by the very presence of the crowd. The liquidation of lack is brought about by at least a partial departure from the very ones to whom the word of God is to be given.

The episode beginning with Luke 5:4 is more ambiguous in terms of the mood created. Initially, it appears that the same sort of sequence will be repeated. The order of society in which fish are caught for the people has been interrupted, but Jesus encourages and enables Simon to catch a multitude of fish in spite of Simon's earlier failures. The reader's satisfaction is premature, however. The very success of the catch invites catastrophe. The nets begin to break. The reader may see this as a repetition of the type of thing which created the lack in the first episode. Too much of what is sought spells failure! Certainly the repetition of the very same type in the sinking of the boats must be seen as comic. The principle of such humor is the "principle that unincremental repetition . . . is funny. . . . Repetition overdone or not going anywhere belongs to comedy, for laughter is partly a reflex, and like other reflexes it can be conditioned by a simple repeated pattern."[95] But repetition in a tragedy may lead to catastrophe, so the reader must contain his emotional response until the final denouement. The completion of the narrative finds the fishermen with their nets and boats safe on the shore. So, as a tale about successful fishing, perhaps in spite of the dangers of the success, the narrative concludes with a comic mood or tone. The reader sees this as a comic genre as opposed to the tragic genre. But this is not pure comedy. It is not ideal comedy which Frye describes as "the vision not of the way of the world but of what you will, life as you like it." Would the reader not see this as ironic comedy which shows the incongruities of the world and yet which holds us to the world? The emphasis is not upon the "all too human" life which is either oppressive or ridiculous, but neither is it the ideal comedy of "what you will."[96]

A reader who is religiously mature and who has a degree of symbolic competence will center upon the episode which forms the crux of the movement from the potentially catastrophic situation of those on the lake to the safe arrival on land. This appears to be Frye's fifth phase of comedy where "the comic ending is less a matter of the way the plot turns out than of the perspective of the audience. . . . In this phase the reader or audience feels raised above the action. . . . We see the action, in short, from the point of view of a higher and better ordered world."[97] In this phase comedy "is part of a settled order which has been there from the beginning, an order which takes on an increasingly religious cast and seems to be drawing away from human experience altogether." Movement is made, then, from the circle of mythoi of Frye into the "apocalyptic or abstract mythical world above it."[98]

In Luke 5:1–11 the movement of the perspective of the reader to a point above the action, the movement away from human experience, is accomplished to the extent that the reader agrees with Simon's assessment of the character of Jesus. The story takes on mythic qualities (myth in the common sense of a story about a god). The narrative is not a simple story about a divine being, however. The epiphany, if such it is interpreted by the reader, is the occasion of Jesus' mandate to Simon and the others present which will enable Jesus to carry out the original mandate of God. The words of Jesus which establish the mandate, ". . . henceforth, you will be catching men," will be read as functioning the same way as Mark 1:17, "Follow me and I will make you become fishers of men." But in fact the statement is literally more of an institution of Simon and those others present than it is an invitation to follow Jesus. With the necessary view of God, providence, and Christology, the saying of Jesus may be read as both a mandate and as an authoritative pronouncement of final success of the mission of the disciples, the mission of Jesus, and, hence, reestablishment of the original divinely ordained society. In such a case the remaining functions are read as merely adding final touches to the narrative.

The modern reader will note the more positive and authoritative form of the mandate to Peter, but he will not see the story as completely finished. The mandate is accepted, but not yet finally accomplished. The mood of ironic comedy which is aware of the incongruities of the world and yet which holds us to the world remains in effect as the narrative is related to ecclesiastical and theological themes.

Interest in the mood or tone of the narrative leads to other affective meaning-effects. There is a volitional meaning-effect in the narrative. The reader relates himself to Simon and his companions in the narrative itself, and to the gospel writer and transmitters of the story which are implicit in the process from God through Jesus to the series of followers. The capstone of the narrative, the words of Jesus which bring reconciliation of oppositions and aesthetic satisfaction, constitute a call to the reader as to Simon.[99] Genuine satisfaction in the narrative is created by the response of Simon and his companions in following Jesus. Genuine satisfaction in the life of the reader and completion of the meaning of the narrative will come when similar response is made. All of the levels of meaning combine to direct and elicit the response. The positive response is affirmation of the presence of God in the narrative and in the life of the reader, appropriate matching of the mood, tone, and emotional satisfaction of the narrative, and the logical consequence of the cognitive content of the interpretation given by the reader.[100]

The Structures Accompanying Plot

The structures used so far in analysis have been related to plot, but the elements of Luke 5:1–11 may be seen to sustain other relationships. The principle governing such patterns is that the creator and interpreter find pleasure and satisfaction in grammatical and other patterns not necessarily related to the major narrative structures. The discovery of such patterns depends in large measure upon the symbolic capacity of the reader, and the process of discovery, as discussed earlier, is often in accord with the law of *Prägnanz* in Gestalt psychology. Jean Delorme finds that spatial patterns of Luke 5:1–11 are significant.[101] Luke 5:1–3 requires a separation of Jesus from the crowd before they can hear the word of God. In verse 4, the space changes. The distance from the bank increases in order for the catch of fish to take place and for the companions of Peter to unite with Peter and with Jesus. This remains the scene until the end of the narrative. The place of the catch is not only fixed horizontally some distance from land, but it is also fixed vertically, for the catch involves the depths of the lake. The nets which break from the catch are let down *into the lake*. The boats sink *into the lake*. Another vertical relationship is that of Simon and Jesus. Simon falls down at Jesus' knees; he asks Jesus to separate himself (horizontal displacement) from Simon. The title of Lord is applied by Simon when Jesus is revealed as Master of the depths. In verse 11 a new spatial relationship is set up in which his disciples follow Jesus to catch men. But the catching of men supposes a spiritual space where Jesus reigns over the depths and where men are removed from the reign of death.

Narrative hermeneutics is not directed toward the determination of an original meaning; the objection that the significations of spatial patterns might not or even could not have been in the consciousness of the writer does not exclude the modern reader from using such patterns for discovery of present-day meaning for himself. A caution, however, is that such significations must either be in accord with the burden of the total narrative seen from the primary perspective of plot or at least not be opposed to that perspective.

Another pattern may be seen from the perspective of Barthes's symbolic code. The symbolic code is the means of transgressing or mediating an antithesis. The antithesis is not that of a complementary relationship or a dialectical relationship, such as empty as opposed to full. The antithesis "separates for eternity" and "is the battle between two plentitudes set ritually face to face like two fully armed warriors."[102] Barthes finds the antithesis of Sarrasine in Garden/Salon and in symbolic readings of the text reinforcing the oppositions such as Dance of Death/Dance of Life, Nature/Man, Cold/Hot, Silence/Noise. The symbolic code which transgresses or mediates this opposition is first seen in the lexia "I was deep in one of those daydreams." The narrator is seated in a window with an elegant party on one hand and a garden on the other. The narrator himself is the mediator. His position transgresses the antithesis (outside and inside, cold and heat, death and life).

In Luke 5:1–11, the words of Jesus ". . . you will be catching men" may be seen as mediating oppositions. The opposition can be set up as that between the lake and the shore: the lake can be seen as the place of success (of teaching the word, of the catch of fish) and of revelation of the divine and the shore can be seen as the place of failure, of the press of men, of misunderstanding, of human attempts to mold Jesus into their pattern (see also Luke 4:42 and 5:15). "Catching men" is a metaphor meaning being evangelists or missionaries, but the denotation of the terms of the metaphor mediates the lake of the miraculous catch and the shore of sinful men. The words of Jesus mediate the antithesis which separates for eternity, but in fact in the narrative it is Jesus himself who transgresses or mediates the antithesis. And Simon with those associated with him are declared to be those who will continue to transgress the eternal antithesis.

Interpretation

The process of reading as outlined by Holland climaxes with the reader "making sense" of the text. The product of the application to the text of the reader's linguistic and literary competency and his "cluster of wishes" is some "literary point or theme or interpretation."[103]

Theoretically, in the interpretation no one level of meaning—historical, existential, ontological-theological, affective—has priority. All levels are involved in the creation and any level may be the focus of attention. The historical level of concern with the original meaning and use can be the initial focus. The historical significance might point to other significations, for the author and reader. Some sort of dialectical relationship between public use of the text and personal meaning can be assumed. The completion of the narrative helps the creator make sense for himself on different levels, but it also has uses at particular historical junctions. To identify use and purpose is not to exhaust or even to define meaning, but it may elicit meaning. Here, source, form, and redaction criticism are useful.

Creation, history, and meaning can be connected by the observation that there is a deep awareness on the part of the creator that the act of creation will provide something new, something needed. "The creative act is judgment on the state of affairs prior to the act."[104] The new and needed information in the narrative is vital enough for the author of Luke that he would reconstruct history on the basis of the "truth" in the narrative. As Conzelmann says, "Luke makes no separation between chronological and soteriological significance." Although the historical sequence "as such is of fundamental importance," Luke is not a modern historian. Luke is a man of faith, who, "when he has discovered the redemptive significance of an event, . . . can go on to deduce from it the 'correct' chronology, which means, among other things, that he can begin to modify Mark."[105]

The interpretations given by modern historical critics vary: the earthly Jesus willed the primacy of Peter and the mission of the Apostles; the Apostles left everything to follow the Master;[106] authentic Christian preaching is to be found only in Peter's church—although others are involved in the mission, they are related to Peter;[107] Jesus willed that Gentiles be a part of his church;[108] the apostolic ministry is based simply on Christ's gracious calling, including forgiveness, not on the religious genius or the worth of the Apostles;[109] to be a disciple is to be a fisher of men; doubt and faith and the presence, forgiveness, and power of Jesus Christ are true of all of the disciples;[110] Gentiles and others on the fringe of the church are reassured that Peter's authority was not simply founded upon a post-resurrection appearance, that Peter was a disciple from the beginning.[111] It is instructive to observe that the critical judgments as to the purpose and meaning of the narrative cited above are also the results of literary responses related to the interpreters' total situation. The readers make both judgments related to historical-critical concerns and literary responses in which their "clusters of wishes" are transformed into appropriate points or themes or interpretations.

Luke 5:1–11 doubtless has ecclesiastical significance for the creator and early readers and modern Protestants and Roman Catholics. These significations depend upon the traditions out of which the readers come. Most significance will be gained by those who are most cognizant of their religious tradition. It is impossible to read the passage and structure it without at least unconsciously bringing ecclesiastical traditions to bear upon it. Since this is inevitable readers should not be hesitant to allow their religious tradition to alert them to new and additional significance in the passage. As the reader comes to a statement of theme or interpretation which is appropriate for him and not inconsistent with the text, the theological question inevitably arises. God is in the narrative as the sender of Jesus Christ. Without God in some sense, however understood, the story probably could not have elicited aesthetic and emotional effects. (The question of the possibility and method of conceiving of ontological and theological levels of meaning will be discussed at a later point.) It must be noted, however, that the statement of interpretation as such is not necessarily the most important result of the process of reading. The emotional, affective, and aesthetic results of the reading may cause the statement to appear rather pale.

A negative conclusion could be made as a result of the analysis: that structural study of narrative does not provide a scientific method of analysis and interpretation of narrative. This conclusion would result from the fact that different structuring is possible, that one clear objective analysis does not result from the work. Our study does not make this negative conclusion because it recognizes the necessity of human perception in analysis and interpretation and it stresses the finite historical nature of human perception, the dynamic evolving human capacity of the human mental structure, and the inevitable relationship of the reader's "cluster of wishes" in interpretation and analysis. In fact, the key to narrative hermeneutics is the very fact that the critical structuring and personal interpretation are related in a dialectical way. Instead of seeing this as a negative fact, we use it as a methodological principle.

Conclusion

The analysis of meanings and structures of Luke 5:1–11 is not an objective statement of *the* original meaning or a neat algebraic-like formulation of *the* profound structures of the passage. This is not accidental, for the major thoughts which inform narrative hermeneutics are in opposition to the postulates behind both of these goals. Narrative hermeneutics unites human creative capacity and the text. In analysis both poles must be considered. Therefore, narrative hermeneutics involves semiotics which, by its very nature, is an endless play of signs and meanings. Analysis must recognize the progressive and dialectical nature of meaning and structures and the multi-level nature of both. Also, the historical and limited nature of the human being and language (regardless of the infinite nature of the ground of being and language) means that narrative hermeneutics (semiotic analysis assisted by the phenomenology of reading or reading assisted by semiotics) will never arrive at finality.

Narrative hermeneutics is not an attempt to determine a final historical meaning. It focuses upon the use which may be made of the text for the development of personal signification. Instead of remaining located at the historical meaning at the time of origin of the text, narrative hermeneutics uses the insights of the structural study of narrative in order to move first of all to the more abstract levels of narrative and narrative logic which the modern reader and original author have in common and then to move back to the historical situation of the reader. The meanings seen in the narrative by the modern reader will vary both from the original meaning and the interpretations others have given in the history of interpretation, but the meanings will be consistent with the structures of the text and will be in continuity with the original meanings.

It is clear that the program of narrative hermeneutics can only be judged operationally. Edmund Leach stated the criterion by which Lévi-Strauss's structural vision could be evaluated for anthropology: "If, by applying Lévi-Strauss techniques of analysis to an actual body of anthropological materials, we are able to arrive at insights which we did not have before, and these insights throw illumination on other related ethnographic facts, which we had not considered in the first instance, then we may feel that the exercise has been worthwhile."[112] Leach judges Lévi-Strauss's method as operationally vindicated. We may paraphrase the criterion of Leach and apply it to narrative hermeneutics. If, by applying structural and semiotic techniques of analysis to biblical material, we are enabled to arrive at literary, theological, and humanistic insights which we did not have before, and these insights illumine other related literary, theological, and humanistic facts, which we had not considered in the first instance, then we may judge that narrative hermeneutics is operationally valid.

STRUCTURALISM, THEOLOGY, AND ONTOLOGY

This work has focused on New Testament narrative, and an apology has been made for the application of structural insights to narrative for hermeneutical purposes. In order for structural insights to assist the study of narrative, narrative must be taken as a level of language and the proposition accepted that language elements function in a system in which they are defined by their relation with other elements. The language system consists of different levels of structure, and at each level (phoneme, morpheme, lexeme, sentence, narrative) the principles of structure are basically the same. The different levels are mutually interdependent, however, with elements of one level combining to form elements of a higher level.

The necessary involvement of the human in the creation of structures and meanings has caused us to reinterpret the structural program as a hermeneutical program relating personal meanings and meaning-effects to structures instead of as a simple positivistic program. The meaning and meaning-effect of the elements of language—including narrative—are dependent, then, not merely upon some objective set of possible relationships but upon those relationships which the reader is capable of "knowing" because of inner developments (the development of his mental structure) and outer developments. The structural program, then, becomes a statement of the way man creates meaning in a narrative text and becomes useful for the program of narrative hermeneutics.

All levels of language and meaning which impinge upon the reader are operative in the process of narrative hermeneutics. Reference has been made to meaning on the level of life, and it will be recalled that Wilhelm Dilthey himself was primarily concerned with the meaning of life, the highest level of meaning to which all other levels point or "refer." What Dilthey sought was the meaning of life itself, the ultimate level of meaning which does not in turn refer to something else. (See below, pp. 30–32.) Can the model of interpretation for which Dilthey has served as inspiration help in the interpretation of life, in ontology and theology? I would propose that the model of narrative hermeneutics may be used as a model for theology by "reducing" life to the level of narrative. The theology which would be related to the narrative of life would continue to be seen as a second level conceptual system, but it would also be seen as a dynamically developing system. The theology envisioned would be related to life at the point where the theologian or the body of theologians or those for whom the theology is addressed are "located." The theology would, therefore, be conceivable and meaningful as much more than a historical statement to be studied historically. Life in such a program would be conceived of as narrative. If one wished to posit some sort of universal narrative of life, it would still only exist in the narrative or narratives of life as they impinge upon individuals and groups. (The groups would be defined not only temporally, but also geographically, denominationally, etc.)

The final meaning of life envisioned as narrative is not seen, for the final meaning of the elements of life and the structuring of the elements can only take place from the "end" of life. Yet, every man reads the narrative of life (i.e., refers the elements of life to things in the "world" and structures the moves and actors in the narrative on the basis of both developments in his mental structure and outer developments) so as to find meaning and be affected by meaning-effects. In the process of discovering or inventing the meaning of the narrative of life, all other narratives which the reader "knows" play a part by means of paradigmatic and syntagmatic relationships.

The protest that the narrative of life is too complex and involved for narrative hermeneutics is to be met by the proposition that stories may be chosen out of the entire narrative to represent the entire narrative. This process is acceptable because the choice of story or stories will inevitably and intuitively involve the entire story as it impinges upon the reader.

Theology is not the hermeneutical reading of the narrative of life or stories which represent that narrative but must be the conceptualization and systematization which make possible and conceivable such a hermeneutical reading and which support the meaning and meaning-effects that result from such a reading.

The present work is not designed as a full description of a narrative hermeneutics of life, for many non-language-oriented questions enter the picture when life is reduced to narrative or particular narratives are taken as a valid representation of life. The personal equation becomes even more significant than it is in narrative hermeneutics per se. Of theological and ontological interest, however, is the existence of structures on the levels which are less comprehensive and perhaps less subject to personal judgment. Some writers argue persuasively that structuralism allows us to account for reality through the structures which are found: Lévi-Strauss affirms that structures really exist in culture and in the human mind, that by means of these structures myths signify the mind that evolves them by using the work of which it is a part and ultimately that culture and nature are one; Brian Wicker affirms that structural linguistics brings us back to the question of God, allowing us to "reach out to God as he is."[113] The relationship of structuralism to contemporary ontological and theological concepts must be examined to determine the validity of a "structural ontology," and if this is not valid, to outline the appropriate help structuralism may give in ontological and theological questions.

Brian Wicker is convinced that "language must reach right out to God as he is, albeit by means of concepts or 'imaginative constructs,' if God is to be worth having," and that modern structural linguistics is a tool which philosophical theology may use to do that very thing. The discoveries of structuralism "imply a whole philosophy of 'Nature' without which the structuralist scheme itself would fall apart."[114] The path followed by Wicker is tedious and leads back to a reevaluation of the Thomistic account of analogical predication and metaphysics. Wicker does not simply reinstate Aquinas in place of newer theologians; however, he makes an important place for the role of metaphorical language. Indeed, Wicker proposes a new synthesis "based upon a marriage of the two partners *metaphor* and *analogy*."[115] The argument of Wicker must be given in some detail for it to be appreciated, but a summary of the argument might be helpful at the beginning: (1) Language and life have paradigmatic and syntagmatic aspects; each aspect is necessary for the other. (2) Metaphor is necessary in language and life; it is paradigmatic in nature and requires for its completion metonymy or analogy which is syntagmatic in nature. In life, man perceives a metaphorical relationship (paradigmatic) between the different species of different levels and uses these relationships to explain his own situation. A syntagmatic relationship, an analogical linking of the human world to the animal world, must exist for the metaphor to be effective. (3) The metaphorical language used by both science and common sense to formulate causal connections, then, inevitably contains metaphysical overtones. In relation to narrative, Wicker asserts that stories are necessary to describe otherwise indescribable inexplicable events in the external world and in oneself. Narrative answers questions which cannot be answered in non-narrative form. The narrative does not merely contain the answer; it is the answer.

Metaphor in the classical scheme was an instrument of rhetoric. Later it was seen as more than style, not just a way of describing things but a way of experiencing things. Metaphor was seen as necessary for describing and understanding. Yet, Wicker says, there is danger in metaphorical language in that it may tend to humanize all things so that the world is "delivered up to the not always tender mercies of man's own thirst for meaning."[116] The corrective presence of the "not human" is needed, the "other" which cannot be manipulated by language; and Wicker sees in structural linguistics just this "counterweight to the dangerous pull of metaphor."[117] The counterweight may be applied by opposing metaphor to metonymic language—instead of opposing metaphor to a supposed literal language.

Structuralism gives the possibility and significance of the opposition of metaphor to metonomy. Wicker uses the syntagmatic-paradigmatic dichotomy of Saussure (whereby a linguistic element has a certain linear, or syntactic, relationship with other elements in the sentence and a paradigmatic, or associative, relationship with other items of the same sort which could be used in its place) and the observation of Jakobson that the two acts of selecting items and combining items rest on different but complementary principles. Wicker, then, sees the structure of an utterance based on two principles or sets of principles in binary opposition.

On one side (the paradigmatic side) is the selection of items which implies the possibility of substituting another similar item in its place. On the other side (the syntagmatic side) is the act of combination which arranges contiguous elements in a particular context. Wicker expands the principles on each side by opposing language-speech (*langue-parole*) and code-message. So he ends with a large number of terms which are necessary to describe the structure of an utterance:[118]

Language	Speech
Code	Message
Paradigmatic relation	Syntagmatic relation
Selection	Combination
Substitution	Context
Metaphor	Metonymy

Wicker sees analogy (metonymy) as belonging on the syntagmatic side of the equation and metaphor as belonging on the paradigmatic side. He does not use analogy as the broad category in which metaphor is classified but in the sense of St. Thomas Aquinas. The problem of St. Thomas was the use of creaturely terms for the creator without degrading him to creaturely status. The solution was to find terms applicable to creature and creator not univocal (identical) or equivocal (unrelated) but analogical (not identical but related). The metaphysics of being allows analogical language. In God alone unqualified being is to be found. While God is elementary being, others *are* in various degrees and in dependence upon the being of God.[119] For Aquinas, the idea of an underlying causal relationship is fundamental to analogy. Aquinas illustrates this by the ancient practice of applying the word "healthy" to a person's urine as well as to the person, much as moderns use the word "healthy" to speak of a person's complexion. The relationship between a healthy urine (or complexion) and a healthy man is a relationship of effect and cause.

Not only does Wicker relate analogy to the syntagmatic side of the equation; he also declares that all of the items on the syntagmatic side have a causal connection. Before modern man can even consider such an idea (that a causal relation exists between items in "*any* syntagm, *any* context, *any* contiguity, *any* message") he must rid himself of a prejudice about causality—the post-Humean prejudice that "the causal relation is a matter of external association of two or more entities and that it must therefore present itself as a temporal process."[120] With this prejudice, it is impossible to conceive of a relation of cause in a coexisting structure such as a sentence. Wicker claims that there is a "form of internal causal relation" or "mutual contextual determination" in a sentence. ". . . it is *because* element A of the total 'context' has such and such function that elements B, C, D, etc. have their particular functions, and *vice versa*. Contiguity in this sense implies causality."[121]

Mutual contextual determination allows us to say at the same time of the sentence "John hits Joe": (a) "that it is because *John* is grammatical subject that *hits* is verb, and because *hits* is transitive *Joe* is object," and (b) "that it is because *Joe* is grammatical object that *hits* is verb, and because *hits* is verb *John* is grammatical subject."[122]

More importantly, there is an underlying causal agency of language itself. Language, then, is not an inert collection of elements and rules; it is an agent, "an active ingredient in the business of communicating in words."[123] Wicker makes plain the implication of the fact of the agency of language: A cause "is not a relationship but a thing: an agent that brings about some effect by the exercise of what can only be called its own 'natural tendency' to behave in a certain way."[124] Causality then involves a metaphysical notion of *nature*. ". . . the discoveries of structuralism in linguistics and elsewhere are not the neutral, value-free, or un-metaphysical propositions they may sometimes seem to be. On the contrary, they imply a whole philosophy of 'Nature' without which the structuralist schema itself would fall apart."[125]

The structuralist reinstatement of analogy in the sense of St. Thomas would reinstate the theological use of analogical language! The particular view of causality which derives from the idea of an agent or "a thing exerted itself, having its influence or imposing its character on the world," or "a thing that is exerting itself according to its *natural tendencies*," distinguishes the pre-Enlightenment transitive concept of causality from the intransitive Enlightenment notion which was expressed most clearly by Hume. According to Hume, to look for a cause is to look for a necessary connection between two or more things, not to look for a thing that is exerting itself according to its own nature. Although the transitive and intransitive views are mutually exclusive, the attempts to combine elements of both (such as that of Mill) are instructive because in such attempts metaphorical language has been necessary. Wicker argues that since "natural tendencies" language is "indispensable both for science and common sense" and since "metaphor is a necessary element in such a language," "there is no avoiding metaphysical involvements." The very fact of metaphor itself implies a metaphysic. Metaphor, then, "asserts a relation between man and a world which is properly called 'Nature'; that is to say, a world ordered and intelligent and subject to discernible 'natural tendencies' inherent in things themselves."[126]

In order to show the relationship between the paradigmatic and syntagmatic sides of the equation in language and life Wicker emphasizes the similarities (or metaphorical relationships) which men see between different species on their own level and on different levels (air, earth, water) *and* the use of this "natural" way of thinking about metaphor by anthropologists such as Lévi-Strauss to study social phenomena. The connection is inextricable "between the perception of similarities in nature and the telling of stories to bring these similarities to life,"[127] between the paradigmatic and syntagmatic, between metaphor and narrative.

In the use of divisions in the animal kingdom to express divisions and tensions in the human community, according to Lévi-Strauss, society may confront its tensions more objectively. "To take one example, any society is liable to generate tensions between females and males, parents and children, fathers-in-law and sons-in-law, etc. By identifying such opposed pairs with pairs of supposedly 'similar' animal species, the society can understand its own problems more clearly."[128] However, more than a simple ratio between the human and animal species must be established for solution of social conflict. "The mere identification of, say, the males of a tribe with the bat and the females with the night owl or the father-in-law with the eaglehawk and the son-in-law with the crow tells nothing about the relations *between* these various pairs." Some link, or some common characteristic that joins the members of each pair together, is necessary. The vertical, paradigmatic relation must be accompanied by a horizontal syntagmatic relation. The myths studied by Lévi-Strauss assert a metaphoric similarity between men and animals which gives insight into the human situations, but it is also possible to emphasize what is common between men and animals in comparison with the "higher world of superior spiritual beings" to show the syntagmatic relation of the totality of the world of the "here below" to the superior world.[129]

Both sides of the equation are necessary, for "an analogical linking of the world here below to the world above would still be inert without a corresponding paradigmatic dimension."[130] The syntagmatic axis sets up analogical relations, but a horizontal, narrative dimension is necessary "to give flesh and bones to the analogical structure, . . . to give the *whole* totality any explanatory power."[131]

Wicker moves from metaphysics, from Nature, which is "a world ordered and intelligible and subject to discernible 'natural tendencies' inherent in things themselves,"[132] to God by means of a theory of narrative derived from metaphor. He is clearly at odds with thinkers who encourage the idea that ultimate reality can be spoken of only in metaphor. Such thinkers fail to see the radical difference between analogy and metaphor and fail to understand that both analogical and metaphorical stretching are necessary, "as necessary to each other as the warp and weft of a fabric, as the melody and harmony of a musical score, as the vertical and horizontal axes of a graph."[133] The thesis of Wicker is that analogy and metaphor are to be regarded as names of the "two poles" of discourse, whether about ordinary things or about God. The divorce between the God "of the philosophers" and the "God of Abraham, Isaac, and Jacob" was caused historically, in Wicker's view, because of the failure to appreciate the real nature of the relationship between analogy and metaphor.

The duality for which Wicker contends is not a duality in God such as the process theologians favor. The answer is not at all in a theory about the way in which we speak of God. Again, Wicker is not talking about the dualism of speaking of God in philosophical terms and in religious terms whereby when we speak of God in philosophical terms the word "God" becomes a common noun and when we speak of God in religious terms we are addressing the Lord and Master. The problem of divorce between the God of religion and the God of philosophy is to be solved by "positing a duality in the language we have to use to speak about God." The divorce will be overcome when philosophical speech about God and poetic speech about God are both accommodated in our theology and brought into a single unified theory.[134]

The way Wicker suggests that the two types of speech be unified is not merely a return to the traditional distinctions between the analogical and metaphorical ways of speaking about God but a proper understanding of the metaphorical way or the narrative way. Philosophical theology will be able to mend the divorce by considering not only the content of narrative but the structure of narrative (in the sense that the structure has paradigmatic and syntagmatic sides). This will allow the accommodation of both philosophical speech and poetic speech about God.

In narrative about God in the Old Testament the basic metaphor is the treatment of God as a quasi-human character.[135] "The poet, or narrator, has taken upon himself to attribute to Yahweh a kind of life which is not that of God, the Most High, creator of heaven and earth, but of ours."[136] The poet does this because he wishes to tell something about the "mighty acts" of God which cannot be told in a non-figurative way. Philosophical problems arise from such action of the poet, questions concerning divine immutability, omniscience, etc. In the story of God's regret for making man, for example, there is a problem with the philosophical doctrine of God's immutability. Aquinas's solution, to argue that God knew all along that the creatures he made would have to be destroyed and that the "regret" of God is only a metaphor, is unsatisfying. The reconciliation of the Most High God with the quasi-human character is a problem in the context in which the story is found, for in other passages in Genesis and elsewhere it is clear that Yahweh is not subject to a change of mind, Yahweh is not *in fact* the quasi-human figure.

The purpose of the narrative about Yahweh is to give a structure to the real world. The structure of the story is projected onto the real world. The structure of the story has a vertical dimension; God is at the top, man is at the bottom, and the two are connected by a "causal nexus of dependence."[137] The character of Yahweh, who is God, but who is also characterized by human limitations, mediates between the top and the bottom of the structure of the story. The *faith* that Yahweh is God causes man to project the story onto the real world. "If Yahweh is God, then it is not a contingent but a necessary fact that the stories about him will be stories about God: and the information they reveal about God will be reliable for that reason."[138]

The act of faith is both a paradigmatic and a syntagmatic matter. Because it is on the axis of choice, "faith, being a kind of voluntary commitment is always a paradigmatic matter. It is the choice either of *this* god out of all the eligible gods, or of this story out of all the eligible stories." The syntagmatic axis, the axis of necessity, follows inevitably from the act of faith. ". . . if the chosen story is a story about the true god, then the god of whom it tells must be God."[139] Both the paradigmatic and syntagmatic ways of looking at the matter are equally valid; each represents a somewhat different notion of what faith is. One begins with a certain concept of the divine and argues to what such a divinity will do. The other begins with a certain sense of the kinds of acts which seem to be especially divinely marked and argues from the stories to the existence of the one God about whom the stories tell.

Wicker asks next of the metaphorical relation between Yahweh, the quasi-human character, and the Most High God. "Yahweh, as the name of a character in a story, is a piece of metaphorical language."[140] Metaphor can work in theology by taking for granted that certain human characteristics may be affirmed of God. Metaphor, in this way, relates God with the world, "but it does so only because it presupposes that we already know that these characteristics are not literally true of God."[141] Before metaphorical speech, then, is an analogical concept of God. The telling of the story must have contained the idea of God, because it is only in light of the idea of God that the metaphorical talk about Yahweh can be understood by us as talk about God.[142] Nothing in the story gives us the basis for the idea. Wicker's answer to the question as to how the stories became a revelation of the Most High God is that "the implicit narrator who is present in the very fact that the story is being told at all is apparently able to tell a story with Yahweh as a character. Now it is in this claim to be able to narrate such a story at all that we can find the notion of God somehow contained in this story."[143]

The teller of the Yahweh story makes explicit claims to know what happened, to be able to report what Yahweh said and thought. If the teller thinks of his gods as men writ large, no presumption is involved. "But if the claim is that the god who is a character in the story is also God, the Most High, and Creator of heaven and earth, and yet the story can report his thoughts and feelings as if they were directly known to the teller, then the claim to be able to tell such a story amounts to the claims to be in the position of God."[144] Since God is the only person who is in a position to tell us what Yahweh thought or felt, "God is after all *in* the stories of Yahweh, but not as a character, or as part of what is told, but as the implied teller."[145] Wicker contrasts the Old Testament narrative with the New Testament gospel narrative in this respect. The Old Testament narratives are anonymous, and it is this anonymity of the Old Testament teller that allows him to assume the "omniscience and the authoritativeness required to be able to tell stories in which Yahweh can figure as a character."[146] It is only a tradition which transcends the teller and imposes a kind of impersonality upon the teller by means of its characteristic narrative form that can authorize the "presumption" implied in placing Yahweh in time and space and involving him in human situation. The gospels are not anonymous in the same way as the Old Testament narratives (regardless of the real relationship the authors named have to the gospels). God, then, does not figure in the New Testament as a character in the stories. He is implied, but he is not named. He is present only as he is related to human characters. He is not present as a character in his own right. For a particular gospel writer to speak of God as the Old Testament narratives do would be "blasphemously presumptuous." Wicker sees the presence of the gospel writers in their books, the "self-conscious art" of each of the writers, as a vitally important difference between the Old Testament narratives and the gospels. The art of the gospel writer is "one which interprets the story of Jesus *as* one about the activity of God in Jesus." The Christian vision, then, is not only radically dependent upon narrative as such but also dependent upon the "distance which written narrative sets up between the author and teller of the tale."[147]

Lévi-Strauss, before Wicker, concluded that structuralism was not merely a model for the operation of analysis but also a description of reality. He does not, of course, posit a transcendental subject. Rather, he dissolves reality into nature. But the criticism of Lévi-Strauss's ontology by Umberto Eco is applicable in part also to the concept of Wicker and may lead us to a legitimate and appropriate use of Wicker's affirmations. Eco sharply criticizes the process by which Lévi-Strauss moved from structuralism as a model for understanding and explaining phenomena to structuralism as an ontological explanation of the phenomena used to construct the model. Structure developed from an instrument to a "hypostatized principle."[148]

Eco sees acceptance of ontological structuralism as leading to the destruction of structuralism and the acceptance of "Heideggerianism." He summarizes his arguments as follows:

> (a) As long as one seeks to make the idea of structure objective and time-less, one comes necessarily to an ontology of the primordial point of origin; (b) an ontology of the primordial point of origin leads to . . . the destruction of the idea of structure; (c) this destruction of the idea of structure is not accomplished by replacing it with the view of history as dialectical process . . . , but replacing it with an "ontology of absence" . . . ; (d) in Western thought this ontology is represented by the philosophy of Heidegger.[149]

Eco points out that a level of deep structures which are discovered to be basic for certain surface structures may themselves be discovered to be grounded by even deeper structures. The final structures discovered, however, may serve for the formation of an abstract logic of relationships which serves "to establish possible instruments for the explanation of reality but not necessarily to account for reality."[150] Ontological structuralism, nevertheless, takes the abstract logical model as the model of reality. It does so because it hypostatizes as philosophical truth what was originally a working hypothesis, that the experience of thought repeats the relationships of reality and that the laws of the mind are isomorphic with the laws of nature. "In other words: the ontological structuralist investigates the *culture* in order to translate it into *Natura Naturata*, in the innermost part of which he recognizes the (once for all time) *Natura Naturans* present and active."[151]

A *final* structure which is the ground of the production of new and original material, however, cannot be identified and defined in some sort of metalanguage or else it would not be the ultimate structure. The ultimate is hidden and unstructured. When it is evoked through a poetic use of language instead of being defined, and the affective components of the investigation of language become included (as is characteristic in hermeneutics), then structuralism is no longer the objective and neutral matter of the study of structuralism. "If one makes a search for an *ultimate foundation* of communication, it means that one is searching in an area which can no longer be defined with structural ideas. Structural models are valid only if one does *not* set up the question of the ultimate source of communication."[152]

Eco's arguments against structural insights *proving* a particular ontology are valid in my opinion. He is correct that the movement of logic would be somewhat circular, that a model is set up on the basis of and to assist the identification of certain phenomena, a structural model, and methodology. Then the model is taken as more than a model. It is taken as an ultimate explanation. Wicker has not accomplished all that he would like. He has not found in structuralism a language that allows us to "reach out to God as he is." If the language of structuralism does not do this what does it do? Where does it reach? From Wicker's own admission, it reaches the human being, the competence or linguistic facility of the human,[153] the structuring experience of the human,[154] and faith. The inability of the human to dispense with the metaphor which logically involves him with the metaphysical does not prove the metaphysical system. The argument from effect to cause, acknowledged as valid for the moment, can cut either way in the matter of ideology, the view of nature as ordered and intelligent and the rational nature of man. That is, ordered nature (or the ordering of nature) and the necessity of God may as well be explained by man as a cause and vice versa. Man may create God or God man.

Proof that our religious language refers to a reality prior to our experience is perhaps too much to ask for, particularly in light of analytical philosophy.[155] John Macquarrie admits, "Frankly, I do not suppose there is any way in which one could prove that the assertions of faith and of theology do refer to a Reality (God) that is independent of and prior to the experiences which we call 'experiences of God.' "[156] It is not possible to get behind the experience or to find a second route to that which is known in the experience. The impossibility of proving God may be paralleled with the impossibility of proving the reality of the "external world" or of other selves.[157]

Perhaps the evaluation of Wicker's attempt to relate the God of the Bible and the God of philosophy in logical terms is too defensive, for the evaluation is from within the community of faith and would like to affirm in broad terms what Wicker affirms, that in our talk about God we are not using a reflexive language to talk about ourselves, that we are talking about ontological reality. God-talk in general, to use Macquarrie's term, may be too much on the defensive. Perhaps we expect too much. Instead of proving that our language is really about God, suppose we take as our task the construction of a language of theology and faith which can be put to such critical analysis and tests as can be devised and not falsified.[158] Or, perhaps more to the point, suppose we construct a language of theology and faith which can speak effectively in our day.

If the work of Wicker and the total program of structuralism do not reestablish the old natural theology, can they help with a new philosophical theology? Macquarrie sets out the task of a new philosophical theology to take the place of the old natural theology.

> It will not set out to prove the existence of God or the immortality of the soul or anything of the sort, but it will show the basic structure of religious faith, what kind of situation gives rise to our talk about God, how this talk is meaningful in the context of that situation, and what kind of validity can be claimed for it.[159]

One approach would be to ask if structuralism gives us any grounds for affirming that our existential language is based on reality. The work of Paul Ricoeur must be considered in attempting to develop a language of theology and faith in our particular philosophical situation. Ricoeur agrees with Heidegger that it is in the poetic work that reality is disclosed. The biblical text, in fact, is to be seen as a variety of poetic language. But Ricoeur distinguishes between religious language (poetic language) and speculative (philosophical and theological) language. In

Western culture, religious language has been exposed to philosophical language, and philosophical conceptions mediate and influence religious experience and discourse. But the two languages are not the same. Religious language is a variety of poetic language, and it is as poetic language that the biblical text allows inquiry. But theology is necessary "to coordinate the experience articulated by the biblical text with human experience at large and as a whole."[160] A parallel distinction is that between semantics and philosophy, particularly as they relate to the relationship of language to reality. Semantics may *allege* a relationship of language to its "Other," to Reality. But philosophy must pose language conceptually as a mediation between man and world, man and man, and man and himself. Philosophy can do this by revising Kant's statement "something must be for something to appear" to: "something must be for something to be said." Reality is the ultimate category on the basis of which all of language can be thought—not known—as the spoken being of reality.

Poetic language should be looked upon as a model. That is, it is a fiction created to make an object easier to handle, but it is a heuristic fiction "inasmuch as we may transfer the description of this better known object to the field to be described on the basis of a partial isomorphism."[161] Poetic language, then, while it does not refer in the sense of ordinary language, is the means of disclosure of new aspects of reality, reality which cannot be spoken of in a more direct way. Ricoeur affirms that even if we agree with Frye that poetic discourse gives articulation only to our moods, moods have an ontological bearing.[162] In "Biblical Hermeneutics," Ricoeur emphasizes that metaphor is not simply an ornament of discourse and has more than an emotional value. He affirms that "it includes *new information*," in that "metaphor says something new about reality."[163]

The key for Ricoeur's search for the ontological explication of reference is the signification of being. In this search, Ricoeur uses the distinction which Aristotle makes between being as power and being as action. In his *Rhetoric*, Aristotle said that living metaphor is the process of making hearers see things, making them see things by using expressions that represent things in a state of activity. The poet gives life to inanimate things. To picture action is to signify power. The poet, then, perceives and pictures power as action and action as power.[164]

The task of speculative discourse, as opposed to the task of poetic language, is to search out the place where "the generation of that which develops" appears signified. It is at this point that Ricoeur's difference with Heidegger is seen most sharply. Heidegger's attempt to see words speaking existence, as flowers, in their blooming, fails to distinguish between speculative and poetic discourse. Heidegger's doctrine of *Ereignis*, the happening by which alone the meaning of being is determined, means for Ricoeur the end of the history of being. It is as if "being would disappear in the *Ereignis*" and this is not acceptable to Ricoeur.[165]

For Ricoeur, poetry in and of itself gives to thought the outline of a conception of truth which is in tension. There is tension between subject and predicate, literal interpretation and metaphorical interpretation, identity and difference. Poetry assembles these tensions in the theory of a redirected reference which culminates in the paradox of the copulative. In the paradox of the copulative, "being as" signifies both being and not being. Speculative thought accepts the contribution of poetry, works on the basis of its dynamic metaphoric statement, and orders it in its own space of meaning. Too sharp a distinction should not be made between poetic and speculative language. Speculative thought is possible because of the process of distanciation, but poetic discourse (from the fact that it is both text and work) prefigures this distanciation. The redescription of reality in the redirection of reference appears in specific figures of distanciation. Speculative discourse then reflects and rearticulates these figures. "That which is given to thought by the 'tensional' truth of poetry is the dialectic which is the most original and the most concealed: that which reigns between the experience of belonging in its ensemble and the power of distanciation which creates the space for speculative thought."[166]

Ricoeur poses continuity as well as discontinuity between poetic language and speculative language, between poetry and ontology, between religious language and theology, and he suggests one method of moving from poetic language to speculative discourse. Ricoeur's poetic and speculative approach to Reality, in which he challenges a major idea of Heidegger's final works, may be improved or at least expanded by a "structural reading" of Heidegger's major ideas. Eco's arguments against structural ontology are valid to the extent that structural philosophy and methods do not *prove* the ontological view of Lévi-Strauss or Wicker. Yet if the model is actually related to the phenomena, if it is constructed on the basis of empirical data, the model should give insight into the cause of the phenomena which are modeled. The structural model, then, may be a heuristic analogical model (heuristic not explanatory). When the structural approach to language is applied to Heidegger's concept of discourse and language, we are confronted with a parallel which at least makes Heidegger's concept more understandable.

Heidegger in *Being and Time* sees language as related to the "discourse" which is an *existentiale* of *Dasein* equiprimordial with understanding and state-of-mind. Later, language becomes more dominant in his thought and becomes itself a mode of revelation of Being. "Language," then, for Heidegger, is not simply equated with the conventional view of language as the tool of man. Yet there is a relationship between the understanding and use of everyday language and the deeper view of language. Structuralism, as we have seen, has come to a view of language which not only emphasizes meaning as the relationship set up by the grammatical elements but a view of language which goes beyond the surface level to a deeper level. Language and literature are not simply to be understood on the level of history, or on the level of tool. The deeper levels which account for the level of manifestation are based on the human (*Dasein*); therefore a homologous relation exists between the mental structure and language and literature. The study of the different levels of language and literature gives us insight into man. Moreover the mental structure has at its core a competence, a positive active capacity which operates to equilibrate the various systems which enter into the mental system.

How does structuralism relate to the ontological search of Heidegger? Does it provide a means to relate epistemology to ontology? That is, do the deep abstract structures uncovered by structural analysis relate to the primordial *existentialia* of state-of-mind, understanding, and discourse? Is Heidegger's fundamental philosophy (which was not related to linguistic or conventional language study in Heidegger) to be seen as tied not only to the level of saying (*reden*) but also to the level of speaking (*sprechen*) by means of structural study which involves not only the structures of the text but also the competence of the human being?

The structures of language and literature appear to be a more satisfying approach to the questioning of *Dasein* and the Reality behind *Dasein* than the poetic approach of Heidegger which Ricoeur finds invalid. Even one who accepts Heidegger's approach as valid must also accept the structural approach as supplementary.[167] The question of the fore-structure (*Vorstruktur*) and as-structure (*Alstruktur*) which are involved in the interpretation accompanying understanding can be understood in the structuralist framework in which there is a mental structure or competence which is innate and "learned" and which operates prior to consciousness in the production and interpretation of sentences and texts.

When the movement of Heidegger toward the emphasis on language is considered, structuralism continues to help. For Heidegger, language speaks as language. Language and Being come close to being identified, and the essence of language is itself expression of Being. The structures of structuralism are not only active in the production of meaning on the conventional historical literary level. They may produce meaning independent of (although related to) the content. The meaning produced by the structures may be identified with the "forms of thought" (poetic thought or forms of experiences) which are produced by both the "syntax-like-mathematics" and the "syntax-like-music" of Donald Davie.[168] The meaning has to do with mood, tone, attitude. It is affective in nature, but no less real.

The meaning of the structures is affective, related to the ideational content of the poetic work, and (as with the meaning in the poetry used by Heidegger) is not possible independent of the human minds who create and read the work. Is it not possible, however, that the language system prior to realization in performance (but which is evidenced in performance) is yet another area for the questioning of Being? In such a case, the work of the narratologists on the level of profound grammar and syntax would provide a field for such questioning. The characteristics which Greimas sees in such a profound level include action and purpose.

In ontological and theological study, however, all levels of language and meaning to which the reader is sensitive remain operative. The historical-literary and existential meanings will be related to the Reality expressed and discovered in the literary work. Just as the affective content of a narrative will influence the historical-literary interpretation, the historical-literary content will influence the affective, ontological, and theological levels of interpretation.

Structuralism does not prove the existence of Reality or God because of the impossibility of such proof in our philosophical and theological situation. The historical and finite nature of man and his mental structure make evidence of Reality and God a matter not merely dependent upon the ontological reality of the structures but also dependent upon the interpreter and his total situation. A contribution of the structuralist approach may be to make conceivable an ontology which supports the language of existence and complements the existing "methods" of interpretation of literature from that perspective. Structuralism can add a dimension not only to historical-literary and existential approaches to literature but also to philosophy and theology.

NOTES

1. One important factor has already been discussed: the prior subjective accommodation of various approaches or stages of development in interpretation. The matters discussed in this section may also be thought of as items which influence interpretation only as they become a part of the total mental structure of the individual. However, the reaction of the individual to these matters is not merely a matter of personal choice, and this discussion will center upon objective factors which have influenced the total theological community.

2. See John Macquarrie, *Principles of Christian Theology* (New York: Scribner's, 1966), pp. 18–21, 35–36, 39–158, for a discussion of the relationship of Christian theology to philosophy.

3. Krister Stendahl, "Contemporary Biblical Theology," *The Interpreter's Dictionary of the Bible* (New York: Abingdon, 1962), I, 422.

4. *Ibid.*

5. *Ibid.*, p. 430.

6. *Ibid.*, pp. 430, 425.

7. Brevard S. Childs, *Biblical Theology in Crisis* (Philadelphia: Westminster, 1970), p. 65.

8. James Barr, "Revelation through History in the Old Testament and in Modern Theology," *Princeton Seminary Bulletin* 41 (1963), 4–14, and *Interpretation* 17 (1963), 193–205.

9. Peter L. Berger, *A Rumor of Angels: Modern Society and the Rediscovery of the Supernatural* (Garden City, N.Y.: Doubleday, 1970), p. 6. For a systematic presentation of this in terms of the sociology of knowledge, see Peter Berger and Thomas Luckmann, *The Social Construction of Reality* (Garden City, N.Y.: Doubleday, 1966).

10. Berger, *A Rumor of Angels*, p. 8. See Berger, "A Sociological View of the Secularization of Theology," *Journal for the Scientific Study of Religion* (1967).

11. Paul Ricoeur, "Biblical Hermeneutics," *Semeia* 4 (1975), 130.

12. Berger, *A Rumor of Angels*, p. 8.

13. *Ibid.*, p. 95.

14. Ricoeur, "Biblical Hermeneutics," p. 130.

15. See John Macquarrie, *An Existentialist Theology: A Comparison of Heidegger and Bultmann* (New York: Harper Torchbooks, 1965), pp. ix, 3–26.

16. Günther Schiwy, *Structuralism and Christianity* (Pittsburgh, Pa.: Duquesne University Press, 1971), p. 11. Structuralism patterns existentialism in its appropriation by both atheistic and theistic thinkers. Existentialism and

structuralism in themselves as methods of study, however, are neither atheistic nor theistic. Much that John Macquarrie says of existentialism in this regard is also true of structuralism. See Macquarrie, *Existentialism* (London: Hutchinson, 1972), pp. 6–8, 34–40, 190–202, 215–18.

17. Schiwy, *Structuralism and Christianity*, p. 32.

18. Mark Pattison, "Tendencies of Religious Thought in England, 1688–1750," in *Essays and Reviews* (1860), p. 257. Quoted in W. Neil, "The Criticism and Theological Use of the Bible, 1700–1950," *The Cambridge History of the Bible: The West from the Reformation to the Present Day* (Cambridge: Cambridge University Press, 1963), pp. 239–40.

19. *Ibid.*

20. W. Neil, "The Criticism and Theological Use of the Bible, 1700–1950," p. 270.

21. *Ibid.*, p. 271.

22. Alan Richardson, "The Rise of Modern Biblical Scholarship and Recent Discussion of the Authority of the Bible," *The Cambridge History of the Bible: The West from the Reformation to the Present Day*, p. 317.

23. *Ibid.*, p. 304.

24. George Eldon Ladd has well expressed the position of the evangelical who would accept historical criticism: "God acted in redeeming history, and God spoke through the prophets as they spoke and as they wrote. The result is not a mere product of history or religious insight; it is a normative, authoritative, divinely initiated and superintended account of who God has revealed Himself to be and what He has done for man's salvation." *The New Testament and Criticism* (Grand Rapids, Mich.: Eerdmans, 1967), p. 216.

25. Richardson, "The Rise of Modern Biblical Scholarship," p. 304.

26. *Ibid.*, p. 297.

27. Walter Wink, *The Bible in Human Transformation: Toward a New Paradigm for Biblical Study* (Philadelphia: Fortress, 1973), pp. 9, 1–2. See James Barr, *The Bible in the Modern World* (London: SCM, 1973), for a fuller analysis and critique of the problem of the status of the Bible in the present day.

28. Hayden White, "Interpretation in History," *New Literary History* 4 (1973), 286–87.

29. See R. G. Collingwood, *The Idea of History* (Oxford: Clarendon, 1946), pp. 239–41, for a similar analysis. Roland Barthes proposes much the same thing as the possibility of and basis for structural analysis of historical narrative: "Historical discourse can be meaningful on at least two levels. At the first of these the meaning is inherent in the historical content—the historian offers an interpretation . . . or draws a lesson, either moral or political. . . . If the lesson is pervasive, we enter the second category, where the meaning is independent of the historical discourse as such and is expressed by the pattern of the historian's private obsessions. . . . In our civilization there is permanent pressure to increase the meaningfulness of history; the historian assembles not so much facts as *signifiants,* and these he connects and organizes in such a way as to replace the vacuousness of the pure catalogue with positive meaning."

Roland Barthes, "Historical Discourse," *Structuralism: A Reader* (London: Jonathan Cape, 1970), p. 153.

30. Karl Schmidt, *Der Rahmen der Geschichte Jesu. Literarkritisch Untersuchungen zur altesten Jesusüberlieferung* (Berlin: Trowitzsch und Sohn, 1919).

31. Martin Dibelius, *From Tradition to Gospel*, trans. Bertram Lee Woolf (New York: Scribner's, 1935), p. iii.

32. Rudolf Bultmann, *History of the Synoptic Tradition*, trans. John Marsh (New York: Harper, 1963), pp. 2–3.

33. Dibelius, *From Tradition to Gospel*, p. 219.

34. Bultmann, *History of the Synoptic Tradition*, p. 322.

35. *Ibid.*, p. 5.

36. *Ibid.*, p. 4.

37. Dibelius, *From Tradition to Gospel*, pp. 13–14.

38. *Ibid.*, p. 76.

39. R. H. Lightfoot, *History and Interpretation in the Gospels* (London: Hodder and Stoughton, 1935), p. 98.

40. Claude Lévi-Strauss, *The Savage Mind* (Chicago: The University of Chicago Press, 1966), pp. 18–19.

41. *Ibid.*, p. 19.

42. *Ibid.*, p. 21.

43. Roman Jakobson, "The Dominant," *Readings in Russian Poetics: Formalist and Structuralist Views*, ed. Ladislav Matejka and Krystyna Pomorska (Cambridge, Mass. and London: The MIT Press, 1971), p. 84.

44. Jurij Tynjanov and Roman Jakobson, "Problems in the Study of Literature," *ibid.*, p. 79.

45. Murray Krieger, *A Window to Criticism* (Princeton: Princeton University Press, 1964), pp. 67–69.

46. *Ibid.*, p. 3.

47. Norman N. Holland, *5 Readers Reading* (New Haven: Yale University Press, 1975), p. 114.

48. *Ibid.*, pp. 115–17.

49. *Ibid.*, p. 119. Holland admits that the principle that the "fantasy" is not "in" the work but "in the creative relation between reader and work" marks a departure from older psychoanalytic concepts which considered each literary work as having a fixed fantasy content. Fantasies, in Holland's view, "are clusters of wishes deriving from the stages in which children develop. . . . What in the child were early and later stages become in the adult 'higher' and 'lower' stages. All coexist, however, and it becomes possible to think of personality at least partly in terms of fixation to one or more levels." *Ibid.*, pp. 117–18.

50. *Ibid.*, pp. 121–22. Dilthey envisions a unified mental structure active in creation and interpretation. He does distinguish between the cognitive, volitional, and affective aspects, however, and he sees the importance of satisfaction on the various levels. See above, p. 18.

51. Philip Pettit, *The Concept of Structuralism: A Critical Analysis* (Dublin: Gill and Macmillan, 1975), p. 116. Although I wish to make a little more of the value of structural insights for hermeneutics, Pettit's evaluation does not

negate the value of structural applications in analysis. He says, "To reduce the aspirations of structuralism to analysis is not to make little of the movement. The model which structuralism introduces, the framework by which it categories the areas for semiological analysis, is an important contribution. . . . The structuralist conceptual framework sets the scene well for semiological analysis, it constructs objects fit for systematic investigations." *Ibid.*

52. See above, pp. 156–57.

53. See Erhardt Güttgemanns, "Einleitende Bemerkungen zur strukturalen Erzahlforschung," *Linguistica Biblica* 23/24 (May 1973), 33–34.

54. Greimas correctly sees human perception as a beginning point in his study of narrative. But this insight must be applied not only to the original creator of narrative on the superficial level but to the reader as creator on the surface level.

55. Northrop Frye, *Anatomy of Criticism: Four Essays* (Princeton: Princeton University Press, 1957), pp. 245–46, 162. In *Kerygma and Comedy in the New Testament* (Philadelphia: Fortress, 1975) Dan O. Via, Jr., has constructed a "nonconventional version of the comic (or tragicomic) genre-structure" (p. 15) into which he places several Pauline texts and the Gospel of Mark for the purpose of a better understanding of the texts. In *The Parables: Their Literary and Historical Dimensions* (Philadelphia: Fortress, 1967), as well as in *Kerygma and Comedy*, Via has done pioneer work in literary approaches to the New Testament text.

56. Wesley A. Kort, *Narrative Elements and Religious Meaning* (Philadelphia: Fortress, 1975), pp. 100, 103.

57. Jonathan Culler, "Defining Narrative Units," *Style and Structure in Literature* (Oxford: Basil Blackwell, 1975), p. 139.

58. Roland Barthes, S/Z (London: Jonathan Cape, 1975), p. 75.

59. *Ibid.*, pp. 75–76.

60. *Ibid.*, p. 76.

61. *Ibid.*, p. 13.

62. In *Maupassant: La Sémiotique du Texte: Exercices Pratiques* (Paris: Seuil, 1976), A. J. Greimas applies a methodological model which he sees as appropriate for contemporary semiotic research. He specifies the general strategy used: ". . . elle consiste, à chaque fois qu'on se trouve en présence d'un phénomène non analysé, à construire sa représentation de telle sorte que le modèle en soit plus général que le fait examiné ne l'exige, afin que le phénomene observé s'y inscrive comme une de ses variables. C'est ainsi que la pratique du texte pourra déboucher sur des considérations théoriques qui dépassent sa singularité, en transformant les 'problématiques' en concepts opératoires et en paramètres méthodologiques, soumis ultérieurement, cela va de soi, à d'éventuelles confirmations ou infirmations" (p. 263). Greimas declares that semiotics offers biblical scholars a metalanguage "qui se veut neutre, c'est-à-dire, une manière de parler du texte tout en s'effaçant devant lui: . . . elle permet à ce discours sur le discours de se distinguer de son objet textuel, elle lui permet aussi de maintenir l'univocité de ses termes et la cohérence, vérfiable, de ses propos. . . . Autrement dit, le bon usage de la métalangue

sémiotique permet de faire parler le texte, en supprimant, autant que faire se peut, la médiation parasite qui cherche à s'insinuer entre le message et son destinataire" (*Signes et Paraboles: Sémiotique et texte évangélique* [Paris: Seuil, 1977], pp. 227–28). The semiotic approach does not offer a unique or definitive reading. ". . . en se considérant comme une démarche heuristique, elle énonce les règles du jeu cansées garantir la présence effective du texte et permettre au lecteur non de s'y refléter, mais de le reinventer" (*ibid.*, p. 228).

63. Frye, *Anatomy of Criticism*, p. 192.

64. *Ibid.*, pp. 187, 214, 223.

65. A. J. Greimas, *Sémantique structurale* (Paris: Larousse, 1966), pp. 192–95.

66. Frye, *Anatomy of Criticism*, p. 34.

67. Daniel Patte provides an introduction to structural methodology and specific methods in *What Is Structural Exegesis?* (Philadelphia: Fortress, 1976). Patte limits his attention to narrative and mythical "deep structures" although he sees that attention can be given to structures closer to the surface of the text. Patte is aware that the methods he introduces complement traditional historical-critical methods and that the end of the exegetical task is hermeneutics. See Claus Berger, *Exegese des Neuen Testaments* (Heidelberg: Quelle & Meyer, 1977), for a comprehensive catalog of models and conceptions of the study of the text which may assist New Testament exegesis. Berger treats over fifteen hundred different titles from different approaches, including German text linguistics and American discourse analysis as well as French structuralism.

68. Henry J. Cadbury, *The Making of Luke-Acts* (New York: Macmillan, 1927), pp. 216, 218, 223–25, 231–32. Cadbury sees Luke as a creature of habit and convention as well as a consciously creative author. A writer's "viewpoint, his use and presentation of his materials, his method of composition, and his style and diction, are only slightly matters of free will or conscious decision." *Ibid.*, p. 113. Writing, says Cadbury, is "a process hemmed in with the compulsion of convention." *Ibid.*

69. Pettit, *The Concept of Structuralism*, p. 48.

70. Perhaps the acceptance of structuralism as the fashion in Paris in the 1960s and the esoteric and sometimes overenthusiastic statements of some of the adherents of structuralism created an early caution and even hostility on the part of some critics. The fact that structural works remained untranslated until recently may also account for its slow reception outside of France. Now that structuralism is no longer the mode, however, it is being seen as a serious method of analysis. D. W. Foster, for example, says that texts on European structuralism in Spanish have had an enthusiastic reception in major intellectual centers of Latin America. ("Consideraciones estructurales sobre 'La Casa Verde,'" *Norte* 12 [1971], 345.) Cesare Segre indicates that between 1963 and 1965 structural criticism "exploded" in Italy and that from 1965 on it has become widespread on all levels. The almost simultaneous founding (1966–67) of two journals devoted to structural analysis is an indication of the growth of structuralism. ("Structuralism in Italy," *Semiotica* 4 [1971], 226–28.) Robert Scholes, in an article stressing the contribution structuralism makes to the

theory of fiction, recognizes that structural analysis has frequently not been known to American and British readers because it has remained largely untranslated from the French and that where it has been known it has been frequently misunderstood. ("The Contribution of Formalism and Structuralism to the Theory of Fiction," *Novel* 6 [1973], 134–36.) He is convinced that structural analysis is sound, even essential, for he believes that "the most important thing we have learned in the past fifty years is a way of thinking called 'structuralism'. . . ." ("Ulysses: A Structuralist Perspective," *James Joyce Quarterly* 10 [1972], 161–71.)

71. In France, biblical scholars early became acquainted with structural analysis. In September 1969, 170 scholars met at a conference at Chantilly (under auspices of the Association Catholique Française pour l'Etude de la Bible) so that exegetes could become familiar with structural analysis. Roland Barthes took part in the conference and three biblical scholars who had become convinced of the value of structuralism read papers. As a result of the conference an Association des Structuralistes and the group "Analyse Structurale et Signification" were formed to apply the method to biblical texts. In February 1971, the Protestant Theology Faculty of the University of Geneva invited Roland Barthes and Jean Starobinski to a colloquium to introduce theologians to the structural method of analysis. Erhardt Güttgemanns, of the University of Bonn, is perhaps the most vigorous advocate of a linguistic-based analysis in Germany. He calls his approach "generative poetics," distinguishing between structuralism and his generative approach. He has made the method an integral part of his more broadly based "Linguistic Theology." Other scholars in Germany, however, have used structural analysis. In America, concentrated, continuing efforts in structural exegesis are being made in the Society of Biblical Literature. A Seminar on the Parables was organized in 1973 and has concentrated upon a study of the parables using the method of Greimas (or modification thereof). A journal, *Semeia*, was founded under the auspices of the society to carry articles discussing and using newer methods. In 1976, a seminar of the international Studiorum Novi Testamenti Societas was devoted to linguistics and semiotics.

72. F. C. Baur, *Paul: The Apostle of Jesus Christ* (London: Williams and Norgate, 1875); *The Church History of the First Three Centuries* (London: Williams and Norgate, 1878). See Charles H. Talbert, *Literary Patterns, Theological Themes and the Genre of Luke-Acts* (Missoula, Mont.: Scholars Press, 1974), pp. 1–5.

73. M. D. Goulder, *Type and History in Acts* (London: SPCK, 1964), pp. x, 34, 61–62.

74. The majority of the work of Güttgemanns appears in the journal *Linguistica Biblica* which he founded in 1970 and of which he is the editor. Important articles are translated and published in *Semeia* 6 (1976).

75. Erhardt Güttgemanns, "Linguistisch-literature-wissenschaftliche Grundlegung einer Neutestamentlichen Theologie," *Linguistica Biblica* 13/14 (1972), 15.

76. Güttgemanns, "Thesen zu einer 'Generativen Poetik,'" *ibid.*, 1 (1970);

"Struktural-generative Analyse der Parabel 'Vom bittenden Freund' (Lk. 11, 5–8)," *ibid.*, 2 (1970); and "Einige wesentliche Denkmodelle der Semiotik," *ibid.*, 3 (1971).

77. Güttgemanns, "Thesen," p. 3.

78. Güttgemanns, "Struktural-generative Analyse der Parabel 'Vom bittenden Freund,'" p. 8; "Einige wesentliche Denkmodelle der Semiotik," p. 17.

79. Erhardt Güttgemanns, "Theologie als sprachbezogene Wissenschaft," *Linguistica Biblica* 4/5 (1971), 9.

80. Erhardt Güttgemanns, "Qu'est-ce que la Poetique Generative?" *Linguistica Biblica* 19 (1972), 4.

81. Güttgemanns, "Einige wesentliche Denkmodelle der Semiotik," p. 14; "Theologie als sprachbezogene Wissenschaft," p. 11.

82. Erhardt Güttgemanns, "Einleitende Bemerkungen zur strukturalen Erzahlforschung," *Linguistica Biblica* 23/24 (1973), 5–9.

83. Erhardt Güttgemanns, "Analyse synoptischer Teste," *Linguistica Biblica* 25/26 (1973), pp. 51–52.

84. See Peter Krausser, *Kritik der endlichen Vernunft: Wilhelm Diltheys Revolution der allgemeinen Wissenschafts—und Handlungs—theorie* (Frankfurt: Suhrkamp Verlag, 1968), for a chronological treatment of Dilthey's views on the mental structure.

85. Wolfgang Iser, "Indeterminacy and the Reader's Response in Prose Fiction," *Aspects of Narrative: Selected Papers from the English Institute*, ed. with a foreword by J. Hillis Miller (New York and London: Columbia University Press, 1971), p. 9.

86. A. J. Greimas, "Les jeux des contraintes sémiotique" written in collaboration with François Rastier, *Du Sens* (Paris: Seuil, 1970), pp. 135–55.

87. See Lowry Nelson, Jr., "The Fictive Reader and Literary Self-Reflectiveness," *The Disciplines of Criticism: Essays in Literary Theory, Interpretation, and History*, ed. Peter Demetz, Thomas Green, and Lowry Nelson, Jr. (New Haven: Yale University Press, 1968), p. 174.

88. Jean Delorme has demonstrated how a structural analysis of Luke 5:1–11 may be related to a study of the history of the redaction of the story in Mark 1:16–20 and a variant of which is found in John 21:1–14. The present analysis is not to be considered a refutation of Delorme's analysis, but a study which organizes analysis for hermeneutical and not for critical or historical purposes alone. See Jean Delorme, "Luc V. 1–11: Analyse structurale et Histoire de la Redaction," *New Testament Studies* 18 (1972), 331–50.

89. Jonathan Culler sees "structuralism's reversal of perspective" as capable of leading to "a mode of interpretation based on poetics itself." He sees this mode of interpretation and ordinary thematic interpretation as different but compatible. Yet he states that in this mode of interpretation "the meaning of the work is what it shows the reader, by the acrobatics in which it involves him, about the problems of his condition as *homo significans*, maker and reader of signs." I have attempted to show that thematic interpretation and the mode of interpretation based on poetics cannot be separated and I propose that narrative hermeneutics is a comprehensive program of interpretation into which

the work of literary critics in general—structuralists and non-structuralists—can be organized and found useful. See Jonathan Culler, *Structuralist Poetics: Structural Linguistics and the Study of Literature* (London: Routledge and Kegan Paul, 1975), p. 130.

90. F. C. Grant, "Jesus Christ," *Interpreter's Dictionary of the Bible* (Nashville: Abingdon, 1962), I, 869.

91. If the desire is the comparison of the abstract structures of the various biblical narratives, interest will be in the formulas, and the formulas themselves take on a value independent of the surface manifestations. If interest is in opening up signification from the signifiers of an individual text, the specific text must be maintained. All possibilities for signification are lost if relationship to the signifiers is lost, if the analysis becomes totally abstract. If, to use semiotics language, readers are interested in the interpretants and in the endless play of signs, the readers must remain with a level which signifies.

92. Claude Bremond, "Morphology of the French Folktale," *Semiotics* 2 (1970), 249.

93. Wolfgang Iser, "The Reading Process: A Phenomenological Approach," *New Directions in Literary History*, ed. Ralph Cohen (Baltimore: The Johns Hopkins University Press, 1974), p. 129.

94. Kort, *Narrative Elements and Religious Meaning*, pp. 100, 103.

95. Frye, *Anatomy of Criticism*, p. 168.

96. *Ibid.*, p. 286.

97. *Ibid.*, p. 184.

98. *Ibid.*, p. 185.

99. See the section following.

100. The future time in the commissioning of Peter and his partners, "you will catch men," will be applied by the religiously and symbolically mature reader as the reader's own time.

101. Jean Delorme, "Luc V. 1–11," pp. 338–41.

102. Barthes, S/Z, p. 27.

103. Holland, *5 Readers Reading*, pp. 121–22.

104. Kort, *Narrative Elements and Religious Meaning*, p. 5.

105. H. Conzelmann, *The Theology of Saint Luke* (New York: Harper, 1960), p. 33.

106. H. Schürmann, "Die Verheissung an Simon Petrus," *Bib Leben* 5 (1964), 18–24.

107. K. Zillessen, "Das Schiff des Petrus und die Gefährten vom anderen Schiff," *Zeit NT Wiss* 57 (1966), 137–39.

108. John Martin Creed, *The Gospel According to Saint Luke* (London: Macmillan, 1930), p. 73.

109. R. H. Fuller, *Luke's Witness to Jesus Christ* (New York: Association, 1958), p. 26.

110. G. Klein, "Die Berufung des Petrus," *Zeit NT Wiss* 58 (1967), 1–44.

111. A. R. C. Leaney, *The Gospel According to Saint Luke* (New York: Harper, 1958), p. 56.

112. Edmund Leach, *Lévi-Strauss* (London: Fontana, 1970), pp. 56–57.

113. Brian Wicker, *The Story-Shaped World: Fiction and Metaphysics: Some Variations on a Theme* (Notre Dame: University of Notre Dame Press, 1975), p. 85.

114. *Ibid.*, pp. 85, 20.

115. *Ibid.*, p. 8.

116. *Ibid.*, p. 12.

117. *Ibid.*, p. 13.

118. *Ibid.*, p. 15.

119. See Austin Farrer, "Analogy," *Twentieth Century Encyclopedia of Religious Knowledge* (Grand Rapids, Mich.: Baker, 1955), I, 38–40.

120. Wicker, *Story-Shaped World*, pp. 17–18.

121. *Ibid.*, p. 18.

122. *Ibid.*, p. 19.

123. *Ibid.*

124. *Ibid.*, p. 20.

125. *Ibid.*

126. *Ibid.*, pp. 50, 58.

127. *Ibid.*, p. 37.

128. *Ibid.*, p. 38.

129. *Ibid.*, pp. 38, 40.

130. *Ibid.*, pp. 40–41.

131. *Ibid.*, p. 41.

132. *Ibid.*, p. 58.

133. *Ibid.*, p. 76.

134. *Ibid.*, pp. 83–84, 87.

135. *Ibid.*, p. 94.

136. *Ibid.*

137. *Ibid.*, p. 96.

138. *Ibid.*

139. *Ibid.*, p. 97.

140. *Ibid.*, p. 98.

141. *Ibid.*

142. *Ibid.*, p. 100.

143. *Ibid.*

144. *Ibid.*, p. 101.

145. *Ibid.*

146. *Ibid.*, p. 103.

147. *Ibid.*, pp. 105–6.

148. Umberto Eco, *Einführung in die Semiotik* (Munich: Wilhelm Fink Verlag, 1972), p. 77. This is a revision and translation of *La struttura Assente* (Milan: Bompiani, 1968).

149. *Ibid.*, p. 394: "a) Solbald man versucht, den Begriff der Struktur objektiv und unzeitlich zu machen, kommt man zwangsweise zu einer Ontologie des *Ursprungsortes*; b) eine Ontologie des *Ursprungsortes* zwingt dazu, den Begriff der Struktur zu zerstören; c) diese Zerstörung des Begriffes der Struktur geschieht nicht dadurch, dass eine Sicht der Geschichte als dialektischer

Bewegung (im Hegelschen oder marxistische Sinne des Wortes) an seine Stelle tritt, sondern macht einer 'Ontologie der Abwesenheit' Platz, die dem marxistischen Historismus entgegengesetzt ist; d) im westlichen Denken repräsentiert die Philosophie Heideggers diese Ontologie." Heidegger's philosophy is not related by Heidegger to the linguistic and anthropological study out of which structuralism developed. Structural ontology recognizes Being as the primordial point of origin which manifests itself conspicuously in the form of structured events. See Eco, p. 394.

150. *Ibid.*, p. 396: ". . . mögliche Instrumente für die Erklärung der Wirklichkeit herzustellen, nicht aber notwendigerweise dazu, die Wirklichkeit zu erklären."

151. *Ibid.*, pp. 396–97: "Mit anderen Worten: der ontologische Strukturalist untersucht die *Kultur*, aber um sie in *Natura Naturata* zu übersetzen, in deren Innerstem er die (ein für allemal einzige) *Natura Naturans* anwesend und wirkend erkennt."

152. *Ibid.*, pp. 411–12: "Wenn man sich auf die Suche nach einer *letzten Grundlage* der Kommunikation macht, dann bedeutet das, dass man diese Grundlage da sucht, wo diese nicht mehr mit strukturalen Begriffen definiert werden kann. Die strukturalen Modelle sind nur gültig, wenn man *nicht* die Frage nach dem Ursprung der Kommunikation stellt." John Bowker seems to agree with Eco as well as move beyond Eco and Wicker in his conclusion that, in terms of structural accounts of religion, "whatever the term 'God' represents would either have to be found within the movement of structures itself, as process theology suggests, or else it would have to be posited as ontologically independent of the movement of structures but creatively involved in those structures as resource and goal." Bowker, *The Sense of God* (Oxford: Clarendon, 1973), p. 109.

153. Wicker, *The Story-Shaped World*, p. 19.

154. *Ibid.*, pp. 36, 40, 46.

155. See John Macquarrie, *God-Talk: An Examination of the Language and Logic of Theology* (London: SCM, 1967), pp. 102–22.

156. *Ibid.*, p. 244.

157. *Ibid.* John Bowker asserts that "the hierarchies of structure which constitute the sense of God could not possibly function" unless "it were *not* [italics added] 'literally meaningless' to talk approximately of what may in reality be the case with regard to God." Yet, "the nearer 'God' comes to being captured, pinned down, ostensively defined, the more he, she, it, or they move back beyond those points of attainment. The theistic structures which exist in the world, as they *do* exist, could not exist unless this were so." Bowker, *The Sense of God*, pp. 111–12. In a very perceptive note, Bowker notes that "God" must stand for the point not yet attained. "Anything less than that leads to what the theistic traditions frequently refer to as idolatry." *Ibid.*, p. 113.

158. This is the perspective of John Macquarrie and is the modern approach to knowledge. Knowledge is never finally proved. It can be stated in an understandable way which does not preclude testing and analysis and yet is not falsified. *God-Talk*, p. 248.

159. *Ibid.*, p. 121.

160. Ricoeur, "Biblical Hermeneutics," p. 130.

161. Paul Ricoeur, "Creativity in Language," *Philosophy Today* 17 (1973), 110–11.

162. *Ibid.*, p. 111.

163. Ricoeur, "Biblical Hermeneutics," p. 80.

164. Paul Ricoeur, *La métaphore vive* (Paris: Seuil, 1975), p. 392.

165. *Ibid.*, pp. 393–94. Ricoeur does cite a statement of Heidegger with which he is in agreement, a statement which indicates the dialectical relationship of the modes of discourse, their proximity and their difference: "Between these two, thought and poetry, reigns a more profound relation which is withdrawn, because these two are devoted to the surface of language and are produced for it. Between these two, however, persists at the same time a profound depth, for they live upon the most separate mountains." *Ibid.*, p. 394. "Entre elles deux, pensée et poésie, règne une parenté plus profondément retirée, parce que toutes deux s'adonnet au service du langage et se prodiguent pour lui. Entre elles deux pourtant persiste en même temps un abîme profond, car elles demeurent sur les monts les plus séparés." French translation from *Was is das—die Philosophie* (Pfullingen: Neske, 1956), p. 45.

166. Ricoeur, *La métaphore vive*, p. 399: "Ce qui est ainsi donné à penser par la vérité tensionnelle de la poésie, c'est la dialectique la plus originaire et la plus dissimulée: celle qui règne entre l'experience d'appartenance dans son ensemble et le pouvoir de distanciation qui ouvre l'espace de la pensée speculative."

167. John Macquarrie comes close to the structuralist concept when he emphasizes that discourse and language not only express but refer and represent. "But how is it possible for language to point beyond itself, or to stand for something? The answer must lie in the form or structure of the language; for language, as distinct from mere noise or sound, has a definite form." Macquarrie suggests that "in some manner, the form and structure of the language bring before us something of the form and structure of what we are talking about." However, he does not follow this fruitful idea because "the number of possible sentence-structures would seem to be much less than the fantastic number of factual structures which we find in the real world and which we might wish to talk about," and similarity of grammatical structure does not always indicate similarity of logical form or of factual structure. *God-Talk*, pp. 71–72. Macquarrie here is distinguishing between the limitless level of manifestation and the more abstract and limited deep level.

168. Donald Davie, *Articulate Energy* (London: Routledge and Kegan Paul, 1955), pp. 65–95.

INDEX